CITY ON
A HILL

Also by James Traub

Too Good to Be True

CITY ON A HILL

Testing the American Dream
at City College

JAMES TRAUB

Addison-Wesley Publishing Company
Reading, Massachusetts Menlo Park, California New York
Don Mills, Ontario Wokingham, England Amsterdam Bonn
Sydney Singapore Tokyo Madrid San Juan
Paris Seoul Milan Mexico City Taipei

To my partners,
E.W.E. and A.E.T.

Many of the designations used by manufacturers and sellers to distinguish their products are claimed as trademarks. Where those designations appear in this book and Addison-Wesley was aware of a trademark claim, the designations have been printed in initial capital letters.

Library of Congress Cataloging-in-Publication Data

Traub, James.
    City on a hill : testing the American dream at City College /
James Traub.
        p.   cm.
    Includes bibliographical references and index.
    ISBN 0-201-62227-0
    ISBN 0-201-48942-2 (pbk.)
    1. City University of New York. City College.   2. Universities
and colleges—New York (N.Y.)—Sociological aspects.   I. Title.
LD3818.8.T72   1994
378.747'1—dc20   94-33054
                                                                        CIP

Cover design by Jean Seal
Cover art by Maria Dolores Rodriguez
Text design by Melissa Kulig
Set in 10-point Palatino by CopyRight, Inc.

1 2 3 4 5 6 7 8 9-MA-98979695
First printing, August 1994
First paperback printing, September 1995

Contents

Preface

"Open admissions" posed a tormenting problem for liberals when it was raised as a rallying cry at the City College of New York a quarter of a century ago, and it continues to torment today. Open admissions is a species of affirmative action; like affirmative action, it advances one cherished American ideal while threatening another. When City College and City University agreed in 1969 to drastically lower admissions standards in order to give access to large numbers of black and Puerto Rican students, they did so in the belief that discrimination had denied these students the chance to compete on an equal footing with the white, largely Jewish population that for generations had used City as a stepping-stone to the middle class. City accepted an obligation to compensate for the effects of historic disadvantage. But can it? Should it? Unlike affirmative action, open admissions creates no victim class, no "angry white males"; but by substituting an entitlement for an achievement— the achievement of satisfying the rigorous admissions standards of another era—it challenges our faith in meritocratic competition and threatens the excellence that that competition makes possible.

City College is a stage on which the dilemma of the affirmative action idea is enacted every day. The abstract questions are invisible; what you feel, acutely, if you spend any time there, is the desperate struggle of the students to exploit the opportunity they've been given, and of the struggle of the college to make that opportunity real without compromising its own commitments to excellence. For many young people, I found, City College still represents an almost miraculous salvation from a life of poverty and hardship. It is, for them, the American Dream in all its glory. A great many others, however, especially those who would not have been admitted under the old standards, flail around helplessly and drop out. And City is often forced to stoop in order to try to raise them up. The truth is that, for all its heroic efforts, City cannot be expected to compensate for the failures of the public schools or of the larger society.

What is true of City is true of college generally. Save for an elite band of highly selective institutions, American higher education operates according to open admissions principles. No country sends so large a fraction of its high school graduates (about three-quarters) to college, and yet the dismal standards that obtain in so many public schools mean that American graduates are less prepared for a college education than students elsewhere in the industrialized world. This is especially true in the inner city, where poverty compounds the problems of low standards and expectations. Open-admissions colleges devote precious energy and resources to remedial rather than college-level programs; however, few of them succeed in graduating as many as half of their students.

Open admissions is a shortcut. As one remedial teacher at City bitterly says, "The great problem with this society is that we don't give a shit about our children. And by the time they get up here, it's too late." If we want to preserve the ideals that made places like City possible, we must do the hard work of development, in schools and communities, rather than offer hollow entitlements. We have to draw serious lessons from success, and we have to be honest about failure.

Part I

The Evolution
of a Great Experiment

1

Too Difficult Life

E very day during the school year thousands of young people swarm out of the IND subway stop at 145th Street and St. Nicholas Avenue, in the middle of Harlem, and toil up a steep hill to the campus of the City College of New York. City is a commuter college, and has been for almost 150 years. The students come from the South Bronx, from East Harlem, from Bedford-Stuyvesant and East New York and Flatbush—from poor and working-class neighborhoods all over New York. The City College student of fifty or sixty years ago was likely to come from the same patches of turf, but in those days the patches, and the students, tended to be Jewish. Now those neighborhoods, and City's student body, consist almost entirely of blacks, Hispanics, and Asians. And so the students laboring up 145th Street, past the truck full of produce and the man who sells African caps and incense from a table and the man who sells English muffins from a grocery carton and the drifting, scowling teenagers with big untied sneakers—these students know the ghetto life around them firsthand. They look on City College as their best chance at salvation from that life. That's a great deal to ask of a college, or of any institution; but those are the stakes. Jim Watts, the

3

chairman of the History department and a City College professor
for almost thirty years, says, "We're charged with creating the middle
class of New York City; that's our mission. And I don't think anything's more important than that."

No, nothing *is* more important than that. No nation has created
so large a middle class, and so prosperous a one, as we have. The
forging of a middle-class nation from the ranks of unlettered immigrants and dirt farmers and the millions in the ghettos, generation
after generation, is arguably America's greatest achievement, and the
crowning glory of industrial capitalism. Our political stability, and
the social equilibrium that has brewed in our melting pot, depend
on the confidence of each new generation of the poor that they, too,
will be inducted into an ever-expanding middle class—the faith that
the American promise applies to them as much as to those who
came before.

Plainly, something has gone wrong with this great process of
assimilation. Poverty has become persistent, and apparently self-
reinforcing, for millions of city dwellers, most of them black or Hispanic. The growth and endurance of this "underclass," despite thirty
years of antipoverty efforts, are corroding our sense of shared purpose and shared interest, and exposing the bombast in our everlast-
ing sense of moral superiority. The middle class feels threatened by
the poor, and politics has shaped itself around resentment and anxiety in a way that would have been unthinkable as recently as President John F. Kennedy's administration. The failure to lift the poor
into the middle class is thus a far graver national problem than the
erosion of middle-class standards and expectations with which we
are now so preoccupied. The market may rescue the middle class;
it is clearly not rescuing the poor. And so we look, with increasing
desperation, toward the institutions that have fostered social mobility
in the past. What can we do—what must we do—to make them work
now? If they're not working, what can we learn from their failure?

In our heavily privatized, free-market society, the schools have
been the public institutions we count on most for the great task of
transformation. As the education scholar Diane Ravitch writes,
"Americans are deeply committed to self-improvement and the
school is an institutionalized expression of that commitment." We

expect the public schools to compensate for the lottery of birth by offering to everyone the basic skills required for middle-class life. But that's not happening. Study after study, most recently Jonathan Kozol's *Savage Inequalities*, has documented the utter failure of the schools to equalize the life chances of the poor and the middle class.

As the public schools' task is set by the shortcomings and failures of the world around them, so City College's task is set by those disadvantages *and* the failures of the public schools to overcome them. The stakes are very high; but that uphill climb is extremely steep. Jim Watts describes City's student body with a grim calculus: "You have a million kids who are going through an incredibly poor public school system, where literally nothing of value is learned; the schools are just holding pens. Maybe half the kids come out the other side. The bulk of those either don't go to college or go to community college." City, Watts says hopefully, gets a "hardy band of survivors." City can't even reach the majority; but what kind of transformation can it work in the survivors, hardy or not? Do the limits lie in the college or in the students? And this, in turn, begs one of the threshold questions of modern American liberalism: How powerful are our institutions in the face of the economic and cultural forces that now perpetuate inner-city poverty?

I first took the IND up to City College in January 1992. A few weeks earlier nine kids had been trampled to death by a crowd pushing to get into a basketball game featuring rap stars in City's Nat Holman Gym. Rap music, basketball, ungoverned energies, violence, and death—it was a moment that crystallized a public view of City College as a menacing site of underclass culture, a grim proof of the failure of sixties liberalism and of the utter collapse of a great institution. But on campus the tragedy had almost no resonance at all. The painfully earnest chairman of the Psychology Department offered grief counseling sessions, but the only people who went were other professors. None of the kids who had died, and not many in the crowd, had attended City College. The tragedy may have opened a window onto rap culture or the culture of poverty that surrounded the campus, but City College was not to be confused with its neighborhood. So far as I could see, the campus was full of students doing

what students do everywhere—studying in the library, gossiping and
playing cards in the cafeteria. It wasn't menacing, and it wasn't slack.

Those first, eye-opening visits of mine took place during the
quiet time between semesters. Not until early March did I attend
my first City College class—World Humanities 101, part of City's core
curriculum. The teacher, Grazina Drabik, had asked me to come fifteen minutes late. She said there was something she had to talk to
the class about. I walked up three flights of swaybacked stone steps
in old Shepherd Hall; listened to my footsteps as they echoed down
a long, semicircular hallway; pushed open a heavy wooden door;
and took a seat in the middle of the class. The classroom itself was
a fine relic of City's bygone age—high ceiling, bare floor, scuffed
wainscoting, old-fashioned desks, and a wall of windows at the far
side. There were about thirty-five students in the class. Drabik was
standing off to the side of the blackboard, and I could see that she
hadn't finished her private session with the students. On the board
she had written two columns of phrases. The first, headed "Student
Problems," consisted of the following:

> too much work
> too difficult life
> small disasters

The second, labeled "Problems with Student Work," included:

> late/absences
> inc. or sloppy work
> disaster of journals

I had arrived at the tail end of the therapy session— "disaster of journals." The students were reading Dante's *Inferno*, and Drabik had
asked them to record their personal impressions as they read. Hardly
anyone had made more than a cursory effort. Merely doing the
assigned reading had been a struggle— "too much work" —and the
very idea of having "personal impressions" of a serious book, impressions worth recording, was alien to many of the students.

And then there was the problem that Drabik, in her Polish-inspired syntax, had called "too difficult life." The students labored under an amazing variety of handicaps. Philip Orama cared for his six-year-old daughter and worked twenty-five hours a week; he was close to flunking out, but if he dropped a class he wouldn't have enough credits to qualify for financial aid. William Okoi, a Ghanaian immigrant, held down three jobs. Ying Wai Hong, a painfully shy immigrant from Hong Kong, lived in terror of disappointing his parents, not to mention his aunts and uncles. "Since the first day of my education," he said to me one day, "I have not experienced any pleasure in books."

One day an older black student, Judy Edwards, peeked in at the door about half an hour late. She was pushing a stroller that held her eighteen-month-old son, Corey, still wearing his pajamas. A single mother getting by on welfare, Judy had lost her sitter and hadn't yet started with a new one. What to do? Drabik hardly wanted a little boy distracting her all-too-distractable class; but because Judy was a responsible student, and because in any case she always erred on the side of compassion, Drabik ushered them in gaily, calling out, "If he cries, we will expulse you from our Hell!" And so the boy darted around the class in his pajamas while Judy struggled hopelessly to throttle him, Drabik soldiered gamely onward, and the students giggled.

There was something enormously moving in the spectacle of black and Hispanic and Asian students, kids from the neglected edges of American culture, working with their Polish émigré teacher to puzzle out passages from the *Inferno*, the first great work of European culture. Drabik was the rare teacher who engaged both students and texts with passionate curiosity. She could make the systematizing scholarship of Saint Thomas Aquinas feel as pressing as today's newspaper. She was wise, and yet innocent, too. She often came to class in what I thought of as her Young Communist League look—white T-shirt with the short sleeves rolled up, a purse clipped onto her belt, and a scarf thrown over her shoulders and knotted over her bosom. With her pale, plump arms and her small mouth and her dark, shining eyes, she looked like she was ready to lead the class in a record-setting dawn harvest. Her students loved her; Judy told me solemnly that she had heard Miss Drabik was world-famous.

Two or three students resonated like a struck tuning fork to Drabik's inspiring music. Several of the foreign students never spoke in class, but I knew from talking to them that they had been well educated at home and were keeping up fairly effortlessly here. And yet there were times I could hardly bear to sit in class. When it came time to discuss *Macbeth*, it turned out that most of the students, including many of the native English speakers, had been utterly stumped by the text. Drabik spoke eloquently, and the class sat quietly. Few of the students had bothered to read beyond the first act. Drabik had them act out the first witches' scene, and then asked what "Fair is foul, and foul is fair" meant. "Like the end justifies the mean," someone said. Another student offered, "Whoever you got to step on to get ahead, go ahead and do it." Everyone agreed with this interpretation, perhaps because its bleak realism lent it a ring of authenticity.

After class I talked to Hernan Morales, a student who had emigrated from Honduras as a teenager. Hernan admitted that he had made it through John F. Kennedy High School in the Bronx, as well as his first year at City, without ever reading a book. He was an English major, and he had never read a book. The trip to the City College bookstore at the beginning of the semester had given Hernan a jolt. "When I saw that the *Odyssey* was a book this thick," he said, placing his fingers about an inch apart, "I thought, 'This is going to be scary.' " Hernan said that he was getting by primarily on Cliff Notes and movie versions of the assigned classics. His friend Elvira Payamps, who was Dominican, laughed at Hernan's bumpkinishness. She had graduated from LaGuardia Community College with an associate's degree in liberal arts. But she admitted that she hadn't been able to make much more sense of *Macbeth* than Hernan had, and like him had gotten the video and Cliff Notes. "I had this idea that Macbeth had killed Banquo," Elvira said, "but I couldn't tell if I was right. So then I saw the movie, and I knew that I had understood."

Drabik called me after class one day and asked how I thought things were going. When I had told her how much trouble the students were having with *Macbeth*, she sighed and said, "It's better I do not know this."

The river of young New Yorkers heading up from the subway swerves left onto Convent Avenue, a narrow isthmus of peace and burgherlike prosperity between a black and a Hispanic ghetto. When the City College campus moved up from downtown Manhattan to Harlem in 1908, Convent Avenue was an elegant stretch of redbrick townhouses with bay windows and carved lintels and fanciful roof lines. And so, for three blocks, it remains. Then the townhouses give way to dowdy apartment complexes with grimy windows facing the street. And then the past, City's fabled past, reappears at 140th Street, where the students walk beneath a gateway inscribed with a crest that bears City College's motto: "Respice Adspice Prospice" — "Look back, look before you, look ahead."

It's impossible, at City College, not to look back. City is perhaps the longest-running radical social experiment in American history. Founded in 1847, City was America's first urban college, and it became one of the great democratizing institutions of an emerging urban culture. Tuition was free, and admission was open to anyone who qualified. And it wasn't second-rate goods, as the poor were accustomed to. A City College education was something fine. And a City College degree was a talisman, a magic key to the good life available in America. For the tens of thousands who went there, and the millions who knew of it, City College was a living emblem of the American Dream. In *World of Our Fathers*, Irving Howe delivered this mighty trumpet blast on behalf of his own alma mater: "Of all the institutions they [the Jewish immigrants] or their children might encounter in the new world, City College came closest to fulfilling Emerson's promise that 'this country, the last found, is the great charity of God to the human race.' "

City was, against all odds, one of America's great colleges. Between 1920 and 1970 more of its graduates went on to receive Ph.D. degrees than those of any other college except Berkeley, despite the fact that City had no graduate program of its own, no research facilities, nor even a very distinguished faculty. Eight graduates received the Nobel Prize, a record for a public institution. Of the cadre of New

York Jewish intellectuals who grew up just before World War II, a remarkable fraction did their undergraduate studies at City College—not only Irving Howe but Irving Kristol, Daniel Bell, Seymour Martin Lipset, Alfred Kazin. Vast numbers of New York's accountants, and physicists, and teachers, attended City. And these graduates still speak of their college days with reverence.

What distinguished City from every other college at its level was its transformative mission. City did not reproduce privilege, as the Ivy League schools did. It gave poor, talented boys (women were not regularly accepted until after World War II) the opportunity to make it into the middle class; it compressed into a few years a process that otherwise took a few generations. City was the most meritocratic of institutions; and because the idea that a man should get ahead according to his abilities, rather than the accident of birth or background, was the core principle of America's free-market society, City had a moral status that no elite college could claim. City was, as Howe's comment implies, a promise that America kept.

But that promise was challenged by new realities. By the 1960s City's rigorous standards had come to seem like a perpetuation of privilege for the well educated, rather than a commitment to egalitarianism. The civil rights movement advanced the idea that blacks and other disadvantaged groups were being denied the right to develop the abilities that would allow them to compete in the marketplace. That was why the great forces of social mobility were failing for this generation of the poor. And City was an almost helplessly faithful register of the world around it: just as the college had symbolized for generations the meritocratic values of a new urban culture, and of America itself, so now it came to stand for the new principle of "equal opportunity," or, in the more contentious phrasing, "affirmative action." In 1969 black and Puerto Rican students shut down the campus to demand vastly greater access for minority students. There were marches and fires and fistfights, and an irrevocable taking of sides. It was a single moment that defined, in a burst of harsh light, the crisis that liberalism itself was undergoing. The racial challenge could not be either repudiated or accommodated without sacrificing cherished beliefs. Liberalism—the self-confident faith fueled by the engines of assimilation and progress—could not survive this shock. It was no wonder that many of those who viewed City as the incarnation of the American Dream reacted to the uprising as if a holy site had been desecrated.

The students won. City's admissions standards were lowered to open the college to those who had formerly been excluded. "Open admissions" shattered City's history into two parts, "before" and "after." But it also arguably represented continuity, or even consummation, for City was engaged once again in a radical social experiment and in the deeply American labor of transformation. The European immigrants didn't need City anymore; it was the black and Puerto Rican citizens of Harlem, the people who for years had looked up the hill at the remote campus, who needed it now. Because of its history, its before and after, City forced a comparison and a question: Could the forces of social mobility work on the new poor as they had on previous generations?

City College's glorious past remains legible, if sometimes only faintly, beneath the accretions of its contemporary life. Decrepit old Shepherd Hall is being renovated at staggering expense. The terracotta gargoyles that once ran along its upper battlements like Harlem's answer to the Cathedral of Notre Dame have rotted over the decades and have been removed for repairs. The dim, clattering cafeteria that sat in the Shepherd basement has been converted into a music library, a cheery space of bookcases and blond wood. The rest of the old campus, low gray stone buildings built like battleships and named like Ivy League dormitories, fans out on the other side of Convent Avenue—Baskerville, Goethals, Harris, Wingate, and Compton. The old piles are ranged around a grassy quadrangle. In the center is a statue of City's mascot, the beaver—symbol of industry and persistence. This is the one and only wholly appealing place on City's concrete campus to sit outside and take the sun, or read, or chat.

The harmony of the place has been wrecked by the grimly functional architecture of the 1970s, a time when open admissions forced City into an overnight expansion. Beyond the southern border of the old campus, which is all of two blocks from the northern terminus, with its scrolled gateway and Latin crest, looms the vast, graceless bulk of the North Academic Center, or NAC, a Pentagon-like polygon that holds the cafeteria and classrooms and office space for much of the college. And the NAC, in turn, faces a three-story cube—the administration building—and City's one skyscraper, the featureless fourteen-story rectangle of the Science Building. It takes about two minutes to traverse the entire campus—this is, after all, New York City, not Mount Holyoke. And if you stand in the plaza of the NAC building, and turn just so, more or less north-northeast, you can see nothing but the old campus, the spire of a church, and Harlem spread out in the distance.

City has a strange, hodgepodge academic identity that comes of this process of simultaneous accumulation and displacement. In certain respects City is very much a traditional liberal arts / professional college. Every student must pass through an extensive core curriculum, including courses such as World Humanities 101. City has a large and fairly accomplished English faculty, a wide variety of history electives, and several hundred students eager to read good books. The majority of students graduate in one of four professional schools—Engineering, Education, Nursing, and Architecture. City has a number of highly sophisticated programs in the sciences, including the Sophie Davis School of Medicine, an elite five-year program that enrolls 200 undergraduate students. At the same time, in recent decades City, like many other undergraduate colleges, has ramified upward into a quasi-university. Now there are 3,000 graduate students as well as 11,500 undergraduates. And doctoral programs in clinical psychology, physics, engineering, and several other fields are located on the City campus, though in fact they serve all students in the City University of New York, of which City College is a part.

But all of this is only the aboveground portion of the great massif that is City College. Hidden from view, and extending far downward, is City's vast remedial underworld. Three-quarters of City's entering freshmen are assigned to at least one remedial class, in language, math, or "college skills." These classes have hierarchies of their own. Students who hope to be engineers or architects may have to take, and of course pass, four remedial math courses. About a third of entering freshmen are admitted through what is known as the SEEK program, which offers access to senior college to students who cannot meet admissions standards and whose family income falls below a poverty threshold. Most of these students take remedial classes in all three fields. And City's English as a Second Language (ESL) program constitutes an entirely separate track, delicately known as "developmental" rather than "remedial." Another third of entering students begin in the ESL program, though owing to overlap the combined ESL/SEEK population is about half of any given freshman class. These students may spend years trudging upward toward the blue sky of the regular curriculum; many leave City College before even reaching core classes like Grazina Drabik's World Humanities 101. The students I saw there, in other words, represented a culled sample of City's entering class. One large body of students stretches below the core; another stretches above. It's only a slight exaggeration to say that City is really two colleges, a liberal arts / professional institution and a remedial / open admissions one.

City is as heterogeneous demographically as it is academically. A study of the 1,240 incoming students in the class of 1991 found that almost exactly half had been born abroad, in a total of seventy-six countries. Although 39 percent of City's undergraduates described themselves as "black" in 1992, a very large fraction, perhaps as many as half, came from the Caribbean or Africa. Another 28 percent of City's student body is Hispanic, but among them students from Central and South America vastly outnumber Puerto Ricans. According to a survey of freshmen, Dominicans constitute City's single largest foreign contingent (followed by students from Haiti, Jamaica, China, and India). Eighteen percent of undergraduates—and almost one-quarter of graduates—are Asian, and the remaining 14 percent are white. This label, too, conveys a spurious impression of homogeneity. Of City's traditional student base—Jewish and Catholic graduates of the New York public school system—only a tiny remnant remains. Many of City's white students are immigrants from Greece, the Middle East, and Russia. City has been revitalized and buoyed up by this immense tide of newcomers. Many of them bring not only immigrant drive and first-generation values but a solid, if narrow, secondary school education.

I used to meet immigrant students by wandering through the corridors of Baskerville Hall, a building across the street from Shepherd that's used as the headquarters of City's innumerable ethnic clubs. At one end of the dim hallway, laughter and shouts rang out from the open door of the Dominican Student Association. At the opposite end was Han Wave, the club for Mandarin-speaking Chinese students. (The Cantonese-speaking club was upstairs.) There nine or ten students sat in a little room with two desks and bare walls. They were silent; they were bespectacled; and most of them were reading texts with titles like *Operating Systems*.

Right in the middle of Baskerville's first floor, in a privileged position just left of the front door, was LAESA—the Latin American Engineering Students Association. Here I found four or five members slouched around a deal table shooting the breeze. They seemed a good deal quieter than the Dominicans and a good deal more relaxed than the Chinese. One of the guys at the table—they were all men— introduced himself as Wagner Ortuno, the president of the club. He was handsome, coffee colored, with close-cropped black hair, dark eyes, a square jaw, big hands. There was a self-assurance about Wagner that I hadn't seen in many City College students; he obviously enjoyed the deference of the other members. They sat and listened while Wagner perched at the edge of the table, folded his arms across his chest, and talked about the club and about himself.

Wagner had been raised and educated in Quito, Ecuador. His father was an auto mechanic, which explained his unusual name. "Wagner is some brand of auto parts that he worked with," he said with a laugh. "I was named after a brake shoe or something like that." After finishing high school in 1986, Wagner had left, by himself, for New York. "I came here to search for the American Dream," he said without the slightest trace of irony. There was something a little bit self-conscious about the way Wagner presented himself. He saw his life in emblematic terms; and his own struggle to succeed, with all its dead ends and detours and scaled heights, had taken on almost heroic dimensions in his mind. "My first year in New York was the most disappointing time of my life," he went on. By now the others around the table had resumed talking among themselves, but quietly. "I thought everything would be perfect—all the streets were straight, and the money was just there. Then I realized that it *is* there, as long as you work for it. I realized that you can't just stay in the neighborhood, you have to go out and learn the language."

Wagner had climbed up the greasy pole doggedly, and methodically. Rather than pursue his education right away, he had taken English classes at night while working as a laborer by day. After a year he had enrolled at City College, which he had learned of through a cousin who was attending. Wagner set his sights on a degree in electrical engineering, and he followed his star with a fervid intensity. He struggled through ESL and bulled his way through math classes. And here he exploited an advantage that more than compensated for his unfamiliarity with English and with New York. In Ecuador, Wagner had had math shoved down him until it had come out of his pores. He was way ahead of most of the New York City public school products who came to City, and he knew it. "I have seen people here who never took trigonometry in high school," he said with something like awe. He hadn't even been able to grasp the fact that many of the students hadn't taken geometry either. That started a brief conversation with the others about the astonishingly low standards of the New York public school system, which none of them had attended for more than a year or two. They couldn't conceive of graduating from high school without having read a book.

Wagner resumed his story. At first he worked thirty-five hours a week while taking a full load of twelve credits. "I used to work at night, get home in the morning, take a shower, and then come here for my morning class," he said. "And I wound up sleeping in class." Wagner was short-circuiting on his own immigrant drive. He was finally saved from a complete blowout when he was laid off from his job. He had never saved a penny anyway, and he found that he could make do with a combination of state grants and student loans. His grades picked up, and he began to enjoy his studies. Finally he could see his way clear to his goal. The rest was just hard work, which for Wagner was second nature.

For all that he kept his nose to the grindstone, Wagner was a person of surprisingly broad interests. He had taken four or five art courses, as well as courses in music and the history of photography. In fact Wagner was taking more credits than he needed for his degree.

"To be educated means you have to have at least a little bit of knowledge about everything," he explained in his sententious style. Roberto Torres, who was sitting across the table from Wagner, said that he thought core courses like World Civ were a complete waste of time. Everyone agreed. But then Hugo Gonzales mentioned that he sometimes thought of writing a book of literary criticism. He loved Spanish lyric poetry. Didn't everyone? "After all," said another student with a wink, "poetry is the language of love." A general discussion of love ensued. The Latins apparently made for more romantic engineers than the Chinese.

Wagner, Roberto, Hugo, and the others had obviously spent countless hours together. Many of them, like Wagner, had emigrated by themselves; the club was their defense against the loneliness of New York, against poverty, and against the strain of academic life. "A lot of us pretty much live in school," Wagner said. The same could be said for Richard and Jeffrey and many of City's immigrant students. "It's a modus vivendi. It's too far to go back home, and sometimes you don't want to be in that neighborhood." Wagner lived in the immense Latin barrio that stretched for two to three miles along Broadway, just to the west of the campus. "I just use my apartment for sleeping," Wagner continued. "I stay home on Sunday, to be with my girlfriend. Otherwise, I'm here. At night we chip in to buy Chinese food, and sometimes we'll collect pennies until we have enough for soda. And then we'll sit around here and have dinner and watch 'Jeopardy.' " Wagner and the others lived in a world as beset with snares as a fairy tale. And they huddled together in the club for warmth, and safety, and the strength that came with family feeling.

City College had a reputation as a caldron of black rage. The newspapers were full of stories about City's militant and obscurantist Black Studies Department, and especially the department's chair, Leonard Jeffries, a racial chauvinist whose mind was filled with dark Jewish conspiracies. Jeffries had a sizable body of followers on campus and a ready audience in the larger black world. He was a menacing figure who made City seem like a menacing place. But in fact City's reputation was largely undeserved. The school's atmosphere was set more by people like Wagner and his friends than by the Black Studies Department. The campus had become increasingly apolitical as the fraction of immigrants had grown. Wagner, who was a political leader on campus, regularly bemoaned the passivity of his peers.

People at City tended to think of the college as a supremely successful experiment in international living. Especially in New York, with its apparently insatiable appetite for tribal conflict, the City College cafeteria—where Haitians and Moroccans and Russians and Puerto Ricans and Sri Lankans and Peruvians and Khmers and African Americans talked to one another like civilized human beings— was an uplifting spectacle. And this was particularly true for many of City's middle-class white Americans, who tended to be far more taken up with issues of multiculturalism than were the multicultural immigrants themselves. At lunch one day I met an English major who had grown up in a small town outside of Lincoln, Nebraska. Cindy had gone to an all-white high school, and when she brought a black friend home one afternoon her father threatened to throw both of them out of the house. Now she was living in a Hispanic neighborhood in Manhattan, taking a Bible study class in Harlem, and dating a Korean guy. It was Cindy's idea of heaven. She looked around at the sea of faces in the cafeteria and said, "What I like about this place is that the smallest minority is blondes."

City's faculty and staff took tremendous pride in the school's diversity, reveling in the sheer variety of the student body. Edward Cody, a World Civilization teacher, kept a map of the world with pins marking his students' birthplaces. Alan Feigenberg, a professor in the School of Architecture, compiled a list of the sixty-four countries from which the school's students hailed, as well as their parents' birthplaces, the twenty-nine languages they spoke, and their twenty-one ethnic or racial self-classifications (African, Afro-American, Afro-Caribbean, Afro-Hispanic, and so on).

But Feigenberg didn't know what fraction of entering students failed to graduate, or what fraction of graduates failed the licensing exam. This pattern recurred often enough that it made me wonder if City's thoroughly justifiable pride in its diversity wasn't also a way of distracting attention from hard questions. Diversity was a goal that City achieved effortlessly, and daily. And it was, in its way, so

stirring an achievement that no one wanted to question whether the
real experiment, an experiment in social mobility and remedial education, not in international living, was actually working. At one point
in my conversation with Cindy she blurted out that her World Civ
class reminded her of "eighth-grade geography." She hadn't been so
lucky in her choice of teachers as the students in Grazina Drabik's
class. It turned out that Cindy was worried about the low value she
had heard that graduate schools placed on a City degree, and had
seriously considered transferring to Barnard, the sister school of
Columbia, two subway stations to the south. But she had found
enough worthwhile classes in City's uppermost reaches to hold her
attention. And when she had asked herself, "Do I want to go to a
party school with a lot of snobby white girls with attitude?", the
answer had been, "Not likely."

After that first World Humanities class, a student caught up
with me in the hallway and said, "In this book of yours" —Drabik
had asked me to talk about my project— "are you going to be writing
bad things about City College, or good things?" It was such a sincere
and artless question that I instantly gave a straightforward answer.
"I really don't know what I think yet," I replied, "but I'm hoping
to write something good." And I was. I *wanted* City College to work.
My sixties liberalism may have been giving way around the edges,
but it was still the basic shaping influence of my beliefs. I had grown
up with the civil rights movement and the war on poverty; and their
shortcomings or bad endings scarcely discredited the efforts themselves in my eyes. I believed in government activism, and I took it
as a premise that a humane society focuses an important part of its
energy on bringing the poor into the mainstream. I believed in the
old-fashioned meritocratic principle that City College had arguably
abandoned with open admissions, but I was also committed to the
ideal of equal opportunity. It was troubling that in City College's
history the two ideals seemed to rise and fall like the ends of a seesaw.
But the zero-sum equation didn't seem inescapable, and in any case
the sacrifice seemed small enough, and the gain great enough, to
justify the bargain.

That was where my dispositions lay. But I had an even stronger disposition not to lose my grip on the fine-grained reality of the college itself and go sliding down an ideological chute. The boxes at either end were all too neat and snug. For the Left, the experiment *had* to work to vindicate the premise that the only thing holding back the inner-city poor was opportunity; and it *had* to fail to vindicate the Right's belief in an unhindered market—in this case the marketplace of abilities—and its half-acknowledged belief that the poor were responsible for their own plight. Ideological purity was against my nature. And in any case it didn't take long to realize that City College was not a story of the struggle of good and evil; it was a place where competing goods collided with one another. That was precisely what made it worth thinking about seriously.

The questions that I needed to answer were "Why did City work so well in the past?" and "Is it working now, and for whom?" And what did it even mean for a college like City to "work"? Were the students being educated in the same sense that they had been fifty years before? Or did the threshold of success have to be put so low that it represented something self-defeating? Could City serve as an antipoverty program or a fine liberal arts college, but not both? The only way to answer these questions was to become a part of City College's daily life, to sit in on classes and read papers and talk to students and teachers and administrators. To put it in the most grandiose terms, I wanted to see for myself the possibilities and the limits of the American Dream as it exists today. As Jim Watts had said, nothing could be more important than that.

2

"Let the children of the rich and the poor take their seats together . . ."

City College was a radical and controversial experiment long before the advent of open admissions. The college came into being in 1847, when the president of the New York City Board of Education, a wealthy businessman and reformer named Townsend Harris, convened a committee to consider founding a municipal high school or college. New York was already a global metropolis and America's commercial capital, swelling daily with a flood of immigrants from Ireland and Germany. And yet its citizens, except for a tiny elite, had no recourse for the education of their children beyond the age of ten or eleven. The city had no public secondary schools at all, and higher education was available only at Columbia College and the University of the City of New York (now New York University), private institutions that charged tuition. And the two colleges enrolled a grand total of 245 students, as Harris's committee noted in its report to the board. "This truth," the committee observed in a transparent attempt to rally civic pride, "would induce the stranger to suppose that we despised education."

In fact the young nation venerated the idea of public schooling, although it was often behindhand about the reality. The Founding Fathers, and above all Jefferson, had absorbed from Rousseau
and other Enlightenment figures the precept that a society of citizens
rested on the powers of education. "I know of no safer depository
of the ultimate power of the society but the people themselves,"
Jefferson wrote, "and if we think them not enlightened enough to
exercise their control with a wholesome discretion, the remedy is
not to take it from them but to inform their discretion." Denomina-
tional schools had been established in New York, Boston, and Philadelphia within a few generations after the colonists had landed; but
the Jeffersonian idea that the school was to cultivate citizens, rather
than worshipers, took shape in the "common school" movement that
began in New England toward the end of the eighteenth century.

For all its glorious symbolism, the common school movement
remained relatively confined until the 1820s and 1830s—the Age of
Jackson—when the rise of new classes, vying for status in an increasingly open society, put a new premium on education. America was
a young giant; education was a means not only of informing its discretion but of refining its dawning powers. Only in the 1840s and
1850s was public education expanded in a large way beyond the primary school. The first common school had been founded in New
York City in 1805, but it wasn't until 1842 that the Board of Education was established with the goal of developing a network of public schools.

Townsend Harris's committee canvassed the available educational options, found them embarrassingly meager for a great city
in a great nation, and proposed that the board "take the necessary
steps to establish a *Free College* or *Academy.*" An academy, at the time,
was usually an institution preparatory to college. A public municipal
college was something unheard of. And yet state colleges and universities had existed from the time of Jefferson's University of Virginia.
The country had 120 undergraduate colleges, according to an estimate
from the president of Brown College. About 25,000 students were
enrolled. Most of these institutions were private, and tiny; but by
1860 twenty states had established college or university systems.
These new institutions reached far beyond the social elite served by

the Ivy League, though the curriculum they offered was almost wholly classical. Not until the passage of the Morrill Act in 1862 prodded the states into establishing land-grant colleges aimed at farmers and mechanics did anything like vocational higher education come into being.

But the principle of a democratic higher education could still be seen as something new and dangerous in 1847. Within a few weeks of the committee's report, letters began appearing in the *Courier and Enquirer,* one of New York's innumerable newspapers, warning the public of Harris's folly. The letters were signed "Justice," and appear to have been written by a teacher or official of one of the city's two private colleges. "Will the new college do away with ill feeling between the poor and the rich," Justice asked, "or will it foster those dangerous jealousies which, at the present day, some are so studiously blowing into a flame?" He also suggested that the Free Academy might threaten an intellectual order predicated on unhurried contemplation—predicated, that is, on the existence of a leisure class. He wondered if there would be any place in the proposed college "for what is called 'liberal education' —that which regards the sciences not so much in their immediate utilities in respect to physical comfort, as in the free and enlarged views they give of human life and human relations." He indulged in a sneering reference to "the manufacture of soap and the composition of paint," which he understood to be an integral element of the Free Academy's proposed curriculum. And this question, whether colleges could preserve their elite, liberal arts character once they became accessible to the ordinary student, was to figure seriously in the debates over open admissions 120 years later.

Harris had, in fact, proposed that the curriculum of the new institution "have more especial reference to the active duties of operative life, rather than those more particularly regarded as necessary for the Pulpit, Bar or the Medical profession" —the only professions that then required higher education. Harris suggested that the Free Academy offer courses not only in Latin and Greek and rhetoric, as all self-respecting colleges did, but in "Chemistry, Mechanics, Architecture, Agriculture, Navigation, physical as well as moral or mental science. . . ." Harris was proposing a new course of study for a new class of students—the sons of artisans and tradesmen, rather than of landowners and clerics. The curriculum would follow the classical model, though only up to a point. It wasn't the liberal arts component of the proposed school that was new, but, as "Justice's" mockery indicates, the professional component.

Harris's ends were actually more conservative than "Justice" understood; he had no intention of upending the social order. The notion that higher education might be a means of social mobility, a premise that City College came to vindicate as perhaps no other college did, seems not to have occurred to Harris. Quite the contrary; should the new academy succeed, he wrote, it "would soon raise up a class of mechanics and artists, well skilled in their several pursuits, and eminently qualified to infuse into their fellow-workmen a spirit that would add dignity to labor." Harris ridiculed the notion that a thorough grounding in "the laws of the mechanical powers" — physics, to us—would render the mechanic himself "disqualified for handling the saw and plane." It would, he wrote, simply make him a better mechanic.

Higher education could scarcely be the means to social mobility so long as only a few traditional professions required advanced training. But if Harris's college was not meritocratic, in the modern sense, neither was it strictly vocational; and it *was* egalitarian. In a magisterial answer to "Justice," an author who styled himself "Plain Truth" and who was almost certainly Harris himself wrote, "Make [the new college] the property of the people—open the doors to all—let the children of the rich and the poor take their seats together, and know of no distinction save that of industry, good conduct, and intellect." Harris was proposing that the democratic, Jeffersonian principles that governed the common school be reproduced at the most elite levels of education. Perhaps "Justice" was right to be alarmed.

In short order the committee's proposal for a public academy or college was passed by the state legislature, signed by the governor, and overwhelmingly approved in a referendum submitted to the voters of New York City. The Free Academy held its formal opening on January 21, 1849, in a redbrick building on East Twenty-third Street. In a speech to the assembled crowd, the first principal of the Academy, a West Point man named Dr. Horace Webster, struck the note of defiant egalitarianism, and of great purposes, which was to become City's watchword: "The experiment is to be tried," he said, "whether the children of the people, the children of the whole people, can be educated; and whether an institution of the highest grade, can be successfully controlled by the popular will, not by the privileged few."

The curriculum offered to the initial generation of students was precisely the amalgam of the classical and the vocational that Harris had envisioned. There were courses in philosophy, Latin, Greek, and rhetoric; in chemistry, physics and civil engineering; and in drawing, stenography, and bookkeeping. Students could pursue a classical program of studies, modeled on the great colleges of New England, which were in turn based on the precedents of Oxford and Cambridge; or they could take the English track, "intended to prepare for the ordinary business of life." By placing the preprofessional on a par with the scholastic, the Free Academy prefigured the shape of mass higher education in America.

Harris had initially proposed that the college not grant diplomas but simply offer certificates attesting to a given student's attainments. And in fact, according to sociologist and City College historian Sherry Gorelick, only 2,730 students graduated in the college's first half century—out of a total of 30,000. This was a source of perpetual embarrassment to the college and fuel for attack on the part of critics in the press. Many of the students were simply unprepared for higher education; others had to go back to work. But it's also true that there was no very compelling reason to stay in college, since a degree was not yet a negotiable commodity in the job market. Students went to the Free Academy for the education, not for the credential.

The very concept of upward mobility was a new one when Andrew Carnegie suggested in 1889 that philanthropists needed to concern themselves with "ladders upon which the aspiring can rise." Not until 1896 would the New York State Board of Regents mandate the establishment of high schools. Until that time teenagers who wished to continue their education in public school could take the academy's entrance exam, and if they passed they would be assigned to the school's "sub-freshman," or preparatory, class. Thereafter the course was extended to three years, which effectively transformed it into an early version of high school.

For its first half century, City College, as it was renamed in 1866, was an odd combination of high school, college, and trade school. The average age of entering students was fourteen, and the usual level of preparation was correspondingly low. West Point men ran the school until 1903, and they ruled over their charges by means of what City College historian Willis Rudy calls "a patriarchal system of benevolent despotism" —including a minutely calibrated system of demerits. The faculty was undistinguished, teaching methods uninspired, and the attrition rate, of course, appalling. The curriculum, which at one time had seemed novel, barely changed from decade to decade. One of the principal innovations came with the establishment, in 1883, of a two-year workshop course—what high schools one hundred years later called "shop."

Only in the early twentieth century did City begin to evolve into a modern college. In 1903 old General Alexander Webb, the hero of Pickett's Charge at Gettysburg, gave way to a new president, John Huston Finley, a professor of politics at Princeton. Finley relaxed the draconian code of discipline and modernized the curriculum. In 1908, after fifteen years of planning and building, the college moved from Twenty-third Street to its current home atop the St. Nicholas Heights in Harlem. Manhattan had swallowed up the old home in relentless urban sprawl, but the Heights was quiet and clean and remote from the frenetic daily life of the city. The great black migration from the West Side—and from the Deep South—had only just begun. The new college, President Finley declared, would constitute "a lofty interior city" within, yet removed from, the larger city.

The college trustees commissioned the architect George Post to design the campus in the English Collegiate Gothic style that had become, at schools such as Yale, a physical symbol of scholastic nobility. By choosing as his principal building material the light gray schist that constitutes Manhattan's bedrock, Post balanced the aristocratic pretensions of the style with a suggestion of ruggedness, a nod to the real life of the city. The five buildings of the campus formed a quadrangle arranged around a grassy plaza, with a great flagpole in the center. The buildings, square and stout, were trimmed in white terra-cotta and topped by gargoyles representing the various scholarly fields. And at each of the four points of the compass stood twin pillars, joined to one another by arms of delicate iron tracery. The archways, which bore the college's grand Latin motto, marked the boundaries of the lofty interior city without walling it off from the great city beyond.

The gargoyles, the battleship buildings, the solemn Latin tag, all spoke of the aspirations of what was, after all, still a modest and rather backward institution. The citizens of New York City had spent $6 million to ennoble their little college, to give it something of the amplitude of the great academies reserved for the wellborn and the rich. The new college was a symbol of the tremendous energies being unleashed in America's great cities, energies that were born of the nation's commitment to the ordinary man.

The children of the whole people did not, at first, enroll at City College. The student body "was predominantly middle-class in its cast," writes Willis Rudy. The largest number of early students described their father's occupation as "merchant." Most were English, Irish, Scots, and German by birth. And so the institution might have remained had not Alexander II, the tsar of Russia, been assassinated as he returned from an inspection of the Imperial Guards on March 1, 1881. Within weeks the anti-Semitism that had been fostered by his brutal predecessor, Nicholas I, burst out in a series of pogroms that brought terror to the Pale of Settlement, the area straddling the current borders of Russia and Poland where the Jews increasingly had been confined. For the Jews, the pogroms appeared to be yet another episode in a timeless history of pharaonic tyranny; and they responded, as they had before, with exodus—to America, the land of freedom. The Jewish flight from Russia quickly swelled into one of the greatest mass movements in human history. Between 1881 and 1924, when the Johnson-Reed Act, inspired by the postwar Red Scare, suddenly turned off the spigot, 2.8 million Jews left Eastern Europe for the United States.

An insignificant fraction of this vast flood of immigrants, or of their children, ever attended City College or any other college. But it took only a small tincture to turn City College quite swiftly into a Jewish institution. Even in the late 1870s and early 1880s City had had a significant population of German and Sephardic Jews, most of them probably members of the middle class. In 1890 one-quarter of the graduates had Jewish surnames, though almost all of them were German. By 1900 the figure had reached 54 percent, and by 1910, 70 percent. And now almost all of the names were Russian or Polish or Hungarian. The fraction of Eastern European Jewish students at City, and at its sister institutions in the Bronx, Brooklyn, and Queens, never went below three-quarters until well into the 1950s.

How is it that City College, a public institution open to all, became a Jewish enclave for almost three-quarters of a century? The simple answer is that Jews went to college at two to three times the rate of non-Jewish Americans—by the early 1930s almost half of the college students in New York were Jewish—and because the over-whelming fraction of those students were poor, they had little choice but to attend a free college such as City. As Nathan Glazer and Daniel Patrick Moynihan observe in *Beyond the Melting Pot*, "Eastern European Jews showed almost from their arrival in this country a passion for education that was unique in American history." Yes; but *why*?

The traditional answer to this question may be summed up in the phrase "the Jewish love of learning." But scholar Chaim Wax-man writes that Jewish "educational mobility was a manifestation of the Americanization and secularization of Jewish values." While in the Old World, learning had been an end in itself—the greatest of all ends—in the New World, it became a means to that end held dearest by all Americans—success. The philosopher Sidney Hook, who graduated from City College in 1923, grew up, he writes in his memoirs, "in a poverty so stark as to be almost unimaginable these days." The word *slack* struck terror in the boy's heart, because unem-ployment was so often followed by eviction and the dreadful sight of a family turned out on the sidewalk. And yet, Hook writes, "above all there was a feeling of hope. The hope was sustained by faith that the doors of opportunity would be opened by education. No generation of parents has ever sacrificed so much for the education of their children."

Education meant *opportunity*—a word utterly new, yet endowed with an almost supernatural power for Jews who had escaped the sudden violence and continual oppression of life in the Pale. The most astonishing feature of Jewish life in the United States was the speed with which these greenhorns left their poverty behind. The average tenure in the Lower East Side was about fifteen years. By the 1920s and 1930s, Jews were leaving Rivington Street en masse for Brooklyn and the Bronx—new ghettos, to be sure, but not so bad as the old ones. Glazer and Moynihan note that while the Irish took an average of three generations to escape poverty, and the Italians two, the Jews managed in one. Most of them moved from being peddlers to salespeople, not lawyers and doctors. Higher education accounted for only a small portion of Jewish mobility. But a remarkably large *number* of Jewish immigrants seized on education as the royal road to success.

Perhaps, then, the question should be taken back one step: Why were the Jews so driven to succeed? One plausible answer is that they were no more driven than the Irish or the Italians, but as urbanites in an urban environment they simply had better survival skills. And yet the burning drive to make it in the New World is a fixture of virtually every account of Jewish immigrant life, whether in fiction or in memoirs. Perhaps, as Chaim Waxman writes, material success meant "national liberation" to the Jews after the forty years in the desert of tsarist oppression. Or perhaps it was the humiliation of life in the tenements of the New World, rather than in the Egypt of the Old World, that cried out for vindication. The Jews of Eastern Europe, for all their poverty, thought of themselves as the heirs of a great tradition. But the Lower East Side was merely squalid—an intolerable affront to respectable folk. In his memoirs, the writer and critic—and City College graduate—Alfred Kazin recalls his parents' desperate hopes that he restore their vanished respectability. "My mother and father worked in a rage to put us above their level," he writes; "they had married to make *us* possible. We were the only conceivable end to all their striving; we were their America." The reason that Asian immigrants are forever being compared to the Jews of another generation is not so much that they both have a timeless tradition of learning and wisdom as that they share a fierce competitiveness, a horror of failure, and a willingness to make almost any sacrifice in order to get ahead.

If the Jewish hunger for success was so often satisfied in the schools, it also had a great deal to do with the transformation of the schools themselves. By the early period of immigration, public education in New York had become systematic, but only up to the age of eleven or twelve. The city's first public high school—Boys' High—was established in 1895. Even in the years before World War I, a period of tremendous growth in public schooling, only one-fifth to one-quarter of Americans received a high school diploma. And no more than one in twenty earned a college degree. At least until the turn of the century, a college education was more a source of intellectual and cultural refinement than of professional advancement.

But the rise of the corporate and public bureaucracy in the early years of the century made educational attainment the key to economic success. Large organizations needed trained accountants, not just bookkeepers. They needed managers and lawyers, and armies of engineers and technicians. The new professions were spawning new forms of postgraduate training—law schools and medical schools and schools of business. And the rapidly expanding public school system itself created a huge demand for teachers. Academic knowledge became valuable as an instrument rather than an end in itself. And the school system itself, with its clear vertical hierarchy, and its testing and its academic "tracks," became an emblem of the emerging meritocracy as well as the prime source of winners. Success in school proved that you were ready to succeed in the new world of bureaucratic capitalism. Alfred Kazin and his parents understood that school was becoming the great sorting device for the emerging professional class. And all you needed in order to thrive was intelligence and determination. It was an impersonal system; it made no difference who you were, so long as you could master its rules. No message could have been more beautiful for the Jews, who since time out of mind had been persecuted precisely because of who they were and whose success was forever being held against them.

The epicenter of the Jewish fixation on higher education was City College, which had accommodated these poor and awkward and insular children of refugees from the moment they had begun to arrive in America. That City College could truly be theirs seemed a blessing of incalculable value. In *The Rise of David Levinsky*, Abraham Cahan's novel of the Jewish greenhorn, the main character reveres City College as a secular temple and a symbol of human glory: "I would pause and gaze at its red, ivy-clad walls, mysterious high windows, humble spires; I would stand around watching the students on the campus and around the great doors, and go my way, with a heart full of reverence, envy, and hope, with a heart full of quiet ecstasy. It was not merely a place in which I was to fit myself for the battle of life, nor merely one in which I was going to acquire knowledge. It was a symbol of spiritual promotion as well. University-bred people were the real nobility of the world. A college diploma was a certificate of moral as well as intellectual aristocracy."

For all his rapture, Levinsky turned out to be too eager to make his fortune to actually enroll at the college. He might have been chastened if he had, since accounts of City from the early part of the century make it sound like a poorly maintained high school. "The classrooms were bare, the chairs and desks of the plainest," writes Bernard Hershkopf, a graduate of the class of 1906 cited by Irving Howe. "The blackboards were grayed over with the chalkdust pressed into them over many years. The library was crowded and old; it had not really been well kept up for a number of years." And yet Hershkopf revered City every bit as much as the fictional Levinsky had. What he loved about the college was that it was filled with young men like Levinsky. "Scores of them thirsted for learning as men long lost in the desert must thirst for water," Hershkopf writes. "None could halt or defeat such deep-rooted determination to learn. We knew it as gospel truth that this plain College was for each of us a passport to a higher and ennobled life."

This is perhaps the earliest statement of a critical theme: City College, as an institution, was incidental to its own greatness. City was a place where bright young men educated *themselves*. If this is so, then City's history scarcely provides comfort for those who believe the college can educate students who arrive without that desperate thirst for knowledge.

The relationship was at the very least mutual. America had worked a profound transformation in this ancient, pious, and backward-looking tribe, and the Jews, in turn, transformed the American institutions that served them. The Jews who swarmed into City College had ambitions that Townsend Harris couldn't have anticipated. They were hoping not to improve themselves but to make themselves new—to become Americans, intellectuals, middle-class professionals. And by their desperate ambitions and their feverish hopes they transformed City from a symbol of Jacksonian democracy to a symbol—perhaps *the* symbol—of the new America of assimilation, competition, and mobility.

The Jews treated City College as the upward extension of the public school system, the apex of the emerging meritocracy. City even had a miniature meritocracy of its own: the old preparatory program had evolved into the Townsend Harris High School, where admission was awarded to the top 200 finishers in a two-and-a-half-hour exam in vocabulary and math. Townsend was at least as heavily Jewish as City. It was as if somebody had finally invented a sport in which the Jews could be world champion.

Townsend boys got into City almost automatically; they had already proved their mettle. Others had to clear a number of barriers. The issue of City's selective admissions policies was later to become a supremely sensitive one, because partisans of open admissions were scarcely willing to concede that City's greatness had depended on the exclusion of the overwhelming majority of students. City's first open admissions president, Robert Marshak, insisted that the myth of "the brilliant Student Superachiever" was overblown, since City's selective admissions policy had lasted only "the short period of three decades." And it's true that during its first half century City had granted admission to anyone who passed an entrance exam. Starting in 1900, when the high school system had begun to be established, any student with a high school diploma was accepted.

But it's also true that in 1900 somewhere between 6 and 17 percent of Americans, depending on which figures are used, were completing high school. *All* colleges were selective at the time. And in 1924, when the high schools were turning out far more students than City could accommodate, the school refused to consider candidates with grade-point averages less than 72. By the late 1930s—the period that Marshak was thinking about—the minimum average was fluctuating between 80 and 83. But these numbers mean virtually nothing in today's terms, since City also required that entering students have completed a minimum of 15 academic credits, including two and a half years of math and five years of foreign languages—a minimum threshold that scarcely any latter-day public school students could meet. In the 1920s or 1930s it meant that students who had attended vocational schools, or had taken the commercial or preparatory track in an academic high school, couldn't get in at all. Even in the academic high schools, City was accepting only the top quarter or so of graduates. In an age when the Ivy League colleges were sharply limiting the number of Jews they accepted, as well as talented, unpedigreed students of all sorts, the City College student body represented perhaps the purest intellectual elite in the country.

A 1944 study of New York City's public colleges, the Strayer report, offers a vivid, and solemn, analysis of a readily identifiable type of young man. "Probably no group of college students of comparable size has a higher level of academic aptitude," the authors noted. All four of New York's public colleges ranked in the top sixth of the country in terms of average student performance on a test of "mental ability." The students were very young. As of the middle of the 1942 school year, 36 percent of City College's entire liberal arts population was still under age eighteen. "Physically," the study found, "they tend to be less well-developed, their average weight and height being well below comparable averages. The proportion of physical defects is also believed to be somewhat higher than that among other college populations."

Almost all of the students came from "lower income groups," the authors noted. "As many as 40 percent of the fathers would classify as unskilled laborers, on relief, unemployed, not living with the family, or deceased." And virtually all of them were first-generation immigrants. Only 17 percent of the fathers and 22 percent of the mothers of City College freshmen who entered in 1938 had been born here. About 10 percent of parents had themselves graduated from college; 40 percent hadn't made it beyond the eighth grade. In socioeconomic terms, these young men were probably more disadvantaged than the students who flocked to City decades later as a result of open admissions.

Two psychological characteristics of the student body especially struck the report's authors. The first was ambition. "Nowhere
is the motivation for getting a college education more intense," they
wrote. They quoted a counselor to the effect that "our students
have enormous driving power arising out of personal ambitions,
family pressures, economic needs and incentives, and the fact that
they are definitely and consciously on the way up the economic
and social ladder." The second characteristic, in part a consequence
of the first, was the students' rank immaturity. Another counselor
was quoted as saying, "Our students are markedly lacking in social
skills, the ability to meet people and to get along with them. They
frequently feel ill at ease in a social situation and cannot engage
in a conversation in other than argumentative fashion." A third
counselor observed, "Even their drive, persistence, and competitiveness, by offending others and especially employers, operate to frus-
trate them."

This, then, is the hothouse that was City College at the zenith
of its glory: a den of precocious boys, at once coddled and driven
by their parents, pale and frail, fierce and argumentative, pushy,
awkward, sensitive, naive, and fearful. Everything about them was
so recently formed—even their bookishness. For all the Jewish love
of learning, most of these students grew up in bookless, semiliterate
households. Alumni from this era recall fathers who read a Yiddish
newspaper, if that, and mothers who neither read nor wrote. Yet
books and ideas seemed almost the most solid thing in their world.

Wilbur Daniel, a graduate of the class of 1942 (who died in
1993), said, "I received an extraordinary education from the public
schools, but also from one other source—the New York Public Library.
I had six public libraries within walking distance of our apartment,
and when I was young I was only allowed to take out one book at
a time, so I would go from one library to the next, taking out a book
from each." When he got older Daniel would go up to Union Square
to hear the debates on Saturday and Sunday. Over at the Communist
Party corner he could listen to the Trotskyists, the Schachtmanites,
and the Lovestoneites play dueling dialectics. "It was the best possible
course in rhetoric, in logic, in marshalling evidence, and in the uses
of obfuscation," he recalled.

It's no surprise that old City College boys often can't remember how they first formed their love of reading; they lived in a world suffused with ideas and debate, as today's world is charged with products and consumption. There were perhaps half a dozen regularly published Yiddish newspapers in New York, and even more English-language newspapers, and Workmen's Circle discussion groups, and literary societies named after great English writers, and of course the library system and the schools. It wasn't simply that the boys who made it to City College had native ability; they grew up in a world where those abilities were fostered and encouraged in a way that would be inconceivable today. In their world, at least, nothing was admired more than being smart. Even the most devout socialist believed in the intellectual elite— "the intelligentsia," as they said in the Soviet fashion.

And for all their poverty, and the sickening fear bred by the depression, the immediate world they were raised in was stable and almost suffocatingly snug. For the first few generations the Lower East Side, where people had been piled atop one another in a density perhaps never before experienced in human history, was an infamous den of crime and disease. But as the immigrant population stabilized, and the immigrants were dispersed across the city, the conservative traditions that had dominated the faith for centuries reasserted themselves. The kinds of pathologies that beset the inner-city poor today were virtually unheard of in Brownsville or East New York. Divorce was extremely rare in poor Jewish families, as were alcoholism, domestic violence, and the like. Many of the fathers, as the figures of the Strayer report indicate, had been unstrung by a combination of disorientation and poverty. But they were present, and often powerfully so. The terrible struggle between the first-generation paterfamilias and the child of the New World, determined to forge an identity for himself out of the materials at hand, was told a thousand times over in the Jewish literature and the memoirs of that era. But this Oedipal combat looks almost like a luxury from the perspective of today's City College, where so many of the students are survivors of shattered families and bullet-ridden neighborhoods, and a sizable fraction have children of their own to support, often without a mate.

And then there were the schools. The New York City public school system of fifty to sixty years ago has been so thickly wrapped in a mantle of nostalgia as to utterly obscure the reality. The dropout rate was high, the facilities were filthy and cramped, and many of the teachers were barely trained. It was an inegalitarian system: good students rose to the top and poor students were left to flounder and drop out. But there's no question that the good students received a thorough academic grounding. For one thing, teaching in the public schools was one of the most secure jobs available during the Depression, so talented men and women who might have gone on to something better wound up on high school faculties. Most high schools were tracked, and students in the honors track were expected to take a rigorous curriculum—three years of math, Latin, French, European history, the classics of English literature. Very few students in today's public schools undergo this kind of regimen; and of those that do, not many elect to go to City College. The grading system of that era looks draconian next to today's vastly more forgiving standards. "A 90 or better was phenomenal," says Bernard Berlly, a graduate of DeWitt Clinton High School and City College. "An 85 was doing really well."

And if you did well in school, and your parents had no money, you went to City College. "In my neighborhood," says Sid Finger, who grew up in the East Bronx, "you went to high school, you graduated, and you went on to City College." By the late 1930s and early 1940s, City College was a far grander place than the overgrown schoolhouse Bernard Hershkopf had known. It had relocated to its Gothic campus in Harlem and had 8,000 students or more studying in dozens of departments or in the schools of business—located at the old address downtown—or engineering. But the campus had already become thoroughly dilapidated. The library facilities were meager, the science departments and the engineering school had to make do with outdated equipment. The intellectuals who have since written about the City College of that era had a low opinion of its academic standards. "For the bright, inquiring student," Irving Kristol has written, "City College was a pretty dull educational place." In his memoirs, *A Margin of Hope*, the late Irving Howe recalled, "Most of the teaching was mediocre" —in his field, English, "quite poor," and in the social sciences, "hopeless."

City simply couldn't compete for topflight scholars. The pay was poor and the working conditions worse. Professors who might have been inclined to pursue original work were left staggering by a mandatory teaching load of fifteen hours a week. City was a municipal institution, after all, with all the limitations that entailed. The Board of Higher Education meddled in faculty selection; until 1937, in fact, the board enjoyed the right to choose departmental chairs, which permitted it not only to discriminate against Jews but to ensure a steady supply of political hacks at the top of City's professoriat. The chairman of the Math Department referred to himself as "the LaGuardia Professor," in honor of his political patron. The meritocracy that reigned among students thus functioned hardly at all within the faculty.

Nobody could call the curriculum innovative; City always lagged a generation or two behind the better schools. A City College education was a thing of breathtaking narrowness and perfect clarity. For their first two years virtually everybody at the college studied the same thing. The required courses for the College of Liberal Arts and Sciences included two terms of English composition; two terms of math; four terms of foreign languages, classical and modern; and a remarkable four terms of speech. "A great many freshmen," the authors of the Strayer report delicately noted in explanation of this requirement, "have developed careless or provincial habits of speaking." "They were trying to get the 'Long Gisland' out of you," as Lawrence Plotkin, a member of the class of 1940, puts it more bluntly. Also required were survey courses in English literature, economics, government, history, science, art, and music. Students had to take one course in biology, chemistry, or physics. And they had to take four semesters of hygiene, or gym—perhaps to counter their waxy pallor and puny stature.

Nor can City be said to have been ably led. The president of the school from 1926 to 1938 was a colorless and stern figure named Frederick Robinson, a sort of efficiency expert at large in the liberal arts. Robinson once told an audience, "Organized business and our government bureaus and offices need competent leaders, lieutenants, and craftsmen who are also scholars." The students considered Robinson a reactionary, and he seemed to consider them a pack of ruffians. His position became untenable soon after he waded into a group of students at a pacifist demonstration, wielding the point of his umbrella.

In many ways the students at City College educated themselves. As Irving Kristol wrote, "The student who came seeking an intellectual community, in which the life of the mind was strenuously lived, had to create such a community and such a life for himself." This was certainly true in the hermetic, flushed and altogether thrilling world inhabited by Kristol and his friends. This was the world known as Alcove 1, the left-wing debating society that thrived in the 1930s and 1940s and has contributed immeasurably to City's mythic status.

Leftism of some stripe was all but mandatory for these poor and working-class Jewish boys. Not only had they inherited a strain of socialism from their parents, but growing up in the Depression they felt, as Irving Howe writes, that "something had gone terribly wrong." Something was out of joint not only in their own families, where able-bodied fathers sat idly in the parlor, but in the system itself. And at least the more intellectual among them transmuted the anxiety they felt into a political program, and into the habit of viewing established institutions and practices critically. They felt a need to reorder a broken world, a need that contributed greatly to their intellectual growth.

Alcove 1 was one of the immensely long tables that bordered the window side of City's vast, gloomy, and grim cafeteria. It belonged, by tradition already immemorial in Kristol's day, to the adherents of the sectarian anti-Stalinist Left. The Trotskyists were the leftmost faction, while the Social Democrats defined the permissible boundary of moderation; and all were united in their staunch opposition to Stalinism, whose brainwashed automata—or so they appeared to Alcove 1—occupied the next table over, known as Alcove 2. In Alcove 1, everything was open to debate. Brilliant, argumentative, and uncouth boys swallowed the cream cheese sandwiches they had brought from home and wrangled endlessly over the correct "line" in literature, anthropology, philosophy, and of course politics. Howe, the de facto leader of the Trots, recalled starting a discussion, leaving for class, returning hours later, and finding the exact same discussion raging with a completely different set of characters. "We made our dark little limbo of Alcove 1 a school for the sharpening of wits," Howe writes.

Alcove 1 has since become a kind of synecdoche for City College in the 1930s, though in fact only a few dozen students camped out there at any one time the way the two famous Irvings did. The other alcoves were occupied by Catholics, Zionists, and various other interest groups. At Lawrence Plotkin's alcove the partisans fought over the relative merits of the Dodgers and the Giants (both, of course, then operating out of New York). But Alcove 1 was important not only because it shaped the minds of some of our leading intellectuals but because it recalls the tremendous urgency that ideas held for young men growing up in the late 1930s. The world was in tumult: The Loyalists were fighting the Fascists in Spain, Hitler was advancing on Central Europe, and capitalism was failing at home and in Europe. A sense of intellectual engagement gripped even City's nonpolitical majority. Lawrence Plotkin, who was a member of City's ROTC unit—the largest in the country, he says—recalls thrilling to news of the great Jewish republic supposedly being established in the USSR. "It had wonderful reviews in the *Daily Worker,*" he recalls dryly.

At the same time, it would be wrong to think of City at its zenith as simply a site where brilliant young men bounced ideas off of each other; the institution *did* matter. Students less gifted than the Irvings speak of City as a transforming experience. "It was an extraordinary education," said Wilbur Daniel. "At the very least, it was the equal of the best schools in terms of the range of subjects and the depth with which they were studied." Daniels's estimate of the school's standards may be colored by nostalgia, but students who went from City to the best graduate schools seem not to have felt ill prepared. Lawrence Plotkin says that his undergraduate psychology notes stood him in very good stead for his graduate studies at Columbia.

For students like Daniel and Plotkin, City was an extension of their high school experience—a place with rigorous standards and high expectations. All candidates for a B.A. degree were expected to master Latin as well as a Romance language. B.S. candidates, even in the social sciences, were required to pass solid geometry, advanced algebra, and elementary physics. Students at Big Ten schools may have been attending pep rallies (at least in the Andy Hardy movies), and Harvard boys may have been clicking martinis in their finals clubs; but City College boys studied. The memory that many of them have is of leaving the campus for a dreary job, and then coming home and studying until their eyes hurt.

The only really renowned scholar at City College was the philosopher Morris Raphael Cohen, a Russian immigrant who had emigrated to the United States as a teenager, graduated from City in 1899, and, after receiving his Ph.D. from Harvard, settled at City for forty years. Cohen was an archetypal City College success story, though it was clear that anti-Semitism had limited his career; no college other than City would offer him a paying job, despite the enthusiastic support of William James and Josiah Royce, among others. Even City's Philosophy Department at first refused him a position, and Cohen was forced to teach mathematics. For several generations of students, Cohen represented the Olympic level of the intellectual sport that they had mastered—or thought they had mastered. Cohen was a brilliant and remorseless practitioner of the Socratic method, although, as he himself conceded, he lacked Socrates' courtesy.

The City College of the 1930s and 1940s, ill kempt and overcrowded, resembled one of the giant public high schools of the time. And yet City had something of the spirit of a small New England college. It was a high-minded place, a monastery dedicated to the secular religion of reason, science, and the study of Western culture. The campus was tiny and self-contained, walled off from the world. It was a place without hierarchies: no graduate students, no exclusive social clubs, no unapproachable academic colossi. Only a handful of people ran the college's affairs. Everyone taught or studied; there was nothing else to do. The only diversions were participating in the occasional political protest, and rooting for the basketball team, coached by the legendary Nat Holman. Even the basketball program was part of City's cult of hard work and overachievement. Year in and year out, Coach Holman molded his squad of undernourished, aggressive Jewish boys into one of the top teams in the city. In 1950

City became the first, and last, college to win both the National Invitational Tournament and the NCAA championship.

The relationship between City College and its students was actually a fairly reciprocal one. The students transformed the nature of the institution; but the institution also put its imprint on the students. Nor was this shaping process wholly intellectual. For all that the student body was almost entirely Jewish, City, as an institution, remained resolutely Christian. And the good Christian souls who ran the college understood their role in missionary terms that would be unthinkable in our own era, when we let a thousand multicultural flowers bloom. The scholar Sherry Gorelick writes, in the modern vein, that "Western elite culture dominated the curriculum at CCNY. It permeated course content and faculty scholarship.... Jewish students commuting between these two cultural worlds subjected themselves to a world of business assumptions and Anglo-Saxon dominance." Gorelick insists that success in such a world was fraught with self-denial: "It required some form of confrontation with a dominant, alien but seemingly all-embracing way of life."

Gorelick would be right if she were describing students today, many of whom consider Western elite culture the ideology of the oppressor. And yet Western elite culture was precisely what most City College students once wanted to master (and what many of City's first-generation immigrants *still* want to master). They were reading not Scholem Aleichem but Tennyson and Pope. Even the rabid leftists didn't think to demand courses in labor history, or in immigration policy. They had been struggling to escape the harsh realities of ghetto life since they were children; and for all the pain they felt when their fathers accused them of spitting at God, they knew that the ultimate purpose of a City College education was to give them escape velocity. For them, as for almost all the children of immigrants, assimilation was *good*. If many old City College boys sport an almost plummy elocution today, despite having grown up in the Bronx, it's because they took to heart all those Christianizing lessons in speech class.

There's a polemical edge to the issue of whether City's greatness lay in the students or in the institution. If it's the former, then there's no reason to believe that the college could achieve anything like its old stature with a less gifted group of students. If it's the latter, then City's history provides some justification for faith in an experiment like open admissions. If City was in fact the author of its own greatness, one could mine its past for evidence of the power of institutions to overcome disadvantage. But in truth the college was only the last of a series of strong institutions that shaped the young men who went there. The family, and the larger community, imparted the values that made them self-disciplined and confident and ambitious. The schools, and the libraries, and the specifically Jewish culture of argument and debate, trained their minds and made intellectual work seem like the most natural thing in the world. Life had groomed them to thrive in an environment like City College's. City's own role was to cull the winners of a meritocratic race, and to channel their raw intellectual energies into rigorous academic labor and soften their rough edges through resolute high-mindedness. The City College of today, however, can neither count on the formative power of those prior institutions nor select the students likeliest to thrive in its own setting. The old City College refined those who came there; the new City College is expected to transform them.

3

Baptism of Fire:
The Birth of a New Order

The City College of 1964 was not immensely different from the City College of 1940. The school was now about two-thirds rather than four-fifths Jewish. Most of the students were second- or third-generation Americans, though still first-generation college-goers. They constituted essentially the last generation of working-class Jewish kids in New York, and they were certainly better off than those titans of yore who had gotten by on cream cheese and dialectics. Many of them came to school in cars, some—or so it is said—in sports cars. A City College education was still free, still about a generation behind the times, and probably significantly better than what had been available twenty-five years earlier. A whole generation of young, largely Jewish academics had arrived in the 1950s, thus bringing the faculty up to par with the students. It was a brilliant, end-of-summer moment at City College.

In his memoirs, *Working Through*, English professor Leonard Kriegel recalls a 1964 class he taught on Emerson as representing a high-water mark of intellectual and social freedom. The chains of the McCarthy era had fallen away; the turbulence of the 1960s, with its insistent politicization and its hostility to traditional scholarship, had not yet arrived. In their openness and vitality the students kindled in the young scholar an overwhelming sense of devotion to the institution. The college remained, in Kriegel's words, "The best that man in his cities could expect in the way of a college education."

It wasn't City, but the world around it, that was changing rapidly. The European migration, and above all the Jewish migration, had ended forty years earlier. And as that great movement of humanity had slowed, another had begun. Blacks in large numbers started leaving the South for northern urban centers in the 1920s. New York City's black population went from 150,000 in 1920 to 450,000 in 1940 to 1.1 million in 1960. And that was only one of two mass migrations. After World War II impoverished Puerto Ricans began to leave the island for New York. The Puerto Rican population of New York shot up from 70,000 in 1940 to 720,000 in 1961. In twenty years the black and Puerto Rican fraction of New York's population went from 6 percent to almost 25 percent. Ten years later it would be close to one-third.

In that short span of time the image of urban poverty—of "the masses"—had changed utterly. The rapid urbanization of an essentially pastoral black population had an overwhelming effect on American society as a whole. The rise of an educated black bourgeoisie, and the dawning of a new consciousness among blacks generally, gave impetus to the civil rights movement, and thereby made black people, and their plight, visible to the American public for the first time. Americans were now forced to recognize that the dismal condition in which most black Americans lived was not an incidental effect of some natural order of things but a consequence of a history of mistreatment. Black urban poverty, unlike the white urban poverty of previous generations, came to be widely accepted as an indictment of American society.

City College had never had many black students (though A. Philip Randolph and Colin Powell were notable exceptions). In the early 1960s probably no more than 2 percent of City's daytime students were black, along with a much smaller number of Puerto Ricans. The other public senior colleges in the city had only a slightly larger minority population, but City operated under a special symbolic burden. The campus was located in the middle of Harlem; and yet blacks who aspired to a better life could scarcely view the campus as the fulfillment of their dreams, as David Levinsky had when City College was a redbrick building on Twenty-third Street. "Our vision was of City College as a white institution sitting up and *over* Harlem, very much like Columbia," says Bruce Hare, a black graduate of the class of 1969 and now the chairman of the Black Studies Department at Syracuse University. Until the age of seven, Hare had lived on 135th Street, and he used to point up the hill to the campus and ask his grandfather, "Who's up there?" And his grandfather, a mailman, would solemnly intone, "The smart people." And Hare understood that the smart people were not his people.

College attendance among blacks had been growing even faster than for the population as a whole, doubling virtually every decade since 1930. But the college-going rate among blacks was still half that of whites, and more than half of black students were enrolled in two-year institutions. Poverty depressed the black college-attendance rate, but so did low high school graduation rates and poor performance on standardized tests. The black presence on campuses with selective admissions policies such as City was thus minute.

A study by Allan Ballard, a black professor of political science at City, offered graphic evidence of the way in which the schools' meritocratic standards made admission almost impossible for minority students. Ballard counted the number of students qualified to enroll at City in the 1968 graduating classes of two predominantly black high schools. At Benjamin Franklin, in Manhattan, 11 students out of 318 met the criteria. At Boys' High, in Brooklyn, the figure was 7 of 353. Black students weren't even getting into the pool. The black dropout rate citywide was 50 percent, as opposed to 13 percent for whites. Blacks were also far more likely to be found in vocational or nonacademic programs than the academic ones required for admission; and only a few black students in academic programs achieved a grade-point average of 83 or more.

In 1965 Ballard and a number of progressive white faculty members at City started a pilot program, known as College Discovery, for about 150 black graduates of high schools in Harlem and the Bronx. The premise of the program was the premise, in miniature, of the civil rights movement and the Great Society: Racism had denied black people their rightful place in society, and had prevented them from fulfilling their potential. Special efforts had to be made to prevent that potential from being wasted. "This was something that was good for the college as well as for the society," says Bernard Sohmer, a math professor who helped devise the program. "There was a whole population out there that wasn't being addressed by the college. And we knew that the program should grow." College Discovery worked like a scholarship program: students who hadn't done well enough to qualify for admission, but had been recommended by their counselors or school officials, were given intensive remedial instruction and counseling in order to prepare them for the regular college curriculum.

City College's reformist impulse converged with a far more powerful, and more pragmatic, institutional drive. Four years earlier the City University of New York (CUNY), incorporating City and the other municipal colleges, had been established. This was a moment of unprecedented growth in college attendance, and CUNY was created to establish in New York City a coherent system of mass higher education, such as existed in most states, including New York. Its initial long-range plan, published in 1962, called for $400 million in capital improvements from the state. The Holy Plan, as it was called after its author, suggested that the senior colleges begin accepting the top 30 percent of high school graduates, rather than the top 20 percent, and that the community colleges be significantly expanded. New York's "new immigrant populations," a phrase apparently intended to refer to Puerto Ricans and blacks who had emigrated from the South, might thus be accommodated with only a small diminution of the colleges' elite status. These proposals were largely accepted in CUNY's master plan, promulgated in 1964 by the new chancellor, Albert Bowker.

CUNY expanded rapidly throughout the 1960s, but almost entirely through the establishment of new community colleges. The four-year colleges neither grew substantially nor relaxed their standards. Minority enrollment at the prestigious senior colleges remained at no more than 5 to 6 percent. And yet it was clear, for demographic if not for political reasons, that the situation couldn't last. Julius Edelstein, then a CUNY vice chancellor, recalls that "Bowker had studied the population projections, and he saw that the elite populations, including the bright people from Jewish homes, were being admitted into the premium colleges. Although CUNY was terribly crowded at that time, he could see that a big fall in enrollment was going to occur if he tried to maintain the senior colleges' traditional standards." Even those better students who couldn't afford private college were enrolling in one of the better-funded colleges of the state university system. If CUNY was going to grow, it had to begin attracting minority students into the senior colleges.

College Discovery offered CUNY officials their first opportunity to catch up with the city's changing demographics. In 1966 CUNY changed the program's name to SEEK and instituted it throughout the system. SEEK grew almost immediately from hundreds to thousands of students, creating for the first time a real black presence on the senior college campuses. Colleges that had prided themselves on their unyielding standards began to offer programs of remedial education, and the principle that the colleges had a moral obligation to provide help to disadvantaged students took root.

The SEEK program was precisely the kind of reform that liberals throughout CUNY had been hoping for—generous, but modest, incremental, and nonthreatening. Theirs was the consensual, optimistic liberalism born of America's postwar dominance and shaped by the civil rights struggle. This form of liberalism was about to go into eclipse. In New York and elsewhere, a new race consciousness was beginning to tear at the seams of the civil rights consensus. In 1967 an experiment in promoting local control over New York's public schools culminated in a showdown between black parents and the largely Jewish teachers union in the ghetto neighborhood of Ocean Hill–Brownsville. The shouting matches, the marches, and the strikes faded away; but the bitterness and disillusionment lingered to corrupt the atmosphere of daily life. Increasingly, as the 1960s wore on, the racial debate took the form of accusation and threat on the one hand, and resentment and repression on the other. White liberals, and especially Jewish liberals, were divided among their sense of moral obligation and guilt, their fear of violence, and a growing sense of outrage.

In October 1968 City's black club, the Onyx Society, convened a conference on black power featuring H. Rap Brown and Olympic sprinter John Carlos. White students were not permitted to enter the auditorium, an unprecedented act of separatism. The student council responded by suspending Onyx's funding. Two hundred club members then descended on a council meeting, where, after a racially charged debate, the club's privileges were restored. Black students were beginning to feel their power—a power that came from a claim on conscience as well as from intimidation and fear. In early December, Stokely Carmichael, by then the "prime minister" of the Black Panthers, called for "armed struggle" in a speech in Shepherd Hall. He repudiated any form of coalition with the Students for a Democratic Society (SDS) or other white radical groups.

In late 1968 a group within Onyx calling itself the Committee of Ten began meeting to formulate a list of demands and to plan a series of escalating protest actions to force the college to acquiesce. By the beginning of the following year the committee had begun to work with a contingent from a Puerto Rican organization called PRISA. On February 6 the group presented to college president Buell Gallagher a set of five demands. The demands were that students in the Education School be obliged to learn black and Puerto Rican history and Spanish; that a separate orientation program be established for black and Puerto Rican freshmen; that SEEK students be granted far greater control over the SEEK program itself; that a separate School of Black and Puerto Rican Studies be established; and that the racial composition of the next entering class reflect the racial makeup of New York's public high schools.

The students demanded a response from Gallagher within a week, and precisely a week later Gallagher issued a statement accepting the Spanish-language demand and offering a search for common ground on the others. The statement, sympathetic but faintly condescending, was suited to an era of comity already long past. That morning a group of about one hundred black and Puerto Rican demonstrators seized the administration building for three and a half hours, booting out white administrators and declaring the advent of "Malcolm X–Che Guevara University." The group had decided to raise the pressure a notch at a time. Four days later black and Puerto

Rican students launched an array of hit-and-run strikes, popping into classes with smoke bombs, dumping gallons of paint down the stairway at Shepherd Hall, slinging food around corridors, and vandalizing equipment. Gallagher neither moved on the demands nor rebuked the students.

A few years earlier these breaches of college protocol might not have seemed quite so portentous; but now they were being played out against the feverish landscape of the late 1960s. The apocalypse, the revolution, and the fascist counterattack all seemed to many ecstatic young people, and terrified older people, to be around the corner. Not only were the Panthers brandishing guns, but white revolutionaries were planting dynamite. Sociologist and ex-radical Todd Gitlin recalls the last years of the 1960s as "a cyclone in a wind tunnel." And the spring of 1969 was the heart of that cyclone, the speeded-up moment of exhilaration, danger, chaos, doom. Gitlin counts "well over a hundred politically inspired campus bombings, attempted bombings and incidents of arson" during the 1968–1969 school year alone.

Buell Gallagher was not the leader City might have chosen for such a moment. He was a tall, gaunt, dark-haired man in spectacles and a bow tie, a man who put some people—not necessarily his friends—in mind of Abraham Lincoln. Gallagher had been ordained a Congregationalist minister, served as president of all-black Tougaloo College, in Mississippi, and devoted himself to worthy causes; but he was accustomed to working on an essentially rhetorical plane, and he retained the minister's habit of orotundity. To his critics on both the left and the right, Gallagher was precisely the kind of clubbable but ineffectual gentleman who had ruled City's affairs since the antediluvian era.

On April 22 a handful of black and Puerto Rican students arrived at City College at dawn and attached a padlock to the gate that gave access to the South Campus, where liberal arts classes were held. White students were not permitted past the gate under any circumstances; white radicals eager to express their sympathy were forced to demonstrate outside the gates. The dean of students ordered the police to come and cut the padlock, but then to leave the campus. The students then held the gates shut. Gallagher had promised to use force if the students closed down the campus, but now he wavered. After meeting with administrators and faculty, Gallagher decided to declare the South Campus closed, postponing a decision about the strikers until the following day.

When white radicals had disrupted the campus in years past Gallagher hadn't hesitated to call in the police. But after a tumultuous meeting in Shepherd's Great Hall, in which students marched around in revolutionary style and outraged faculty members stormed out in a collective huff, the president announced that City College would remain closed, that the students would not be evicted, and that negotiations would commence. The idea of forcibly breaking up what was arguably a civil rights protest may simply have been repugnant to Gallagher. But he was also frightened. Gallagher felt that he knew the black community; and he sagely warned the Board of Higher Education, according to another professor present at the meeting, that "if the forces on the South Campus were let loose, the riots in Watts and Newark would pale by comparison." In fact, as Gallagher himself was told, the students took it for granted that they would be evicted and had decided to go peacefully; none of them had even brought a change of clothes. But he refused to change his mind.

Many black and Puerto Rican members of the faculty and administration, especially those involved with the SEEK program, sided with the students. A contingent of whites called Faculty for Action did so as well, sending negotiating formulas and chicken soup over to South Campus. Conservative members of the faculty, however, saw the takeover as the garroting of the humane tradition of which they had been the final carriers. The radical students, black and white, were "Nazis"; the administration, their craven appeasers. But most faculty members found themselves roughly in the same position as President Gallagher—appalled by the takeover, but mortified by the prospect of toppling a black protest by force. The day after the Great Hall meeting the faculty adopted resolutions deploring the forcible halt in classes but urging that the police remain off campus and the college itself remain closed. Four days later the faculty reversed that decision, and then reversed it once again. For a few days the faculty and students of the Engineering School, located on the

North Campus, defied the ban on holding classes, with the tacit permission of the school's dean.

City found itself in an ideologically agonizing position. No other college in the nation had the tradition of radicalism that City had. And the postwar generation of faculty generally had a strong leftward tilt. But many of these same teachers were alumni of City; they revered the school and what it stood for. The brandished fists, the nonnegotiable demands, the fixation with symbolism, the separatist language—it all violated a cherished image of the school and an ideal of the life of the mind. On April 24, during one of many interminable, anguished meetings in the Great Hall, Stanley Feingold introduced a resolution calling for classes to resume, "with the least possible violence either to persons or to the spirit of learning." The resolution was an earnest and forlorn attempt to reaffirm the ancient norms. Feingold wrote, "In a society that claims to be free, revolutionary action is justified, if not morally obligatory, where dialogue is suppressed and decision-making precludes the consideration of significant and deeply-felt interests." But City College, he pointed out, had gone to great lengths to sustain debate.

Feingold was a City College figure of classic vintage, a working-class boy made good. He had graduated from the college in 1946, studied political science at Columbia, and then returned to City to teach without ever bothering to get a graduate degree. For years he had taught the course American Political Thought to upperclassmen. He loved what he did, and he was considered a dedicated teacher. He was also an outspoken progressive. He had participated in anti-war sit-ins and had taken on President Gallagher over the issue of loyalty oaths. Feingold felt that knowing justice, and doing justice, were the core of his profession. And now he found himself defending an entrenched interest that he deeply believed in. "The conduct of a college is as instructive as the teaching of its faculty," he wrote. "If, by whatever euphemism, it pays a ransom price for the return of its buildings and resumption of its classes, it can only inspire further bitter and disruptive activities."

In 1969, New York's mayor, John Lindsay, who had delighted white and black citizens soon after his election in 1965 by walking through Harlem, was up for reelection, and the mood of the city had changed considerably. Lindsay's chief opponent, city comptroller Mario Procaccino, was part of a cadre of white ethnics who were making their way in big-city politics by appealing to frightened and angry white voters, as President Richard Nixon and Vice President Spiro Agnew were doing on a national level. Procaccino, as it happened, was City College class of 1935. And in the City College takeover he saw a potent political issue. Declaring that it was "criminal" to allow protest to halt the education of thousands of New Yorkers, Procaccino announced on May 1 that he was seeking a court order compelling the administration to reopen the college. That same day the militant Jewish Defense League, as well as a group of students, obtained court orders requiring President Gallagher to show cause why the school should not be reopened four days hence.

The college held its collective breath as the court orders were served; but the students had long since agreed among themselves that they would leave peacefully. On Monday evening, May 5, the 250 students marched out from behind the gate without incident. Now, however, a miniature version of the race riot that Gallagher had predicted exploded on campus. On May 6 several white students were attacked by blacks; at least one was robbed. The following day was much worse. In a story carried on the first column of the front page, the *New York Times* reported that "a bloody pitched battle between club-swinging black youths and white counterprotestors erupted at City College yesterday shortly after the school had been closed for the day because of a previous series of violent incidents." Seven white students were injured; three were taken to the hospital with head wounds. A crowd of blacks, many of them high school students or not students at all, swarmed into the library and classrooms, ordering white students and professors to leave. One white girl who refused was beaten up by ten members of the crowd. Another white girl was robbed at knifepoint.

President Gallagher was at last forced to call in the police—a decision he must have found crushing. But even with 200 police officers on campus, the violence continued. Fistfights broke out all day between blacks or Puerto Ricans and whites. White radicals and counterdemonstrators pelted each other with eggs and rocks and bottles. A crowd of about 2,000 people surged up and down the campus and along Amsterdam Avenue, shadowed and sometimes blocked by detachments of police. At 2:33 P.M. a fire broke out in the Finley Student Center. Before it was brought under control an hour later the fire had destroyed the college's auditorium. Pictures of the blackened building, and the billowing smoke, made the top of each network newscast. The Procaccino campaign exploited the footage in its campaign commercials as if it were *Kristallnacht*. For many City College alumni, it was.

The following day, a Friday, Buell Gallagher tendered his resignation as president, effective Monday. It was widely believed that he had been fired by the Board of Higher Education. He had become, by then, a melancholy, isolated figure. He had occupied what he thought was the honorable position; and there he had been stranded. As he said in his characteristically lofty resignation statement, "When the forces of angry rebellion and stern repression clash, a man of peace, a reconciler, a man of compassion must stand aside for a time and await the moment when sanity returns and brotherhood based on justice becomes a possibility." There was a terrible, hard truth in that windy cascade of words. Gallagher understood that, whatever he did, he would violate his principles. The liberalism that had guided him had become impossible to practice.

In his memoirs, *The Education of Black Folks*, Allan Ballard recalls an early and unsuccessful attempt to change City's admission policies. It was April 1968, and Martin Luther King, Jr., had just been assassinated. Riots had broken out in Washington, Chicago, and other major cities; there was an overwhelming feeling that something had to be done to give black youth some hope of a better life. Ballard writes, "I called together a group of the most 'radical' white faculty members and asked them to support a proposal that would have mandated that the freshman class of September 1968 have a 25 percent composition of black and Puerto Rican students to be drawn from Harlem and East Harlem." This would be a drastic change from the SEEK program, which was still viewed as an appendage to the college itself. Ballard was shocked at the reaction: "Only one of the ten radical leaders in the room agreed to the proposal. One of those who opposed the plan stated that he would leave the university since these students would most certainly destroy the traditional academic standards of CCNY."

Ballard thought that he was asking nothing more than consistency; in fact he had touched a hidden fault line. Those activists had joined the candlelight vigil at Gracie Mansion, the mayor's home, to protest King's death. They were committed to the cause of racial justice, and City College's status as a white island in a black sea had left them feeling increasingly conscience stricken. They supported SEEK and were eager to see it grow. At the same time, they believed devoutly in "standards," and in the meritocratic admissions process that allowed the college to uphold those standards. They wanted City College to be academically exclusive but ethnically inclusive. And if they had to sacrifice the one to attain the other? That was where the fault line lay.

Ballard's proposal, like the Committee of Ten's demand the following year, reversed familiar terms of debate. Quotas had been the chief obstacle to equality of opportunity for the upwardly mobile urban poor who had flocked to City College forty years before. Freedom, for them, meant freedom from the laws that had confined their ancestors to the ghetto and excluded them from education and the professions. America was the land where people were judged according to what they did, not who they were. And City College, where no distinctions except those of ability and industry would matter, was the great symbol of that promise. Even the devout socialists of Alcove 1 believed in the free market of abilities.

The situation was different for black Americans. With the waning of Jim Crow, and the passage of civil rights legislation in the 1960s, they, too, faced no formal obstacles to success. But because of their history of enslavement and exclusion, not in Russia but here at home, they entered the marketplace of opportunity on a deeply unequal basis. As President Lyndon Johnson had said in 1965, "You do not take a person who for years has been hobbled by chains and liberate him, bring him up to the starting line of a race and say, 'You are free to compete with all the others,' and still justly believe that you have been completely fair." Black Americans *deserved* special benefits as compensation for past discrimination, and they needed those advantages to help them overcome the effects of that discrimination.

Johnson declared a "War on Poverty," to be waged with jobs, housing, urban renewal, and programs like Head Start. These programs were designed to remove the shackles so that black people could reach the starting line on an equal footing. But these were long-term, developmental programs. What could be done to equalize the competition *now*? By the late 1960s a consensus had developed among mainstream civil rights groups that a system of preferences, or targets, should be built into decisions on hiring, contracting, and college and graduate school admissions in order to ensure proportional representation for blacks. This was the principle of affirmative action, which President Richard Nixon's Labor Department adopted in 1969, without great controversy, as a set of enforceable guidelines.

The logic of affirmative action turned the meritocratic argument on its head: Impersonal "standards" perpetuated a discriminatory system. Only through quotas—of inclusion, not of exclusion—could equality of opportunity be guaranteed. The affirmative action principle could be applied to virtually all economic or social goods. But in the case of higher education it acquired a special force because a college degree had become the indispensable passport to the good life. A bachelor's degree was worth approximately 60 percent more than a high school diploma in the job market. Unionized blue-collar jobs were dropping from year to year, and an increasing fraction of middle-level jobs were becoming unavailable to nongraduates. Black parents understood the system perfectly well. A 1966 study found that while 79 percent of white parents wanted their children to attend college, among blacks the figure was 96 percent. As Julian Bond, then a Georgia state legislator, wrote, "Higher education can no longer be regarded as a privilege for the few, but must be seen as a right for the many."

The affirmative action argument didn't question the validity of distinctions of merit, but insisted that higher education had become too valuable a good to be parceled out according to these distinctions. But at the same time white scholars on the left were questioning the meritocratic premise itself. In their highly influential *Academic Revolution*, published in 1968, sociologists David Riesman and Christopher Jencks argued that meritocracy served as a legiti-

mating device for a deeply unequal society. Higher education, with
its various devices for testing and sorting, sustained the myth that
economic success was being distributed according to ability rather
than birth. In fact, they said, while high school graduation had
become more democratically distributed in recent decades, college
entrance and graduation had become, if anything, increasingly correlated with prior socioeconomic status. Higher-class parents were
passing down to their children the abilities that made for college success, as once they had passed down trust funds or WASPy affilia-
tions. Moreover, Riesman and Jencks weren't even convinced that
social mobility was such a good thing. "What America most needs
is not more mobility," they wrote, "but more equality."

Riesman and Jencks considered the question of admissions
standards irrelevant. Employers faced with a more democratically
distributed pool of college graduates would simply discriminate on
the basis of grades, which would continue to be correlated with class.
College-level remediation, they argued, "being of limited duration
and coming late in life, can almost never undo more than a fraction
of the damage done by earlier neglect." Moreover, they insisted, colleges would never devote their precious assets to students so unlikely
to succeed.

But it was possible to turn the critique of meritocracy against
the schools themselves. Jerome Karabel, later a professor at Berkeley,
noted, "Universities are irrevocably committed to the business of con-
ferring awards, and, once this fact is recognized, their exclusive
stance, based on an idealized image, becomes less defensible." Like
Riesman and Jencks, Karabel didn't really believe in meritocratic
distinctions at all: "A frenetically competitive inegalitarian system,"
he wrote, is scarcely preferable to "an ascriptive society [one based
on inherited status], which, at least, does not compel its poor people
to internalize their failures." But unlike the authors of *Academic Revolution*, Karabel believed that opening up higher education to all
students could strike a serious blow at the unequal social structure
that it sustained and appropriate the resources of the elite for the
use of the many. Karabel's hope was the realization of "Justice's"
nightmare 120 years earlier: that higher education could be used to
upend, rather than confirm, the existing order.

But here was the rub: City College was either an exception to the claim made by Riesman and Jencks, and by followers like Karabel, or its refutation. Indeed, the very idea that higher education might redistribute goods from the wellborn to the academically worthy depended on the legendary reputation of City College as much as of any other institution. City had turned poor boys (and by now girls) into successful professionals. Perhaps New York City had run out of bright, underprivileged Jewish kids. But weren't there plenty of other students, many of them black and Puerto Rican, who could be fed into City's meritocratic machine? Moreover, the entire anti-meritocratic argument, which often appeared to be conducted by upper-class whites feeling guilty about the good fortune they had inherited, irritated City's faculty and administration, so many of whom were City boys who still felt in their bones the immensity of their struggle to succeed, and felt as well a corresponding pride in their achievement.

Philip Baumel, a professor of physics, had been born into grim, Depression-era poverty. His father, a nonunion housepainter, had contracted sciatica when Philip was seven, and the family had eked out a bare living in the Bronx on workmen's compensation and income from his mother's hospital job. But Philip had been accepted into the prestigious Bronx High School of Science and had graduated from City College in 1953. For Baumel, belief in the system of merito-cratic advancement was indistinguishable from self-respect. "I taught myself a foreign language," Baumel says proudly. "It was called stan-dard English. I learned it by reading." And Baumel didn't just believe in the abstract idea of distinctions of merit; he believed devoutly in City College as an institution predicated on those distinctions.

For men like Baumel, and for others more skeptical of the glories of the system than he, the demands of the students consti-tuted an attack on values they had scarcely even questioned before. To lower admission standards would be, in effect, to devalue the cur-rency in which their diploma had been issued. This was the visceral reaction that Allan Ballard had encountered the year before. In one of the innumerable Great Hall resolutions, two professors declared that "an admissions policy based upon racial and ethnic quotas rather than academic achievement would destroy this College and . . . such an admissions policy if implemented would in fact perpetrate a cruel hoax on the young people so admitted." It would destroy the college because City would have to sacrifice the standards that had made it what it was. It would be a cruel hoax because City would not be able to undo the damage these young people had suffered. In years past City had been only the last of a series of institutions that had shaped its students; it could not be asked to do the work that other institutions were now failing to do.

Or could it? Fran Geteles, a counselor in the SEEK program and former stalwart of Faculty for Action, asks, "Which is the stronger truth: That you are locked in by your background, or that you have potential?" For Geteles and others, *potential* was the magic word, the answer to all the talk about standards. Potential was the underlying quality that the hardships of ghetto life had obscured but not destroyed. If you looked, you would find it. In a magazine article in the summer of 1969, an associate professor of English, Leo Hamalian, noted, as many others had, that "the planning and organization that went into the strategy of seizure by the BPRC was masterful." They had taken over the South Campus in a surgical strike, they conducted negotiations with great self-assurance, and, unlike white radicals, they hadn't trashed property or raided liquor cabinets. If these students, many of them from SEEK, didn't belong at City, Hamalian said, "then perhaps we should examine the academic process itself rather than the student." Hamalian also noted that a study in East St. Louis had isolated a quality in ghetto youth— " 'hipness' for lack of a better term" —which, he said, "may be an indication of educational potential." Hamalian offered a cautious endorsement of these alternative gifts. "With massive supportive services," he wrote, "many such youngsters are performing passingly well in college."

For the Jewish liberals who made up so large a part of City's student body, faculty, administration, and alumni, there could be no easy resolution to the debate between merit and potential, or between standards and access. But most black students and faculty members considered the entire discussion demeaning. "The whole notion that we were endangering the college's standards was racist," says Bruce Hare. "Those were just excuses, and the excuses were serving to keep the joint white." If black students had done less well in school than the white students now at City, it was because of the low expectations that teachers had for blacks. And if black students performed far less well on the SATs than whites, it was because standardized tests were culturally biased. Bruce Hare hadn't done well enough in high school to be admitted to City. He had spent three years in the evening session before transferring to the supposedly far more rigorous day session. And he hadn't been all that impressed. To his grandfather, who had told him that "the smart people" went to the school up on the hill, he had said, "Grandpa, you were wrong."

Negotiations on the five demands resumed on May 19, after the new college president, Joseph Copeland, agreed to withdraw the police from campus in exchange for promises from white and black militants to end the disruptions. An earlier set of discussions had already led to acceptance of the first three student demands, an agreement to set aside the issue of a School of Black Studies, and a stalemate on the fundamental question of admissions. The students wanted a black and Puerto Rican quota equal to minority enrollment in the public high schools, then about 40 percent. The faculty negotiators accepted the idea of a separate track of nonmerit admissions, like the SEEK program, but balked at the numbers.

Now those agreements had been nullified, and the faculty negotiating team replaced, on orders from the Board of Higher Education. The new three-member team included Stanley Feingold, who had made his opposition to the takeover very clear, but who was hoping to find some sort of middle ground on the critical issue of the quota. But the legitimacy of the quota demand had been granted in advance—it was a demand, after all—and only the means remained to be discussed. Feingold recalls that the students presented one ingenious formula after another designed to raise the fraction of minority students at City to 40 percent. None of them involved explicit ethnic quotas; all of them, Feingold felt, amounted to the same thing. Feingold could not accept a quota at City College. On May 22, as the group was reaching agreement, he quietly resigned his position.

It was a wrenching moment for Feingold: He stood sharply defined against a background that was all too schematic. Conservatives welcomed him as a convert. Pro-student faculty members accused him of losing his nerve. And radical students vilified him. Feingold had always thought of himself as a radical egalitarian, and City as a radically egalitarian place. But old-fashioned egalitarianism, with its implicit faith in competition and the marketplace, had come to seem like the mask of domination. And so, by standing in one place while history spun by him, Feingold had become something he never could have imagined: the enemy of potential.

In mid-June, Feingold was asked to testify before the Board of Higher Education, and he took the opportunity to map out the place in the middle where he stood. Yes, he agreed, the students were "sincere," but to say so was condescending, since "neither the manner nor the appearance of the students had anything to do with the merits of their case." The question was not who had the moral upper hand but how best to achieve "equality of access without diminishing excellence in standards." It wasn't enough, he argued, to accept students merely on the basis of minority status, because potential was not something that belonged to all students, or to all minority students. The colleges would have to reach down into the high schools and identify and nurture the students who showed signs of special abilities.

Feingold proposed that CUNY institute a system like California's, where the top 12.5 percent of high school graduates were eligible to attend the elite "university colleges"; the top third of graduates, the state colleges; and the remainder, a two-year community college. In fact CUNY chancellor Albert Bowker had previously worked in the California system and had devised a version of the state's master plan in which the three tiers were, in effect, dropped down one level each. According to CUNY's 1968 master plan, the senior colleges in the system would accept one-quarter of high school graduates— slightly less than the Holy Plan had anticipated—in addition to several thousand others enrolled through programs like SEEK; the next 40 percent of graduates would be admitted to community college; and the remainder, including dropouts, would be eligible, according to their academic level, for vocational, apprenticeship, or college transition programs in Educational Skills Centers. The master plan was scheduled to be implemented in 1975.

The tiered system was designed to reconcile equality of access with excellence. Feingold was scarcely the only faculty member to have suggested one: Others, including several of the archconservatives, had proposed some sort of college preparatory institute, where students would be given remedial instruction; survivors of the course would be enrolled at City. Another group recommended the establishment of a high school affiliated with City, as Townsend Harris once had been. All of these proposals assumed a careful act of selection; underachieving students with the potential to succeed at City would be culled from the many who had fallen too far behind.

But Feingold had a deeper point to make. City College, he insisted, was not, and could not be, the place to make a stand against inner-city poverty. Feingold says, "I believed then, I believe now, and I will continue to believe that the problem was being attacked from the wrong end. The place to create equality of opportunity is birth through secondary school, not beginning at the college level. If you tried to deal with the problems of a child before the age of six, which is really where you should begin, you would be talking about cataclysmic changes in the society. But nothing short of cataclysmic change will ever produce equality of opportunity in the United States. Higher education is vulnerable to change in a way that the rest of society is not; but by that time it's too late to make a difference."

To the actors in the open admissions drama, City College appeared literally to be determining the course of history. But of course they lived inside history, and events were being driven along by larger historical forces. Throughout the twentieth century the United States had moved, with incredible speed and consistency, toward the idea of universal access to higher education. The Morrill Acts of 1862 and 1890 established the system of land-grant colleges; billions of dollars of expenditures by state governments produced a vast, if patchwork, system of public colleges and universities. Unlike City College, very few of these public institutions practiced selective admissions policies. Most accepted any student within the state who had completed an academic course of study in high school; and their standards tended to be governed by their egalitarian commitment. As far back as the mid-nineteenth century the president of the University of Minnesota proudly declared, "The State Universities hold that there is no intellectual service too undignified for them to perform."

Higher education was remarkably accessible, even when few Americans availed themselves of it. In 1900 only 4 percent of eighteen- to twenty-one-year-olds were attending college, largely because so few young people graduated from high school. But as public school attendance became mandatory, and as graduation thus became commonplace, the number of college students increased astronomically. By 1920 the fraction of eighteen- to twenty-one-year-olds in college had doubled to 8 percent. By 1940, when high school enrollment had reached 73 percent, the figure for college had almost doubled again, to 14.5 percent. And by 1950, with the huge release of veterans from the service, the college-going rate had doubled *again*. Almost 2.5 million young people were attending college. Four and a half million veterans ultimately took advantage of the GI Bill to pursue higher education.

In the years immediately after World War II, policy makers asked a question that had never been seriously posed before: How many Americans should be able to go to college? President Harry S. Truman appointed a commission to look into the question, and at the end of 1947 the Zook Commission, as it was known for its chairman, delivered the kind of supremely confident answer that was a hallmark of postwar America: "at least 49 percent" of college-age Americans had the "mental ability" to complete a two-year post-secondary school education, and at least 32 percent were up to the demands of a liberal arts college or professional education. "Mental ability" was postwar bureaucratese for "potential." The report, titled *Higher Education for American Democracy*, called for free and universal access to schooling through the fourteenth grade, as well as an immense expansion of four-year college facilities.

The report's very title was a statement: Higher education had to serve the larger purposes of American democracy. In the postwar years, Americans would need "education for peace," for "international-mindedness," for "self-understanding." Most important of all, higher education had to accept its role as the credentialing device for the new middle-class society emerging from the war. The authors

recognized that a college degree had become, as never before, "a prerequisite to social and economic advancement" —the insight that
Riesman and Jencks would formalize a generation later. And yet, the
commissioners wrote, "for the great majority of our boys and girls,
the kind and amount of education that they may hope to attain
depends, not on their abilities, but on the family or community into
which they happen to be born or, worse still, on the color of their
skin or the religion of their parents."

Part of the problem was cost, for City College was unusual not
only in being selective but in charging no tuition; thus the recommendation that the first half of a college education be free. Another
part was accessibility, and so the commission had proposed a boom
in campus construction. But perhaps the most intractable obstacle
to mass college attendance was the elite character of the college itself.
Many private colleges, and some public ones, had become increasingly selective as the number of applicants had skyrocketed, and had
made their rigorous standards a selling point. The Zook Commission, like the sixties leftists, counted selectivity as another form of
discrimination. The authors wrote that colleges "cannot continue to
concentrate on students with one type of intelligence to the neglect
of youth with other talents," such as "social sensitivity," "motor skills,"
and "mechanical aptitudes and ingenuity." Higher education for
peace and self-understanding required a new kind of student, as did
higher education for the ordinary citizen. America needed mass
colleges for a mass society.

The Zook Commission's triumphantly middlebrow, anti-
intellectual tone infuriated many people, especially in the academy.
Another study, commissioned by the Rockefeller Foundation and
staffed by scholars and administrators from the elite colleges, stoutly
defended the academic tradition. "The primary purpose of higher
education," the Rockefeller group wrote, "is the development of . . .
intellectual promise and . . . [the capacity to] deal with abstract ideas."
It was this traditional purpose, rather than the new credentialing
function, that must determine the scope and character of higher education in the United States. Higher education would contribute to
society not by widening the circle of pedigreed young people but
by contributing "the trained experts, the scholars, and the leaders"

America required. The study put the number of Americans who could benefit from some form of higher education at 25 percent. A 1952 report titled *Who Should Go to College?* reached the same conclusion.

Higher education in the United States was too heterogeneous to allow one to say that one or the other of these models ultimately was adopted. But the Rockefeller panel's suggestion that college be limited to those prepared to master a liberal arts education never had a chance against the sheer national faith in the value of a college degree. The state never agreed to guarantee education beyond high school, as the Zook Commission had hoped; but it didn't matter. By 1960, 3.8 million students, and 34 percent of eighteen- to twenty-one-year-olds, were attending college. And by 1970, in a burst of growth unprecedented even by the awesome standards of past decades, the number of college students increased 124 percent, to 8.5 million. Even without the governmental inducements that the Zook Commission had proposed, the numbers had outstripped the commission's own predictions. As a report by the Carnegie Commission on Higher Education boasted, "The United States is creating a society in which more people will have had more education than ever before in history in any nation."

The negotiators whose ranks Stanley Feingold quit ultimately accepted what was known as the "dual admissions" formula: half of the next incoming class would be selected from essentially all-minority high schools in Manhattan and the Bronx, and the other half according to traditional criteria. It was a zero-sum solution in Solomonic form: instead of deciding between two principles, they had divided the school into two parts. But for many people who thought of City College as one of the great institutions of American culture, half a principle was almost worse than none. Every mayoral candidate, including Mayor Lindsay, denounced the accord. Representative James Scheuer called it "a shameful violation of the basic principles of a free society." The American Jewish Committee labeled the proposal a transparent form of quota. City College alumni, including the Nobelists and the left-wing intellectuals, reacted with horror. Alfred Kazin pronounced himself "thoroughly unhappy." The head of the alumni association said that his group was "violently opposed" to the new system. A *Times* editorial criticized the plan for placing faith in "educational magic."

But for all the noise, the dual admissions plan was simply the prelude to an ultimate solution. Admissions standards could be decided only by the Board of Higher Education. When the board began to review the demands in June, it was clear that something drastic had to be done. Virtually every campus in the system had been rocked by violence and strikes. The board had to find some way of accommodating the demands for access, and it had to be done on a systemwide basis.

And yet one drastic solution contradicted another. The board couldn't adopt the quota system discussed by the City College negotiators and rejected by the faculty. Quotas were abhorrent, especially to the Jewish voters whom Mayor Lindsay was courting in his reelection bid. But neither could the board embrace Bowker's master plan, with its three tiers of educational opportunity. Minorities wouldn't stand for it. State senator Basil Paterson, then the most important black political figure in New York, had said, "I will not be able to support any system of open admissions which turns out to be a continuation of the second-class, vocationally-oriented, dead-end policy prevalent in our public high school system for Black and Puerto Rican youth."

And at this point the particular set of circumstances that had produced City's racial standoff was overtaken by the larger dynamic of growth, both within CUNY and nationally. There were constituencies that had no interest in the civil rights issues, but great interest in expanded access to higher education. Harry van Arsdale, the immensely powerful president of the Central Labor Council of the city's unions, had opposed the quota proposal but observed that the senior college's high standards had denied admission to "thousands and thousands of youngsters who do not have the marks, but who might become good students"—the children, that is, of his largely white ethnic members. And what constituencies were there to support the principle of high standards when it was opposed, not by fist-brandishing militants, but by working-class New Yorkers upholding the national tradition of ready access to higher education? None, except the faculty, students, and alumni of the colleges. And so the obvious solution was to admit more minority students into the senior colleges *and* more nonminority children, thus circumventing the dangerous issue of equity and threatening only the colleges' standards.

In early July the board announced its decision: "We have concluded that the City University should initiate an open admissions policy as soon as practicable." This last phrase meant that open admissions would be instituted not in 1975, as the master plan had foreseen, but in 1970. Nor was the board merely accelerating the Bowker plan. The board directed that admissions criteria be designed so that all high school graduates could enroll in a college program; "standards of academic excellence" be maintained; all colleges be ethnically integrated; and no student be denied a place he or she would have had under the previous criteria. The board, in other words, insisted that all of the contradictory impulses that had propelled the debate be simultaneously accommodated. Ethnic integration meant that minority students would not be confined to the lower reaches of a hierarchical system; the Skills Centers had been dropped altogether. The last stricture meant "no losers." The system would simply expand—the deus ex machina of the 1960s.

Since there really was no way to reconcile open admissions, integration, and standards, the board, like the City College negotiators, came to no conclusion on how best to do it. That was left to a Commission on Admissions, which spent the summer and fall wrangling bitterly over the details. The commission discovered that it would be impossible to achieve an acceptable level of integration simply by lowering the required grade-point average, because so few minority students graduated even with a 75 average. Class rank would have to be included as well. But even taking all students in the top half of the class would be insufficient, because too many minority students were concentrated in the bottom half of their class.

In the scheme finally adopted by the board, every student with an average of 80 or more or a standing in the top half of the graduating class would be assured a place in one of the senior colleges. Full integration would be achieved by admitting thousands more through special programs like SEEK. Everyone else would be guaranteed a seat in a community college. The system not only was much less stratified than the one that obtained in California but also was less concerned with protecting standards than with helping students achieve their ambition. In California it was very difficult to move from the two-year to the four-year system; in CUNY's open admissions plan, community college graduates would be automatically accepted at senior college with full credit. And while half of each freshman class routinely flunked out at many midwestern universities that functioned under a state-mandated open enrollment system, CUNY agreed to give all incoming students a one-year grace period. In other words, CUNY committed itself not only to accepting a vast cadre of new students but to advancing them toward a bachelor's degree.

The open admissions plan was to be implemented in the fall of 1970, a year from the time it was conceived. The change was so drastic, and the time given to adjust to it so short, that many of the students' supporters accused CUNY of trying to discredit the reform by introducing it in an impracticable way. They hadn't sought open admissions, they pointed out; they simply wanted to increase the representation of black and Puerto Rican students. But if they got more than they bargained for, it was because they hadn't fully reckoned with the historical forces that lay behind their own demands. Open admissions lay at the convergence of several powerful trends— the century-long movement toward mass higher education, the changing demographics of the American city, the critique of meritocratic distinctions, a growing sense of obligation toward the black poor, and CUNY's own expansionism.

City College's admissions policies *had* to change, although the old guard couldn't admit that this was so. But they didn't have to change in the way that they had. Without the lockout, City's, and CUNY's, admissions policies would have evolved over a period of years rather than being dismantled overnight. More important, CUNY would have adopted a different model—the 1968 master plan, or the California model, or one of the alternatives devised during the debate. Any of these models would have reflected more conservative assumptions about what a college education could do for ill-schooled eighteen-year-olds. But the lockout, and the ensuing negotiations, produced a fait accompli that could not be undone. It fostered an atmosphere of intimidation and blackmail within which realism came to sound like racism. And it provoked larger forces that transformed the demand for affirmative action into a demographic free-for-all. And so open admissions, in the form it took at CUNY, became perhaps the most improbable and radically idealistic experiment in the history of American higher education.

4

Paradise Lost

I n the fall of 1970, open admissions hit the City College campus like the D-day landing. The previous fall 1,752 new students had registered for class; now the figure was 2,742, an increase of almost 60 percent. The freshman class would peak in 1971 at 3,216, and then fall off, for the simple reason that City College was not built for the volume of students considered normal in the Big Ten. Chaos reigned: Students stood in line for hours, sometimes for an entire day, just to register. The college rented space in a building down the hill at 134th Street to accommodate overflow classes. Great Hall, the cavernous space in Shepherd where grand and bitter debates had been staged for sixty years, was divided by partitions into a dozen classrooms. City had always been bulging at the edges and out at the elbows; but now the school felt like a rushing, bellowing madhouse. If the Board of Higher Education had decided to punish City for its impertinence, it had succeeded admirably.

But even monumental inconvenience seemed trivial compared to the change in the school's demographics. By 1969, City College was no longer all white, but most of the black and Puerto Rican students lived in the separate world of the SEEK program. In 1970

the number of SEEK students almost tripled, to 2,000; and the number of non-SEEK minority students tripled as well, to 15 percent of
the entering class. Nowhere else in the CUNY system were the
changes quite so stark; City's location in the middle of the black
ghetto, and adjacent to the black and Hispanic slum areas of the
Bronx, meant that it received a disproportionate number of minority
students. The fraction of Catholics at City also rose from 23 percent
to 43 percent. The Catholics, ironically, were numerically the greatest
beneficiaries of the Board of Higher Education's decision to lower
admission standards rather than to institute a minority quota. Some
left-wing members of the faculty were heard to grumble that they
hadn't planned to teach "white trash." But Harry van Arsdale had
gotten the drop on them.

Family income among CUNY students had been creeping
toward middle-class levels in recent years, but open admissions
returned the school to its proletarian past. In 1970, median family
income among Jewish CUNY students was $12,000, and among
Catholics, $10,300; but among black open admissions students it was
$6,700, and slightly less for Puerto Ricans. These students not only
were economically disadvantaged but were, by definition, academically disadvantaged as well. The number of incoming students with
high school averages under 80 went from 124 in 1969 to 1,473 the
next year. Among SEEK students the median average was close to
70, since they now had to fall below the new admissions standards.
And the A students started going to Queens College, or SUNY, or
private colleges. In a pattern that held ominous implications for the
future, the better a student did in high school, the less likely he was
to choose to attend City. By 1972, well over half of the student body
had scored under 80 in high school.

The faculty and staff had a year to brace for the vast tide of
unprepared students, but they still were swamped. City had never
needed a remedial program before; freshman composition had been
abolished, in a burst of liberal reform, just before the open admissions
battle. Now remedial programs were drawn up in math, writing, and
"college skills." All entering students were given evaluation tests. In
the first year of open admissions, 90 percent of those 2,700 incoming
students were assigned to at least one remedial course—a fraction

that implied either that many traditional City students needed special help or that the remedial standards were too strict. By the next year the figure was down to three-quarters.

City College's academic mission changed overnight, not by design but by sheer force of circumstance. Seventy percent of English courses had traditionally been given in literature, and 30 percent in writing; open admissions reversed the ratio. Electives in English and some of the other humanities fields rapidly became vestigial, because the new students viewed education in almost exclusively instrumental, vocational terms. Older faculty members, especially, were appalled. One of the shibboleths of the time was that physics professors taught graduate seminars in the morning and algebra in the afternoon, though in fact almost all of the remedial math teaching was conducted by the Math Department. But the underlying truth was that scholars who propagated "the best that is thought and said" — or at least felt that they did—found themselves training students in the fundamentals.

It was in many ways the worst of times, and in no way the best. Conservatives on the faculty enjoyed the grim satisfaction of seeing their predictions of catastrophe realized in full. Their memoirs bear titles such as *The End of Education* and *The Death of the University*, testifying not only to their bitterness but to the implicit assumption that City College had a symbolic dimension that gave a global significance to local events. What they recalled of that time were sneering, illiterate students and fellow-traveling junior faculty, the collapse of standards, and the demise of an old reverence for learning. Many older members of the faculty felt that the commitments of a lifetime were being mocked and belittled. The wounds from the sixties' revolt against authority were still fresh when they turned to face the crisis provoked by open admissions.

Warfare raged within the faculty. At a debate held at the Bronx High School of Science, Howard Adelson, a rather magisterial historian of the Middle Ages and a former officer in the Air Reserves, an Old Believer in the City College orthodoxy, told a packed hall of students and parents, "City College is decaying. It is no longer the school it was, and its future is bleak." For generations Bronx Science had supplied City with a constant stream of brilliant students, just as

Exeter and Andover had done for Harvard. In recent years the contingent had shrunk to a dozen or two. Now Adelson recommended that Bronx Science graduates go not to City but to Queens, the whitest and most middle-class of the senior colleges. City College president Robert Marshak, who had come to debate Adelson, angrily insisted that City College had a new mission, and that it was performing it ably under trying circumstances. Marshak never forgave Adelson for what he considered an act of treachery; Adelson, in turn, savaged the college president regularly in his column in the *Jewish Press*.

The History Department, where Adelson had been teaching for twenty years, broke down under the sheer weight of ideological difference and personal hatred. The fact that they were historians only made matters worse, since the Left and Right factions naturally interpreted the events they had been witnessing in completely opposite terms—as a capitulation to racial fear and racial politics on the one side, and as a new phase of empowerment, of class self-assertion, on the other. The invective came to a head in a battle over control of the department, a mock-epic war that might have come straight from the pages of *Tom Jones*. One of the conservatives, Stanley Page, claimed that he had been punched in the stomach by the chief of the radicals, a woman. Liberal and left-wing members of the department denounced Page in the letters column of the *Campus*; one questioned whether he was "mentally competent" to teach. It would be many years before hostilities subsided.

And it was still a bad time for the people in the middle. The career of Theodore Gross, who became chairman of the English Department in 1970 and was later dean of humanities, became a sort of cautionary tale of the decline of the liberal center. Gross's academic field was black literature, and like Stanley Feingold he considered himself a member of City's liberal wing. But it was also his job to oversee the new remedial writing program, and he was stunned by the near illiteracy of many of the new students. In his 1980 memoirs, cautiously titled *Academic Turmoil*, he wrote that "the problem of Open Admissions students that controlled all others was a weak command of the language." Gross accepted the validity of teaching basic language skills in college; but the effort, he concluded, simply didn't work:

When we failed to bring students to the accepted level of literacy, we blamed ourselves—we hadn't been adequately trained or we lacked patience or our standards were set too high too quickly.

But in fact we had false expectations.... [The students'] entire miseducation and bookless past rose up to haunt them, and all the audio-visual aids and writing laboratories and simplified curriculum materials we tried could not work the miracle. The mistake was to think that this language training would be preparation for college education when what we were really instilling was a fundamental literacy that would allow social acculturation to occur. We were preparing our students to be the parents of college students, not to be students themselves.

In 1978 Gross wrote an essay titled "Open Admissions: A Confessional Meditation." In January of the next year it appeared in *Saturday Review* under the title "How to Kill a College." The cover of the issue showed a dagger, dripping in blood, plunged into the facade of a college building. Gross was not, in fact, a member of the death-of-the-university wing of the faculty, and he was horrified at the treatment; but in his essay he disclosed his deep sense of ambivalence about open admissions. Among the more impolitic passages was his observation that many of the new minority students came from families "in which television and radio were the exclusive sources of information."

Gross had said nothing that many, perhaps most, members of the faculty considered wrong; but he had said out loud what until then had been conveyed in whispers. Like Stanley Feingold before him, he had violated the taboo against discussing the limits of the remedial process. And, like Feingold, Gross became an enemy of the people. At a mass demonstration in his office, militant students denounced him as a racist; faculty members did their denunciations by mail. Gross desperately pointed to the work of a lifetime to show that he was scarcely unsympathetic to the plight of minority students. It was fruitless. In a letter to the *Saturday Review*, President Marshak declared that "Dean Gross's use of sexual, racial and religious stereotypes is profoundly offensive to our student body and faculty."

Marshak felt that Gross had betrayed his trust and the college itself. In late April, Marshak informed Gross that he was fired as dean. Gross left on a sabbatical and never came back.

In *Academic Turmoil* Gross went to far greater lengths than he had in the magazine article to underscore his belief in open admissions, criticisms notwithstanding. "Educating the parents of college students," he wrote, "is a worthy social function for any institution of learning." He spoke of the historical inevitability of open admissions and described it as an experiment "fundamentally in the American grain." A conservative book reviewer accused Gross of losing his nerve. Perhaps he had; he had felt the tightening of the screws of ideological compliance. But Gross was also an agonized liberal, like Buell Gallagher and Stanley Feingold, and he was torn between an a priori faith in that American grain—the grain of optimism and inclusiveness—and the terrible evidence of his own eyes. Open admissions was an easy call for the Left and the Right; for liberals, it was torment.

It was impossible to dispute Gross's claim that City College was not the place it had been. Students still took courses, or even majors, in philosophy and history and physics; but the task of City had become increasingly a remedial one. By 1975, 45 percent of students were beginning their careers in remedial math, writing, *and* reading. And very few of them were emerging from these courses as traditional City College students. A 1972 study found that the College Skills course made a "small but significant difference" in student performance in nonremedial courses, and Basic Writing made none at all. Three-quarters of students going from remedial to nonremedial math flunked. Averages were dropping every year, as were graduation rates. In the late 1960s between three-quarters and four-fifths of students graduated, generally in four years. But after four years only one-third of the class of 1970 had graduated; only a half remained in school. A 1981 study put the graduation rate for black open admissions students at 22 percent, and at 19 percent for Puerto Rican students.

There was an alternative point of view about open admissions: that City College *shouldn't* remain the place it had been. City had to be a new kind of college for a new kind of student. In a 1974 article in *Daedalus* Robert Marshak argued that it was time "to redefine the traditional model of the 'educable' by reaching out to students of all ages, backgrounds and degrees of preparation in the metropolitan area and to turn out well-educated graduates who will serve the city with diligence and dedication." Marshak took up a call first issued by Clark Kerr, president of the Carnegie Foundation, for the establishment of the "Urban-Grant College," an inner-city version of the land-grant colleges. Marshak embarked on a campaign to transform City into the first such school, dedicated not only to educating underprivileged youth but to dealing with problems of urban blight. He was trying, in effect, to reimagine higher education in the democratic and egalitarian form envisioned by the Zook Commission. But the "urban educational model," as Marshak called his grand design, was never realized, owing in part to public skepticism and in part to a lack of money.

The fierce debate over the virtues of open admissions in the 1970s, a debate that took place not only in dueling memoirs but in innumerable symposia and foundation reports and scholarly studies and magazine articles, offered a kind of recapitulation of the positions taken by the Zook and the Rockefeller groups. The question of who should receive higher education was an indirect way of asking what higher education was *for*. Conservative critics continued to argue that the purpose of college was the propagation and the pursuit of learning. Martin Trow, a Berkeley sociologist, wrote in 1970, "I believe we are seeing the consequences of the profound error of prescribing for half, and in some states for 70–80 percent, of the age-grade a form and content of education that closely resembles the bookish, traditional academic education that was designed for 5–10–15 percent of the age-grade."

Not only the Left, but some traditional liberals as well, asserted that this bookish tradition was an anachronism, and probably a myth. Timothy Healy, the vice chancellor of CUNY and later the president of Georgetown University, claimed in a 1973 article in *Change* magazine that the "patronizing collegiate stance" of selectivity and standards had more to do with institutional self-aggrandizement than with scholarship. For several generations, Healy noted, colleges had been a willing adjunct to the labor market: "In addition to keeping the nation's culture, the colleges also keep the keys to the treasure chests." And this being so, "the pressure on students to get in is a matter not of prestige but of survival."

Healy was echoing the point made by Jerome Karabel: Once it was understood that colleges had long served a credentialing function, their defense against the claims of open admissions vanished. How could higher education refuse its role as a weapon in the war on poverty if it already served as a middle-class entitlement program? Higher education was reinforcing likely outcomes instead of altering them. Alexander Astin, a careful student of admissions policies and the demographics of higher education, compared the selective college to a funnel, with good students going in one end and out the other, and the typical admissions officer to a handicapper, "picking winners." Astin suggested an alternative model, in which colleges would select those students most likely to be positively affected by the experience rather than most likely to succeed.

And yet neither Astin nor Healy nor Marshak nor Karabel believed that the new model of higher education required a wholesale reduction in academic standards. They felt that colleges could be far more inclusive without becoming less intellectually serious. Healy admitted that "there is little that open admissions can do to turn the high schools around," but he was confident, as Marshak was, that open admissions would vindicate the educability of the new student. The question itself struck Healy as a form of obfuscation raised by the guardians of the status quo—just as it had Bruce Hare and so many black students at City College. But this was too easy a form of dismissal. Riesman and Jencks, for all their attack on the academic meritocracy, had also expressed a dim view of the powers of remedial education.

City College's own experience seemed to be confirming the fears rather than the hopes. Yet there were tantalizing hints that remediation might not be quite so futile as Gross and others took it to be. Mina Shaughnessy, the director of City's Basic Writing program, said that after less than a year of remedial work a group of her students had outperformed nonremedial students on a writing test. Shaughnessy had gathered a group of gifted and idealistic teachers around her; their experiments in teaching writing to semi-literate students offered thrilling anecdotes to those who believed that higher education could make winners rather than simply pick them. Healy wrote of Shaughnessy's efforts, "A straw in the wind? Perhaps, but also a demonstration that new methods and good teaching can work wonders."

But the experiment came to an abrupt end. In 1976, with New York City having come within a whisker of bankruptcy, CUNY's budget was slashed by a third. The system actually shut down for the first two weeks in June. City fired fifty-nine nontenured faculty members, including virtually the entire cadre of dedicated teachers whom Shaughnessy had assembled. And it wasn't only the remedial commitment that was circumscribed. To reduce the flow of students to the senior colleges, and to raise their level, admissions standards were changed to admit the top third, rather than the top half, of graduating classes. And in a decision that was no less shocking for being inevitable, CUNY ended its tradition of free tuition. That tradition, at City College, was over 125 years old. Tuition would be only $900 a year, and state grants were generally available to cover much of the cost; but a higher education was no longer available to all who qualified.

Open admissions was dead, or so said its partisans. Technically, of course, open admissions had never applied to the senior colleges, but only to CUNY as a whole. At a place like City the phrase really denoted the vastly greater ease of access that came with lowered admissions standards and the huge increase in the SEEK population. Despite the imposition of tuition and the tightening of admissions standards at the senior colleges, CUNY still offered a place to every high school graduate, and City was still radically more accessible than it had been before 1970; and so it was appropriate to keep using the term *open admissions* in its loose sense. But what the partisans really meant was that the open admissions experiment was meaningless without massive funding for remediation; to cut off funds was to preclude success and instead to establish a self-fulfilling prophecy.

But was that so? If the cuts had never happened, would the Basic Writing program have proved that potential, like rocky soil, is perfectly cultivable so long as you have the right tools? Or did the problem also reside in the hardness of the job itself? Open admissions proved to be a chastening experience for some of the most idealistic people at City College. Leonard Kriegel, the English professor who had rhapsodized over his 1964 class on Emerson, was an ardent champion of open admissions and a barn-burning orator in the late 1960s. He had eagerly signed up when Mina Shaughnessy asked him to teach Basic Writing, and he dedicated his memoirs of the time to her. Now Kriegel says, "You wanted so desperately for this to work. The educational Left decided that potential was reality. Never mind that the kid was functionally illiterate; he's really brilliant. Anyone who says that the students I was teaching in 1974 were as good as the students I was teaching in 1964 is either a liar or is perpetuating an out-and-out illusion."

Kriegel was another poor Jewish boy from the Bronx who had made good. He was a well-known essayist and an authentic member of the New York intelligentsia. And his politics were founded on a visceral identification with the disadvantaged. He couldn't deny the evidence of his senses, as so many ideologues could; but neither could he abandon the ideals represented by open admissions. And so Kriegel, like Ted Gross, came to feel that open admissions didn't work but was the right thing anyway. "The previous system was immoral," Kriegel concludes, "and that made open admissions necessary. You knew that the standards were changing. You had to have the honesty to admit that, and know that it was worth it. I compare it to the 40 years in the wilderness. They had to have a long transition period."

In the early 1970s open admissions was a burning, bitter issue for policy intellectuals, fraught with symbolic overtones. Like school desegregation, the other great issue of the day, it represented a massive attempt by the state to transform the lives of the poor by giving them access to a good enjoyed by the middle class. In fact open admissions was often posed as the means to desegregate higher education. For people on the Left, open admissions represented the commitment, begun in the civil rights era, to confer full citizenship on black Americans. For conservatives it represented the vanity of social engineering and the breakdown of the liberal state in the face of impossible demands. And this was especially true for the neoconservatives who considered themselves the heirs of an abandoned tradition of postwar liberalism. Many of the neoconservatives were City College alumni like Irving Kristol and Seymour Martin Lipset. For them, City College's demise was of a piece with what they saw as the collapse of national values in the 1960s.

In 1972 the Council for Basic Education, a Washington-based think tank, sponsored a symposium on open admissions in which Kristol was one of half a dozen panelists. Kristol denounced open admissions as "a fraud." And it was, he continued, a fraud with a critically important moral: "To think that you can take large numbers of students from a poor socio-economic background, who do badly in high school, who do badly on all your standardized tests . . . who show no promise, and who do not show much motivation—to think you can take large numbers of such students and somehow make them benefit from a college education instead of merely wasting their time and their money, I say that this is demonstrably false. . . . Schools just cannot do that much and colleges simply cannot accomplish this mission." Kristol conceded that his skepticism about the power of institutions "runs against the grain of our American ideology—by now an American instinct—which asserts that it is always in man's power to abolish injustice and inequity, if only the will to justice and equity is strong enough." But, he said, "that proposition, quintessentially American though it be, happens to be false."

This was too much for Kenneth Clark, the black psychologist whose research had been instrumental in shaping the Supreme Court's decision in *Brown* v. *Board of Education*. Clark had taught at City College for decades, and he insisted that Kristol and others were gilding City's past with retrospective glory in order to discredit the present. Like so many other supporters of open admissions, Clark asserted that higher education had never performed the intellectual function that the neoconservatives were now urging on it. He had, he said, "given up" trying to infuse scholarly values into higher education, "because I think a more concrete and immediate battle is to open up higher education in America on what I consider questionable values . . . to a larger proportion of the American people." Here was the argument for credentialism in pure form—open admissions without illusions.

But Clark had devoted his entire career to proving that disadvantaged children were victims of their environment, and to arguing for reform of that environment. If he was cynical about the values of the academy, he was deeply idealistic about the human capacity for change and growth—about potential. "Institutions, and particularly schools, do perform miracles," Clark retorted to Kristol. "And one of the miracles which I think he is ignoring is the miracle of taking a precious human being and dehumanizing him.... A kind of amoral cynicism permits this miracle to continue when it actually could be remedied and solved, and I think those of us who believe that institutions are important in affecting lives of human beings cannot permit ourselves to be seduced by your perspective."

Open admissions was one of those fundamental questions about which, finally, you had to make an almost existential choice. Realism said: It doesn't work. Idealism said: It *must*.

Part II

The Remedial Underworld

5

Starting from Zero

I realized that if I wanted to get to the heart of the open admissions experiment I would have to become, in effect, a student, sitting in regularly on classes, seeing the same students day after day, and watching as the transformative process took hold—or didn't. A social scientist might have found a less time-consuming way of reaching conclusions, gathering data rather than direct experience. But as a journalist, I placed great value on sheer immersion, on the particular words and acts of particular people, and on the evidence of my own senses. Statistics mattered, greatly; but the questions I was asking were too textured to be answered merely with numbers. And so I decided to climb up the ladder of City College, starting at the lowest rung.

Every morning, Monday through Thursday during the summer of 1992, I went to the basement of old Townsend Harris Hall to sit in on an ESL class, where students at the lowest level of English-language proficiency were learning to speak, read, and write a language with which they were almost completely unfamiliar. It seemed like a staggering task for a college student, and it was one that City had never even attempted until recently. In earlier years City had

had no need for an ESL program, because students arrived already speaking English. City had been a college for second- or third-generation immigrants, not for the greenhorns themselves. And because, at the time, the virtues of acculturation and assimilation were accepted almost without question, even the recent immigrants rarely graduated from high school without having mastered English.

In any case, immigrants straight off the boat would not normally have been accepted in the days before open admissions, because either their language skills or their high school record would have been considered inadequate. Open admissions made it vastly easier for foreign-language speakers to be admitted into a CUNY college. But what created the ESL population was the vast surge of immigration, from the Caribbean, from South America, from Asia, the Middle East, and Russia, that began in the late 1970s. By 1990 the national immigration rate was triple what it had been in the 1960s; New York City alone received 850,000 immigrants in the 1980s. And these new Americans arrived in a country in which higher education had become immensely accessible as well as virtually indispensable. CUNY, which could no longer weed out students on the basis of language proficiency, adjusted by creating second-language programs, and by training admissions officers to translate the scoring system of the public schools in Port-of-Spain or Mogadishu or Quito into their New York equivalent.

Three or four hundred of City's 1,100 or so entering freshmen now begin their career in the ESL program. They are sorted into one of three levels, which together offer six courses. Students who begin at the bottom of the ESL ladder typically take two years to emerge into the regular curriculum, if they emerge at all. The dropout rate is harrowing. As of a few years ago, two-thirds of ESL students were leaving City before completing the freshman composition class that follows the ESL sequence. But the figures have been improving, and, given the magnitude of the problems its students confront, the ESL Department is a relatively optimistic place.

On a hot, bright morning in early July, I walked down the steps of Townsend Harris and found the lab-style room where the ESL class met. It was clean and quiet, carpeted and air-conditioned, and the students were gathered at six round tables. Looking around the room, I was immediately struck by the sobriety of these under-graduates. They wore shoes rather than sneakers, and khakis and buttoned-down shirts and, in one or two cases, despite the heat, V-necked sweaters. Only about half of them looked to be normal college-freshman age, and a few were clearly in their thirties. They were courteous to their teacher, Gloria Silverstein, a silver-haired mother hen figure, and to one another. Fernando Morales, a Domin-ican student from an upper-middle-class family, had the courtly habit of shaking hands with everyone at his table. There was the air, in the classroom, of adults engaged in a collaborative exercise.

Silverstein was offering a combined version of the two lowest-level classes, ESL 10 and 11, in a highly concentrated dose: the class met six hours a day, four days a week, for six weeks. Students who passed would be able to begin the fall semester on the second rung of the ESL ladder, and those who showed the most promise would go on to an accelerated class in which she and another teacher com-bined the next two levels of the program. The survivors would thus would be ready for City's regular curriculum by the spring. As I listened to the students marshal their meager fragments of English, the idea that some of them would be sitting in freshman composi-tion in February seemed positively bizarre.

The class had five speakers of Spanish and three each of Rus-sian and French-Creole; one student each spoke Korean, Mandarin, Urdu, Somali, and Arabic. At the outset of the class, none of the Russian speakers could express themselves in English; they had learned a little bit in school, and not much more in their few months in the United States. The same was true of two of the Haitians and one of the Spanish speakers. In theory, says Carole Berger, the direc-tor of ESL, "you must have some language skills to enroll; but the college wants the FTEs, so you've got to take them." (FTE stands for "full-time equivalent"; it's a way to measure the total number of credits being compiled at an institution.) One student spoke English fluently; the others could form simple sentences, although usually not without some forethought.

Since 1987 the ESL Department has used a pedagogy called "fluency first," a whole-language technique that focuses on comfort rather than technical correctness. The premise of fluency first is that students ought to learn a new language more or less as they learned their own tongue (known in the trade as "L1"), through immersion rather than through a conscious mastery of rules. Adele MacGowan-Gilhooly, one of the founders of the program, has written that "when learners do abundant reading and writing, talk about both, enjoy both, exercise a good deal of control over both, and are not overly concerned about correctness, literacy development, like L1 acquisition, is enjoyable, successful and almost effortless." In ESL 10, students thus read books rather than ESL texts, keep extensive reading journals, work together in groups, and exchange ideas.

Silverstein had her own version of the method. She showed the class a videotape based on an Isaac Asimov novel called *Caves of Steel*. The somewhat involved story line concerned a group of colonists from outer space who dominate the Earth with their robots; it culminated in an attempted murder, which the students would be expected to solve. Every day Silverstein would play fragments of the tape over and over, giving the students a chance to hear the different accents used by the actors and working on their oral comprehension. The students were to produce an exact transcript of parts of the tape, and to work with clues to deduce the identity of the villain. At the same time, they were reading the original Asimov novel, copying passages from the book, and commenting on their meaning.

On one of my early visits to class I sat at a table with a Yemeni student named Hammeed Assaidi, a Dominican girl named Sandra Andujar, and Yaffa Pavlanova, who along with her sister Larissa had emigrated from Armenia six months earlier. Hammeed was a dark-skinned boy with a thick mustache and a crescent-shaped scar on the left side of his head, just below the hairline. He had been in New York for eighteen months, and in that time he had acquired a version of English that was a parody of the fluency-first ideal. He stammered explosively, his scar flushing scarlet, and rather than pause to get things right in his head he simply talked without stopping or even breathing. He was almost completely incomprehensible, although once your ear got used to the violent cascade of his language you could begin to pick up some sense. Hammeed also misunderstood the simplest words.

Sandra and Yaffa, on the other hand, didn't speak at all; they knew almost no English. When Silverstein switched off the tape and asked the students to write down a clue, they were simply lost. Silverstein read slowly, fully articulating each syllable: "Escape route—hole blasted in archway." Sandra kept her pen poised above her notebook; she wanted to write, but nothing made any sense to her. She stared at the page, scribbled something, then looked at me beseechingly. She had written "how wasted in" and then a hapless scramble for "archway." I pronounced the words even more slowly for her, and then spelled them out one by one. Sandra looked at me with the same mute, helpless expression. Finally I had to write out the sentence. And Yaffa was just as flummoxed. When I asked who she thought had committed the crime, she smiled and said nothing. A moment later she replied, "I am no understand."

Few of the students were starting from zero, but they were close. They needed massive amounts of practice speaking English and hearing it spoken, and Silverstein, in line with the fluency-first pedagogy, encouraged conversations on diverse topics. One morning she asked the class why it was that some people had darker skin than others. Servio Villalone, a Dominican student, went up to the blackboard and drew a picture of a monkey inside a circle. Servio had finished high school in New York and was one of the more accomplished speakers in the class. He also loved to talk. He was an actor, with florid, Latin gestures and a brilliant smile. "One of the theories is that man come from the monkey," Servio said, wrinkling his brow in a satire of scholarly gravity. "The son of this monkey is going to continue walking. And the skin of them was from place." Servio flashed a smile of triumph; apparently he had proved his point.

Abukar Abukar, a Somali student and another one of the better speakers, understood Servio to be saying that sunlight causes pigmentation, which may very well have been what he meant. If that's so, Abukar asked, "how comes it that in some hot countries you have light-skinned people?" Servio started to say something, then stopped, then laughed and said, "In Spanish, I explain everything." Next to me, Mones (pronounced Mo-*nes*), one of the Haitians, kept opening his mouth to speak, but nothing came out. Like Servio, Mones knew what he wanted to say, but only in another language. Finally Abukar, a tiny man who always dressed with the utmost care, said, "My idea about the color is: The human being, they came from Adam and Eve. I'm not sure, I think one is white, one is black."

It was obvious that these students had an incredibly daunting climb in front of them, but most of them, like Wagner Ortuno, had been more rigorously educated than the average student entering City College. They came from countries where not only college attendance but high school graduation was a relatively elite attainment, as it had been in the United States through the 1920s or so. Abukar, for example, had left Mogadishu only when he failed to get into the premed program at the university. When he came to New York in 1989 he enrolled at a community college, where he compiled a near-perfect academic record despite what must have been profound problems with language. He was so proud of himself that one morning, on some flimsy pretext, he brought a copy of his transcript to class.

Several of the students had attended college before emigrating. Fernando had a degree in accounting. Mones and Hyunsun, the South Korean, had diplomas in engineering. Other students had obviously been standouts in high school. Atikul Khan, the Bangladeshi student, had edited a journal of student poetry. Boris Glukhovsky had been born into the intelligentsia: his father had been the principal of a music school in Kiev. And Ericson Pierre and Jean Thelusca, the other two Haitians, had both benefited from the discipline of a lycée education. Apparently the same had been true of Hammeed, who said that back in Yemen students who failed a single course had to repeat the entire year. When he came to New York in the middle of his junior year he assumed that similar standards obtained at Park West High School, where he enrolled. He did his homework diligently. "But all the other kids, they were like laughing at me," he said. And so he slacked off, and despite the fact that he spoke virtually no English, he got excellent grades.

The class represented a rarefied sample of ESL students, many of whom have received haphazard educations in provincial backwaters. Silverstein had chosen students who said that they planned to major in engineering or the sciences, and whether through luck or careful selection she had found students unusually likely to succeed. Even in the first few weeks of class I could see incipient signs of progress—the kind of progress you would expect from students familiar with the routines of learning. Hammeed continued to speak uncontrollably, shouting, "Teacher, teacher, teacher!" to get Silverstein's attention; but he had begun fashioning a homemade dictionary by folding sheets of paper vertically and writing words on one side in Arabic and on the other in their English equivalent. His spelling, which had baffled Silverstein, was almost perfect. Derek, the Chinese student, wrote down words he had read in the *New York Times* but didn't know—*torture, manufacture, ideology, contempt*. He was especially fond of the words he found in articles on soccer—*flat-footed, duck-hook*.

Often it was hard to tell from classroom performance whether students were improving or not, since about half the class lived in terror of having to speak. Even here, though, there were tiny signs of improvement. Mones, for example, began peeking out of his shell of mortification. One day Silverstein explained that *robotics* was the noun form of *robotic*. "What about *robotocist*?" Boris asked. "Yes, what about this?" Mones cried with sudden academic fervor. Silverstein then asked for the adjectival form of *artist*. And Mones, no doubt translating from the French, fairly shouted, "Artistic!"

The students progressed at very different rates, and in ways that reflected their prior experience as well as their training. The Spanish students had all been in the United States longer than the Russians or Haitians, and most of them spoke with greater confidence and elan. Even by the end of the semester neither Mones nor Ericson could speak without great forethought and painful effort. Ericson's lips would tremble so that it seemed almost cruel to engage him in conversation. The lycée was a prime example of old-fashioned fluency-last pedagogy. But their inability, or reluctance, to speak was not a sign of an overall language problem, or of an intelluctual problem. Because they had been relatively well educated in their mother tongue, they were comfortable with writing as a form of expression. They were likelier to work out their problems with language on the page than in class.

Mones often sought me out for help with his written work. He was so concerned about the *mot juste*, or even the accepted usage, that not only could he not bring himself to speak, but he could spend hours laboring over a few paragraphs. He reworked everything he wrote until he had hit the right note of Gallic pedantry. And he was finding more and more words with which to express himself in English prose. He began one essay, "One of the most meaningful strengths of science fiction is its ability to supply a fictional world that can be manufactured for the investigation of several sociological and moral principles."

The students kept double-entry journals. On the left side of the page they wrote down passages from their reading verbatim, and on the right they were to reflect on the passage in their own words. The left-hand column really was an exercise in diligence, and since most of the students were diligent it changed little from week to week. But the right-hand column was a record of growth, though of a very uneven kind. The passages got longer and longer, the sentence structure and verb forms more complex. The writing was still heavily coded in a foreign tongue, but it was becoming more supple. Silverstein was very proud of the journals, and she used to beckon me over for a glimpse at her favorites. Early on, for example, Abukar had said of an episode in the movie, "I think Baley is trying to tell Daneel that he is not human being. And ones the riot people know that he is robot, that is it nobody can stop the riot." After a month, he wrote, "Mr. Clausarr is really rude. I mean, how can someone extended hand and didn't shake. For me, if my enemy extended his hand, I would shake it. It is a simple thing not to be proud like this circumstances."

The Spanish-speaking students had, in general, the greatest problems with writing. Sandra wrote as if she were transliterating from speech, though at a lower level of fluency; she was very close to illiteracy. The courtly Fernando, who unlike Sandra conversed in English, not only translated directly from Spanish in his writing but did so in a kind of headlong tumble. He began his essay on the characters in *Caves of Steel*, "I detective Lije was in my office like every days, I was listen the news in my TV office, and then call me R. Sammy, he tell me the Commissioner want to see me."

With the exception of Fernando, the Spanish speakers had not been particularly well educated at home; most of them had finished their schooling in New York City. They lacked the academic habits and the self-discipline of some of the others; their relative fluency masked deeper problems. Gloraida Malave, for example, was the exact opposite of Mones or Abukar. Gloraida had been born in Puerto Rico, moved to New York when she was nine, moved back to Puerto Rico at fifteen, and returned to the States with her mother in 1991. Gloraida had been shaped by the inner-city culture that the others had avoided. "When I came back to New York," she said, "all of my friends were pregnant. Nobody was going to school or doing anything." Gloraida *was* going to school; but she seemed out of place among these driven immigrants. She often showed up late for class, and she chewed gum and tossed her ponytail and whispered and giggled with Servio. Gloraida spoke English effortlessly, but she had been placed in ESL 10 because her writing was so rudimentary. She repeated whatever she read, and in the simplest possible constructions. She was surprisingly prone to get her transcriptions wrong.

But even for the best of the students, the handicaps of immigrant life were every bit as threatening as the hardship of language learning. Whatever they had been at home, now they suffered from the poverty and dislocation that came with their sudden upheaval. And the dislocation was all the greater since they were trying to combine in a single generation a series of experiences that once had required two: finding your feet, and moving up. Only about half the students lived with one or two of their parents, and few of them could count on financial help. How could they support themselves, and sometimes their families, and still go to school? How could they find a job when they couldn't even speak English? Boris lived with both of his parents, but his father sat at home, helplessly becalmed and bitterly lamenting his lost life. The best job Boris had been able to find was distributing handbills for discount stores at $3.75 an hour; he saved money by bringing his lunch of liver sandwiches every day. Hyunsun, the South Korean, worked in a beautician's shop. Hammeed worked in a deli, Jean at a McDonald's.

At least they had jobs. Mones, constrained by his pride as much as by his lack of English, had been able to find only occasional work tutoring Haitian students in English. Somehow he managed to send some money every month to the wife and two children he had left

behind in Port-au-Prince. Mones was an educated man. He had
received a degree in civil engineering from the Ecole Normale
Superieure in Port-au-Prince. Since Haiti had virtually no jobs for
engineers, Mones had become a teacher in lycée. He took pride in
his former status; perhaps that was why he couldn't bring himself
to risk an error. Now Mones was hoping that he could acquire a
graduate degree in computer science from City and resume his
teaching career in the United States.

I could scarcely believe that Mones was only thirty-five. He had
a gray beard, and the lines on his broad brow were deep. Mones
smiled whenever he was addressed, but it was a smile designed to
ward off ill fortune and to disguise unease—the propitiatory smile
of the downtrodden. Mones's gloom was almost palpable. During
a break in class one day I asked him why he had left Haiti. Mones
always paused, translating in his head, before he spoke. "You know
about the political situation," he finally said.

"Did you get in trouble with the politicians?" I asked.

"I told my students . . .," he started to say, and then backed
up to try again. "In my class I say the truth. When the students ask
me about the *gouvernment*, I say the truth."

I asked Mones if he had been threatened. He said that he had.
With death? Yes. And how had he left Haiti? Mones smiled at me,
in lieu of giving a direct answer. "I don't like to talk about it," he
said. He smiled again, that smile of solicitude and pain, and turned
his eyes away.

Every day Mones came to class in a short-sleeved dress shirt
and shiny black tie-up shoes. But his gentility barely covered the
ferocity of his struggle. One Monday morning I asked how his weekend had been. "Not so good," he said ruefully. "I had a headache."
This was Mones's way of hinting at his monstrous migraines. Sometimes they lasted for three days; sometimes, intermittently, for two
weeks. His head would explode, and his field of vision would contract until he was almost blind. When Mones was an adolescent he
sometimes had to walk up to strangers and ask them to take him
home. Migraines still incapacitated him on a regular basis. Mones
saw me listening button-eyed to his tale of woe, and he broke the
mood with a mirthless little laugh. "It is my darkness," he said gently.

Practically everyone in the class lived in a state of anxiety. One morning Thelma Mason, the director of the financial aid office, came to class to explain the aid regulations. "You must be either a citizen or a permanent resident in order to qualify for aid," Mason explained. "A permanent resident is one who has continuously resided in New York State for one year or more." This caused a stir. None of the Russian speakers had been here that long. What was worse, Mason explained, tuition for nonresident students was $2,400 a semester, or twice the regular cost. Boris, sitting next to me, was getting more and more agitated. Boris was only seventeen, but his waxy complexion and thick, square black glasses made him look like a member of Brezhnev's Politburo. Now he raised his hand, but when Mason called on him Boris began to stutter. It was a moment of sheer frustration: he simply didn't have the words to express himself. Finally Boris tapped himself on the head with his papers, rolled his eyes in a gesture of despair, and said nothing.

Other students were trapped between self-reliance and technical dependency. Hammeed raised his hand and said, "What if you are here with no family, not brother even, but you are *with* a family?" Hammeed was staying with family friends. His parents were not supporting him, but Mason explained that until he was twenty-four he would be considered a dependent, and his father's income would be counted in determining his eligibility for aid. Jean was in an even worse fix. Jean had come to New York with his father and stepmother, but he and the stepmother had been at daggers drawn. Jean had moved in with a friend of his late mother, and his father had cut off all support. Jean was a gentle soul, and almost childlike. He wasn't very disciplined to begin with, and the loneliness and instability of his life seemed to be wearing away at his work. Mason delivered the bad news: he was still a dependent.

Everyone had problems; and yet the class developed a sense of esprit de corps that came of their common struggle to learn English. Most days the male members of the class ate lunch together; Gloraida often joined us, but Yaffa, Larissa, and Sandra were either too shy to join the group or too habituated to a second-class status. At lunch one day about a month into the semester, Servio told his first joke in English. Halfway through he realized that the joke turned

on the Spanish word for crackhead—*pipero*—but he told it anyway.
Then he told his second English joke ever, and his third. The others,
who were faintly in awe of Servio's lack of inhibition, desperately
tried to follow. When anyone laughed, the others laughed as well.
Then Abukar said, "I have a joke, too," and he told a story with a
punch line in the middle. Then he told another with the same structure. Apparently Abukar didn't know what a joke was; he thought
it was an amusing tale from real life. Hammeed, who had been listening with twitching impatience, then told a dirty joke. It was completely incomprehensible, but everyone laughed anyway.

During those summer mornings I also sat in on a course called
Language Arts that was meeting across the hall from the ESL 10 class.
The class was offered, on a voluntary basis, to incoming students
in the SEEK program whose scores on a writing assessment test had
assigned them to the lower of the two levels of English remediation.
Their performance would not be graded, and would not, by itself,
land them in a higher level of remediation in the fall. The course
was designed to give them a running start on their steep uphill climb
through the curriculum. These were students who by definition had
not done well in school.

When first founded, SEEK accepted any student from one of
several neighborhoods with large concentrations of minorities. Some
of those students had excellent academic records; none were accepted, at least in theory, with a high school grade-point average
under 70. But the lowering of admissions standards meant that many
of those students would be admitted to a CUNY senior college without the benefit of SEEK. And so starting in 1970 SEEK qualifications
became strictly negative: students had to come from a family whose
income fell below the poverty level, and they had to have compiled
an academic record that would not qualify them for admission to
senior college. GED students could be enrolled through the program,
as could students with high school averages in the low 60s.

The language arts class had been assigned to one of the traditional classrooms in Harris, a big room with high-school-style desks
where voices echoed off the high, bare walls. The first morning that
I walked into the class the teacher, Charles Frye, was writing on the

blackboard. He had the high school teacher's habit of writing down practically everything he said; many of the students, as he knew very well, had never learned to take notes from the spoken word. Frye wrote the words *independent clause* and *subordinate clause* on the board. He turned to the class and asked, "Have you seen these words before? Any of you that went to Catholic school and studied grammar?" Facetiousness in a teacher is usually a bad sign; it's a way of cushioning frustration. There was silence; Jenny Villegas, sitting next to me, punched *subordinate* into her computer speller, and found that it meant "inferior." "Okay," said Frye wearily, "does anyone want to take a guess as to what this has to do with *grammar?*"

"With who?" That was Renato Lopez, a big kid with a striking, pre-Columbian face—soft and rubbery, like a child, with a *campesino's* air of stoicism around the big, dark eyes and thin mouth. Renato presented himself as a child: he wore madras shorts attached to suspenders that dangled around his waist—a version of the ghetto teenager's unlaced-sneaker look. He carried on a friendly running dialogue with Frye, and stabbed at whatever questions came his way. But his banter was a way of distracting attention from the issue at hand.

Frye hadn't planned to focus on grammar. Initially he had brought to class the reader that he had used in English 2, the second-level remedial course. He had planned to have the students read passages, discuss them in class, and write essays. But the first few readings he had assigned had produced an ominous silence. Those students who had done the reading hadn't made any sense out of it. Frye had never before taught college students at this level; he was taken aback by the scantiness of their skills. And so he had retreated to the basics. He still assigned writing, but he handed out grammar worksheets and went over the answers in class.

Now he repeated his question: "What's a clause, Renato?" Renato admitted that he didn't know. But he wasn't alone. Nobody in the class knew that the word *in* was a preposition. Frye drew a piano on the board, and then placed a bouquet of flowers variously under, on, and next to the piano to illustrate the function of the preposition. The class wrote and identified sentences using prepositions. At the end of the class Frye turned to Paula Sarmiento and said, "Okay, Paula, what part of speech is *in*?" Paula looked up at the board, looked down at the worksheet on her desk, looked even farther down, as if into the desk itself, and said nothing.

As I shuttled between the ESL and the SEEK classes that summer, I often felt that I was passing from one world to another. There were, it was true, any number of superficial similarities. Both groups of students were starting their careers at City College, and both were starting at rock bottom. About half of the students in the SEEK class spoke English as a second language. They had been born in Cambodia, China, Ethiopia, Ecuador, the Dominican Republic, Haiti, and Puerto Rico. In fact three or four of them had such limited English skills that they probably belonged in the ESL program. But most of them were lifelong products of the New York City public schools; their problems were the problems of the schools themselves. Renato, Paula, and Jenny were Ecuadorean; but Renato had been born in New York, Paula had moved there nine years before, and Jenny, seven. It was L1 that many of them hadn't mastered, not L2. They had graduated from high school with only the barest degree of literacy.

The two classes were also poles apart in atmosphere. The SEEK students seemed barely socialized to school: they giggled, and whispered, and flirted, and did their best to avoid eye contact with Frye. Even when it wasn't hot in the unair-conditioned room, which it often was, the climate felt torpid; Frye often couldn't get an answer to the simplest question. These were students who had drifted through high school with an implicit contract: I won't disturb you if you won't disturb me. The premise of the contract was that education was something that happened to you rather than something in which you were an active participant. None of them devised the sort of educational aids that Hammeed or Derek had thought up. Lessons were forgotten from one day to the next; homework assignments went undone. In fact many of the students assumed that schoolwork was something you did only in school itself. When I asked Nancy Anokye whether she had had to do homework over the weekends, she looked at me like I was daft. "So how much did you do during the week?" I asked. Nancy thought about it and said, "I usually finished my work at school." And Nancy had gone to parochial school.

Frye did his best to instill some life in the class, but I could see that he was having trouble keeping his head in the game. Every once in a while he would idly practice a left-handed tennis swing. He was a large black man in his mid-forties, balding, with a mustache, which he sometimes absently smoothed, wire-rimmed glasses, and a deep and penetrating voice. He had the ironic, amused manner of a high school teacher, which he also was. But this class was clearly getting under his skin. One morning he launched into a long, grim monologue about the demands of college. "One day very soon," he boomed, "a man or a woman will stand in the classroom at ten minutes to two on a Friday and say, 'Read *Hamlet* for Monday.' "

"The *whole* thing?" asked an incredulous Renato.

"That's what *you're* going to say," Frye shot back with an air of triumph. "And she'll say, 'Yeah, the whole thing.' " Actually, no such thing ever happens at City College, and probably not at Yale, either; but that was a detail. As Frye saw it, the students were like a pack of Cub Scouts about to be shipped off to the Pacific theater. They needed a mighty wake-up call as much as they needed to learn the parts of speech. And as far as he could tell, he wasn't reaching anybody just yet.

Once a week or so Frye assigned an essay on a topic that he thought might engage the students. The results had not been encouraging. One day he asked the class to discuss "the most vivid memory of your graduation." One student wrote, "My high school graduation was on a long and hot morning. The graduation had almost about everything but it had to go on a scedual. It had marching down the isliles, singing the school almata, which I never heard before, and the color guards." Another essay read, in its entirety, "The most vivid memory I have of my graduation is went my graduation of P.S. 115 I graduate from six grades we sang." Few of the students wrote more than a paragraph.

Midway through the summer Frye instructed the students to divide themselves into groups to plan and compose a narrative. I sat with Nancy Anokye, Gail Farquharson, and Mercline Augustin, three black girls who always sat together in the rear corner of the class. They were stymied by Frye's suggestion that they work jointly. At first they sat around and talked idly, and then Gail started writing a story about a girl getting pregnant. Gail was a big girl whose hair was a fantastically complicated maze of braids and buns and bangs and green plastic studs and streaks of copper and rust. She hadn't really thought about where her story was going, or even where the sentences were going. Every once in a while she would show me the page and ask where she should stop a sentence. She had a sense of how to use commas, but not periods. She and Mercline and Nancy talked about whether the Gail character should keep the baby.

"Is this baby going to bring you more closer to your boyfriend, or is he going to ignore you, or what?" Mercline asked, playing the best friend. "How's he going to support this baby? He going to get a good job?"

Gail dug in her heels under attack. She said, "Yeah, he's going to get a good job." She didn't want to part with the baby, or the boyfriend, and she didn't appreciate being pressed to think about it. "I want you to like him," she said, idly scratching the writing arm of her desk with the back end of her pen. Mercline plainly thought that Gail was living in fantasyland.

Everybody was doing more or less the same thing: woolgathering on paper, rather than plotting out a story. Frye realized that the students needed more guidance, and the next day he talked about the construction of a narrative. On the board he wrote, "Developing a Conflict." Then he turned back to the class and said, "Tell me about conflict. Gail?" Gail almost never spoke in class. Now she looked down at her hands and said nothing. Frye searched for a way to get through to her. "Gail, you see movies?" Gail said that she didn't. "You read the Bible?" No, said Gail, "not since I was a kid." Frye was getting exasperated. "What do you do with your spare time?" From what she had told me, Gail hung around with her girlfriends, gossiping and looking at boys. But instead of saying anything she gave Frye that blank, bovine look that can drive teachers crazy, though it often comes of fear rather than indifference. "Is it a secret?" Frye deadpanned. "I'm glad to see you can make bail every morning."

That was a mean-spirited crack, but if Frye was hoping to get a rise out of Gail, he miscalculated. Gail just looked at him and said nothing. Now Frye's dander was up, and the lesson of the day was rapidly heading out the window. He crossed the room, stood in front of the board, and thought for a moment. There was something more important to say. "I'm begging you," he said, "*imploring* you, to stop fooling around. In thirty days things are going to start accelerating here faster than you can believe." Frye was standing before the board in his crisp purple polo shirt, waving his broad hands. For once, everyone was listening. Frye talked about grades, and credits, and workloads. He was working himself up into a lather. "You know about January clearance?" he asked. "What that means around here is all the people that begin in September that leave in January. This is not high school, folks. They don't *play*."

The January clearance story, like the *Hamlet* story, was a bit hyperbolic. But Frye's urgency, his sense of peril, was all too real. Frye had a strong "there-but-for-the-grace-of-God" feeling about his own career. "I was lucky," he said to me one day after class. "I went to this very progressive primary school connected to Columbia Teachers' College, and I went to George Washington High when it was still a good school. I took all the Regents courses I could." Frye was proud of the fact that he had been admitted to City in 1964, before open admissions or SEEK. But then he had goofed off in school, been put on probation, lost his academic deferment, and been drafted and sent to Vietnam. That had been *his* wake-up call. When he left the army he returned to City, hit the books, and got his bachelor's in English Literature. When he looked at the students he saw them standing at the same fork in the road where he had once stood. But of course they hadn't had his education. Frye never ceased to be amazed by how little they knew, how unfamiliar they were with the basic routines of school.

Now he was warming to his theme. "If you talk in class," he said, in his deep, ominously quiet voice, "the professor is going to tell you to be quiet. If you continue talking, he's going to ask you to leave. And if you don't leave, he'll call security. And your counselor is not going to help you. Nobody's going to be watching out for you. You can't come back in with your mom." Frye was ironic most of the time; now he was dreadfully serious. "Remember," he said, "people go to this college so they can get a job, so they can make money. This is the last chance for many people to break the cycle of poverty. *And you can't afford to waste it*."

Nobody said a word. Were they shocked? Were they insulted? Were they taking it in at all? I wondered if Frye weren't wasting his breath. And then Sabour Clarke interrupted him. Frye was expounding on the dangers of holding down a job while taking a full load of courses; Sabour thought that he was implying that only rich kids could handle college. "If it comes too easy," he said, "people slack off, right?" Frye was in no mood for Socratic dialogue, and he irritably resumed his oration. And then Sabour, remembering the question that had launched the monologue in the first place, said with a sly look, "Mr. Frye, are we in conflict?" It was a virtuoso needle; and it was an indirect way of saying that *he* could have answered the question had he been asked.

Until that moment Sabour had seemed to fit perfectly into the demoralized atmosphere of the classroom. He had scarcely spoken, and I had taken his silence as acquiescence or passivity. The mistake was mine. Sabour wore high-top sneakers, a baseball jacket, and a blue "Duke" cap that he never took off, perhaps because he was self-conscious about his shaved head. He wore his name in a big brass nameplate around his neck. Sabour was tall and thin with extremely long hands and fine fingers. He reminded me instantly of Michael Jordan; I found out later that the resemblance was a point of pride with Sabour. He had something of Jordan's features, but even more of his movements, liquid and slow. Sabour spoke slowly, too, and he had a rather unnerving dead-level gaze. He wasn't skittish, or sullen, or timid, as so many of the others were. His life had been just as isolated as theirs, and his education just as bad; but he moved, and spoke, with the self-assurance of someone who knew where he was going.

Sabour showed, in tiny ways, that he didn't need Charles Frye to tell him that his time was precious. For one thing, he took notes—slowly, but methodically. When another student floundered helplessly before some elementary matter of grammar, Sabour handed over his notebook and explained the point. He was almost painfully deliberate, and he was often confused; but he watched the world keenly. I was often struck by his delicate sense of manners. When Maritza Hernandez, the class siren, came back from the blackboard with chalk on her hand, Sabour sprang up to Frye's desk, plucked a tissue, walked over to Maritza—and then stood there mutely, trying to think of the polite words. Finally he made a noise, and Maritza turned around, uttered a little cry of thanks, and took the tissue.

Most of the students ran away from me when I tried to talk to them; I think they saw me as some kind of extension of the teacher. But not Sabour. One day when I sat down next to him he asked if I would like to see his drawings. It turned out that Sabour's father, whom he hadn't lived with since he was young, had been a contractor, and through him Sabour had developed an interest in building and design. Now he wanted to be an architect. "When I was in high school," Sabour said, "I used to buy architecture magazines on the street. And then I would go through them and just copy things." He had taught himself perspective, and he showed me a stack of drawings he had made of dressers, desks, bookshelves, and toy chests, viewed along sharp, if sometimes wayward, orthogonals. He had drawn up a blueprint of a spacious suburban house: garage, living room, dining room, big kitchen, three bedrooms. "I'm going to build this house when I'm successful, and I'm going to live there," he said, dead serious. But he also said that he would never abandon Harlem, even when he was making $100,000.

Sabour was an eddy of life in the midst of a sea of lethargy. Every once in a while another ripple disturbed the surface. Harold Saintelus, a Haitian student, was reading Steinbeck's *The Pearl* on his own, to improve his English. Yin Phors, a Cambodian student whose family had fled to Laos and Thailand before finally reaching New York when Yin was thirteen, had read several books about the CIA and had decided to return to Cambodia as an intelligence agent. (Nancy said, "I hope you change your mind. It sounds too dangerous.") Julissa Martinez wrote a story about a girl who wanted desperately to be a model but feared that she was overweight. "I personally considered her belumptious," Julissa wrote. *Belumptious?* Julissa said that she had heard the word in a movie. "It means beautiful, but too big." Finally I realized that she meant *voluptuous*. It was a big word, and it combined two other words, and it sounded like what it meant. It was a wonderful word, and Julissa had appropriated it in the form in which she had heard it.

Julissa, Maritza, Yin, and to a lesser extent Sabour made real efforts to plan out and then revise their stories; the others largely tagged along. The stories had the melodramatic plot lines of comic books or soap operas. Sabour and Yin wrote action-adventure stories with plenty of gunplay; Yin's was called "Die Traitor Die," and featured an American agent who is infiltrated into Southeast Asia to prevent a communist takeover. The girls wrote about domestic rather than military violence. Julissa's belumptious girl ultimately took diet pills to make herself beautiful, went into a coma, and died. She worked into this tale a series of fragments written by the other girls, including one in which a perfectly innocent child is beaten by her parents, locked in a closet, and treated like a slave.

Maritza was the most literate of the students; her story sounded like a combination of *Romeo and Juliet* and *Slaughter on Tenth Avenue*. Light-skinned, well-born Carmen falls in love with Carlos, who "lived in a wooden house and had a lot of animals and walked barefoot." Carlos and Carmen leave narrow-minded Puerto Rico for New York, where Carmen falls in with a drug dealer, starts to snort coke, and winds up turning tricks on the street. When Carlos finally discovers Carmen in bed with his hated uncle, "He couldn't believe his own eyes he went crazy, he grabbed a machete from the side the door and started to cut them all up there was blood all over the place, he felt so frustrated he ended up hanging himself." And then the final, cheery touch: "The End!"

During the last few days of the term, Sabour spent a lot of time in the computer room working on his story. He had managed to get through Louis Brandeis High School without writing anything longer then four or five paragraphs. He said "patriism" for "patriotism," and wrote "respect kids" instead of "respectful kids." He didn't know math beyond arithmetic. In fact Sabour had arrived at City College with almost no school learning at all. He had no idea how little he knew. And yet he had something else—self-discipline, alertness, a habit of listening. There was something slightly uncanny about Sabour's intuitions. When he got up from the computer screen to tell me about his story, which involved an accused killer being chased by the police, I said, "Everybody seems to be writing about crime and violence." Sabour fixed me with that reckoning gaze of his and said, "This report of yours could lay on a lot of stereotypes."

"Like what?"

"Like about kids write about violence so they must come from violent backgrounds." Touché. Sabour said, "I live up on Lexington Avenue and 129th, and I don't think it's a dangerous neighborhood. I've never gotten hurt. If you don't bother no one, no one bothers you." He would not be typecast.

Sabour was the kind of student in whose name the open admissions struggle had been waged. He had "potential": not only unexplored ability but a sense of direction, a focus, that would allow him to explore those abilities. But he was the exception, not the rule. So many others in the class seemed sunk in apathy, or despair, or confusion. And while Gloria Silverstein had been able to focus on the task at hand, Charles Frye had not; he not only had to teach his students but had to scare them sober. Perhaps he should have been doing something more affirmative. But it's not easy to reverse at age eighteen habits that have been building since five.

The final assignment for the ESL 10 class was for each of four groups to write, and perform, their own play solving the mysterious attempted murder in *Caves of Steel*. At first the class met the request with utter bafflement. Ericson whispered to me, "What is a *play*?" Boris, however, was fascinated by the whole idea of writing narrative, something he had never done in Russian, much less English. He would compose sentences like "The robot came to him and said loudly. . . .'' Boris had sincerely believed that nothing except math and engineering held the remotest interest for him, but now he seemed to be proving himself wrong. One morning he said to me, "Is possible in English?" and showed me a sentence in which he described a character "bombling" his hamburger.

"I don't think it's a word, Boris," I said.

"But you said this word," Boris replied. "You said Enderby was bombling his food." I thought back, and realized that I had described the character as a "bumbler." Boris had somehow understood the word as meaning "eating absentmindedly," an expression that, he

said, corresponded to a specific word in Russian. Like Julissa, Boris
was assembling a language of his own. He was making the kind of
creative mistakes that learners, whether adults or children, always
make. Boris was, in fact, the star of the class. His fluency grew from
week to week; toward the end of the summer I caught him whisper-
ing quips to his neighbors. Boris's writing improved so rapidly that
Silverstein could scarcely believe that he had written his first draft
of the *Caves of Steel* script himself.

When the students finally performed their playlets—in front of
a television camera—there were a few unexpected standouts. Henry
Arias, who never spoke in class, recited his lines almost flawlessly
from memory. Mones held himself as stiffly as a nineteenth-century
tragedian, and filled his lines with sentiment. Boris clutched his script
but never looked at it. After it was over he was wearing a goofy grin
of relief that even his Leonid Brezhnev glasses couldn't hide. He said,
"That was the most nervous moment of my life." But Derek was
almost incomprehensible, Sandra could barely bring herself to speak,
Ericson was inaudible and his French-style ellision made his lines impossible to follow. Yaffa spoke each word separately: "I . . . don't . . .
chave . . . time. I . . . want . . . you . . . leave . . . now." Hammeed
gave himself all the lines, and fell all over himself saying them. He
was still writing the way he talked: "At the moment of the ending
of the time that have been given to the earth people to find out who
commit the murder of Dr. Fastolfe, Baley was the responsible of the
investigation."

After the last class, the students decided to hold a farewell party.
Atikul and Hyunsun and Servio went out and bought huge quan-
tities of terrible Chinese food, and lots of soda, and we sat at our
round tables and talked in little spasms. It was still painfully hard
for many of the students to sustain a conversation. But it was a festive
moment. They had been together four days a week, morning and
afternoon, for eight weeks, engaged in an arduous and often tedious
joint exercise. They had eaten lunch together and told jokes together
and slowly learned how to communicate with one another. There
was a sense of camaraderie in the room. I asked for everyone's phone
number, and then I had to photocopy the list because everyone
wanted my number, and Gloria Silverstein's number, and each other's
number as well.

Virtually everyone in the class had made significant progress in some form of expression. Their progress had a great deal to do with the subject matter itself: second-language learning consists in large part of sheer exposure, especially at the outset. And the students had probably shown the most improvement in oral comprehension, the aspect of language learning in which immersion matters the most, and conscious effort the least. The fluency-first approach had done what it was supposed to do. Their writing, with some exceptions, had also grown in ease and complexity. And this, too, was a consequence of sheer experience and of the pedagogical focus.

But it also had a great deal to do with the students themselves—their academic habits, and their relative mastery of L1. These were not the students whom the champions of open admissions had envisioned, the inner-city kids whose gifts had been ignored by the public schools. They were disadvantaged, but they were not the victims of the system. They had, for the most part, succeeded in their own systems, and they were ready, and eager, to exploit this one. Perhaps what they resembled most were the very early generations of Jewish students at City.

Silverstein was immensely proud of the class. Everyone had been promoted; and she had invited all of them except Yaffa, Larissa, Sandra, and Derek to move into her ESL 20/30 class, which meant that they would be ready to take up the regular curriculum by the spring semester. But money problems would keep out some of the students who had surmounted the academic hurdles. Abukar had decided to skip the fall semester in order to put away some savings through his job as a manager in a movie theater. Mones needed the morning, when the accelerated class would be taught, to earn his precious keep through his tutoring, so he would be advancing only to the regular second-level class. Yaffa and Larissa couldn't afford the $2,400 nonresident tuition, so they postponed enrollment until the spring, when they would qualify for residency.

Boris would be leaving City College as well, but for an entirely different reason. He had fretted about his poverty, and his father's inertia, and his hateful job, until one day just before the end of the summer he announced that he had received a five-year scholarship to study engineering at Yeshiva University. Like some crazy story out of *The Rise of David Levinsky*, Boris had landed, suffered, floundered, and been saved, all in a matter of months. In fifteen years, if all went well, Boris would be driving his proud, idle father around the New Jersey suburbs in a Lincoln Continental.

The ESL Department does not keep pass rate figures for all of its courses, but there's no question that 100 percent was an amazing figure for ESL 10 and 11. Clearly, this was no ordinary class. Silverstein had no SEEK students in her class, for example, though about a third of ESL students have come through the SEEK program. This is the most multiply disadvantaged group at City. One of City's SEEK counselors, Shen Tien, conducted a study of 155 SEEK students who had been placed in the ESL program. After six years, only seven of them had graduated. After seven years, another half dozen or so had graduated. Even projecting out a decade, it seemed that no more than 15 percent of the group would graduate.

Silverstein's class had been, in effect, a laboratory where second-language problems were separated out from the host of other academic problems that afflicted students at City. And the experiment had demonstrated that the lack of English, by itself, was the least crippling of the liabilities that the new students brought with them to college. But it was still a huge problem. It was easy to forget how far these students had to go. Many of them had been virtually innocent of English a few months earlier. Few of them could carry on a conversation even now. They had never read a difficult book in English, or written an essay of more than a page or so. Perhaps, after another semester of language instruction, they would be ready to forge ahead in math. But would they be ready for a World Humanities class, or even freshman composition, in four months? It didn't seem likely.

The language arts class had a party, too. But the impetus came from Frye, and some of the students drifted away even before Nancy and Mercline came back from the cafeteria with ice. After fifteen or twenty minutes, the big classroom with the bare walls was empty. There was no sense that a great adventure, or even a frightening one, was about to begin. It was hard to say what kind of a difference the class had made. The students took the writing assessment test again, but only Maritza passed it. She would start her City College career in the freshman composition course. The others would all begin in English 1 and College Skills 1. They would also take a remedial math course—in many cases Math 71, which consists of arithmetic and elementary algebra—as well as a slowed-down social science course designed for SEEK students and a course called Freshman Orientation. It would be boring work, and they would earn a grand total of 1 credit for all their pains. In the spring they would move up one rung on the remedial ladder. Despite Frye's lecture about the day of reckoning—he called it, " 'Oh, Shit' Day"—most of the students would survive their first year at City, because they would be living almost entirely inside the nurturing and nondemanding environment of remediation. But what would happen after that?

Charles Frye was not sanguine. I asked him how many students he thought would graduate. We were sitting out in the glorious sunshine of Yankee Stadium, where we took in a ballgame after another depressing day at the office. Frye looked out at the field while he slowly ran down a mental list. "Two," he said. "Maybe three." Frye assumed that the recent immigrants had a better chance of surviving than the others. "At least," he said, "they have good values." The stern lectures were intended to help instill those values, but Frye didn't put much store by his own oratory. He said, "I tell them the same thing every year, and every year they come back and say, 'You were right, Professor Frye. We should have listened to you.' "

Frye sometimes spoke fondly of the students at A. Philip Randolph, the high school on the City College campus where he also did some teaching. On the subway ride up to the stadium, he said, "I think I'd really like to be a high school principal."

I was shocked. I said, "I thought that was one of the worst jobs in the public schools."

"Not to me," said Frye over the racket of an incoming train. "At least I feel like I might be able to *do* something. Maybe you can reach those kids when it's still possible. Here, forget it. I'm not making much of a difference in their lives. Maybe it's too late."

And Frye was not alone—far from it. The teachers and counselors in the SEEK program were the most discouraged people at City College; they tend to sound like doctors on an oncology ward.

There was a widespread feeling among them that they were being asked to do the impossible—and they weren't producing any miracles. One administrator said sadly that he considered SEEK a waste of money. "If this were being run by private industry," he said, "it would have been dead a long time ago." The graduation rate among SEEK students was about 17 percent, half the rate among regular admission students.

The need was great, and the resources were scanty. SEEK students received a stipend of $400 per semester, and had access to their own tutors and to courses in areas such as language arts. SEEK was developed as a remedial empire, with a curriculum of its own, classes limited to 12 to 15 students, and in-depth counseling. But after the drastic cuts of 1976, SEEK was largely folded into the remedial curriculum, and its funding shrank. Once there had been a counselor for every 50 students; then the number rose to 100. By 1992, it had reached an absurd 145. Class size reached a hopelessly unwieldy 25 to 30 students. If the premise of open admissions was that higher education could transform the outcomes of inner-city students, given enough resources, then the SEEK program vindicated the argument that open admissions had been abandoned before it had been tried.

But it wasn't only a question of money; it was the task itself. One afternoon I sat at one end of a conference table in the Special Programs office, as the SEEK department is diplomatically called, and listened to eight or nine of the counselors talk about their students. I had expected defensiveness and brittle idealism, but I was wrong. These were people steeped in realism to the point of bitterness. "These students are brainwashed in high school," said Rufus Davis, as the others nodded. "They've been told, 'You can write. You can read.' Then they get here and they're shocked. They're just not prepared." Ralph Evans, like Charles Frye a proud graduate of City in its selective era, asked, "Can you bring a student from a fourth-grade level to a twelfth-grade level in three semesters, when he's already eighteen years old? Just how much can you remediate? That's the big question."

The group agreed that the students coming from the public schools were getting worse and worse. Most of the counselors were black or Puerto Rican, but they didn't hesitate to point out that

African American and Puerto Rican students had been disappearing from the program, and those who came seemed to have an especially poor chance of survival. It had something to do with skills, and something to do with expectation and hope. They agreed with Frye: it was the students who hadn't gone through the public school system, and hadn't grown up in New York, who seemed likeliest to make it.

Experience had taught them all an ethnic hierarchy, a scale of expectations that was politically very incorrect; but they were past caring. "If there's a Korean student in my program," said an administrator, "he'll graduate." Chinese, Haitian, and West Indian students came next. Dominican and South American students had a chance of success if they had been raised in an urban center and had attained "academic fluency" in their own language, as many of them had not. African American males came last, though all of them were native speakers of English. The lack of English was a relatively trivial disadvantage, as I had inferred from Gloria Silverstein's class, when compared with a student's values and academic orientation. "We have a joke around here," said Ramon Berenguer, the director of the SEEK program, "that ESL students will stay until we tell them to leave." ESL students in SEEK had a *higher* retention rate after one year than non-ESL students.

Perhaps it was unfair to compare the students in Gloria Silverstein's class with those in Charles Frye's class: the gap in school experience between them was too great, and the difference in subject matter was overwhelming. It was so much easier to make progress in learning the rudiments of a foreign language than in gaining mastery over your own language. But the contrast pointed up a truth that virtually everyone at City College recognized, although scarcely anyone spoke of it directly: the very students whom open admissions was designed to help were arriving at college so deeply disadvantaged, psychologically as well as academically, that City was virtually unable to help them.

6

The Apostle of the Possible

"For anyone who has watched the success of many young men and women who were taught to fail, the widespread pessimism over whether Open Admissions can 'work' ... is baffling," wrote Mina Shaughnessy, the director of City's writing program and a beacon of hope in the early days of open admissions. Shaughnessy believed in the new student, and his or her potential, with a luminous passion. Her work, and her person, came to symbolize the moral and intellectual principles on which the open admissions experiment rested.

Shaughnessy was an English literature scholar and composition teacher who was hired to teach writing to SEEK students in the spring of 1967. That summer the head of the writing program suffered a heart attack, and Shaughnessy was appointed in his stead. At the time, the writing program was conducted much as it was on other campuses where remedial education programs had been developed to educate the new cadre of poor and inner-city youth being admitted to college: the teacher distributed a grammar book and plowed through it in the course of the term. The educational reforms of the 1960s, which focused on process rather than product, on the

111

learner rather than the lesson, were only just beginning. It was obvious to Shaughnessy that students needed to be encouraged to write and to read more than they needed to have their knuckles rapped. And so she began to change the curriculum to focus on reading solid works of fiction, and gaining experience and confidence with writing. And she gave the program a telling new name: Basic Writing.

The first transformation Shaughnessy had to work was in teachers, and in their sense of purpose. City's English faculty in the late 1960s was not very different from the faculty of the late 1930s— tweedy, Anglophile, steeped in the traditional ideals of connoisseurship. The sweaty labor of social uplift required by the SEEK program constituted almost an affront to the department's concern with parsing and preserving the classics of English and American writing. Math professors had no problem teaching SEEK students; English professors did. Bernard Sohmer recalls that when he went to the English Department to ask for volunteers to teach remedial writing, he was told, "That's not our job. We have our Ph.D.'s in literature, not in writing."

But Shaughnessy swiftly gathered a devoted team of linguistics scholars, radicalized young English professors like Leonard Kriegel, writers, and poets. She was a uniquely persuasive figure. "She was the best person I knew," says Edward Quinn, an English professor who heeded the call. "We all felt that if she was doing it, it was the right thing to do. There was a quality to her mind, and a clarity, that was remarkable. She was extraordinarily charming, and it didn't hurt that she was beautiful."

Shaughnessy was a tall blonde from rural South Dakota in a world that was largely male, Jewish, and working class. In a place where the dress code was based on the premise that no one should ever notice what you were wearing, Shaughnessy would appear before her class of impoverished black and Puerto Rican students in designer outfits, in high heels and capes. "The students know that I dress for *them*," Shaughnessy would explain laughingly. And she could get away with it, in that grimly ideological moment, not only because she was beautiful but because her commitments were so self-evidently moral. She had graduated from a Lutheran Bible college back home, and at one time she had seriously considered becoming a nun.

Respect for the students' abilities was an axiom for Shaughnessy; but it was not an abstract political principle, as it was for New Left critics who were prone to view minority students as the vanguard of a revolutionary order. Shaughnessy was an anthropologist of the new student. From her first days in the SEEK program she amassed a collection of thousands of essays written by students in the lowest reaches of remediation, most of them, she later admitted, "stunningly unskilled." But as she studied the work and came to know the students, Shaughnessy found evidence to corroborate her essential faith. She came to feel that a logic, a web of intentions, lay just beneath the screen of error; and thus that people like Theodore Gross, who had been overwhelmed by the students' language problems, were blinded by the traditional preoccupation with technical proficiency. Over time Shaughnessy devised an interpretative method by means of which she read backward from error to its source, a sort of literary version of the Freudian method of reading backward from pathology to cause.

Shaughnessy was herself a tormented writer, and she had her hands full after she became director of City's immense remedial writing program in 1970; it was not until 1977 that she published a book based on her research into basic writing. The book was called *Errors and Expectations*, and its central premise was that "BW [Basic Writing] students write the way they do, not because they are slow or non-verbal, indifferent to or incapable of academic excellence, but because they are beginners and must, like all beginners, learn by making mistakes." This was an immensely powerful, if scarcely self-evident, assertion. The image of the beginner, and of the new beginning, is probably central to any project of reform. Beginners are not captives of their past; they are eager to learn, and able to learn. Shaughnessy not only denied that past failure would govern future effort; she tried to put to rest some of the terrible fighting words of open admissions, such as *standards* and *ability*.

Shaughnessy had the liberal's faith in the force of nurture. She assumed that what distinguished people was not innate talent but training. Literateness was a teachable skill, not an attribute. She looked for analogies in other skills routinely mastered by adults. Thus she said in a speech that basic writers are "exactly in the same relation to writing that beginning tennis players or piano students are to those skills; they are adult beginners and depend as students did not depend in the past upon the classroom and teacher for the acquisition of the skill of writing." In other words, Irving Howe and his friends didn't need City College in order to attain intellectual self-realization, but Sabour and Jenny, and Fernando and Ericson, would.

Errors and Expectations was probably the most influential work of pedagogy to emerge from the world of open admissions. Shaughnessy was an elegant, even a lapidary, writer; but what made the book so remarkable was the way she marshaled evidence. *Errors and Expectations* contains literally hundreds of passages of the kind of writing that friends of open admissions generally tried to hide from the public. Perhaps many of those friends believed in the principle rather than in the students. Shaughnessy believed in the students, and the patience and the infinite care with which she translated these passages was itself a sign of her respect.

Shaughnessy quotes the following passage from a student essay: "But many colleges have night classes so you could have worked and gone to college also pay for your education although some other programs to help pay on some where you don't pay or some where you don't pay at all so you were lazy." The sentence trails off into incoherence, and most readers would abandon it with a shrug around the word *although*, or at best the second *pay*. People for whom writing is second nature assume that having something to say and being able to say it are one and the same thing. But Shaughnessy insists that if you scrape away the mistakes you can clearly spot the meaning. What the writer is trying to express, she writes, is: "A person who wants to go to college but thinks he can't afford it has several choices: he can work and go to school in the evening; get help through some program; go to a free-tuition college. A person who doesn't go to college therefore is lazy, not deprived." The writer, that is, already possesses the complex thing—the thought —but lacks the means to express it.

What went wrong? The errors of basic writers, Shaughnessy argues, have to do not only with "the accidents of transcription in an unfamiliar medium" but with "differences between spoken and written sentences," especially when "the writer's own speech is non-standard." Basic writers tend to reproduce speech patterns in their writing, unlike people habituated to literacy. Speech, Shaughnessy argues, "is more likely to follow normal word order and to tolerate a high level of redundancy and loose coordination. It is perfected in the dynamics of dialogue, not at the point of utterance. Writing, however, withholds utterance in order to perfect it." And perfecting requires what Shaughnessy calls "consolidation"—the rearrangement, foreshortening, and balancing of ideas in order to produce logic. "The impulse to consolidate often exceeds the ability to do so," Shaughnessy writes, but should be recognized as a form of "responsiveness to the writing situation." Thus her translation of the passage above is essentially an expansion, a filling in of blanks left by an inexperienced writer.

What Shaughnessy did in *Errors and Expectations* is to rethink the act of writing, and the choices made by writers, so that errors come to be seen as logical choices, if wrong ones, rather than proofs of cognitive failure. Shaughnessy explained error; but she did not dismiss it. She never accepted the argument, even more fashionable then than it is now, that all forms of expression, all variants and dialects, are equally valid (a principle codified in the "Students' Right to Their Own Language" resolution adopted by the chief organization of composition scholars in 1974). She thought that Standard English could be, and should be, taught to all students.

For all her radical attack on conventional pedagogy, Shaughnessy believed in the traditional mission of English departments and liberal arts colleges, and her own sense of language was conservative. She had received her master's in English literature from Columbia, and among her favorite authors were John Milton and Francis Bacon. She was also a fine, meticulous poet, though she refused to be published. Shaughnessy represented a merger of two great American traditions: The high-minded progressive and the radical populist. A former colleague, Robert Lyons, wrote that Shaughnessy recognized the difference between herself and her students, "but she did not think the difference condemned either the student or traditional academic values."

The Basic Writing program was a thrilling place to be in the early 1970s. While history professors were tearing one another to shreds, and English professors were seeing the end of the world around every corner, the young writers and scholars who worked for Shaughnessy were reading Noam Chomsky and the psycholinguists, charting the grammatical structures of Spanish, Chinese, and Creole, learning about the patterns of black English. The department had its own publication, the *Journal of Basic Writing*—the first issue was on "error" —and published an annual anthology of students' work. Visitors from other programs would come to City as the fountainhead of writing instruction; members of the department were invited to discuss their findings at professional conferences. This one corner of City College was alive with a sense of possibility.

But the program went into eclipse in the mid-1970s. In 1975 Mina Shaughnessy left City to run a new research body established by CUNY. The following year the budget cuts came, and the junior faculty and adjuncts who had poured their energy into the Basic Writing program were forced to leave. English teachers returned to the English Department; graduate students went back to scholarship. By the time *Errors and Expectations* appeared in 1977, Mina Shaughnessy was suffering from cancer of the kidney; she died the following year. Though she was fifty-four, her career had barely begun. Her premature death symbolized the feeling, inside CUNY, that open admissions had been extinguished before its promise could be realized. She was mourned both for who she was and what she represented—a passionate idealism grounded in a keen sense of reality. Shaughnessy had persuaded a great many people of something they might have wished to believe but didn't really think was true— that the poor and poorly educated black and Hispanic youth now streaming into college could gain the same kind of power over their words, and thus over their thoughts, that past generations of City College students had achieved.

Shaughnessy was a heroic figure—a brilliant writer and by all accounts a splendid teacher and leader. But was she right? She herself acknowledged the limits of the transformative process, though not in print. "She was what I called a tough-minded optimist," says her friend and colleague Alice Trillin. "She really believed in the good, but she was smart enough to see all the problems. I think she felt that this was the only thing worth doing, so maybe we had to oversell our success a little bit to get people to see what was possible." That, perhaps, was the dilemma at the heart of the open admissions crusade itself: all one's hopes for a fully democratic society were bound up with the idea of imparting the power of literateness to impoverished, inner-city youth; and yet success was so hard to come by. Some students blossomed, and their vivid examples made their way into the *Anthology of Basic Writing* and into Shaughnessy's moving anecdotes. They vindicated her theory of the adult beginner; they proved what *could* happen. But the statistics that she deplored showed what *did* happen. And the effect of Basic Writing on overall student outcomes appeared to be marginal. It was far from certain, even under ideal conditions, how much the gap between the possible and the actual could be closed.

Shaughnessy never developed a pedagogy of her own. She believed that what basic writers needed was sympathetic and intelligent attention. They needed teaching premised on their potential, not on their supposed deficits. Alice Trillin says that Shaughnessy died before she could tackle the problem of encouraging critical thinking, which she recognized as a serious obstacle to academic progress. But in her writing and speeches Shaughnessy did not dwell on this problem; perhaps that was a necessary part of salesmanship. She argued that basic writers have not learned how to translate their critical insights into prose.

Composition theory since Shaughnessy has all but anathematized the imagery of deficit. David Bartholomae, one of the leading figures in the field, has described basic writing as a "variation of writing, not writing with fewer parts or more rudimentary constituents. It is not evidence of arrested cognitive development, arrested language development, or unruly or unpredictable language use." Shaughnessy has, if anything, been attacked from the Left, for according too much respect to the university and its codes, and too little to the student and his or her codes. In 1992 the Mina Shaughnessy Award, decided by the editors of the *Journal of Basic Writing*, went to Min-zhan Lu, who derided what she called Shaughnessy's "politics of linguistic innocence" and urged writing teachers to harness their students' "oppositional" tendencies.

What do these theories have to do with reality? Sabour Clarke, the one African American male in Charles Frye's class, was perhaps the most oppositional student as well, at least in terms of his attitude toward authority figures like Frye—or me, for that matter. But Sabour had also committed himself to school, and accepted its disciplines, in a way that most of the others had not. Frye saw this same commitment in some of the immigrant students in class. And of course everything I had heard from the SEEK counselors, and seen in the ESL class, showed me the overwhelming importance of this fundamental orientation. It was the ESL students who seemed to be beginners in Shaughnessy's sense; flailing and confused, but eager and willing to learn. The SEEK students, with a few exceptions, seemed self-absorbed, unfocused, mired in apathy. It was tautological to call that attitude "oppositional."

It was possible to describe the difference between the SEEK and the ESL students in cognitive terms, and thus as a matter of deficit, or as a question of values and habits. It doesn't really make that much of a difference, and in any case no bright line separates these "hard" and "soft" ways of describing the problems that remedial students face. But in the field of composition, reverence for the beginning writer, with his supposedly oppositional tendencies, is so obligatory that the mere suggestion of developmental concerns can bring down the thought police. A group of composition scholars describing a classroom observation criticized an obviously dedicated and thoughtful teacher for saying, "A lot of these kids have problems with connections between things." The problem, they noted tartly, lay with "the system," not with the kids.

Remarkably enough, a few scholars have had the temerity to suggest that these students *do* have intellectual shortcomings. One, Andrea Lunsford, has written that basic writers "have not attained the level of cognitive development which would allow them to form abstractions or conceptions." Basic writers, Lunsford argues, may be able to apply abstract thinking to everyday problems, but because they don't engage in self-reflection they have trouble forming the kinds of generalizations that "are basic to mastery of almost all college material." Lunsford does not by any means assume that developmental problems are insurmountable. She goes on to propose a curriculum designed to promote cognitive growth. In recent years many of Shaughnessy's descendants, including scholars who would never avail themselves of the dreaded "deficit metaphor" or the almost-as-bad "developmental metaphor," have urged basic writing teachers to try to foster the growth of critical skills, as Shaughnessy apparently might have been inclined to do herself.

At least this sort of pedagogy acknowledges the gravity of the remedial task. The basic flaw of Shaughnessy's metaphor of the beginner is that it minimizes the obstacles that the sort of students who come to City face. Learning how to think critically is not like learning how to play scales on the piano so much as like learning how to play a sonata. And it's a matter not only of the material but of the person. Students who haven't learned how to think critically haven't learned how to learn. The students in Frye's class had arrived with a set of values and habits that separated them from school rather than bound them to it. That was why Frye wound up teaching attitude as much as grammar. The attitude had to come first. And Frye had very little confidence in his ability to transform attitudes. Maybe Mina Shaughnessy could have succeeded where he failed, but there was something wrong with a method that depended on a teacher of incomparable powers.

The metaphor of the beginner holds up better in the face of reality than does the polemic of opposition, but, like open admissions ideology in general, it still seems to glide too easily over the space between the possible and the actual. In the end, even some of the very people Shaughnessy inspired suffered a devastating loss of faith. Leonard Kriegel was one of those who all but worshiped at Shaughnessy's shrine, but later came to feel that he had deluded himself about the remedial project—that the educational Left confused potential with reality, in his words. And Shaughnessy's former colleague Marilyn Maiz, now a researcher at CUNY, says, "At the time I was very idealistic. I believed in open admissions. With hindsight, I'm not so sanguine. There's a limit to what you can do."

Shaughnessy was without doubt a brilliant and original epistemologist of error, and of writing generally. Her work still casts a strong light. No one who has read *Errors and Expectations* can lightly dismiss the open admissions student. Shaughnessy made a whole range of common snap judgments seem dangerously simpleminded; she compelled the reader to distinguish between deep causes and superficial effects. But it's also true that there are deep causes with which Shaughnessy herself never fully reckoned.

7

A Miraculous Survivor

arilyn Sternglass, the director of City's master's program in composition, was dumbfounded that I could harbor serious doubts about the remedial ideal. Sternglass shared Mina Shaughnessy's faith in the potential of open admissions students, and she fumed when I told her about my experience in Charles Frye's class. "How can you draw *any* conclusions from that sort of pedagogy?" she asked. Sternglass was a full generation older than I, and I felt thoroughly uncomfortable when she accused me of having too harsh a view of human prospects. If I did, I certainly wasn't taking any pleasure in it. I *wanted* to believe in the students in the same way that she did; but what I had seen in the classroom had been trying my faith.

Sternglass had been following the fortunes of a group of fifty-three students since the fall of 1989, when she had taught one class each in English 1, English 2, and English 110, the mandatory freshman composition course. She made a point of interviewing them twice a year in order to talk about their lives and the role of writing in their education. They gave her copies of the papers they had written, and she kept close track of their academic record. Eager to convert me, Sternglass let me sit in her office when her students came in for interviews, so long as they consented. Even she admitted that the students who kept coming in to see her after three years were the most successful, and the most impressive, of the group. Digna, a Dominican woman who had gotten straight A's the previous semester, was now taking several master's courses in psychology, despite working twenty-five or thirty hours a week in one of her mother's two restaurants in New Jersey. Roberto, a chemistry major who had grown up in Puerto Rico, was about to stay up all night to read *The Odyssey*, and was thrilled at the prospect of discussing it in class the next day. Sternglass put them through their paces for my benefit. "Roberto, could you tell Jim about your feelings about a liberal arts education?" she asked. And Roberto obliged by talking, with passionate conviction, about the power he had gained from learning to see a problem from multiple points of view.

One day in the middle of the fall a black woman named Tammy arrived punctually in Sternglass's office—a rare achievement in itself for City students. Tammy was quiet and demure, serious, and rail-thin. She sat very straight in the chair next to Sternglass, her books resting in her lap. Tammy wore very thick glasses that enlarged her eyes; a straight gold bar across the top obscured the view of the upper part of her face. She looked like the kind of girl you would have met at a church social. Sternglass, smiling encouragingly, asked Tammy if writing had helped her in the learning process. Tammy brightened, struck by a happy thought. "Oh, yes," she said, "I learned to use these words like 'therefore' and 'moreover.' "

"Really?" asked Sternglass. "How?"

This was a topic that Tammy had given some thought to. "I learned from listening to professors," she said, her vowels stretched out with the faintest traces of a southern accent. "You know what I found out? That teachers really like it if you imitate them. Last year I had this psychology professor who said 'in that,' 'moreover,' and all that kind of thing, so I started using them in my papers. And I got an A. And then I started using those words in all my papers." Tammy was a careful listener; she had figured out how to play, if not beat, the system. And it sounded like she was educating herself as well: what had begun as clever mimicry had over time become genuine self-expression.

Tammy was a SEEK student. She was beating the odds merely by lasting into her fourth year, an achievement matched by only one-third of SEEK students. Tammy had a kind of self-awareness I hadn't seen in most of Charles Frye's students, though she had none of the intellectual self-confidence, or sophistication, of Digna or Roberto. She got up to go; but I had started asking about her life, and she was becoming more and more animated. And now Tammy stood in the doorway of Sternglass's office, talking about the catastrophic world that she had somehow survived with her gentle, church-social manner intact—about her brother who was homeless, and her sister who was an alcoholic, and the projects in the South Bronx where she lived with her mother. I was a perfect stranger; but I had the impression that Tammy would have delved deeper and deeper into this well of sorrows, so long as I cared to ask. Sternglass was listening, with little expressions of grandmotherly sympathy. Tammy's almost picaresque tale of disaster hadn't fallen within the ambit of her research.

And then Tammy said, "I promised myself I would *never* turn out like them." Now there was something almost fierce in her soft, slow voice. "The college is the only thing I have," Tammy said, "and I'm *not* going to let anyone take it away from me." She looked over at Sternglass, who knew exactly what she was referring to: Tammy had already failed the math assessment test four times, and the dean of academic standards had warned her that she had to pass this year. "I'll take that test over and over and over until I pass," Tammy said. Her voice was brittle. She wanted to sound angry, but it came out fearful. *"She can not take that away from me."*

Tammy agreed to talk to me further, and to let me read the papers that she had given over the years to Sternglass. It was only when I sat down with a sheaf of Tammy's work that I understood how miraculous her survival was. Her story could have served as a case study of cross-generational wreckage for *The Promised Land*, Nicholas Lemann's book on the formation of the black underclass. In her sophomore year Tammy had written a paper for freshman composition, "The Struggle of Family Life in the South," in which she noted, "My family has a history of early teenage pregnancies, going back to my great great grandparents. Everyone semed to bear their first child at seventeen." Tammy's mother, Mary, had been born in Greenwood, South Carolina, the first of ten children. Tammy was the last of ten. Mary married the father of her second child, and while she held down two jobs to keep the growing family in food and clothing, her husband, who was an alcoholic, would go to bars and, Tammy wrote, "spend up his earnings with various women." Finally, after years of humiliation and abuse—and seven more children— Mary packed up the family and fled to New York.

Tammy's memory of her early childhood was of her parents squabbling and scuffling. Her father never lived with the family and scarcely acknowledged Tammy's existence. Her mother couldn't control the boys. "My brothers would drink a lot," Tammy said as we sat in the cafeteria one gray morning in mid-October, "and they would start reacting to the drink. They would argue and fight." The drinking would start on Friday—payday—and subside on Sunday night. Tammy would cower in the closet, sometimes for hours, until the noise died down. It wasn't poverty that she recalled from her childhood so much as helplessness. The gentleness, the shyness, and the seriousness that I saw in Tammy were the survival skills she developed in the midst of that tumult.

Tammy was the youngest by six years, and her brothers and sisters scattered to the streets. All but one of the girls had a baby in their teens; all but one of the boys fell prey to alcoholism or drug abuse. Tammy's mother was the only port in this perpetual storm. Mary was one of those southern pillars of strength who keep the ghettos from collapsing altogether. By the time Tammy was ready to begin high school, her mother could no longer afford their house in an integrated neighborhood in the West Bronx, and the two of them moved to the projects. Tammy now lived in one of the worst slums in America. She enrolled in Adlai Stevenson High School, a school full of kids with backgrounds like hers. "Most of my friends dropped out," Tammy said. "Now they're dead, they're on crack, they have kids all over the place. And if they're not, they're into something they shouldn't be into."

Tammy herself had skirted disaster once or twice, but in the end she had graduated, hadn't gotten pregnant, and hadn't gotten hooked on anything stronger than diet pills. In Tammy's neighborhood, that was an achievement. Tammy assumed, with her average, that she would have to go to a two-year college. She was all ready to go to La Guardia Community College when she learned about the SEEK program, and found, to her amazement, that she was eligible. She was admitted to City; only one other person she knew from Stevenson wound up attending with her. Virtually no one Tammy knew had ever received a degree from a four-year college. "I was so *proud* to get in here," Tammy recalled. I thought, 'Oh boy, I'm going to *City College*.' "

Tammy was unprepared for the academic demands of college. She had never done a lick of homework; never taken notes, except for what the teacher told her to copy from the blackboard; never written anything more than four or five paragraphs long. She had scarcely read a book. Within a few months, in fact, she developed eyestrain so severe that she needed therapy, but she had to give that up after a year when Medicaid stopped paying. Like the other SEEK students I had met earlier, Tammy assumed that high school rules applied in college. In her second semester she arrived late one day for her World Civilization class. The door was locked, but a student opened it for her. The teacher immediately asked her to leave; he did not tolerate lateness of more than five minutes, he said. It was like a moment out of one of Charles Frye's grim lectures.

"But I just came from 45 minutes away," Tammy protested.

"I'm sorry," he said. "You'll have to leave."

"Fine," said Tammy on her way out the door. "I'm not coming back." And she didn't, thus preserving her pride and earning an F. "I was a lot more laid-back then," said Tammy, by which she meant that she had no idea what was at stake. "Now," she said, "I would *never* do a thing like that."

Tammy didn't want to resist the institution; she just didn't understand it. In fact for all that she was unprepared academically, Tammy was emotionally ready for the demands of college. Suffering, persistence, and sublimation were branded into her character. In the English 2 class in which she encountered Marilyn Sternglass, Tammy would write draft after draft. In one of her essays, Tammy compared her own drive to succeed to that of Booker T. Washington, who she viewed not as a sellout but as a model of personal persistence. She had been out of work for four months, she wrote, but she had hunted and hunted until finally she had heard of a position at the Martin Luther King Health Center, near her home. "I was determined to get that job," she wrote. "But later they told me that there weren't any openings. They told me to call in every day to check. I did this for an additional two months. Finally they informed me that they had a position open for switchboard operators. I filled the position."

Tammy had the energy that comes of desperation. But with it came anxiety, and even dread. She couldn't even feign a sense of ease; whenever we talked, it was the fear that I heard, not the hope. As we sat in the cafeteria between classes Tammy suddenly put her hands to her head and said, "I feel like I'm under so much pressure." She often talked about pressure as if it were coming from the outside: "It's like everybody is expecting something from me." This was the burden that City College students of another generation had felt, and that many immigrant students, and above all the Chinese, still felt. Tammy actually suffered from a lack of expectations: her world was sadly quiet, unpopulated, and lonely. She often said that her mother and her boyfriend Jay were her only friends. But she projected onto them, and "everybody," the terrible pressure she felt within.

Tammy was not thriving, like some of Sternglass's prize pupils; she was just getting by. Her grade-point average hovered at around C plus. Her eyesight had become a chronic problem. "I can read for about ninety minutes, and then I just have to stop," Tammy said. "When they assign seven chapters, I can only read about four." Sometimes in exams, when she was bearing down hard, the words would start to swim before her eyes. Tammy wondered if that explained her problems with the assessment exams, which she had to pass before reaching the halfway point in her career. It wasn't just the math exam; she had also failed the reading test twice, and she might have gone on failing it had a SEEK counselor not taken pity on her, Tammy said, and let her spend extra time on the test beyond the allotted thirty minutes. Tammy's problems may have had something to do with her eyesight; but her performance indicates that she was reading at a level barely above junior high school.

Tammy's courageous and solitary journey through life could not have been much more different from that of the students of the class of 1940. They, too, had been "disadvantaged," in the sense of being socially and economically marginal. They, too, had needed to call on reserves of willpower and self-discipline. But the veterans of City's Golden Age did not owe their success to merely personal qualities. Every institution they had encountered on the way to City had prepared them emotionally and intellectually. They had had two parents, stable households, safe neighborhoods, orderly and rigorous schools. They had reached City College without even making any conscious effort. And once there, they had succeeded fairly effortlessly as well. Tammy, however, had succeeded, insofar as she had succeeded, despite her environment. Circumstances had conspired to derail her, as they had derailed almost everyone else she knew. Tammy's survival was a testimony to purely personal characteristics.

The academic literature on college retention barely seems to apply to students like Tammy, or to those I had met in Charles Frye's class. It assumes that in college, as in high school, the dropout problem lies with the institution, not with the student. Vincent Tinto, probably the leading authority in the field, doesn't even use the term *dropout*, which he considers misleading as well as stigmatizing. Only about 15 percent of students who leave college, he estimates, have been forced out by poor grades. The literature stresses that student departure can be predicted by what Randi Levitz, a consultant to college retention programs, calls "a cluster of affective variables," which include "academic boredom and uncertainty about what to study, transition/adjustment problems, limited and/or unrealistic expectation of college, academic unpreparedness, incompatibility and irrelevance." This is a milder and broader version of the "oppositional" thesis: Students drop out not because they can't hack college work but because there's something wrong with the "fit" between themselves and the institution. It's the institution's job to adjust the fit.

But for students like Tammy, failure was the norm; only the few with exceptional personal characteristics hung on until graduation. And the word *affective* scarcely did justice to the nature of those characteristics. A better word was *values*, with its inference of personal choice and personal responsibility. Tammy knew that if she got pregnant she would probably repeat the destiny of her sisters and her mother and her grandmother and most of the girls she knew. She knew how much was at stake. She even hinted that she had remained a virgin, risking losing Jay rather than losing her hopes in life. Girls who get pregnant in high school enormously decrease their chances of graduation. And City College students with children, and especially single parents, had an incredibly hard time juggling schoolwork with the responsibilities of child care. There wasn't much City could do to lighten that burden; more importantly, City couldn't instill Tammy's values in students who arrived without them, the students whom Charles Fryé had watched come and go. It had never had to do so in the past. That was a problem that lay in the institutions and the culture that had shaped these students long before they had reached City.

And while it was true that most students who left City were academically eligible to remain, there was an overwhelming and scarcely surprising connection between departure and academic performance. A 1989 CUNY study found that retention was strongly correlated with high school average, performance on the assessment tests administered at the time of admission, and college grade-point average. Most of these students hadn't flunked out, but their problems with college-level work had a great deal to do with their departure. Indeed, the distinction between affective and academic, or cognitive, problems was specious. Virtually all of the SEEK students, and many non-SEEK students as well, had arrived at City College with such profound academic problems that almost any jolt from another part of their life could knock them off the path to a degree. If Tammy dropped out, the likeliest cause would be depression, not her grade-point average. But although City College was the focus of all her hopes, it was also true that Tammy's continuing academic problems, and especially her fears about the math assessment exam, were an important source of her depression. Tammy had the tenacity and the focus to cling to school with all her might; others didn't.

Marilyn Sternglass used to get especially short with me when I wondered whether students like Tammy would be truly educated even if they managed to get their degree. "What does that *mean?*" she asked. "How are you measuring education?" I didn't have a clear answer to that question. It was easy to say that students who left without a degree had failed; it was a much weightier charge to say that students might have gotten what they wanted—a degree—and still in some sense be considered failures. Of course, if no such possibility existed, the college's sole function was the issuing of degrees. And no one at City College, including Marilyn Sternglass, sought to justify open admissions strictly as a credentialing device—at least not openly. What Sternglass and I were disagreeing about was whether the mere fact of improvement, from any baseline, was enough to constitute success.

Writing scholars like Sternglass tend to use a developmental model based on the work of Jean Piaget, the Swiss psychologist who argued that children pass through four distinct cognitive stages. The problem of remediation is often posed as that of moving students from Piaget's third stage, of concrete operation, to the last phase, which Piaget called formal, or propositional, operations. A concrete thinker is tied to particular data; a formal thinker operates hypothetically. Piaget illustrated the distinction with this example: If you give a child a pile of poker chips of various colors and ask the child to come up with all possible different-colored pairs, the concrete thinker will come up with many groupings, whereas the formal thinker will devise a system that will exhaust all the possibilities. Concrete thinkers tend to be egocentric rather than abstract. Thus one composition scholar, Annette Bradford, notes that with remedial writers, "hypothetical, theoretical questions based on reading yield confused and concrete responses, usually based not on the reading, but on the readers' own lives or experience."

The problem with accepting this model is that Piaget placed the onset of formal operations at eleven to twelve years, and its firm establishment at fourteen to fifteen. Thus it would seem that college freshmen who don't think propositionally suffer from some sort of cognitive deficit. Academics in the field have had to tie themselves into some serious knots to escape this conclusion. Bradford, for example, argues that the stage of formal operations "may extend into early adulthood" for some students. Others insist that remedial students think every bit as well as academically proficient students, but haven't mastered the "reasoning/reading/writing conventions" that govern the classroom.

In her own research Sternglass measured students' intellectual progress along a scale of nine "acts of discourse," beginning with "narrative, with or without commentary, of events in the writer's life," and ending with "analysis/interpretation of all or part of a work of art." She thus avoided the nettlesome questions raised by the Piagetian model, while still establishing a trajectory toward greater levels of intellectual complexity. When she ran the work of her fifty-three students through this model, she came up with some shining examples of improvement and self-discovery, whom she featured in her scholarly work. A student whom Sternglass called Linda had moved from one end of the scale to the other in three and a half years, and was writing fairly self-assured essays about issues such as gender roles. Linda's work, Sternglass concluded, showed "the kind of progress that is possible for students of this background."

What about Tammy? She had arrived at City with a bare grammatical sufficiency, enough to place her in English 2, ahead of Sabour or Renato. Her prose wasn't obscured by error; it was timid, unventuresome, and flat. Tammy had self-awareness enough to recognize her weaknesses. At the very beginning of her second semester she wrote, "I feel, my biggest problem in writing is, my sentences seem awkward to someone who reads it. When I want to make a particular statement, I tend to get caught up with words. Sometimes I'm aware of the confusions. Unable to find a better set of words to express what I'm saying, I leave the words as is. . . . My teachers make comments on the paper that many times I can't understand. Since he's my teacher, I guess he knows best." By "a better set of words" Tammy seems to have meant the ability to express more complex thoughts in writing. But she was also apparently feeling intellectually out of her depth. She was beginning to leave her remedial courses behind, and she was feeling unprepared for the demands being made of her.

But Tammy was also changing in ways that she probably didn't recognize. A semester earlier she wouldn't have written a sentence beginning "Unable to find . . ." And she had made one much more noticeable change. In her first semester she had written in a straight-up-and-down script in which letters huddled into one another and each line lapped up to the one above it. Tammy's writing was so illegible that this added barrier to comprehension seemed at least subconsciously willed. By her third semester Tammy had begun using a typewriter, or one of the City College computers.

Tammy was also picking up on the expectations of academic life. In the fall of her second year she wrote a nine-page paper, "Impotence in Males," for a class in human sexuality. The paper began with an outline, ended with a conclusion, and in between enumerated the various causes and treatments of impotence. Tammy understood the convention of offering "your own view," but she clearly wasn't comfortable with the practice. She hazarded only the tiniest, and most cautious, opinions. She also didn't have a clear idea of what it means to prove an argument—categories four and five of the "acts of discourse." One of her teachers wrote, "You didn't really do everything you said you did in your conclusion." She could state facts adequately—category three—but she tended to hug tightly to frameworks—lists, definitions, authorities. When Tammy reached for something larger, a synthesis or a generalization, she often stumbled into a vague, fuzzy space.

Tammy's writing continued to become more "academic"; the language itself was something she could cling to. But her writing was also growing slightly more supple. Her vocabulary broadened, and she no longer strapped all of her sentences onto the same Procrustean bed. She was now organizing larger amounts of material. For a paper she wrote on Korean art—this was soon after we met—Tammy described several different aesthetic movements, historical periods, and artistic media. This constituted the sixth of the acts of discourse—"presentation of essential data about a historical period, social condition, political structure, and so on." And she made a game, although halting, effort to interpret the data: "With Koreas' discovery of the western culture, this country experienced having

CITY ON A HILL

new ideas relating to their fascinating artwork, which put their old values in the back seat of society."

After four years at City College, Tammy's writing had improved dramatically. She had, after all, completed what would be an entire career for most college graduates, though she herself was only two-thirds finished. But even after all this time, Tammy shied away from making critical judgments. On one of her last psychology papers her professor wrote, "I looked for your opinions and ideas in this report and didn't find much—there is no critical evaluation." And yet every once in a while Tammy moved far enough away from the data to make connections at a more abstract level. In a World Humanities paper she wrote that "Pangloss inspired Candide's optimism because he attributed what we would call in Psychology a Halo-effect to every experience in life, meaning, there is good in everything and everyone."

Tammy had grown intellectually, but the imitation of academic forms took her only so far. She had barely passed the reading exam, and she still hadn't passed the math exam, and neither of them was pitched at much more than a tenth-grade level. It was hard to imagine that Tammy would achieve her dream of earning a Ph.D. in psychology, though it would be a mistake to underestimate the role of persistence. But from another point of view, it was remarkable how very far Tammy had come: she had graduated from high school, she had piled up close to 80 credits, she had learned to write in the forms used by academics.

Was that enough? By Marilyn Sternglass's lights, it surely was. Sternglass did not accept the logic that lay behind the word *enough*. But what if you did hazard some rough definition of what it means to be an educated person? For example, in his memoirs Theodore Gross wrote, "If he does not know something of philosophy and history; if he has not developed the critical skills that enable him to distinguish the moral from the immoral, flatulent language from genuine art from artifact—then he is not educated. Discrimination is essential—intellectual discrimination." Tammy had not developed intellectual discrimination, and she certainly knew virtually nothing of philosophy and history. And it was unlikely that she would before she left City College.

I wouldn't dispute Gross's definition; but neither could I imagine denying Tammy the right to enroll at City College. And this was so not because City had an obligation to all disadvantaged students, or because it had no choice but to accept its credentialing role, but because Tammy deserved it. She was special; she had committed herself to her education in the most serious way. And it was just this kind of commitment that City's admissions policies made it possible to honor.

At the same time, City's commitment to the new student presented it with a series of impossible choices. In their official statements, City College and CUNY routinely claimed that traditional standards could be maintained despite the remedial obligation, that students like Tammy were no less likely to become "truly educated" than were the strivers of another generation. Perhaps Marilyn Sternglass believed this as well. But as Leonard Kriegel knew, and Ted Gross knew, it wasn't so. And what were you to do about it? If you were Tammy's philosophy teacher, and you knew the story of her struggle against hardship, would you fail her if her work deserved it? Or would you measure "desert" according to the honesty of Tammy's effort—according to the form of merit that Tammy truly had? Or would you delude yourself about her performance? And what if you lacked the capacity to delude yourself? You might see City's commitment as something at once unavoidable and unsatisfiable.

8

Can You Understand My Pain?

udi Gedamke used to argue with Mina Shaughnessy. Gedamke was a reading specialist who had been hired in 1971, when a vast tide of students had begun to course through City's remedial program. He was as passionately engaged a teacher as Shaughnessy, and as a German immigrant who had graduated from City in the late 1950s, he had a genuinely romantic attachment to the college's historic mission. But he was, by temperament and intellect, a realist, and he insisted on the distinction between what was and what ought to be. At times Shaughnessy would assemble the remedial faculty for a dose of inspirational oratory. "*Everybody* can be educated," she would say. And Gedamke, playing the spoilsport, would twist around in his chair so that she could see him and say, "Yes; but at what level?" Where Shaughnessy conjured up the imagery of improbable success, Gedamke, immersed in the daily reality of the classroom, saw the hard fact of limits. "I couldn't see eye to eye with Mina," Gedamke says today. "She was a very good academic, but when it comes down to the classroom the shit flows differently."

For the last twenty years Gedamke had been teaching in City's College Skills program. At the beginning of his classes Gedamke often tried to estimate the steepness of his uphill struggle by asking students to explain something relatively straightforward. In the spring of 1992 he presented a new batch of kids with a headline from the *Campus*, the student newspaper: STUDENT TURNOUT NIL AT GAMES. He asked for a simple translation. Gedamke had cut out the answers and pasted them one on top of another. One student wrote, "he/she is not good for nothing." Others tried, "Students spend most of their studies time as their leisure times" and "Students are getting addicted it toward it." Others made a real stab at translation but probably didn't know what to make of *nil*, and so wrote "Students act uncivilized at games" or "Student turnout facinate at games." There was only one answer that he could deem correct: "no one didn't go."

Gedamke did not, as Shaughnessy had, find a rich bed of meaning under the bramble of error. Nor did he chalk up the errors to ignorance of the conventions of academic discourse. Gedamke was indifferent to the niceties of scholarly debate; he knew a cognitive deficit when he saw one. "The problem," he said, "is that these students can't deduce the whole from the piece, the way you would puzzle out a French sentence just by knowing a few words. If they don't get it right away, they make hopeless stabs." His students were focusing on each individual word rather than on the whole. "A lot of these kids read at about 40 words per minute," he said. "We speak at maybe 210, 220, words a minute. You can't process data if you read that slowly. You can't hold onto it." The average American, said Gedamke, couldn't read a sentence longer than twelve words, which was dreadful enough. Millions of Americans were reeling beneath a combination of bad schools, the decline of literacy, and the wholesale destruction of the national attention span wrought by television and the whole jazzy, frantic, momentaneous consumer culture; and his students worst of all.

It was early August, not long before the farewell parties in the ESL and language arts classes I had attended, and we were sitting in Gedamke's tiny, windowless office in the NAC building. Gedamke kept the door wide open; he wanted to make sure that students felt welcome to wander in. He was an intense man with an unwavering and almost unsettling gaze; he kept his glasses perched on his brow, as if he didn't want them to interfere with his attention. He was warm and polite, but just a little bit pugnacious; it wasn't hard to imagine him putting his head in the lion's jaws. He had a deep, steady voice, and you could catch traces of his German accent. But for a German he seemed awfully Mediterranean: he was a man who ran hot rather than cool.

Gedamke was a widower, and he may very well have been too bound up with his teaching and with his students. In recent years he had come to feel that he was pouring all his energies into a lost cause. Other teachers in the remedial program felt the same way, and they had become bored or burned out, or they had retreated into their own garden. Gedamke couldn't accept that failure; and the fact that others did, or that they averted their eyes from a painful truth, made him angry. One day in late March he sat down and wrote a memo to his superior, Dean Alan Fiellin, in which all the dammed-up feeling came cascading out. "There is a fire in my gut," Gedamke wrote,

> that tells me that what we are doing has little to do with education. Or learning. Or teaching. Something has gone wrong here, and the student who arrives at our door here with a fourth-grade reading level, and the administrator who herds him into a CSK [College Skills] class of twenty-five students, and the professor who teaches that course, and the committee who designed it, and the curriculum committee which approved it are all locked into a silent contract of fraud.
>
> When I document in my CSK 2.0 class [the higher of the two remedial levels] that less than 20% of the students can understand the headline "Student Turnout Nil At Games," I am met with a sympathetic wall of silence. I am told that we are caught in force fields not of our own making—black holes in the educational sky named politics, the Board of Higher Education, rotten high schools, dinosaur administrations and racism. By what sort of mental alchemy can we justify our silence?. . .
>
> I know, you ask for statistics. But I will not succumb to academic dust-grubbing. Instead I think of students once in my

care: Sharon, Tisha, Frank, Yolanda, Elizabeth, Andrew, Novena, Lorna, Getulio, Soledad, Ying-Li, Horatio, Marshall, Marie, Nicole, Lucian, Ali, Fel, Ramon, John, Mac, Ginger, "Tiger," Gina. All are gone now. Who knows where. All failed. Broken by our silence. If my children were treated the same way at their universities, I would sue for fraud....

I somehow can't face the thought of looking at City College and seeing instead of a university a poorly run junior high school. Can you understand my pain?

Dean Fiellin, an administrator since the dawn of open admissions and by nature a diplomat, responded more or less as Gedamke had expected: "While I might define the issues somewhat differently, I do, nevertheless, share with you and others an interest in clearly identifying the deficiencies in the existing system and proposing viable solutions to the appropriate authorities...." Fiellin proposed the compiling of a report. The dean did suggest that such a report might compel CUNY "to reexamine both realistically and compassionately our admissions procedures and our standards." Gedamke then tried to convene a conference of remedial teachers, but nobody was interested. His accusations of fraud might have offended some of his colleagues and seemed overblown to others. Perhaps he was viewed less as a courageous whistle-blower than as an irritating gadfly. What was the point of documenting so minutely a pathology they felt powerless to treat?

During the fall I sat in on Rudi Gedamke's CSK 2.0 class, which met four days a week at 11 A.M. just down the hall from the room in which Charles Frye's language arts class had met over the summer. He had twenty-six students—a normal figure, but an appalling one for a remedial class, a consequence of City's perpetual budget crisis. On the first day of class Rudi handed out not his headline test but a sheet asking the students some questions about themselves. All but six of them, it turned out, were in their first semester at City. A dozen or so had come through the SEEK program. The majority were taking a remedial English course as well as College Skills. Most were native English speakers; six had been speaking English for seven years or less. Rudi asked, "What books or magazine articles have you read lately that have impressed you?" Only nine mentioned a specific book or article, although others wrote down the names of magazines, like *Time*. The average number of hours the students reported watching television every week was seventeen, though the figures ranged as high as forty.

Many of the students wrote painfully candid answers to the question "What are your strengths and weaknesses in reading/studying?" Yesenia, a SEEK student who had been speaking English only five years, wrote, "My weakness is pronouncing words, vocabulary. Also writing about topic. I don't like to read a lot." (The students asked that I not use their last names; in one case I have altered an unusual first name as well.) Margaret, at thirty-eight the oldest student in the class, wrote, "My strength in reading is finishing the book. My weakness is I can't remember what I have read." Many of the students admitted that they could not understand what they read. A few chose the route of braggadocio, but their self-awareness got the better of them. "I can 80% of the time instantly memorize anything I read the first time," wrote Che, who planned to be an engineer. "The disadvantage I usually read comic books and draw."

Their expectations were not much different from those of college students everywhere. Most answered the question "What will you be doing ten years from now?" by writing that they hoped to have a family, a stable job, and a home— "a beautiful home in a suburban area and a Lexus," as Yvonne, a Guyanese student, wrote. Sherry planned on having an entertainment company of her own. Simeon expected to have degrees in physics and electrical engineering, "with alot of funding for my research projects." Many had dreams of helping the world, whether as an architect or a teacher. Others just wanted to get rich. Sometimes a tiny note of desperation crept into their grandiose plans. "I wish I can be a happy person by that time," wrote Janet.

Students are placed in a College Skills course by virtue of their performance on the reading assessment exam. The class is designed to help them to improve their reading skills as well as to learn how to write outlines and take notes. As Rudi taught it, however, College Skills was the most fundamental of courses. His goal was explicitly cognitive: he wanted to develop critical skills in students whom he believed had reached college without them. He wanted to teach them how to extract meaning from texts, how to structure their thoughts, how to make an argument about something. It was very much the sort of developmental pedagogy that composition scholars and learning theorists prescribe for remedial students.

On that first day Rudi also handed out a sheet that laid out the sequence of intellectual abilities he hoped to cultivate: intake skills, storage skills, retrieval skills, critical analysis skills. There were boxes and columns and arrows going down and across. The sheet itself illustrated a basic element of Rudi's personal epistemology: information cannot be used until it is structured. This is one of those submerged concepts that is normally learned as an incidental consequence of learning other things. But much of College Skills, at least in Rudi's class, consisted of trying to teach explicitly concepts that educated people don't even know that they know. Rudi felt that many of his students didn't know what it meant to think rigorously. "A lot of these kids don't really think," he said. "There's a lot of daydreaming-type thinking."

In the initial stage, intake skills, Rudi explained how to make sense out of information. "What is communication?" he asked in one of the first classes of the term. Rudi was pacing back and forth across the class, his glasses perched on his broad brow. He had been a soccer star as a kid in Germany, and he had the chesty build of an athlete. His tweed jacket was too tight; the look was macho rather than scholarly. "Does my *shirt* communicate anything?" Someone snickered. "Bad taste, okay. How about my position? I'm standing, you're all sitting. Does that communicate anything? Authority, maybe? And then sometimes I kneel down to help you with your work. Am I trying to say something different? What about space? *I* have all this space up here, and *you're* sitting close together. How would I react if you tried to get into my space?" Rudi had the habit of dicing up his sentences into staccato flashes, and piercing them with innumerable questions and hesitations designed to be filled in by students. He was, in fact, trying to get them into his space, though he wasn't having much luck.

Communication, he explained, had three "levels": topic, generalization, and supporting details. "In order to understand something," he said, "you have to focus on something"—the topic. But "you would be overwhelmed by data if you couldn't form a generalization. Notice how a generalization is a kind of classification system"—how, that is, it establishes a hierarchy of information. Details organize themselves around generalizations. And Rudi wanted them to understand that information could be decoded not only from the abstract, school-worn forms of written language, but from the living world, from shirts and postures and commercials. He held up a tattered Salem ad showing a couple sheltering under a bright red umbrella. "What's it about?" Rudi asked.

"Cigarettes."

"Cigarettes, yes; but beyond that?"

"Salem." Rudi brought out more ads, discussing the whole idea of implicit meanings. Finally someone said that the real meaning of a Kent ad was "Smoking is cool."

Rudi found that students generally had as much trouble assigning meaning to pictures as to paragraphs. He was skeptical of the theory, promulgated by Marshall McLuhan and some of his followers, that a new generation had become "image-literate" rather than "word-literate." The real problem, he thought, was that students lacked the habit of forming generalizations, of thinking critically. Images, in any case, were a poor replacement for language, since research showed that students retained less of a message in televised form than from even the most turgid lecture. And so he spent the first few weeks of class assigning passages from a College Skills textbook and trying to give the students an intuitive feel for the differences between a topic, a generalization, and a detail.

Rudi also harped constantly on language. "Talk to me in whole sentences," he said one morning. "By the end of the term I want you to talk to me in whole paragraphs." If the students were to think in more complex terms, they needed a more complex language; if they were to operate in an academic environment, they needed to get into the habit, as Tammy had, of using a more academic form of speech. But Rudi also used language learning as an "intake" skill, a way of learning about the organization of knowledge. He explained that because words, like any other unit of meaning, had structure—roots, prefixes, and suffixes—they could be learned by system, by logic, rather than one by one. Meaning could be deduced from structure. From there he moved on to the idea that meaning is mutable, that words live within a context of other words, that they have connotations.

But Rudi didn't want to lose them through abstraction; he wanted them to feel the tang of language, the sheer play and variety of it. One of the regular assignments in class was to make a list of new words and phrases. Every morning before class the students were to go to the board and write down the ones that were especially strange and wonderful. This turned out to be an instructive, if slightly demoralizing, experiment. Nobody knew the meaning of *inoculate*, or why *fourplay* was misspelled. Among the words that wound up on the board were *reckon*, *subtlety*, and *habitual*. Most of the phrases the students came up with were jingles and slang. Andrew, a Ghanaian student, wrote down the cryptic, "To be a winner you got to drop a chicken dinner." Che offered, "Your batteries are Elvis." Their language came from talk, and from television, not from reading.

As much as Rudi worried about his students' lack of academic language and reasoning skills, what really upset him was their attitude. Where was the hunger for learning that had propelled him, or the hope of redemption that had driven the young men and women of Alfred Kozin's day? "High school teaches them to be passive," Rudi said. "The schools are doing a better job of weeding out the druggies and the bad guys, so the students who come here are nice kids. And in high school being nice was validated as an academic skill." And in fact the class, like the language arts class I had attended down the hall, was full of students who sat politely but ventured nothing. Many of them seemed to make a point of keeping their jackets on even though it was warm inside, as if they were planning only to drop by for a minute or two. By the second week of class Rudi was already worried that he was losing them. "A lot of you are not functioning," he said one morning. A new admonitory tone was creeping into his voice. "A lot of you are just drifting by."

He peered into the depths of the back row, where five or six black kids always sat, and said, "What is *wrong* with you?" Rudi's tone was plaintive rather than angry. But the question was met by dead silence.

Rudi had a special gift for using the attendance roll to reel in his wayward students. "Mario?" he called out one morning. "We're making progress. You're still sitting in the back, but at least you don't have that *attitude*." Mario was at least making eye contact. That morning he was sitting next to Curtis, who unquestionably did have that attitude: His eyes shone angrily beneath the bill of his cap. The cap never, ever came off, and Rudi knew better than to try and get a rise out of him. "Cantina?" he continued. "Come talk to me. I'm losing you." Cantina had joined a remote, all-female fastness under the windows at the far wall. Rudi was losing them, too. "Anton? Anton's going to give me a hug before the end of the term—and he's going to *like* it." Anton grimaced, and Rudi flashed him a mocking grin.

Anton and his friend Aisha were the only really bright-eyed citizens of the isolated back-row nation. Anton was wiry and spare, with sharp cheekbones that made his face diamond shaped, a wispy goatee, close-cropped hair, and small, round ears. Sometimes Anton came to class with his cap on backward and an expression on his face that said, "Don't get near me." At his vocational high school, Transit Tech, Anton had walked around with a major chip on his shoulder. He told me proudly how he had taunted an English teacher, who responded by flunking him. He was forced to make up the class with an independent study. "That teacher was a pushover," Anton said; "so I pushed him over." But Anton was smart enough that the only problems he had had in school, at least in the baby pool of remediation, were the ones he made for himself.

Rudi made quick, intuitive judgments about people, and he decided right away that he could take the risk of shaking Anton up, flicking the chip off his shoulder. Anton was, like Curtis, the sort of "oppositional" student celebrated by the academic Left; but Rudi loathed the reduction of individual characteristics to political categories. In Anton he saw a wary young man who was afraid of dropping the cool pose he had carried until now. Anton needed to know that he could be accepted, even embraced; but Rudi had to keep it light or Anton would bolt. He seemed to make a point of taking two steps backward for every one step forward. One morning Rudi said, "Did anybody find a new word?" and Anton said, "Yes."

"Could you tell me what it was?"

"No."

"Did you write it down?"

"Yes." Anton still had the idea, from high school, that he could play on his own terms. Sometimes he studied, sometimes he didn't; he spoke when the spirit moved him. He tried to toy with Rudi, and with his friends in class. And he was good at it. One day Rudi asked if the habit of being critical was more natural to some cultures than to others, and Anton said, deadpan, "Broads are the most critical." This started the closest thing to a real discussion that the class had yet conducted. Aisha, sitting next to Anton, kept the game going: guys, she said mockingly, criticized girls' appearance just as much as other girls did. It was mostly a joke, a little game of verbal tennis; but Mario, forever earnest and often out of his depth, said that Anton was right. "They forever seeing something they want; that's why they shopping." With only the lightest hint of archness, Anton said, "What you basically are saying is that it's imprinted in them, and then it's developed through shopping."

Like Rudi, I was determined to break into the impacted mass of the back row. I often took a seat there in the hopes of making conversation, but I rarely got far. It was true that, except for Rudi, I was the only white person in the room; but the air of reserve didn't seem at all racial. The students barely talked to each other, and the students in the back were the most isolated of all. Curtis barely acknowledged my existence. I couldn't get more than a word or two from Che, who like Curtis almost never spoke in class. Andrew, however, came from a different planet. His African upbringing had obviously included lessons in deportment toward elders. He was a shy young man with a round moon face and skin so black that it made his eyes look yellow, like vellum. After class one day Andrew and I walked across the path that separated Harris Hall from the cafeteria in NAC, bought our lunch, and sat down.

Andrew spoke so softly that it was hard to hear him over the racket of chairs scraping and trays rattling. He said that he hoped to be an engineer. Back in Accra, he said, "I read something that mentioned computers. I thought, 'What is computer?' So there was a store I found that sold computers, and I talked to the salesman in the store. He showed me how to do graphics on the computer, and he drew a plane. Ever since I was a little kid I loved planes. So I decided I wanted to do something with computers and planes." At fifteen Andrew moved with his family to Brooklyn. After graduating from high school, he said, "I was about to go into the navy, but then I had this friend who was at City College who said that if I go into the navy it will take me years to rise up, but if I get a college degree I can progress much faster."

Andrew hadn't done well in high school, but had been admitted to City as a SEEK student. The prospect of college terrified him. "I thought, they're going to use all these big words. I'm not going to know what's going on." But over the summer he had taken a full load of courses, and he had decided that he was college material. Now he spoke with quiet confidence. "I know I can do the work," Andrew said, "as long as I can get the time." That didn't seem like an immodest hope. Andrew was a serious young man, with the immigrant's exaggerated respect for authority. In class he never played the fool, never challenged the teacher. After we had sat talking for half an hour, he asked permission to be excused. Andrew reminded me of the ESL students I had met over the summer.

It took me a lot longer to sit down with the silent Che. It was Che who had said that he liked to read comic books and daydream, and there was, in fact, something childlike about him. He had big, dark eyes in a long face, and he often seemed to be separated from the rest of the class by some sort of mental gauze. He wasn't sullen, like Curtis, or testy, like Anton; he was dreamy. Che didn't always bother to do his homework, rarely studied for quizzes, almost never betrayed signs of interest. Outside of class, though, he turned out to be loquacious. Che had grown up in Brooklyn. His father had abandoned the family when Che was seven or eight—fathers often seemed to be an extinct species at City College. Che insisted that he hadn't missed his father at all, but I had to wonder. At Samuel Tilden High School Che had been the class clown—a low-grade form of Anton's more explicit rebellion.

"I had this one teacher who made me sit in the front of the class to keep an eye on me," Che admitted rather proudly. "My economics teacher would be saying something and then he could just feel that I was going to come out with a joke or something, and before I could even open my mouth he'd say, 'Che, shut up!' " When things got intolerable one of the teachers would call Che's mother and ask her to speak with him. "I'd be okay for a few weeks and then I'd go back to the same old thing," Che said, as if describing an addiction.

Che had made it into honors classes on the strength of passing a ninth-grade Regents exam, which in New York State certifies an academic course, in biology. But he had done badly, and he had also come to City as a SEEK student. "When I was graduating," said Che, "six different teachers came up to me and said the same thing. They said, 'Che, you're a smart kid, but you've got to get serious.' " And so Che had taken their advice to heart. He had decided that once he got to college he would simply close his mouth; and he had made good his vow. He had, perhaps unconsciously, formulated a new style of disengagement. He said, "I went back to Tilden after a few weeks, and my teachers came up to me and said, 'Che, have you changed your ways?' And I said, 'Yeah, I have.' And they said, 'How are you doing?' I sort of evaded that question."

Che realized that he had somehow made another wrong move. He wasn't doing well in his other courses, and he saw that Rudi didn't believe he was taking the class seriously. Che thought that that was unfair, but he seemed to have no idea of what was required of a college student. Nor did he seem to grasp the peril that he was in. He missed class on the day of a test—the subway broke down—and then came in so late the next day that Rudi couldn't talk to him or give him a makeup test. I asked Che if he was keeping up with the reading, and he said that he did most of it on the subway. I wondered whether he could really concentrate on a rattling, crowded subway car. "I can't study when it's silent," Che replied.

In late September, with the leaves beginning to scuttle around the maple trees in the quadrangle just beyond Harris Hall, Rudi gave his first full-dress exam. He asked the students to define twenty roots and use them in a word, to deduce the meaning of unfamiliar words from roots, to rearrange the scrambled paragraphs of a passage into a logical sequence, and to demonstrate the proper use of an outline, which he had spent a good deal of time teaching them. I dropped by Rudi's office the day after the test and found him sitting behind his desk with the tests splayed out in front of him. When I asked how the students had done, he picked up a sheaf of papers with an angry jerk and waved them at me. He had had some hopes for the class; but now he felt the first stirrings of despair.

Stephen and Paul, two of the three Chinese students, had gotten 90s. Anton had scored an 86. But Che, Curtis, and Andrew had scored in the 60s. Though Rudi had been going over the same ground again and again, losing time rather than losing students, sixteen of the twenty-three students who took the test had still scored under 70, and four under 50. Rudi was in a state. "What really upsets me is how many of these kids have *no idea* what's going on," he said. "What am I supposed to say to them? That you're not going to make it? I guess I should. Look, look at this one." He thrust Simeon's paper at me. Simeon was the opposite of the back-row crowd. He sat in the front of the class and talked without stopping, driving the other students nuts. Simeon had missed every single root. His outline was meaningless. "His problem," Rudi said, "is that he can't *read*. It's clear that he has dyslexia, but he won't deal with it. Look at this one." Margaret, the thirty-eight-year-old, had earned a 29. She had done fine on language, but she simply had no idea what the subject of a paragraph was, or what the difference was between a generalization and a detail. She hadn't learned either the symbols used in outlines or what outlines did.

Rudi put the papers back on his desk and ran a hand through his silver-brown hair, which seemed to have been flattened by thousands of such anxious gestures over the years. He said, "The problem is that these kids are coming out of school *damaged*. It's not just that they haven't learned properly, or they haven't taken the right courses. You've got these kids who are so passive, they get a 10 or 20 on an exam and I tell them to come in and see me, but I never see them. What are they thinking? What do they think is going to happen to them?"

The metaphor of damage was Rudi's answer to Mina Shaugh-nessy's image of the beginner. The students he was seeing now were starting not at zero but below zero. School had trained them to hunker down, to disengage. And it wasn't only school. The over-whelming struggle of daily life, of a life lived on the edge of disaster, had absorbed so much of their intellectual energy. "We don't even have the racial thing anymore," said Rudi. "Eight or ten years ago, kids came in with a real attitude, but at least you could *build* on it." Rudi liked oppositional students; he was a pretty oppositional type himself. "Now," he said, "there's nothing to build on. There's no content."

"Maybe they know a lot about nonacademic things," I ventured.

"We tried that!" Rudi cried. "We talked about black issues and rap music and so forth, but when you push them there's nothing there but the soft stuff. Sure, they may know the names of lots of songs and the singers and so forth, but can they *analyze*?"

Rudi's anguish was genuine. He derived, so far as I could tell, not the slightest satisfaction from seeing his most dire predictions fulfilled. Whatever Rudi thought about the mass, he believed de-voutly in the individual. Every time I went to visit him I found stu-dents waiting outside, or coming in to borrow books or a typewriter, to pick up a reference for a job, to talk about a paper he had volun-teered to read for another class—or just to drink up Rudi's fortifying broth of praise and support and tough love. He knew about their brothers and sisters, and boyfriends and girlfriends, and their hopes and worries. Rudi was the only teacher many of these students could turn to for help, and he knew it. He left his home in New Jersey at dawn four days a week in order to reach the campus by 7 A.M., so that he could meet with students before classes began. And he spent about $20 a week calling them from home.

One day Aisha told me, somewhat hyperbolically, "Professor Gedamke calls me practically every day. He drives me totally crazy. He calls me in the morning, he calls me at night. One time he even had Anton call me, because he couldn't find my number." Aisha was a smart girl, but, like Anton, sometimes she seemed to be not quite there. She was taking a tough schedule, and Rudi felt that she needed to be egged on and watched over. And he thought it might not be a bad thing for Anton to take some responsibility for his friend. It all sounded more like high school than college. But like Charles Frye, Rudi felt that his students needed counseling—and attention and support—at least as much as they needed teaching.

Rudi identified with his students—perhaps too much. One day, after another set of dismal test results, he stood in front of the blackboard and, in the urgent and plaintive tones that I was hearing more and more, said, "The strange thing is, I see *me* in *you*. I see my kids in you. I see my working class in you. What do I mean by working class? None of my people went to college—none—ever! The highest anyone ever went was eighth grade. The system didn't *want* me there. And it doesn't want *you* either. It doesn't know what to do with difference. But that means you have to fight *so damn hard* to get even with the system. So if I'm emotional, maybe it's because I'm talking about *me.*"

Rudi was something like them, but he was even more like earlier generations of City students. He had grown up outside of Hamburg, a tough, smart, working-class kid who played soccer and hung out on the docks. At ten he was inducted into the Hitler Youth, and he and his pals would swagger around, singing rousing tunes like "Jew Heads Roll in the Gutter." Then Hamburg was obliterated by bombing, and the war ended, and the Allies came. One day the GIs gathered the townspeople to watch film clips of the death camps. "I remember a lot of the guys were laughing," Rudi says. "I just came out of there crying." Rudi thus had early in life the educational experience of disillusionment, which was to become something of a motif with him.

Just after the war ended, when he was fourteen, Rudi was shunted off into the apprentice system, as his father had and his father before him. Apprenticeship in Germany stretches back to the medieval era of the guilds; by Rudi's time it had taken on a meritocratic gloss, but it was in fact a caste system. "It was a world where you never moved," he says. "You didn't even try; you knew you'd only get shat on if you did." Rudi was not about to accept the harness as meekly as his ancestors had; and yet the system was not altogether onerous. Vocational training was not a diluted form of education, but a specialized one. Rudi went to trade school one day a week, where, as an apprentice carpenter, he learned physics and math— much as Townsend Harris expected his mechanics and artisans to do. "I could have walked through a college physics course and laughed at it," says Rudi. And the remainder of Rudi's education was filled in by a fellow worker. "He was a guy with a big, round head, and he came over to me and said, 'You got smart eyes.' I liked that— smart eyes. This guy was a member of the Communist Party, and at lunch time we would go out to the dock, open our lunch boxes, and talk about Karl Marx."

In 1950 Rudi boarded a ship for New York. He spoke no English when he arrived, but after three months in night school he took the Regents exams in the major subjects and passed with flying colors. To satisfy the principal of the school he applied to City College; and in due course a letter arrived informing him, to his utter amazement, that he had been accepted. Rudi loved to recall his first sighting of City's Gothic spires. One morning he said to the class, "When I got to the bottom of the hill and looked up, and I saw that beautiful campus, I cried. I could not believe that a person like me, an immigrant, could go to college."

For all that, Rudi quickly contracted a case of intellectual alienation. He dropped out of City after a year, served in the army, returned to City, and graduated in 1959. He entered a Ph.D. program in English at Columbia, but again dropped out after a year. Graduate school brought out the Eric Hoffer in Rudi, the left-wing, working-class scorn for intellectual nicety. "I couldn't balance a teacup on my knee and talk at the same time," as he puts it. Rudi began teaching at a reading clinic, which, he found, satisfied his need to do something solid and useful. He also found that he was good at it. He became a student of developmental psychology and reading theory. And after knocking around for a decade he came to rest at his alma mater. Rudi had been, at various times, a coffeehouse poet and an amateur philosopher, but nothing really came of it. He wrote some textbooks, but scholarly production was not his thing. At some point Rudi seemed to have accepted the fact that he would never satisfy his intellectual ambitions. Perhaps a residue of disappointment disturbed the clarity of Rudi's soul. And yet the acceptance was real; he loved teaching, and he loved his students.

Halfway through the term the class had separated into a very small group that didn't need much help, a large group that desperately needed help, and a third group that seemed beyond help. At the top were students such as Stephen, who like almost all male Chinese students at City College was single-mindedly pursuing an engineering degree. I was more interested in Paul, a shy boy who peeked out from under a sheaf of straight black hair. One day I caught up with him on Convent Avenue as we were both emerging from the subway. I asked Paul about his family. "It's hard for me to talk to my parents," he said. "They've been here thirty years, but they don't really speak English, and I don't speak Chinese. I have to use a lot of hand signals and stuff."

It was a fine day in mid-October, and the sun was lighting up the splendid brownstones that had made the neighborhood so gracious when the campus moved to St. Nicholas Heights. Paul plodded uphill with his own private cloud. He said that he was barely on speaking terms with his older brother and sister, though they lived at home. He hadn't had many friends in high school either. "Mostly I would go to school, come home, do my homework, and go to sleep," he said. "I wasn't very active." On his questionnaire Paul had described what he hoped to get out of City College: "I like to be able to express myself and build up my self-confidence without everyone condescending on me." Paul often knew the answer to one of Rudi's questions, he said, but couldn't bring himself to blurt it out, and scarcely even to raise his hand. To listen to Paul you would think there was an intense competition for class speaking time.

Rudi felt that many of his students suffered from serious depression, and Paul appeared to be a perfect example. Music, he had written, "is the only thing in my life now that's worth something. Music takes me to another world—my world—and in this world only good things happen. There's no worry at home, school or at work." Now Paul was taking a piano class, though he didn't have a piano at home and had to visit a friend in order to practice. He was also taking fencing, just because it was new and different. Maybe it allowed him to express aggression in an acceptable form. In his first bout he actually knocked over a kid from Yale, which seemed like a fine working-class response to the aristocratic etiquette of the sport.

Paul said that he wanted to go into advertising, but he really didn't know much about it and didn't particularly like to write. It's possible that he didn't think he was good enough at math to do engineering.

Paul always sat right behind Yvonne, another of the better students. They never spoke, because Yvonne was almost as shy as Paul. She was a slight girl, with a dazzling smile, and every time Rudi saw her in the library—she was often there—he would tell her that she was cute. He did it for the same reason that he called Aisha all the time—to shore up an ego where he felt it needed shoring. Rudi distributed both literal and metaphorical hugs. It's also true that he was something of a sexy older guy, with his silver hair and his barrel chest and his disarmingly personal style; he liked to violate an implicit classroom taboo by talking about sex. It often worked like a dose of smelling salts.

Yvonne had gone to school in Guyana until her family moved to New York when she was in eleventh grade. She had a solid base in an English-style educational system. So did Andrew, but Yvonne had gone two or three years longer. Yvonne was much more conscientious than Andrew. I saw her in the library one afternoon, and she talked with wonder about the atmosphere of DeWitt Clinton High School, where she had gotten her diploma. "It was so violent, and everyone was running around and almost crazy," Yvonne said. "I didn't feel comfortable there." Yvonne also had a big, intact family. Many of the students had a dreary Thanksgiving; Yvonne had a giant family gathering.

In class Yvonne never did quite so well as Stephen or Paul, but her confidence grew as she realized that the work was easy for her. One day toward the end of the semester Paul called Yvonne at home to ask if she wanted to study with him. She was stunned speechless. "Yes," she said, as soon as she had composed herself. Paul was interacting; he was overcoming his timidity. And when the two of them got together, Yvonne was shocked again to see how hard Paul worked. "Sure," said Rudi when she told him about their tête-à-tête. "Paul reads everything five times."

What was it that separated the few students in the top bracket of the class from those on the bottom? In cognitive terms, the better students were able to operate at the level of abstraction required, for example, to reduce a passage to an outline, whereas the others were not. Did that mean that the one group was "smarter" than the other? Perhaps, by definition, it did. It certainly seemed that something irreducible, something that could be called "ability," if not "intelligence," separated the top of the class from the bottom. Rudi once asked the class to comment on a passage he had assigned. The usual uneasy silence ensued. And then Aisha said, "Poorly written." Rudi, who had been walking toward the front of the room, whirled around and gave Aisha a high five. She had only said two words; but the words implied that she had not only absorbed the passage but assessed it in the global way required to appraise style. Very few of the students in the class could have made such an appraisal.

Aisha was smart but unfocused. In most of the better students, however, "ability" was inextricable from experience and attitude. Like many of the ESL students I had met, or like Wagner Ortuno, the Ecuadorean engineer, they had arrived at City with good study habits and a certain comfort level with school itself. The larger group at the bottom included students who were virtually illiterate, but they also seemed never to have made real contact with school. I asked Mario, the big, amiable kid who sat with Curtis and Che, how he was doing in class. "I'm doing good," said Mario. Then, when I asked about the work Rudi had been assigning, Mario waffled a little bit. "If the outline is in the first sentence of the paragraph, then it's easy," he said. "But sometimes it's in the middle, and I don't know where to find it." The class had just begun talking about outlines, and Mario had confused the idea with that of the topic sentence.

Mario had gone to a vocational high school, which, so far as he could recall, offered virtually no math or science. He had not been a particularly successful student. But he had gotten a prize for his work in a dental technician's class, and he had settled on that as a profession. Mario had enrolled at City because he thought that he needed a college degree, as well as a graduate degree, to work as a dental technician, but in fact he needed only technical training. Mario seemed to be in a fog much of the time. Aisha tried to help him with his writing, which she assessed at about a fourth-grade level. She would make corrections, and Mario would dutifully write them down, and then he would make the same mistakes again.

Across the room, in the Hispanic girls' section, sat Yesenia, a doll-like figure with a perfectly round face, perfectly wide eyes, and delicate, perfectly arched eyebrows that gave her a look of perpetual surprise. Yesenia, who had written that her weakness was pronunciation, vocabulary, and "writing about topic," was a SEEK student. She never spoke in class, and never seemed to pay much attention to the goings-on. One day I sat next to her and noticed that on an inside page of her notebook she had pasted a photograph of a baby. Yesenia spent much of the class gazing at it dreamily.

After class Yesenia told me that the little girl's name was Taisha and she was ten months old. Taisha was part of a sad, tangled story. "I came here before," Yesenia said in her soft and timid voice. "It was two years ago. But then my mother got sick and she went into the hospital. It was bad, and the doctor said she was going to die." Meanwhile, Yesenia had gotten pregnant. Her boyfriend was a cop. "He didn't want me to have the baby, so he said he wasn't going to have anything to do with it. But the way I grew up" —as a good Catholic girl in Puerto Rico— "we didn't believe in abortion, so I had the baby anyway." The combination of her mother's illness and her own pregnancy was too much for Yesenia, and she dropped out after only one semester. Her mother died days before Taisha was born. Her boyfriend had at least begun to support the two of them, but Yesinia was surviving on welfare and living in a project in East Harlem. She answered all my questions with a gentle smile and an air of long-suffering patience. The one time she expressed any passion was when she said of the projects, "For me it's not so bad, but I don't want Taisha growing up there."

Yesenia said that she was doing fine in class, though in fact she was failing. She had never been to see Rudi, or her SEEK counselor; in fact she didn't know who her counselor was. She was hoping to get a degree as a physician's assistant, but she hadn't yet asked anyone how she could get into City's special program in the field. Yesenia seemed confused and distracted; her mind was elsewhere. After fifteen or twenty minutes, I could see that she was getting fidgety. "Usually I go home right after class," she explained. "I have all my classes in the morning, and my babysitter finishes at one." In her mind, Yesenia was already with Taisha.

It was late October, and Rudi was reviewing a quiz. He had included a reference to Ghana, in honor of Andrew. "By the way," he said, "where's Ghana?"

"In India," someone said. "In South America," corrected Jose, who was from the Dominican Republic. "Near Venezuela." Jose was thinking of Guyana. Anton turned on the worldly contempt. "Ghana is in Africa, kid," he said.

"Oh," said Rudi. "Where in Africa?"

"Central? Is it coastal? I don't know."

Rudi wasn't trying to embarrass Anton, and he didn't even care much about geography. He wanted to instill the habit of absorbing information; he wanted them to build up a storehouse of knowledge. He drew a time line on the board. When was Christ born? When did Columbus discover America? When was the Civil War? There were nearly as many random answers as right ones. Rudi felt that it was virtually impossible to think complex thoughts without a wealth of specific knowledge, as it was without a storehouse of words.

Rudi agreed with E. D. Hirsch, a former follower of Mina Shaughnessy, who argued in his highly controversial *Cultural Literacy* that "a consistent lack of necessary information can make the reading process so laborious and uncommunicative that it fails to convey meaning." Hirsch, in fact, insisted that there was no such thing as "general, transferable skills in problem solving, critical thinking or in any other field," a claim that amounted to heresy in progressive pedagogical circles. He suggested that teachers teach information—cultural literacy—rather than developmental skills. Rudi did, of course, try to teach skills directly. But he felt that students would not be able to deploy these skills without the scaffolding of data. How could you fathom history if you had no sense of chronology? Chronology was a structure, and you needed structures to think. "Frameworks," Rudi said. "*Contexts.*" He was in the habit of speaking highly flavored one-word sentences.

The class moved on, though students seemed to be dropping off left and right. After the section on "intake" Rudi discussed "storage" and "retrieval." He used these terms to mean the capacity to retain information and to reproduce it in a meaningful way. Here, as before, Rudi taught techniques of learning that are intuitive to most

well-educated people but that his students, he knew, had never absorbed. He talked about the effective use of time, mnemonic tricks,
and various kinds of tests. He continued to harp on the intake skills
of underlining and note taking. Taking good notes, he explained,
was not some freestanding academic skill, but a consequence of
understanding what was primary in a lecture or a reading and how
ideas were related to one another. Rudi was trying to bring them
to build a representation of the structure of a given passage in their
notes and above all in their minds.

A few days after the quiz Rudi asked the students to write a
350-word take-home essay explaining the main points of a passage
they had read on the traditional male role. Rudi was now nudging
them toward the kind of work they would be expected to do in
freshman-level courses. What he got back, though, showed how very
unready most of them were for college work. "Some of these papers
really hurt me," he said in class. "Why? Because you had *so many*
good ideas in there, but you couldn't get them out. You couldn't do
the writing." Lakisha and Mario virtually copied the original text.
Jose had taken some notes, but in his paralyzed sentence structure
you could see the struggle he was waging with written English. "In
the American society," Jose had written in his careful, upright hand,
"males & females have been in a disputes for many years, because
of the male role in the American society. Many females belief that
American males have it easy. I agree that males have it easy because
man have been free to exercise legal and social powers."

Curtis did the opposite: he paid no attention to the text and
wrote two paragraphs of his own thoughts on manhood. And he
used the opportunity to express things he never would have said
in class. He wrote, "We all try to become like all the heroes in the
comic books, or in the T.V. or in the books. But in alot of cases, we
twist that vision and turn it into something even worst. We try to
act macho, showing no true feelings, thinking that they are gods.
And they show this when they attack their children + wife. Hiding
their emotional side, so that no one will think that they are gay."
Curtis was letting himself off easy by noodling about his own feelings
rather than thinking through the text. And yet he almost seemed
to be offering a critique, and a devastating one, of his own persona;

perhaps he felt trapped inside it. And his self-criticism, if that's what it was, didn't stop there. Underneath he wrote "YUCK!!" And underneath that piece of self-criticism he wrote, "This sounds confusing. I'll give up another one on Wednesday." That was a revealing locution. By the time Wednesday rolled around, Curtis had apparently forgotten his offer.

The strangest essay came from Simeon. His letters lurched forward and back, and forward and back again, as if they were being sloshed around in a glass. Apt observations dissolved into a shapeless welter. One of his sentences read, "Whereas the male by which society has played him to be the sole provider, protector, and he will to take risks concerning the wealthfare of the family." Perhaps Mina Shaughnessy would have divined Simeon's meaning. Rudi did not consider the effort as rewarding as she had, but neither did he believe in discouraging his students. "As always you have interesting and exciting ideas," he wrote, "but the grammar, spelling and organization need a lot of work. We will have to work together on this."

Simeon was, in fact, a highly intelligent young man. He was the only one in the class who seemed to know things about the larger world. He knew what Greenpeace was, and the geodesic dome, and sado-masochism, and even supply-side economics. He seemed to have remembered everything he had ever heard. And his gifts were not merely mechanical: he understood intuitively how to formulate concepts. When Rudi asked whether it was possible to have memories that predate the acquisition of language, Simeon said that he thought not, "Because you wouldn't have any words to describe it to yourself." It was a plausible hypothesis, even if it was wrong.

And yet Simeon flunked virtually every exam, often by a mile. He couldn't sustain an idea beyond a sentence or two. He could absorb an individual concept, but not the overall concept of organization. He was like a living refutation of Hirsch's theory that knowledge produced skills. In effect, Simeon could function only on an oral level; in fact he suffered from a verbal compulsion. Simeon sat directly in front of Rudi and shouted answers before Rudi finished his questions. "Do you know what this means?" Rudi would ask. And Simeon would say, "Yeah, yeah," as if it were the most obvious thing in the world, and then fire off a wild guess.

Simeon was so desperate to stand out that he would show up in all sorts of strange costumes. For some time he wore a kind of neosharecropper outfit—denim coveralls with one shoulder strap hanging down, fancy sunglasses, and a leather, multicolored "X" cap worn backward. Later in the semester he switched to a thickly padded black leather jacket, which he wore in class with one arm in a sleeve and the other out, as if he were throttling himself. By then, in fact, Simeon *was* throttling himself. Perhaps he had finally taken a hint after being shushed by Rudi as well as some of the students; or perhaps his repeated failures had taken their toll on his ego. Midway through the term he stopped sitting directly in front of Rudi, and his magpie chattering diminished.

Rudi thought that Simeon was dyslexic, but Simeon himself refused to acknowledge any problems. He had long since learned to use his gift of gab to mask them, probably even from himself. Until now he had breezed his way through school, having attended a vocational school that was undemanding even by New York City standards. "We were supposed to read books," Simeon said, "but you didn't have to. The exam was just about the plot of the book, and I could remember that from what the teacher said. I considered it like a sin to study." In fact Simeon hadn't done all that well in high school. He appeared to be a SEEK student, although he said he didn't know if he was or not. He had a facile, and transparent, explanation, for everything—his handwriting, his poor showing on the reading assessment test, his problems in math class. I remarked, "High school gives a lot of people a false sense of security." Simeon shot me a look of recognition and added, "In high school you could just roll with the punches. Here you're getting hit in the face."

In the middle of the term Rudi gave an exam on note taking. He had asked the students to read and annotate five passages at home. The exam covered the material they had read; they were allowed to use their notes. In years past Rudi had given the exam in one class session; now he was stretching it over two periods, because students had complained that it took them too long to read the passages themselves. The morning after the second session, when everyone shuffled down the dingy basement hallway of Harris and into the classroom, they found that Rudi had written an equation on the blackboard: "I'm overworked + I'm underloved + your tests = I'm hurting." *Hurting* was a word that Rudi used a great deal; he pronounced it without the *r*.

This almost abject confession shattered another classroom taboo, in fact several taboos: Don't sacrifice your authority. Don't call attention to yourself. Don't lay a guilt trip on your students. But Rudi felt that he had to let them know that it was safe to open up, to connect, to allow themselves to be engaged by school. It was they, Rudi thought, who were underloved. "A lot of you don't know how to be loved," he had said. Again and again he had invited them to come to his office for help, with the class or anything else. And they had not come, or they had sat across from him and pretended that everything was fine. Maybe the whole idea of having an emotional bond with a sixty-year-old teacher with a German accent struck them as weird. But that was what Rudi was offering.

The real source of Rudi's hurt was a column on the right-hand side of the board: the range of test scores. Even after giving 20 free points simply for having shown that they had read the passages he had assigned, Rudi had given no one so much as a 90. Four students had scored 80 or above, four more had scored 70 or above, and the other ten who had taken the test had come in below 70, including three students in the 20s. Throughout the semester Rudi had been hinting at his growing dismay; now, as he had when he wrote his memo, he opened the sluicegates, and his pent-up emotion came rushing forth. He pointed to the numbers on top, his tweed jacket hiking up on his arm, and he said, "These scores here are on standard. What does that mean? That once they left College Skills and went out into the college they would be average students—65, 70, 75, maybe a bit stronger. What looks good in here for the college at large is just what? Survival skills. But if you're starting to pull 30, 40, 50, what am I saying? *That you're just not making it.* You're not motivated enough. Those motivations may have been good enough for junior high school, but they're not good enough for college."

I was reminded of Charles Frye's lecture about "January clearance." Rudi, too, had been driven to shock tactics. He was pacing back and forth; his agitation was mounting. He was running his hands through his hair, and flipping his big aviator glasses back and forth from his brow to the tip of his nose. "When I give you a one-page test," he continued, "and you take the whole hour to read it, I say you cannot read." He looked around, and perhaps he registered the anger he had provoked. He said, "You cannot read *at the college level*. Now how can I say that? How *dare* I say that? How dare I make such an assumption?" Rudi pointed out that all the students who did well had finished the reading in plenty of time. It was a myth, he said, that people could read equally well at any speed. Once you slowed down far enough the context would become invisible.

The class had been sitting in stunned silence until Aileen spoke up. Aileen was one of the better students, as well as one of the most assertive. She had big dark eyes and fine lashes, and she kept her thick hair pulled severely back. Now she said, "Don't you think that's kind of insulting to the people who did okay?" The tension was so great that Aileen's voice was almost strangled. "I mean, they didn't get a 90, but . . ." Aileen couldn't get anything else out.

Rudi just said no. He was not in a mood to hug anyone, or even to meet anyone halfway. "A lot of you are playing with a totally un-realistic sense of what the standards are," he said, still pacing at the front of the class. He talked about the high dropout rate and the pressures they would be facing as they left the cocoon world of remediation. "I *worry* about you," he said, and the hard edge of his voice softened. "I worry that some of you will not make it, and you will be worse off than when you came here. Why do I say that?"

"Self-esteem?" That was Che.

"Yes," said Rudi. "I hurt for that. I *know* what's down the road for you; you don't. You're dreaming. *You have got to wake up!*" Rudy wasn't shouting—he never shouted—but he was in a passion. Once again he had gained complete silence. Aileen was so nervous that her whole body was bobbing up and down as she chewed gum. And then Rudi went back to his desk and did something I never would have expected—he read his memo to Dean Fiellin. Halfway through, incredibly, I could see that the class was woolgathering, as if the fail-ures the memo discussed so brutally weren't theirs as well. But by the end, when he compared City College to a junior high school, Rudi had a gravely attentive audience.

And then Rudi talked about how he saw himself, and his children, in them. He wanted them to know that he, too, had faced adversity, that he knew how hard it was, that he was on their side. He was saying that he cared about them too much to let them feed on self-delusion. And all that was true. But would the truth set them free—the truth of their own dreadful shortcomings? Or would it confirm their worst fears? After class I rode the escalator up to Rudi's office. He looked stricken. The lines that ran from the corner of his mouth to his chin seemed to bite deeply into his flesh. "I don't know if I did the right thing," Rudi said. "Frankly, I don't know what to do." He talked about triage, about the diminishing number of students that he felt he could save. As I was getting up to leave, he said, "What you see here is a whole system failing."

The test produced a few tiny glimmers of good news. Curtis surprised me by reporting that he got an 81, one of the highest scores in the class. It turned out that Curtis was paying more attention than he let on. Curtis never deigned to speak in class, but sometimes, Rudi told me, he would come up after class and ask what a word or phrase meant. Sometimes he even showed Rudi a paragraph or two that he had written. I was reminded of that "Yuck!" and of something Curtis had said to me earlier. We had had a very uneasy conversation in the cafeteria after class one day. Curtis had placed his book bag on the table between us, so that I could barely see him. He kept his cap on, and his eyes, as always, were narrow and veiled. He answered my questions with monosyllables and shrugs, waiting impatiently for the ordeal to end. I wasn't going to learn much about Curtis, or Curtis's anger.

Then I asked about writing, and Curtis began talking. At Louis Brandeis High, he said, "Me and my friend Jason used to have this competition where we would write something really disgusting and show it to our English teacher. We even wrote some stuff for the principal." Curtis said that he and Jason used to crib their ideas from Stephen King and Clive Barker. "Jason," in fact, may have been a horror-movie nom de plume. Like Che, Curtis was also an avid reader of comic books. "I got this really weird assignment from my English teacher," Curtis said. "We're supposed to put ourselves in the mind of the opposite sex." Curtis thought the idea idiotic, but he was working on a story that would have made Jason proud. It involved several serial killers, disemboweled corpses hanging from trees, skinned fetuses, Vietnam flashbacks, statues that come alive to commit murder, and so on. Curtis recited his tale with an air of detached connoisseurship worthy of Hannibal Lecter. He was trying to gross *me* out. It was a completely adolescent, comic-book story, with just the elements of overblown macho that Curtis had been deriding in his essay. But at least it was a story; at least Curtis was trying to move his reader, even if only to disgust. And then the story was over, and the hard, glinting mask came back on, and our conversation ended.

Andrew offered a surprise of a different sort. He had stopped partway through the exam and written, "Owing to personal problems, I can not finish the test." Andrew's test scores had been dropping to dangerous levels in recent weeks. A few days later I saw him hurrying ahead of me as I walked away from the campus toward the subway. I caught up with him and asked about his route home. Andrew lived in a very bad part of the South Bronx. "Most of the people I knew in school dropped out," he said. "A lot of them are selling drugs or on drugs or in jail. But I keep away from those guys. I go to school, do my work, come home. That's where my values come in." Andrew had the habit of speaking in homilies; he had staked out a role as model student and dutiful son. It was true, he said, that his life had gotten complicated recently. He had been shuttling back and forth between his father's home in Brooklyn, where he felt unwelcome, and his mother's home in the South Bronx. "But that's okay," he said. "I can deal with it."

I noticed that Andrew, a big, soft boy, was sweating heavily, though it was a cold day. And as we walked down the stairs and stood on the platform at 145th Street, waiting for the D train to come, Andrew finally dropped the pretense that he was okay. "When I was in Brooklyn," he said in the piping voice of West Africa, "I had such big ambitions for myself. I thought I would be a pilot. Now I don't know; maybe I won't even make it through college." It was soon after they moved to New York, when Andrew was in ninth grade, that his parents had split up. "I couldn't take it," he said. "In Africa I used to always have this hope that they would stay together, no matter what. . . ." Andrew looked out over the tracks with his soulful yellow eyes. "I was an A student," he went on. "And the year my mother went away my average went down to 67. That's 32 points." He said it as if each point had been a dram of blood.

Now he had to be strong for his little brother and sister, and for his mother. And who would look out for him? "Sometimes," Andrew said, "I sit at my table and I'm like crying inside. I ask myself, 'Why me? I'm only nineteen.' I feel like I need to have my father with me, but I'm all alone." Andrew's work was suffering not only because he found it hard—he wouldn't admit that he did—but because he could barely concentrate. That week his parents were in court; their long drawn-out custody battle was finally coming to a head, and the pressure on Andrew was almost intolerable.

Rudi felt that many of his students had no idea they were heading for a crack-up. But when he asked them, toward the end of the semester, to write an essay about themselves as college students, he found that they could acknowledge on paper what they often hid from him. The notes of bravado, of glib self-confidence, that many of them had sounded in their answers to his initial questionnaire were now muted, almost inaudible. College had exposed weaknesses they had been able to ignore in the past. Even Simeon wrote, in his pitching and yawing hand, "I constantly am causing my own slow-self-destruction. In many ways I know why I do these things or rather I say behave like I don't care about what happens to my existance. Well one way I see it is lack of motivation on my part in particular. . . . This lack of motivation sounds good but, it could just be very bad habits ones that reward bad behavior. This is also self-destructive but more or less a character flaw." Andrew wrote, "I want so much from college but I do so little. . . . I have study disorder which is very fatal as a college student. . . . When I really spend time on writing most of the time I write beautiful essays, stories, and letters. Is just that I dont have or make time for all of this great major factors I need to be a successful student." He was hoping, he said, that tutoring "will help me study more and overcome my study disorder."

Many students also wrote about their language problems with a terrible candor. Eddie, one of the Chinese boys, wrote, "I never open my mouth or ask question in class that feel needed answers. Whenever I called on I feel fear or just get numb." Cantina, a Hispanic, wrote, "I think if one person from my house (my mother, my sister or one of my two uncles) will want to come to college, I will advice them to first learn English and then come to college. Because it's to difficult to on a place where you're the only one who feels out of place." Even the pitch of ambition had become less steep since the beginning of the semester. Eddie wrote that what he wanted above all was "to keep my parents off my back" —a sentiment that might well have been repeated by half the male Chinese students at City College. Stephen said he hoped to become "an average middle-class person." Cantina wrote, "Even though my English it's not strong I will keep on trying. Because I want to be someone important in the life and I don't want to work in a factory."

And in a few of the essays, you could feel the kindling of new life. Yvonne, who seemed to unfold a new petal every week, wrote, "As I search myself for strengths, I couldn't find any." She had written virtually the identical sentence at the beginning of the term. Now she went on to say, "But as I search deeper and deeper I stumbled upon endurance. Even though I get frustrated very easily, I do not give up. I am the first child in my family to attend college and I want to be a positive role model to my sister and cousins. I want to show them that you can be successful and make big bucks; no matter where you came from." It was Yvonne who, at the beginning of the term, had hungered after the Lexus and the suburban house. And she had something to prove to her father, who "always tells me . . . that I am not confident enough about myself, I do not have the strength, eagerness and aggressiveness to fight for life. I want to show my father that I have more than what it takes to become successful." Rudi had asked the students to edit one another's papers, and Paul, who had read Yvonne's, corrected the line to read, "I have more heart and determination than you think." Paul must have heard the words coursing through his own blood.

Paul himself wrote modestly that his greatest strengths were his "ability to get to class on time" and the fact that he could "easily get along with all types of people." But, he wrote, "my weaknesses overweighs my strengths when it comes to studying. My first weakness is that I get easily distracted when I study. If I hear a good song on the radio, I would stop to listen." In the margin, Yvonne wrote, "Turn the radio off." Paul concluded with the reflection, "To be successful in life or in college, you must set goals for yourself. In order to accomplish these goals, it must not be set too high." Yvonne underlined the last phrase and drew an arrow to her comment: "Doesn't make sense."

In the last month of class Rudi focused on critical analysis, although he knew that many of the students, if not most, hadn't gone beyond the stage of literal reading. Rudi talked about persuasive devices, about the whole idea that information can be organized or manipulated to advance a point of view or a hidden agenda. One morning Mario walked in with a letter he had received from Publishers' Clearinghouse, offering a "guaranteed" prize. Rudi read the letter to the class. Should Mario call the 900 number? Everyone agreed that it must be some kind of scam. But why did it work? How did it work? "Listen to this," Rudi said. "You will be disqualified if you do not respond within thirty days. 'Disqualified' —do you hear how that's being used to coerce you?" Rudi wanted them to practice critical thinking by decoding the world around them. One day he taped a Benetton ad on the blackboard—two black hands clutching a bone; a semiautomatic weapon slung over a shoulder. What did it convey? Pictures were shorthand; they conveyed meaning without ever stating it explicitly.

The Benetton ad required a much higher order of interpretation than the Salem ad that Rudi had taped up at the beginning of the course; the one was modern poetry, the other traditional narrative. Still, it was discouraging that no one had ventured even a wild guess. Perhaps E. D. Hirsch was right: in the absence of "cultural information" about hunger, warfare, and tribalism in the Third World, the students hadn't been able to read past the local elements of the text to generalize a meaning or a hypothetical narrative. Or, as Rudi would have put it, they lacked frameworks. Certainly the sequence of cognitive skills that he had tried to foster throughout the term had not raised students' interpretative abilities from the level of Salem to that of Benetton. And perhaps it was absurd to think that so small-scale an academic experience could have so broad an effect. But that was, after all, the effective premise of College Skills. Students were expected to read at a "college level," as defined by the reading assessment test, by the time they had finished. The remedial ideal assumed that such a transformation was possible, and not just occasionally but regularly. But in the classroom, as Rudi found, the shit flowed differently.

In the final weeks of the course, students began to sort themselves out. Yesenia stopped coming to class. One day she dropped by Rudi's office with Taisha, but she refused to be drawn into conversation. Rudi never saw her again. Simeon announced that he would not be in college next fall: he was enlisting full-time in the Army Reserves, where he worked as a dietitian. Simeon still insisted, against all plausibility, that he would graduate from City as an electrical engineer. Mario turned out to be flunking most of his classes; Aisha, who had a soft spot for Mario, was sitting in the library with him and taking him to see his academic adviser. She led him around as if he were an overgrown puppy.

One day after class Curtis went storming into Rudi's office, closed the door behind him, and began to complain bitterly about the grade on his most recent quiz. Rudi said, "Open the door, and sit down, and then we'll talk." Curtis opened the door an inch. Rudi, still sitting calmly behind his desk, said, "Don't try to pull that physical stuff on me." Rudi was the wrong guy to try to intimidate. Curtis pushed the door open and sat down, still glowering. Rudi talked to him for a minute and then said, "Come back and talk to me when you've calmed down." And in fact Curtis came back that afternoon, and Rudi discovered that on the exam Curtis had faithfully reproduced the information in his notes, but that the notes themselves were all wrong. They had a rational conversation. Curtis was not about to give Rudi a hug; but he might allow himself to be reached.

On the last day of class Anton seemed possessed by some private fury. Aisha bent over him solicitously; Aileen tried to make him laugh. Rudi said, "Anton is full of rage today. We're back where we started." Rudi talked about the final, which he would count only if it improved a student's overall grade. And he admitted that midway through the term he had stopped asking for their vocabulary work. "This is the first time ever have I pulled out of vocabulary development," he said in one of his occasional German-sequenced sentences. "You remember what happened? Whenever we talked about vocabulary development, you all sat there like this" —and he slumped into a chair with his arms folded across his chest. "I thought, 'Does it really make sense to keep going with this stuff if that's the way you feel?' "

Rudi's chastisement modified, bit by bit, into a plea. "Gang," he said, "you've *got* to reach out a little more. Any student I've worked with even once is my student, they're my family." He invited them, again, to come to him for help. "You know what a tough guy I am, but when I go to graduation and I see my students, I cry a little bit inside." He talked, again, about the need to accept love, to be hugged. The students snickered, made some jokes, and Rudi clenched his broad jaw and said, "Damn it, I lost my point." He was dead serious; he wanted to hold on to the emotion. He wanted to leave them with something real. And so as the class, and the term, came to an end, Rudi told a story that lightly summed up the conflict that he had wrestled with for twenty years. "A few years ago," he said, sitting on the edge of his desk, "I went on a sabbatical, and I was out on a sailboat crossing the Atlantic by myself. And I was out there under the moon, bailing water, throwing up, and I suddenly thought, 'What the hell is so-and-so doing? Has she graduated? Is she making it?' And that's what made me come back to the college."

Rudi did not like giving out grades. He knew of another College Skills teacher who had passed all twenty-two of his students. But that seemed to Rudi not so much an act of generosity as of surrender. To pass everyone was to accept the situation he had described in his memo with a shrug. Rudi cared too much about the college to simply stamp the papers of students who could barely read. But he cared too much about the students to block their passage forward unless he felt that he had no choice at all. And so he negotiated with himself, and sometimes tortured himself, and he erred on the side of generosity.

Rudi had developed a system he called "the contract." He would pass a student with the proviso that they would work together in the following semester. So long as the student committed him- or herself to improve, Rudi would keep the passing grade; if not, he would change the grade to F or R, for "repeat." Normally Rudi gave out three or four contracts per class. This time, though, he gave contracts, with a C grade, to six students, including Che, Andrew, and Margaret. Margaret clearly belonged in College Skills 1—she had been placed in Rudi's class by a clerical error—and Rudi offered to give her a passing grade if she would return to College Skills 1, pass the course, and then pass the reading assessment test. Even this seemed unlikely.

Rudi also used the contract for students he couldn't bear to fail. A black student named Sherry had scored between 33 and 60 on her exams, but she soldiered on, never complaining, always looking to Rudi for help. She was thirty, had been in and out of community college, and spent much of her time caring for a grandmother with Alzheimer's disease who lived with Sherry and her mother. The three of them eked out a life on public assistance. Sherry's life seemed to have come from a Dickens novel; and, true to melodrama, she had somehow preserved a child's pristine imagination in the midst of a nightmarish landscape. She wrote stories about angels fallen to earth. She gave me a poem she had written: "A world without women/is like a beach without sand/or like a boat/that won't float/on dry land. A world without a woman is like God without his heaven/like a king without a crown. . . ." Rudi couldn't bring himself to grade Sherry either according to her performance or according to his fondness for her. And so he put Sherry on contract, hoping to persuade her to go back to a two-year college.

Rudi considered F a punitive grade, and he almost never gave one out. Nor did he normally hand out D's. But he gave seven students an R, including Mario, Eddie, and Simeon. Rudi didn't feel that they were less able than the students he had put on contract; it was more that they hadn't made a serious enough effort to survive. They hadn't reached out. Five other students, most of whom were failing, had withdrawn from the class. Rudi gave Yesenia a WU, a grade that denoted withdrawal without the proper formalities. One of the stars of the class, a black student named Eric, had left early in the semester to transfer to a private college to which, he said, he had been given a full scholarship. Rudi had great hopes for Eric—until he showed up again at the end of the semester, hoping to get back into class. Eric could barely make eye contact with Rudi; the scholarship, and the private college, went unmentioned.

Rudi awarded only two A's—to Stephen and Paul. He gave B's to Aileen, Yvonne, Aisha, Anton, Curtis, and one other student. Rudi was delighted with his few success stories. But he had prevented a dozen students from receiving credit for the course—and he wondered if even that ruinous casualty rate were high enough. "If I made a decision in terms of what College Skills ought to be, then two or maybe three students would have passed," Rudi said—the same dismal ratio that Charles Frye had considered appropriate for *his* class. The others had such rudimentary skills, or such poor study habits, that he assumed they would not survive City College.

It was possible that Rudi's predictions were too dire. City could be a very forgiving place. Simeon's English 2 teacher, incredibly, had given him an A. Rudi was seeing more and more of this. Finally he sent a letter to Barbara Gleason, the head of the Composition program: "Attached please find copies of essays a student wrote during the final week of my CSK 2.0 class. This same student passed her English 110 course with an A." The essays were on the level of Margaret's or Mario's, which is to say that they were semi-literate. "How is it done?" Rudi asked in the letter. "With mirrors?" This was what Rudi meant when he said, "The whole system is failing."

Rudi had been an angry young man and a teenaged Marxist and an enemy of privilege. Now, like Stanley Feingold during open admissions, he found himself mounting the ramparts of "standards." He was attaining a prophetic bitterness in his old age. "We're validating a kind of illiteracy by giving degrees out," Rudi said in his cramped, paper-strewn office. "We can do all the finger-pointing at the high schools; the problem is, we're doing the same thing." Rudi wanted to tell students like Mario to go to vocational school, no matter how undemocratic, inegalitarian, or elitist it might sound. He believed in vocational education, even though he hated the class system that it helped support. Above all, he wanted to find *something* that would help kids whom he felt he was failing. "What is the phrase for doctors?" he asked. " 'Do no harm?' Maybe we should adopt that. Because I wonder if we aren't doing more harm than good. When these kids don't make it here, it's a confirmation of themselves as nonstudents, as failures." I wasn't sure that was true, and Rudi himself was only guessing. But he certainly wasn't doing much good for the students who dropped out.

Rudi thought a lot about quitting to join the Peace Corps, or to sail solo around the world, but it always ended in conversions under the moonlight. He remembered sitting around with a few friends during the mid-70s and saying, "We should all get ourselves fired so we can go to a junior high school, where we could really make a difference." Maybe Charles Frye had been sitting there, too. Rudi was a succinct man, and he summed up his view of the world as follows: "The great problem with this society is that we don't give a shit about our children. That's where the problem lies. And by the time they get up here, it's too late."

9

Prepared for Disappointment

I n 1970, when higher education had been freshly democratized at City University and at private and public colleges around the country, the Carnegie Commission on Higher Education, in a report called *A Chance to Learn*, concluded that "it should not be necessary for colleges and universities in the year 2000 to provide compensatory education programs or to struggle over flexible criteria for admissions and grading." The "should not" was meant not only normatively but predictively: the authors of the report felt that open admissions would itself go a long way toward solving the remedial problem. The open admissions institutions would dedicate themselves to improving the conditions of the public schools from which they drew. And high school students would apply themselves as they hadn't before, knowing that real opportunities lay before them.

Things didn't work out that way; and the optimism of that era can't help seeming terribly naive to us now. The education historian Diane Ravitch has argued that the lowering of college admission standards starting in the mid-1960s led to a corresponding *decrease* in high school requirements, for the commonsense reason that it had now

171

become easier to get into college. And this, in turn, produced the exact opposite of what the Carnegie report had predicted—a large increase in compensatory education. Between 1975 and 1980 the number of students taking remedial math in college increased 72 percent. About one-quarter of entering college students now take at least one remedial course.

By most indications, American high school graduates have become less well educated over the last quarter century or so, even as they have gone off to college in increasing numbers. Scores on the combined math and verbal SATs have dropped 80 points since 1963, when the averages were 502 for the math and 478 for the verbal test (though they are currently inching back up). Scores also declined regularly on most achievement tests. Although over three-quarters of adult Americans have graduated from high school or received a GED degree, the National Adult Literacy Survey, completed in 1993, found that almost one-half of adults lacked the literacy skills to identify two occurrences of a broad theme in a text of ten paragraphs—the sort of task that a decently educated ninth-grader might be expected to perform. At the *uppermost* range, this group was able to "make low-level inferences based on what they read and to compare or contrast information that can easily be found in text." Three-quarters of African Americans and over three-quarters of Hispanic Americans, as well as one-half of *all* high school graduates, functioned at this level. Only 3 percent of Americans were performing at the highest of the survey's five levels of "prose literacy." And young adults were measurably less literate in 1992 than they had been in 1985.

Why were students leaving the schools with such scant learning? Clearly the problem was not entirely the fault of the schools, especially in systems like New York's, where poverty, ill health, family instability, and neglect had taken their toll on so many children long before their first day of kindergarten. The tight correlation between socioeconomic status and academic performance had been documented in James Coleman's massive 1966 study, *Equality of Educational Opportunity*, and confirmed again and again since then. Other baleful influences lay in the culture at large: the rise of the electronic media, the distractions of the consumer culture, the low regard for learning and for teachers. And there was, of course, a staggering literature detailing the shortcomings of the schools themselves—the loss of authority and sense of shared purpose, poor teacher training, bureaucratic gridlock, reactionary pedagogy, lack of parental involvement, shortage of funds, and above all the decline of "the basics."

One of the most compelling, and widely shared, explanations for the decline of standards was the eclipse of a rigorous curriculum. Students simply weren't taking academic courses anymore. Progressive critics such as Theodore Sizer noted that schools had become so diffuse in their functions that they had lost sight of their academic core. Conservatives, including the authors of the Reagan era report, *A Nation at Risk*, complained of an indolent national culture that let students off too easily. The authors, in fact, borrowed from Sizer and others the phrase "cafeteria-style curriculum" to describe the consequences of the sixties' assault on traditional pedagogy.

A Nation at Risk, with its tone of cold war alarmism, gave the argument for a rigorous high school curriculum a bad name. "If an unfriendly foreign power had attempted to impose on America the mediocre educational performance that exists today," the authors memorably claimed, "we might well have viewed it as an act of war." The truth actually *was* alarming. In 1982, the year before the report appeared, 12 percent of high school seniors had taken trigonometry and 5 percent had taken calculus; 14 percent had taken physics, and 31 percent, chemistry. Among minority students the figures were, predictably, much lower. Six percent of black graduates had taken trigonometry; 7 percent had taken physics. The following year Diane Ravitch wrote that "all French adolescents receive an education by the age of 15 or 16 that is the equivalent of what the American student covers by the end of the sophomore year in college." And it was certainly true that the American curriculum was incredibly undemanding by European standards, at least for the ordinary student.

The situation in New York City was even more extreme. The best students, who attended one of the few selective schools, received the equivalent of a high-quality prep school education. But the great mass of students were drifting through, as Che or Simeon had done. A 1990 study found that 45 percent of the students who had graduated the year before had not passed the state Regents exam, signifying proficiency, even in ninth-grade math. Only a quarter of graduating seniors earned a Regents diploma, a number that dropped still lower when GED recipients were included. At many of the schools in Manhattan and the Bronx that served as feeder institutions to City, 5 percent of students, or fewer, graduated with a Regents diploma.

The rest of the students opted for the general rather than the academic track. It was a dirty little secret, in fact, that the schools were tracked at all, since officially the practice had been abandoned as inegalitarian. Students who opted for the general track normally took what were known as modified courses. These included English courses with no serious reading or writing, social studies courses pared down to vague "concepts," math courses with no real math, and so on. Students like Mario had taken Consumer Math and Business Math, but never so much as geometry, and sometimes not even algebra. In the old tracking system it had been assumed that most students weren't going to college; they received a commercial or preparatory degree, scarcely even seeing the academic elite except in shop and gym. In the new, unofficial, equal-opportunity tracking system, the great mass of students received a degree that would get them into college, but an education that would leave them deeply unprepared.

The New York City comptroller's office took the measure of that failure in a 1992 report titled *Prepared for Disappointment*. The study found that three-quarters of the 10,000 New York public high school graduates entering CUNY had failed at least one of the three skills assessment tests governing college placement. (The numbers became slightly lower when only senior college entrants were counted.) "The findings are made more distressing," the report's authors observed, "when standards for passing CUNY's entrance exams are examined." Those standards had been pitched at a tenth- or eleventh-grade level.

In September 1990 a new chancellor, Ann Reynolds, was installed at CUNY headquarters on East 80th Street. In her previous job, as chancellor of the California State University system, Reynolds had gained a national reputation by working to upgrade the academic standards of entering freshmen; and on her second day in office she announced that she would institute in CUNY the program she developed in California, known as the College Preparatory Initiative. The CPI, as it became known, stipulated that as of the 1993 school year freshmen arriving at senior college would be expected to have completed 11 academic courses; community college students would be expected to arrive with 9 such credits. These figures would rise over the next eight years until all incoming students would be expected to have completed 16 academic credits.

Thus by the year 2001 students would be expected to enter CUNY with the kind of academic preparation that they had had in the days before open admissions. Business Math would not be good enough. Students would have to have taken three semesters of sequential math, as well as two lab sciences, which was one more than the great majority of high school graduates were now taking. They were also to have earned 4 academic credits in English and social studies, and 1 in the fine arts. It wasn't quite clear what effect these requirements would have, since there was no precise equivalent of Business Math in the humanities. The CUNY administration had, however, established a very ambitious set of competencies to serve as standards for academic courses in the various disciplines.

In the spring of 1992 the new initiative was circulated throughout the CUNY system, where it met with cries of outrage from students and faculty. A group calling itself the CUNY Coalition of Concerned Faculty and Staff issued a statement arguing that "implementation of the CPI will have profound negative impact on access, particularly for students attending ghetto schools." The coalition went so far as to allege that "the CPI will return CUNY to the days of segregated campuses." Half the members of the coalition taught at City, which remained the prime keeper of the open admissions flame, and in early May the group called a press conference in the NAC building to publicize its sense of betrayal. Unfortunately, I was the only journalist who showed up, though I was told that after I left a reporter from the militant black radio station WLIB arrived. I gathered up some literature and was introduced to Walter Daum, a mathematician I had seen handing out Socialist Worker literature on campus. Daum was an owlish man with flyaway hair and thick

glasses—a born mathematician—and for the last several years he had
directed City's remedial math program. We agreed to meet again later.

It turned out that Daum was not at all happy with his job.
"When they asked me to take over the program," he explained, "I
said that I would, but only under one condition: that I could make
it clear that I thought that the whole idea was a fraud. We try to
do one year of high school math in three and a half months. It's obviously impossible. The only part we can teach successfully is the
rote material." This depressing experience had led Daum to conclude
that the CPI was similarly doomed to failure. The high schools, he
said, just couldn't do it. There weren't enough qualified math
teachers, there wasn't enough money. The high schools had to be
changed fundamentally, and that wouldn't happen by decree. And
so the students with the weakest background—minority students,
above all—would arrive at college without the required academic
courses, and would have to do even more remedial work than they
did now. Or they wouldn't make it to the senior colleges at all, and
CUNY would return to "the days of segregated campuses."

The odd thing about Daum's argument was that his view of
remediation was much closer to Rudi Gedamke's than to Mina
Shaughnessy's. He had concluded, he said, that remedial math
worked well enough for students who were going on to the liberal
arts and so needed only a course or two, perhaps a refresher, but was
a failure with students who wanted to go on to engineering, which
was a good part of the student body. It was fanciful to think that
students could come to college with virtually no background in math,
and then learn geometry, trig, precalculus, and calculus, and move
on to the deeper waters of physics and engineering; it just didn't
happen. But as a devout socialist Daum believed that the problem
could be solved with money; and as a good radical, he considered
outright failure preferable to letting an unjust system legitimate itself
through half-assed reform.

"In that case," I asked, "what should be done?"

"There's nothing that we *can* do," said Daum, with what seemed
like stunning nonchalance. "There's no ideal."

"And if there's no ideal, then it's better to keep doing what
you're doing now?"

"It's better to keep doing what we're doing." Daum did not flinch from the despairing logic of his own argument. I had to admire his candor.

The alternative argument against efforts to raise standards was that the "literacy crisis" was a giant hoax fostered by the Right in order to exclude minorities from the fruits of education. This line was often repeated in the scholarly journals of composition and rhetoric instruction, and was usually accompanied by ritual denunciations of "the deficit model." One beleaguered dissenter, Donald Lazere, rehearsed all of his progressive credentials before timidly observing that "my own experience and that of most other teachers I know is that there is [a literacy crisis] and that it has been detrimental to all social groups except the most privileged." The progressive position, in other words, was to confront the remedial problem, not repudiate it. Lazere argued for "a restored emphasis on basic skills and knowledge" in the high schools.

Daum and the others had too strong a sense of reality to deny the problem; it was the solution, they insisted, that was a hoax fostered to exclude minority students from higher education. There was one overwhelming problem with this theory: the CPI was not mandatory. Students who had not chalked up the minimum credits in high school were not to be barred from entering college, but rather would have to take makeup courses, or otherwise demonstrate their competence, once they got there. The CPI was an exhortation masquerading as a demand; it had no "or else." And this was no accident. Ann Reynolds understood that the open admissions commitment was sacrosanct; no measure that might have had the effect of limiting access to CUNY could be expected to survive public scrutiny. In the very first line of the resolution authorizing the CPI, the CUNY Board of Trustees reaffirmed the commitment to offer every public school graduate a place in a CUNY college.

The claim that the CPI was a blow against access was a canard. The underlying truth was that open admissions had taken on such transcendent status that any attempt to raise standards was seen, at least in some quarters, as a retreat from egalitarianism. Standards were necessarily the enemy of access. Of course this couldn't be said explicitly, so the critics focused on the impracticability of the plan.

They pointed out, for example, that the high schools simply didn't have enough qualified teachers to offer real math courses. And it was true that accredited math teachers were in short supply. But according to Ronald Berkman, a CUNY dean who was responsible for the CPI, "the demand is so slack in academic math courses that you could probably double the number right now without stressing the math faculty." The greatest problem lay with the culture of the schools. Their overwhelming imperative was to graduate students, come what may—a response in which cynicism and despair were mingled with sympathy for the terrible problems with which the kids were burdened. That was why the new tracking system had developed, and why students like Renato and Margaret had graduated from high school in a state of virtual illiteracy.

And so the real question posed by the CPI was this: Could the culture of mediocrity, of low expectations, of mere survival, that flourished in the public schools be changed? And could it be changed by an exhortation from above? Ann Reynolds, a figure of boundless self-confidence, insisted that it could. Students would conclude that it was easier to take academic courses in high school than makeup classes in college, as they had in California. Between 1982 and 1987 the number of California public high school students taking algebra, geometry, calculus, biology, chemistry, and physics had increased by an average of about 20 percent. The program had, in fact, become mandatory after eleven years, at which point so many students had taken the required courses that the issue of exclusion became essentially moot. But Cal State was not CUNY. Most of the campuses were located far from the inner city, and the demographics of the system were more like SUNY than CUNY—white and middle class. Minority students tended to be heavily concentrated in the separate community college system, where the new standards did not apply, and few of them transferred into the senior colleges. CUNY represented a more radical experiment in social reform and social mobility than did Cal State. The CPI thus would have to accomplish greater miracles in New York City than it had in California.

For the last several years the New York City public schools had been trying to raise standards, as had school systems around the country. All students were now required to take at least one year of sequential math. Could this momentum be sustained? Would the schools now teach rigorous courses where they hadn't before, and would they demand that students actually take them? Joseph Fernandez, the schools chancellor who had initiated the change, had been forced out of office over issues that had very little to do with education, as had several of his predecessors. The schools, in fact, seemed almost incapable of self-governance or self-reform. The public schools *had* to turn out better-prepared graduates; but could they?

The CPI had struck to the heart of the problem of open admissions. What did it mean to offer a college education to all high school students when many of those students hadn't received a high school education—in some cases not even the rudiments of such an education? And this was hardly a problem confined to CUNY, or to inner-city schools. Over half of entering students at the nation's two-year colleges read at an eighth-grade level or below. Slightly over half of the nation's high school graduates enroll in college (two-thirds of them in four-year institutions), yet an equal fraction cannot pick out a simple theme from a brief passage. The premise of the CPI, which Reynolds had been courageous enough to admit, was that colleges could not be expected to give students a secondary as well as a higher education. Open admissions could not work so long as the public schools routinely turned out, in Rudi Gedamke's phrase, "damaged" students.

The CPI was an honest attempt to repair that damage. The hidden premise of much criticism of the initiative was that high school students *couldn't* rise to a higher standard—a strange view for people who believed devoutly in the open admissions ideal. It could be argued that the damage started so early in life that high school was already too late, just as Rudi felt that college was too late. Clearly, school reform had to begin in the earliest grades; but CUNY could exercise no control prior to the level of the high school graduate. Moreover, the high schools had a great deal more room for improvement, in terms of standards, than did City College.

The real limiting factor of the CPI was its voluntary character. The credit requirements probably should have been mandatory, at least for admission to the senior colleges; but they weren't, because that would have made admission much more difficult. Especially in the ghetto schools that City drew from, large numbers of students might have been disqualified. The schools might not have been able to offer courses that would pass muster. The students might not have done well enough to preserve the 80 average that guaranteed senior college admission. CUNY really would be doing what the Coalition of Concerned Faculty and Staff had accused it of doing. Students— many of them black and Latino—would have had to make up their academic deficiencies in community college or elsewhere. But would that have been unfair? What scarcely anyone inside the system was willing to say was that the right to an education for which one was hopelessly unprepared was not much of a right at all.

10

Here We Come, Ready or Not

One day in the middle of the fall term I dropped in on Gloria Silverstein's ESL 20/30 class. Silverstein had placed twelve of her seventeen ESL 10 students in this special accelerated class. Four hadn't been able to attend. The eight who remained were joined by a roughly equal group of students who had been placed directly in the class on entering City. In addition to this course, which focused on writing, they were taking a reading course and a speech course—a total of thirteen hours of ESL classes per week. It was a heavier load than they had had over the summer, especially since most of them were taking a math course and one or two other courses as well. For the reading course, ESL 21, they were required to read four books, including *The Right Stuff* and *The Double Helix*, both of which the students found very tough sledding.

I was again struck by the atmosphere in the class, which would have made a perfect advertisement for the virtues of immigration. The students were well dressed, respectful, good natured; they joked with each other, helped each other, knew one another's names. Their problems, of course, hadn't vanished since the summer. Hammeed, of the explosive stammer, still could barely read aloud, though at least he was exercising some impulse control; his outbursts were much less frequent than they had been. Gloraida, who had spent years in New York and had picked up some of the worst habits of the school system, was still waltzing in late. Ericson, a Haitian student who hid his shyness and self-doubt behind a brilliant smile, still trembled whenever he was called on.

When I talked to Silverstein a few weeks later, she was projecting a high casualty rate for the class—a tone I hadn't heard from her before. Gloraida wasn't serious enough, and Ericson, she said, "seems trapped between two languages, though he's certainly trying hard." She also worried that Jean, another Haitian, was "falling through the cracks." Jean, tall and handsome and boyishly charming, was working at McDonald's three nights a week and wasn't doing his homework. Jean had finally won a protracted struggle to qualify for financial aid, but it hadn't been enough to cover tuition, books, and transportation, much less the meager cost of surviving from day to day. He was earning $4.70 an hour and taking home a grand total of $50 a week. The rent on his portion of an apartment in the projects in central Brooklyn was $150.

And yet by the end of the term everything had somehow come right. Silverstein had arranged twice-weekly tutoring sessions in writing for Hammeed, Ericson, Jean, and two other students. "I was convinced that none of them would make it," Silverstein said. "And I saw unbelievable changes, literally in the space of a week and a half." And the changes were not all academic. Jean had moved in with his mother and stepfather, quit his job, and started handing in his homework. Hammeed had befriended another Arab student who had proved to be a stabilizing influence. "His behavior has changed completely," said Silverstein, "and his writing is getting better."

For her final, Silverstein handed out a chapter on poverty from a sociology text, *Social Problems*, by Robert H. Lauer. The text was quite straightforward, but it included graphs and charts, and made some fairly sophisticated arguments about the origins and effects of poverty. The students had the chapter well in advance of the final, which consisted of five questions; they were to answer one question in a 500-word essay. Apparently the tutoring sessions had been well worth the effort. When I had last read Hammeed's work, at the end of the summer, he had cleaned up his random spelling, but his writing was only barely comprehensible. Now he began his essay by writing, "According to the Lauer article, there are myths which diminish the dignity of the poor. Discrimination against the poor by the nonpoor leads to contempt of the poor and attacks their pride as human beings. The nonpoor disparage the poor with many myths such as the poor are lazy, people on welfare have it good, welfare is draining us." After only his first full semester at City, he had gained a grasp of English syntax, as well as some command of academic language. "There is no evidence to support the notion that poverty is caused by laziness," Hammeed wrote.

All of the others wrote more clearly and comfortably than they had even at the end of the summer. Hyunsun Bang, the Korean student, wrote about as crisply as Hammeed, and made a more or less equal number of wrong choices in language and punctuation. The others still had serious problems, and not merely in surface matters. Servio's sentences were very simple, and after making one or two observations he essentially repeated himself. Ericson never answered any one question, and his writing sometimes wandered off aimlessly. "In one word," Ericson wrote, "in America they talk about poverty as a comparison between people who are better off or less well off than others. Americans think this way they can have a better life than now, so that poverty will become extinct and not ravage society by causing complex and enormous problems." Jean's writing was equally hard to follow, digressive, and in some cases simply confused. And Gloraida, the one student who had begun the summer speaking English more or less fluently, had made almost no progress at all.

Nevertheless, fifteen of the eighteen students passed the exam. Because the exams had been graded by other ESL teachers, the students' remarkable achievement couldn't be chalked up to Silverstein's enthusiasm. She had culled the better students from her ESL 10 class, and handpicked the others, producing something of an ESL elite. On balance, they were an even more impressive group than the ESL 10 class had been, in part because the new students, who had placed directly into the class, had better language skills, and possibly a stronger academic background, than the original class. Most of these students were ready to succeed academically; but I wasn't convinced that their language skills were equal to the demands of college. Some of them had been speaking, reading, and writing English, or at least school English, for six months. Most of them spoke virtually no English once they left the campus. When I walked up to Ericson in the cafeteria, his smile vanished and his lips started to quake; the very thought of having to switch from Creole to English filled him with anxiety and all but paralyzed his tongue.

Students graduating from English 2 or ESL 30 traditionally had been required to pass the writing assessment test in order to be admitted to English 110. But the writing skills required to exit the ESL sequence were way short of those needed to satisfy the requirements of the exam. In 1991 the average ESL student who passed the exam at all—many did not—required two and a half tries. The figure was down from four and a half tries eight years earlier, but it was still a source of tremendous frustration to the students, who had been led to believe that they had attained some sort of proficiency in written English. The ESL faculty felt strongly that the test itself was unfair. And so rather than ensure that students were not leaving ESL 30 without the writing skills required to pass the SKAT test, the test was abandoned as a prerequisite; now Ericson and Jean and Servio would be able to advance directly to freshman composition, though none of them had passed the writing test (which they would have to do at some point later).

If the writing test had, in fact, failed to capture the ESL students' real ability, presumably they would prove it by their performance in their regular writing class. But freshman composition, like the writing test, assumed a level of competency that few of these students had attained. By 1991 three-quarters of the ESL students who began at the bottom of the ladder were completing the sequence without failing a single course, a testimony, apparently, to the success of the whole-language approach. But only 6 percent of the students were passing all three courses and freshman composition as well. (It was likely that a larger, perhaps much larger, fraction of students who began higher up on the ESL ladder were passing the writing course.) These students were reaching the regular curriculum and then falling off a cliff. Did that mean that freshman composition, too, was taking an unfair sounding of their abilities? Or that even the improvements wrought by the new pedagogy (the 1983 figure had been 2 percent) were scarcely enough to make students who arrived at City with little English minimally competent writers by the standards of the English Department?

Gloria Silverstein had not promoted her students with the same sense of hope-against-hope with which Rudi passed Che and Andrew and Cantina; they had upheld their end of the bargain by working hard and making impressive progress. But was that enough?

I also tried to keep up with the students from the language arts class, who had now scattered across the remedial program. The student I most wanted to see was Sabour Clarke, the Michael Jordan lookalike with the dead-level gaze. One day in late October I visited Sabour in his English 1 class. The class was discussing an essay by the historian William Manchester on the savage battle for Okinawa. "What does Manchester say?" asked the teacher, Ann Tabachnikov. And Sabour, to my surprise, was the first to speak. He seemed to be making a conscious effort to use academic diction. "William Manchester talked about the experience he had on the beach of Okinawa," said Sabour in his soft, sleepy voice. "It was a really major battle. It was one of the worst battles of the war.... That's as far as I can go." It wasn't very far; but it was at least as far as anyone else in the class was prepared to go.

Most students in the class spoke in monosyllables, filling in the blanks at the tail of leading questions—a skill they had perfected · in high school. When Tabachnikov asked open-ended questions, she rarely received an answer. Sabour, however, spoke up often, and in more or less complete sentences. Sometimes he stated the obvious, and sometimes he was wrong; but he was curious, and he made connections. He understood, for example, that Manchester was placing the Japanese soldiers on an equal moral footing with the Americans. Tabachnikov gave the class ten minutes to think of an essay topic. Most of the students offered such cryptic suggestions as "I would explain myself like he did." A number of students hit on an easy way out, saying they would summarize the story, or their feelings, or some other thing. When Tabachnikov came to Sabour, he said, "I'd like to explain how would you feel if you killed someone in hand-to-hand combat."

Sabour showed me the final draft of his typewritten 400-word essay; he was obviously proud of his performance. "War, it not what the literature in the history books makes it out to be," the essay began. "War is a harsh, fierce and deadly action that a country may engage in. When two countries engage in war for a single purpose; they send there soldiers to protect there countries rights." Sabour then talked about "the gore of battle," as Manchester had described it. "In contrast to hand to hand combat," he wrote, "modern technology has taken war out of context." Sabour's real topic was the way what he called "technical weapons" disguise the horrors of war. Either way, he concluded, "War commits none other than 'Genocide.' " This was a far cry from the cartoonlike gangster story he had written for Frye.

Sabour was making a conscious effort to turn himself into a college student, and he took enough responsibility for his work to try to revise it. Tabachnikov had written on the bottom of his paper, "This is *radically* improved over the previous drafts." Sabour cared about academic form; he had also compiled a lengthy, and accurate, bibliography for another of his classes. At the same time, he had started his career at City College even lower on the remedial ladder than Tammy. His written language was far more flawed than hers had been at the outset; his thoughts were very simple and clichéd. Unlike the better ESL students, Sabour needed not only a new means to express himself but something more to express. It was hard to imagine him reaching the top of the scale that Marilyn Sternglass used to measure writing growth. But it was not quite as hard to im- agine Sabour graduating. I think he would have scored high on the cluster of affective variables.

I wish that I could have said the same for many of the others from Frye's class whom I spent time with in the fall. Six of them had been placed into a new program of "linked classes," in which the same group of students move together from class to class, as in high school. The idea was that their teachers would be able to help them more by virtue of working together, and that they would enjoy the familiarity, and benefit from the ego support, of their classmates.

The students traveled together from College Skills 1 to Freshman Orientation to Social Science, a course that offered a once-over-lightly tour of the field.

A month or so into the semester I visited the Social Science class, which was working its way through psychology. When I arrived, the students were milling around in the hallway, hoping the teacher, Arsenio Martinez, known as Pete, wouldn't show up. Once class began, Jenny, Paula, and Julissa, who had been an inseparable threesome over the summer, whispered back and forth, keeping their notebooks open to feign engagement. Jane, the only black student of the six, sat by herself, silent and almost rigid. Monet, a Puerto Rican girl who had sat through Frye's class with an air of smoldering resentment, sat in the back, bickering and giggling with Renato. I felt that I had returned to the almost adolescent world I had seen over the summer.

Martinez was reviewing material from the last class. "What do we call the ability to feel other people's emotions?" he asked.

"Isn't it 'primary group'?" That was Renato, still entertaining the class with wild guesses. Martinez asked Monet to take a stab at it, but when Monet turned to the part of her notebook where she thought the answer might be, she couldn't read her notes. Martinez gave the answer and plowed ahead. "What is 'the generalized other'?"

"Isn't it a repetition?" tried Renato. Martinez rolled his eyes. And so the class went on, Martinez running through a stack of abstract terms, the class mostly sitting in silence. Sometimes a student would make a grammatical error in the course of an answer, and Martinez would counter with a prim correction. He wrote a few basic terms from social science on the blackboard—*impartial, arbitrary, simultaneous, serial*. No one seemed to know them. He used the word *discreet* and drew a blank. He asked Jenny if she knew the word. No. Paula? Silence. Then Monet piped up with a crisp definition. But for the most part Monet kept her usual sullen silence.

Later I ran into Jenny/Paula/Julissa. I asked them if they felt they were getting anything out of the class. Jenny said no, and laughed. Paula said no, and clucked with embarrassment. And Julissa, by far the best student of the three—it was she who had coined the word *belumptious*—said, "Maybe it will help me decide on my major."

Martinez had just finished grading the last test, on which he had asked the students to define a list of terms in a few sentences and one brief paragraph. The average score had been 48. Julissa had gotten a 70, Renato a 40, the others in the 20s. Martinez, unlike Rudi Gedamke, felt that he should be teaching an academic subject—his field was Persian history—rather than remediation; he was a bitter man, and he took a thoroughly unvarnished view of his students' prospects. "Anyone who passed the test is going to do okay," he said. "The low fails are not going to make it. They have attitude problems and cognitive problems that they're just not going to be able to overcome. The ones in the middle may survive, but you don't know what's going to happen once they leave the SEEK classes."

As the term wore on, the test scores rose slightly, though the atmosphere of the class remained the same. Martinez apparently had shocked the students into reading the textbook before exams. He and the other two teachers in the linked program had decided, as Martinez put it, "to scare the bejeesus out of them at first, and then make it easy for them to have the perception that they were doing well. We would alternate between trying to boost them up and giving them sermons. And then the idea was that at the end of the semester we would really challenge them." The improving test scores had given them some hope. And so on his final, Martinez asked the class to study eight or nine chapters, rather than two, of the turgid Social Science text. And the scores plummeted back to their early-semester level. Only if you peered very closely could you discern signs of growth in most of the students.

In the end, Martinez gave Julissa an A minus for the class. Monet had broken her leg falling down the stairs earlier in the term and withdrawn from school rather than hop from class to class. The others had flunked the final and their grades had averaged in the 30s and 40s, but Martinez passed them anyway, with D's or D minuses. He had, in fact, found a reason to pass everyone in the class, as had his two colleagues. Neither Renato nor Jane nor Jenny nor Paula had heeded the dire warnings Charles Frye had issued over the summer, but they had survived January clearance nonetheless. Even Renato, who had driven his teachers to distraction, would be back. "I want to give Renato a chance to be in the group," Martinez said. "I think even if he doesn't graduate from City College he has a chance to be a better person, to be better socialized."

Here was a new minimum threshold for promotion—it might make you more mature. This was a particularly flimsy sounding rationale coming from Martinez, who took such a dim view of his students' prospects. Silverstein may have been too ready to believe in her students' development, but she considered them good learners, and with reason. Martinez thought that most of his students didn't belong at City College; then again, he said, neither did most of the students in his World Civ class. Promoting them all was an act of surrender, a throwing up of hands—the sort of thing that Rudi Gedamke sometimes railed against. Underneath the putative hope for improvement was a very different kind of logic: it wouldn't do them any good to repeat the class, so why not send them on their way? And that rationale was not easy to challenge. What good would it do Paula or Jane to take the same classes again? It might well be a devastating blow to their ego, and to their hopes, as Rudi felt that dropping out often was. Promoting them wouldn't help either, but at least they could stay with their friends. And that might help them become better socialized.

This was, of course, the same logic that had allowed these students to be waved through high school in the first place—the same combination of compassion and futility. And what made matters more complicated was that City College had chosen to educate precisely such students as these. By the logic of open admissions, the failure of the students implied a failure of the institution. Or, alternatively, it called the remedial ideal itself into question. And even people like Martinez, who scarcely believed in the ideal, were reluctant to act on their convictions. And so, unless you were as conscience ridden as Rudi was, it was better to pass everyone and then let nature take its course. Up in the regular curriculum they would be hopelessly out of their depth, and they would be felled by frustration, self-doubt, poor grades, insufficient credits, and all the daily ills that came their way. But it wouldn't happen on your watch.

11

At the Barricade of Standards

If it's critical for high schools to adopt a culture of high standards and high expectations, surely the same must be true at a place like City College, which has set itself the task of raising students up to the level required for a college education. City's vivid memory of its own past, and the high caliber of much of its faculty, ensures that those standards will not be abandoned. But the promise not only to admit but to transform woefully undereducated students presses City to kneel down rather than to lift up. Unlike the contradiction between the old meritocratic ideal and the new egalitarian, affirmative action one—which was solved, for better or for worse, by the open admissions policy—City has to deal every day with the conflict between rigorous standards and the students' continuing academic problems. There's no perfect solution to this problem—any more than there is to the admissions problem—merely a continual set of adjustments that try to reconcile these ideals or favor one at the expense of the other. When they hand out grades, and give or withhold promotion, teachers are inescapably confronted with this dilemma. But grading and promotion are personal choices. The issue of standardized testing has brought the student's "right" to continue the

191

education to which he or she has been granted access most nakedly into conflict with the college's commitment to an academic ideal.

The assessment tests, in reading, writing, and mathematics, are themselves an artifact of the struggle over standards. The tests were instituted following a decision by the CUNY Board of Trustees in 1976 that students were being advanced through the system too easily by colleges desperate to show that open admissions was working. The tests were originally designed as "junior year-rising" measures, to ensure that upperclassmen had attained proficiency in the various subjects. Over the years, though, the colleges came to use them as devices to sort incoming students into remedial courses, and sometimes to stand as gateways between the remedial and nonremedial programs. Thus at City College the only way that students in remedial English, or in the upper-level ESL class, could advance to freshman composition and the core curriculum was by passing the writing assessment test. And with some exceptions students could exit from the ESL reading class only by passing the reading test. Prospective majors in architecture or engineering who failed the math test could not begin their professional training until they had completed a sequence of remedial math courses.

The tests had all sorts of problems. They were used for too many different purposes. They created an obsessive pass-rate mentality among teachers. They served as prerequisites for courses or fields that didn't really require them. They measured specialized skills rather than general ability. But the real problem with the tests was that many students couldn't pass them, even *after* remedial work. A 1990 study at City College found that, over a four-semester period, 58 percent of College Skills 2 students and 62 percent of ESL 21 students failed the reading test, while 40 percent of English 2 students and 51 percent of ESL 30 students failed the writing test. The study took comfort from the fact that test groups of nonremedial students failed the exams at almost the same rate; but this could have meant either that the test groups weren't taking the exams very seriously, or that they, too, needed help.

In early 1990 a CUNY research official named Howard Everson published a report suggesting that many students were failing the reading test because they weren't being given enough time to finish it. Everson had administered the reading test in both its standard thirty-minute format and in an identical forty-five-minute version to 1,360 freshmen at nine CUNY colleges. He found that less than three-quarters of students were able to complete the test in thirty minutes, but virtually all finished it with fifteen extra minutes. Pass rates rose astronomically—from 28 percent to 55 percent of the sample, in one version of the test. Everson concluded that the test was "misclassifying" 15 to 25 percent of the students. "Apparently," he wrote, "many of our students do not complete the test simply because they run out of time and not because they run out of ability."

Everson's report arrived at a propitious moment for a group of ESL teachers and administrators who had joined together two years earlier to form the Language Forum. The group was concerned with the fate of CUNY's foreign-language students, who were swiftly replacing African American and Puerto Rican students as CUNY's largest bloc. ESL students had become CUNY's new disadvantaged minority. They suffered from an overwhelming attrition rate: no more than half survived their first year in a four-year college. The Language Forum, along with another group called the ESL Council, lobbied for programs that would improve retention among second-language students and speed their progress out of the remedial and into the regular curriculum. And when the Everson report began to circulate, the Language Forum seized on it as proof that the reading test was condemning ESL students to the remedial underworld simply because they read slowly. ESL teachers and administrators began to lobby CUNY officials to have the reading test lengthened. Edith Everett, a member of CUNY's Board of Trustees who served as a sponsor of the Language Forum, took the case to other board members and officials in the chancellor's office.

The university officials responsible for freshman assessment were strongly opposed to anything that smacked of lowering standards. Until the Everson study, in fact, the principal concern about the reading test was that students were laying their hands on it in advance, especially ESL students, who tended to pool their work. The scores, in other words, were *too high*. "The reading test measured minimal competence, and the stress is on the word *minimal*," says Harvey Weiner, then the university dean for academic affairs.

The test was already pitched at a tenth- or eleventh-grade level. It consisted of fifteen brief passages, each followed by three multiple-choice questions. A typical passage (this from a practice test) read: "Everybody's always referring to America as *the* melting pot, but our ethnic mixture pales in comparison to that of Zaire. This young African nation, four times the size of Texas, is populated by more than 250 distinct ethnic groups who converse in not only five official languages—Linsala, Swahili, Kokonso, Tshiluba, and French—but several hundred dialects."

The questions consisted of statements to be completed: "The main point of the paragraph is that...," "The population of Zaire is...," and "Zaire is called a melting pot because...." The first question required the reader to distinguish between a detail and a generalization: the right answer was "America is not the best example of a melting pot," while one of the wrong answers was "Zaire has more than 250 ethnic groups." The second question contained the tiny wrinkle of asking the reader to identify what wasn't there: the correct answer was "not specified in the paragraph."

Weiner didn't think it was too much to expect a college student to answer slightly less than two-thirds of such questions correctly in half an hour. "The standard," he says, "was, 'We have some confidence that you will be able to survive in a college environment.'" While he took seriously Everson's claim that the test was "speeded," Weiner, like Rudi Gedamke and many reading specialists, considered reading rate an important aspect of reading ability, not an independent variable. "Every reading situation has within it a temporal element," says Weiner. Everson had not, in fact, found that ESL students suffered more than others from the time limits on the test, though they did less well than English-language students. He had found that black and Hispanic students gained more from the added time than white students who were, on average, more proficient readers.

The real problem, Weiner felt, was the very nature of the remedial process. "Students were not showing dramatic enough progress in reading comprehension," he says. "It wasn't particularly shocking, but it was a matter full of despair for students and teachers. The teachers felt that they were doing a good job of teaching and that the students should be progressing, and that if they weren't, the fault must lie with the test." Weiner was "a true son of Mina," as he puts it, a Ph.D. in Renaissance literature who became a convert to Shaughnessy's faith, an author of several books on composition; but his commitment to remedial teaching did not dispose him to minimize its difficulty. "Mina understood that problem very well," he says. "She knew that you can have progress, but it's a matter of time and an enormous amount of effort. Reading is the slowest skill to show improvement; and one semester of College Skills is not going to make that much of a difference."

Everett looked at the problem differently. "I believe very much in high standards," she says. "On the other hand, we have to look at this university. People are different, times are different, needs are different. We have a very large immigrant group, in the city and coming in to the university. We need to educate them. Many of these students come to school very motivated—that's a big leg up. You may have quite a bright young person but he simply can't read that fast. Are you going to give him a few extra minutes, or is that a real reason to prevent him from going on with his work? Why would you want to have him postpone his life indefinitely?"

Everett saw herself as the champion of a new kind of student— the motivated, well-trained immigrant, eager to get ahead and lacking only fluency in English to do so. She was thinking, in short, of students like those in Gloria Silverstein's class. This was a group within a group, and it wasn't clear how many of them were being held back in the way ESL lobbyists described. Everett distinguished, at least in her own mind, between these students and those who arrived at CUNY with a real academic or cognitive deficit, though she may have been inclined to inflate the size of the first group and minimize the size of the latter. She says, "We have to see who needs what kind of help, and also be honest with those who aren't going to make it."

The Language Forum, however, took the position of the academic Left. "Arguments predicated on the notion of deficits do not impress them," they wrote of themselves in a paper advocating the extension of the reading test and other reforms. The motivated, well-trained immigrant was not a subgroup of students but an archetype of all students. All students arrived at CUNY with a mix of strengths and needs; and if some students were failing to advance and drop-

ping out, it was not because remediation hadn't been able to cure
their weaknesses but because CUNY hadn't bothered to capitalize
on their strengths. Eric Nadelstern, the chairman of the Language
Forum, says, "If you look at the 50 percent freshman retention rate
in CUNY, if you look at the graduation rate, then it's clear that we
have to rethink the structure of the university." Far from erecting such
barriers as the assessment tests, Nadelstern and other ESL activists
hoped to transform instructional method so that students who placed
into ESL or College Skills or remedial English could take credit-
bearing courses and move into the mainstream of the college as soon
as they arrived.

Just as this debate over assessment and remediation was heat-
ing up, in mid-1990, a report titled *The Condition of Latinos in The
City University of New York* was published under the imprimatur of
CUNY's vice chancellor for academic affairs—Harvey Weiner's boss.
The report had been written by Ricardo Otheguy, a specialist in bi-
lingual education at City College. Otheguy posed the same questions
that the ESL groups had, only specifically with reference to Hispanic
students. Why were they failing the SKAT tests in such large numbers? Why were they dropping out at a higher rate than any other
ethnic or racial group? Some part of the problem, Otheguy acknowledged, could be traced to such "social and economic factors" as the
need to hold a full-time job. "But to a considerable extent," he concluded, the problem was of CUNY's own making. Otheguy blamed
the asessment tests for stigmatizing Latino students and stranding
them in the remedial backwater. He made explicit the idea, often
buried in the debate over standards, that students had a right to be
promoted. CUNY, he said, was violating that right: "Open admission into an ESL program, if it does not lead to entry into significant,
credit-bearing content activities within a reasonable time for reasonable numbers of students, is not open admission." Otheguy thus absolved ESL students of the obligation to perform well enough to gain
access to the regular curriculum.

Because Otheguy, like the Language Forum, did not accept the
notion of deficits, he found the high rate of failure on the assessment tests inherently suspicious. CUNY, he pointed out, had never
proved that the tests measured general ability, or that they predicted

later performance in the subjects they were designed to assess. Thus, Otheguy concluded, the test results were "arbitrary" in regard to actual skills levels. He suggested that they were measuring not the ability to read or write but the ability to reproduce information in a culturally acceptable way. Otheguy relied on Everson's findings to argue that the reading test discriminated against second-language students, and thus against Latinos. The tests might thus be sorting students not according to ability but according to race and ethnicity, and thus driving minority students into an academic cul-de-sac. Studies had shown that the more assessment tests a student failed, the likelier that student was to drop out. The conventional explanation, Otheguy noted, was that "the same underpreparation that prevents students from passing the tests later makes it impossible for them to succeed in college." But that was an explanation from deficits. Otheguy suggested that the problem lay not with the causes but the effects of failing the tests—the sense of demoralization, the despair that comes of being marooned in remediation.

Otheguy pointed out many serious flaws in CUNY's system of testing and sorting incoming students. But his single-minded insistence on lifting the taint of remediation, of "deficit," from Latino students compelled him to ignore the obvious and to distort some of the research findings that he cited. The reading test was not, in fact, discriminating against ESL students any more than against other slow readers. The fact that the tests had flaws, even serious ones, scarcely made the results arbitrary. They clearly were, in fact, measuring the kind of underpreparation that led to academic problems in college. Latino students were failing the tests, and dropping out of CUNY, because so many of them suffered from academic problems *and* language problems—and economic and psychological problems as well. A CUNY report published in 1989 concluded, "Blacks and Hispanics are more likely than whites to come from low-income families, enter college with poor high school grades, complete fewer units of academic course work and pass fewer skills tests on entry to the university. . . . Each of these characteristics is associated with persistence and retention."

The Otheguy report, which appeared to be an official document from the vice chancellor's office though in fact it reflected only

Otheguy's own view, had a major impact both on the debate over the reading test and on the larger debate over testing and remediation. It galvanized many ESL teachers; it provided plausible-sounding arguments to those who were already convinced. Pressed to respond to Otheguy's arguments, CUNY chancellor Ann Reynolds impaneled a Committee on the Freshman Year, which ultimately accepted many of the reforms suggested by Otheguy and the Language Forum, including the use of nontest criteria for freshman student placement and permitting students in remedial courses to take a wider array of regular credit-bearing classes. Another group, the Chancellor's Task Force on Reading, seemed to take a much harder line on the issue of standards, stating in a mid-1991 report that "the University should mandate 'competence' rather than 'minimum competence.' " But the task force, citing the Everson study, accepted the recommendation that the reading test be extended fifteen minutes. Doing so, it suggested, "would help to counter the criticism leveled at the university."

By 1991 Harvey Weiner and the reading specialists he worked with had agreed that the reading test could be extended fifteen minutes without lowering standards, so long as the test was "renormed" —that is, so long as the passing score was raised to reflect the additional time. The idea, after all, was to remove time as a factor, not to make the test easier. But Edith Everett, as well as the Language Forum and the other ESL groups backing the change, wanted to retain the old passing score. "Harvey tried to hold the line as long as he could," reports Marilyn Maiz, Mina Shaughnessy's former colleague and an official in CUNY's Office of Institutional Research. "The whole thing started taking on a symbolic dimension when it moved from education to politics," says Weiner, meaning the politics of ethnicity, as well as the educational politics swirling around the issues of remediation, language use, and so on. The complex question of whether the reading test was speeded had gotten lost in an assault on standards and remediation. Renorming the test was thus seen as compounding the original offense. "No one gave me an ultimatum," Weiner says, "but it was made clear that this was the sentiment of the trustees and the university administration." And so in late 1991 Weiner agreed that the reading test for the following spring would be extended fifteen minutes, but the passing score would remain the same.

The results were not earth shattering, but people close to the epicenter felt the shocks clearly. The pass rate among incoming students at City College went from 66 percent to 73 percent after the new test was administered in the spring of 1992. Rudi Gedamke began to see more students who couldn't decipher STUDENT TURN-OUT NIL AT GAMES. And other students were moving directly into the regular curriculum—as Otheguy and others wished—who had not had to confront their reading problems. Even in its thirty-minute form the test had measured so low a degree of competency that City had assigned students who scored a low pass to College Skills 2. Now many of those students were advancing directly to English 110. In 1993 the SEEK program made College Skills mandatory even for the few students who scored a high pass, because few of them seemed ready to handle the regular curriculum. The system was either rejecting them or adapting itself to their level—thus Rudi's angry letter to the head of the composition program, asking how a semiliterate student could be getting an A in English 110.

The struggle over the reading test was reenacted in 1993. After fifteen years the university had finally decided to change the exam. And now reading teachers, who had largely sat out the debate on the extension of time, asked whether the new test would be normed according to the old thirty-minute passing score or the new forty-five-minute standard. In an April 1993 letter to the new dean for academic affairs (Harvey Weiner having left for a position at Hofstra University), the coordinators and faculty of CUNY's various reading programs asserted that "certification in reading currently represents reading skills that are below high school levels." The reading specialists asked, in strikingly blunt language, that the university "not corrupt the new examination by linking it to the questionable standard of the old test under the extended time limit."

This time the other side won. After testing the test on several campuses, CUNY decided to require a passing score that would be roughly equal to the score on the old thirty-minute exam. Students would be expected to read at approximately an eleventh-grade level, according to figures supplied by the Educational Testing Service.

Because the new test was considered slightly more difficult than the old, the number of students assigned to remedial reading might actually be slightly greater than it had been before the test was lengthened. It wasn't clear how the campuses, and especially the ESL community, would react once they made this discovery.

But the new test would be used only to place incoming students, whereas the old exam, all forty-five minutes of it, would continue to be used as a minimum competency test to be passed by students prior to their 61st credit. Moreover, the assessment tests had ceased to function as barriers to the remedial curriculum on many campuses. At City, ESL 30 students no longer had to pass the writing test to enroll in freshman composition; nor did students in English 2. This change probably did more to advance students through the system than had the fifteen-minute extension. Reformers in both English and ESL were convinced not only that the writing test measured glibness and technical correctness rather than real powers of expression, but that no test should function as a barrier to the regular curriculum.

Thus most students in English 2 are now graded according to their performance on a portfolio of writing. Portfolios are a much more flexible tool of measurement than tests, and have been the subject of endless discussion and refinement in the academic literature and in the classroom. But it's no coincidence that as a result of the change more students are "slipping through" to freshman composition, as English Department chairman Joshua Wilner says. The underlying ethic of the reformers is that more students *should* slip through, because otherwise the institution is restricting what Otheguy called their right to advance into the regular curriculum. Wilner is a member of the department's small avant-garde, and a firm, reflective proponent of the commitment to the new student. But he says that he "remains to be convinced of the wisdom of the change." Doing away with standardized measurements of ability makes him nervous.

Wilner is a serious scholar, and he doesn't want to see City's academic mission compromised by its remedial obligations. But the true believers in ESL and in the remedial world have trouble seeing these reservations as anything other than a form of obstructionism. Adele MacGowan-Gilhooly, who helped create City's fluency-first program, agrees with Otheguy and the Language Forum that ESL students should be able to move directly into the regular curriculum. City would simply have to cease being an English-language institution. Non-English-speaking students, she insists, should be able to take chemistry, math, or psychology courses in their native languages—of which there are several dozen. And core courses, such as World Humanities or freshman composition, should be held off until a student's junior or senior year. "These courses are too demanding linguistically and conceptually," she says. The college, presumably, would have to stop calling them "core courses."

Gilhooly is suggesting that City transform itself rather than its students, admitting the impossibility of overcoming their handicaps in the limited time now available. City should kneel down in order to raise up. This new vision of the open access college is one taken very seriously among the people who fought the battle over the reading assessment test. To Eric Nadelstern, the chairman of the Language Forum and a City College graduate, circa 1972, CUNY must either move backward, to a discredited elitism, or forward, to a "radical restructuring" by which the university would remake itself in the image of the new student. "All I hear," says Nadelstern, "is people invoking the mission that the university had prior to open admissions. In my view the mission ought not to be to compete with the private and state schools."

Meaning that CUNY can't afford to have high standards?

"There's a difference," Nadelstern says, "between high expectations and high standards. You should have high expectations for every student, but you can't have standards that serve as terminal gateways." Standards, in other words, must be reduced to the status of hopes. How, then, will excellence survive? Nadelstern has a curious answer: "I would say that you need to keep excellence as a standard for faculty performance, but high expectations as a standard for students." In other words, CUNY has a right to demand that its professors teach at a college level, but not that its students learn at a college level.

Nadelstern's position is based on the candid admission that places like City College cannot be expected to eradicate the gross disadvantages that students arrive with. He would rather see the

college sacrifice its intellectual standards than see the students fail
to get a degree. Nor is Nadelstern's position extreme; one finds it
as well in the literature on student retention. Colleges have devised
all sorts of programs to keep at-risk students from dropping out;
scholars in the field occasionally worry that such programs threaten
to supersede the college's academic mission. "Lest we forget," writes
Vincent Tinto, the expert on dropout issues, "the point of retention
efforts is not merely that individuals be kept in college, but that they
be retained so as to be further educated." Tinto also writes, "Regret-
tably, the view has spread that it is the duty of higher educational
institutions to attempt to educate all those who enter, regardless of
their goals, commitments and capacities.... To absolve, in effect,
individuals of at least partial responsibility for their own education
is to make a serious error."

But Tinto's is a minority view. Far more common is the anti-
intellectual premise of the Zook Commission report delivered to
President Truman in 1950: The ultimate mission of the college is to
satisfy the needs of students. A professor of education named
Leonard Valverde has observed that "high-risk students prefer formalized instruction, teacher-directed lessons, predictable academic
routine, group-directed learning goals, and certain types of tests and
reading assignments," and would have "negative experiences" in
more flexible settings. The college, Valverde suggests, should not
shatter this submission to drudgery and routine but recognize it as
a legitimate "cognitive style" and institute programs of "bicognitive
learning" for *all* students. Valverde also notes that since "low-income
students are often preoccupied with satisfying low-level needs," the
college should offer them "external incentives" —presumably money—
thus "making it materially worthwhile for them to learn." Valverde
goes on to suggest a whole range of changes in curriculum, pedagogy, and attitude, which together "should reflect that all students
are equally qualified when we are willing to look at their situation
from an alternative perspective." This last sentence might easily have
been written by the Language Forum, with its brief for the second-
language speaker.

What Valverde and Nadelstern are proposing is a new model
for higher education—the remedial college. Gone altogether is Robert

Marshak's blithe assumption that the needs of the new student can be assimilated to the intellectual ambitions of the traditional college. Marshak's idealism here gives way to a bizarre combination of harsh realism—indeed, cynicism—and vogue multiculturalism. This grim new vision of the role of higher education seems to offer inadvertent confirmation of the conservative argument that the intellectual values treasured in the academy cannot survive the onslaught of the new student. It is to City College's great credit, though, that it has not surrendered to the remedial college model.

The whole debate can be recast in the form of a single question: What should we do about high dropout rates? When the question is asked of high school, the answer clearly is, Change the schools. And this is so because we believe that everyone ought to have a high school diploma; no modern society, and no democratic society, can accept a lesser goal, even if we know we're a long way from achieving it. (The high school graduation rate is about 75 percent.) Bad schooling is not, in fact, nearly as important a cause of dropping out as is low socioeconomic status, but because high school attendance is mandatory, and because graduation is a minimally acceptable standard, we don't hesitate to insist that schools reform themselves to increase graduation rates.

Is the same true of college? Is Otheguy right in saying that the high dropout rate of minority and foreign-language students is an indictment of the racism or nonchalance of the institutions? Dropout rates *are* high, though exactly how high depends on how you calculate them. Because so many students at a place like City work part-time or full-time, and because many students "stop out" and then return, four-year or even five-year graduation rates are meaningless. Only 3 percent of students entering City in 1984 graduated in 1988; by 1992, after eight years, the figure had reached 28 percent. A plausible final figure would be 30 percent. But many of the students who left transferred elsewhere. The actual fraction of entering City students who graduate from a four-year college might be as high as 45 percent, which would put it close to the overall CUNY average. CUNY officials point out time and again that the national graduation rate is no higher, though that's not quite the case. About 45 percent of students graduate from the four-year college in which they enroll;

another 15 percent or so, according to Vincent Tinto, transfer and graduate from another senior college.

CUNY's record, and City's, is not as poor as it is because the institutions discriminate against the students they enroll, but because the students themselves are so heavily disadvantaged both socially and academically; every study of retention vindicates that conclusion. The figures actually show that City and CUNY are doing a relatively good job in overwhelmingly adverse conditions. But in absolute terms, a college dropout rate of 55 percent is still stunning (so is the national rate of 40 percent). What is to be done to solve this massive problem of "fit"? It won't help to *raise* standards, since City already loses students because of its standards. The premise behind proposals to raise standards in the high schools, such as the College Preparatory Initiative, is that it is the student, and not the institution, that must change. The dropout problem might well be eased by *lowering* standards, however, as in various ways the partisans of the new student have proposed.

Why insist, as with the CPI, that the student rise to the level of the institution, rather than having the institution sink to the level of the student? Why not make it easier to get a degree, when a degree means so very much? There can be only one answer: Because if you do, you will no longer have a college. You will have a job-training institute, a social-service agency, a passport-stamping office. Higher education's overwhelming economic importance leads it into precisely these roles. But the intellectual values that have traditionally informed college life pull it in the opposite direction, toward engagement with ideas rather than with students' disabilities.

City College lives at the intersection of these two principles. It cannot fully satisfy both. The only way to ensure that it flourishes as a fine professional and liberal arts institution, as it once did, is to recognize the limits of its social mission. City, and any other college that aspires to high academic standards, cannot be asked to educate large numbers of deeply disadvantaged students, as Ann Reynolds understands. It's not unreasonable to ask that students who complete high school without the academic credits detailed in the College Preparatory Initiative complete them elsewhere, presumably in a community college. Programs like SEEK, which permit students to enter without having satisfied admissions criteria, should stop functioning as entitlements and accept only those students who show special promise. And City cannot allow its commitment to remedy disadvantage to lead to the sort of "social promotion" that has such a demoralizing impact on the high schools. City must accept students who have a decent chance of succeeding, ply them with help, and then insist that they satisfy not only high expectations but high standards.

12

Meeting Them Where They Are

T here would have been no need for the ideologues of open access to do battle with people like Harvey Weiner were it not for one simple truth: The academic handicaps that students were bringing with them to school were very, very stubborn. That was why, as Weiner said, it was a matter of "despair" for serious, dedicated teachers like Rudi Gedamke that they could not solve the problems of students who had had so little experience of academic life. Perhaps, as Weiner felt, it was a function of time: one semester, or two, or three, were not enough to overcome years of bad training. Remediation was not working within the confines of the current system, as even people like Walter Daum, the foe of the College Preparatory Initiative, conceded. Perhaps the system needed to be radically overhauled; but City was not about to blot out its traditions and adopt the model of the remedial college.

But neither would the college tell the students it hadn't managed to equip with reading or writing skills to go home, to find another life; that would violate City's social mandate. It would, instead, clear away obstacles to their passage, like the assessment tests. And so those students who were able to keep coming to school—except for the most hopelessly overmatched—were promoted to the regular curriculum. There, in the *Purgatorio* of City's academic hierarchy, a different sense of mission applied. In the core curriculum, and in freshman composition, a college education was to begin—the academic regimen for which these students had been prepared. And if they *hadn't* been prepared? Would the college kneel down to them, would it raise them up, would it hold to a level and insist that they reach it? And if not there, then where?

The core curriculum was the great democratic middle of City College, where it was possible to find students headed in all directions and of almost all levels of ability. (A large fraction of students from the SEEK and ESL programs had dropped off before reaching the core.) City had a large and wide-ranging core that accounted for fully one-third of a student's credits. The battles that had raged elsewhere over the displacement of the European American experience, the dethroning of dead white males, hadn't really registered at City, which might have been excused for tumbling head over heels into multiculturalism. As a result of a curriculum revision in the mid-1980s, some Third World epics had been shuffled into the canon, and courses once known as "Western" this or that were now called "World," but the mix seemed reasonable. Much more surprising was that City was one of the very few colleges that required a semester of philosophy for all students, no matter what their field.

Because City remained very much a teaching rather than a research institution, no stigma attached to teaching core courses, and some of the college's most gifted professors willingly conducted World Humanities or World Civ classes. The sheer size of the core overwhelmed City's faculty, so most of the classes in fact were taught by adjuncts—freelancers paid by the class—but some of them were quite talented as well. Grazina Drabik, the exuberant Pole who taught the first class I ever attended at City, was an adjunct. Drabik gave herself unreservedly to her students, as even a teacher like Rudi Gedamke, with his scars and his corrosive doubts, could not. "Let me *look* at you," she would say fondly, surveying the class, as if for the first time, from her perch by the windows. She believed in her students, as Rudi could not—she was teaching a more select group, after all—and she never condescended to them. She assigned a great deal of reading, which most of the class duly ignored, and she tackled the texts with as much intelligence as urgency. When the class read the *Inferno* she spoke of how Dante fused the passion for knowledge and structure of Saint Thomas Aquinas with the intense inwardness of Saint Francis. When we reached *Macbeth*, she asked a student to read the "out, out brief candle" soliloquy, and then, leaning into the class, her eyes alight, she said, "This is the voice of modern man speaking, three centuries ahead—the despair, the irony, the loneliness."

The class had one or two real stars. When Drabik asked the students to write an essay in which they would put their own sinner in the appropriate circle of Dante's Hell, one of them, a Jamaican girl named Alicia Edwards, wrote a story about Madonna in a rough approximation of Dante's own terza rima. And there were occasional moments of revelation that repaid Drabik's lavish outlay of enthusiasm and spirit. Andrea Price, an Irish Catholic girl, told me that reading the *Inferno* had reawakened an old fascination with religious doctrine; Dante seemed to offer a much more humane and nuanced version of her grandfather's stern disquisitions on matters of faith. Andrea had bought *Purgatorio* and *Paradiso* and read at least parts of them on her own, and had discovered something that even Drabik didn't know—that each book ended with the word *star*.

By and large, however, the class was silent. The students supplied so little that Drabik often wound up lecturing by default; the class never conducted a sustained discussion of a book. Part of the problem was "too difficult life"—many of the students were so overburdened with work or child care or responsibilities of one kind or another that they simply didn't do the assigned reading. Halfway through the semester Drabik stopped administering spot quizzes, and as a result the students read even less. Drabik, ever sympathetic, understood their quandary. "They make a rational choice," she said. "They have to cut something out, and they cut out reading." But it wasn't just a matter of time. Many students just found the reading too hard. One said of *Don Quixote*, "It was just too deep for me." Like Hernan Morales, the English major who had never read a book, they were being asked to operate at an analytical level that they had never known of before. And so when Drabik delivered her

marvelous peroration on Shakespeare, I had to wonder how many
students got it.

Drabik wasn't exactly blind to this reality; she simply refused
to let it impinge on her faith. When I told her of the problems the
students were having with *Macbeth*, and she sighed and said, "It's
better I do not know this," could I say that that wasn't a better course,
spiritually as well as pedagogically, than Rudi's terrible honesty?
Drabik did not view her class as a failure; quite the contrary. She
loved teaching these classes; she believed in the mission, and in the
students, as ardently as Mina Shaughnessy ever had. Had she let
herself be deterred by doubt, she would not have been so devoted
a teacher. And so she had persuaded herself, as Shaughnessy had,
that the students' problems had to do with inexperience, too little
time, and too difficult life.

Drabik's attitude was a kind of realization of Eric Nadelstern's
proposal that the open admissions college have high standards for
its faculty, but high "expectations" for its students. Drabik asked a
great deal of herself, and, like Marilyn Sternglass, seized on any sign
of progress with her students as proof of success. She tallied up the
revelations, and put all the signs of apathy and bafflement out of
mind. In a survey she took at the end of the term, the students gave
themselves poor marks for class participation. They deserved no
better; but Drabik saw an altogether different moral. "These students
are developing the habit of self-criticism," she explained proudly.
"They are taking a sense of responsibility for their work." The final
papers, she conceded, had been poorly written, but they had been
much more heavily edited than the first ones had been. "They know
that they just can't put anything down on the page," Drabik said.
"This is *their* work, it's not something separate from them."

Drabik was an extraordinary teacher, and she perhaps proved
Mina Shaughnessy's assertion that the new student needed good
teaching in a way that the old had not. For all the lethargy, at the
end of the class several students said that they had learned how to
read, and even to think, in a way that they had not before. In other
core courses I attended that spring and the following fall I found
even less of an exchange between teachers and students. In a World
Civilization class, Edward Cody, an old and rather weary veteran,

was giving out a high school–style map quiz on the ancient world. After the students had handed in their tests, Cody asked if anyone could describe the Athenian idea of freedom, which they had just been reading about. This produced a silence that stretched out to an excruciating length. Cody then answered his own question, launched another query into the silence, and so on.

Later Cody told me that I had seen a fairly typical class. "You can't teach these kids the way you would a college class," he explained, "with a mid-term and a final and a term paper. You would lose them. I say, meet them where they are" —with regular quizzes, modest reading assignments, simplified class discussion. Drabik, of course, worked in the exact opposite direction, lighting up serious ideas and serious texts with her personal fire. I asked Cody if meeting students where they were actually worked. Maybe not, he said with a shrug. "I have to say, when I'm finished with them I'm not sure that I've done much for their writing."

One student in the class had been operating on a separate plane from the others. When Cody described the death of Socrates, and his famous refusal to flee a fate that had been democratically determined, the student raised his hand and said, "This is probably just a cynical, twentieth-century view, but it's just too good to be true. I tend to believe that the story was glorified to support the system or something. I'm sure Socrates said something, but I doubt he said that." This cynic turned out to be a twenty-seven-year-old Israeli—it figured—named Ronen Wilk. We talked after class. Ronen was an unhappy fellow, in fact a deeply disillusioned one. He said that he felt like a college student in a high school. "I had thought of education as something . . . exhilarating," he said. "But the students here don't think. They just shoot from the hip." Ronen had learned that he could operate on cruise control and still excel. "I got straight A's last semester," he said. "I'm probably going to get straight A's this semester. And I'm not that good."

This was a plaint I heard from good students again and again. Middle-class Americans like Cindy, the girl from Nebraska who was living out a multicultural fantasy, only reluctantly admitted that their core classes felt like baby stuff, since they were ideologically committed to City's democratic principles. Immigrants, however, could be devastatingly harsh. Jackie, a Trinadadian student from a middle-class family, said that she hadn't attended a single class with students whom she considered "acceptable," much less "well prepared." Jackie felt that the standards had sunk to the level of the students. She had taken the honors class in introductory philosophy and found it "a joke." And she had dropped out of World Civ in disgust. "It was absurd," she railed. "Do you know how long we spent on Napoleon and the French Rev? Half an hour! In Trinidad we spent *a year* on the French Rev." Jackie considered the level of her core classes a standing indictment of American public education. "The whole system has to begin at the base," she said. "In Trinidad, if you teach at elementary school, that's something. You are well paid and well respected. Here you're nothing; you're a babysitter."

Jackie, or Ronen, or any of a dozen other immigrant students I knew, would have jeered at Grazina Drabik's standard of personal responsibility. Standards, in their mind, had to do with intellectual rigor, not self-realization; as far as they were concerned, City College, and the whole public education system, had sacrificed standards at the altar of equal opportunity. They were ruthless meritocrats. And some of them voted with their feet: Kris, a Turkish Cypriot I met in Drabik's class, finally transferred to Hunter College because he felt that he was not getting a decent education at City.

I, however, couldn't be quite so ruthless. I wasn't sure how much equal opportunity I was willing to sacrifice in order to raise standards. Whenever I tried to balance these competing goods in my mind, I thought of students like Tammy and Sabour. Given the stakes, given the honest efforts and the poignant hopes of these very real young men and women, wasn't even the very little that Drabik asked quite enough? Jim Watts, the chairman of the History Department, who had described City's task as the forging of a new middle class, asked me one day in his usual hectoring tones what I actually proposed to do with the "hardy band of survivors," in his generous phrase, who came to City. "Are you going to say that, a priori, in the name of standards, they're not going to get the opportunity to go to college?" Watts said.

It was an easy call for Watts; he simply refused to acknowledge that there was any cost to extending that opportunity, or that there was any contradiction between City's social and academic missions. When he said "in the name of standards," he really meant "in the name of a mere abstraction." Unlike Leonard Kriegel, or so many others, Watts did not believe that City's intellectual level had sunk as a result of its commitment to the new student. "The fact that we have such a high failure rate is a measurement of how serious we are," he observed. Watts was saying that, though City was graduating fewer students than it used to, the graduates were as good as they had been thirty years before, when he first came to City. And unless, like Rudi Gedamke, you believed that failure exacted a cost of its own, there was nothing to lose by admitting students who eventually dropped out because they couldn't meet high standards. But Watts's premise was wrong, as those disillusioned immigrants would have been happy to tell him. Students were passing through the remedial program with their handicaps unremedied. They were arriving in their World Humanities class unable to make sense of a literary text. They were, presumably, continuing onward from there. There *was* a cost; and it had to be honestly reckoned.

During the fall of 1992 I sat in on a freshman composition class, known as English 110, almost as regularly as I attended Rudi Gedamke's College Skills class. The English class met in a windowless box at the end of a narrow corridor on the sixth floor of the NAC building. The students were either freshmen who had passed the writing assessment test and thus been placed in the course directly, or veterans who had already taken and passed remedial English or ESL classes. English 110 was intended to prepare students for the kind of writing demanded by college, and beyond that, or before that, to make them comfortable with writing as an activity. I had already seen dozens of examples of student writing, but I wanted to get a clearer idea of the intellectual skills that students possessed as they moved on into their specialized fields; and I wanted to know how far City could develop those skills.

Ann Tabachnikov often asked students to read in class the essays they had written at home. One morning she called on Mike, a quiet, eager-to-please student of Puerto Rican background. Mike was such a halting reader that when he read passages from books

Tabachnikov sometimes had to recite them again herself to make sure that everyone else understood. He rolled his eyes when Tabachnikov called on him, but he gamely plunged in (I quote from his written text): "Mothers of the past decades are more difficult to comprehend. It seems that they matured in age, yet, they did not change with the times of today. They still treat us young adults as if we were children of medieval times. What I mean by this is that this is not Little House on the Prairie, this is reality. They are to strict, to demanding and especially to possessive; unlike todays mother which are far more understanding. And still, you have to live with them and bare their non-sense all the time. As for me, I love my mother with all my heart. I know that in reality, there's no other woman that can take her place. There's no one like her. There are no two mothers alike. I guess that's what makes them so unique."

Mina Shaughnessy had taught me to look past such surface features as Mike's incomplete stops and his mistaking of "to" for "too." They were, in any case, fairly trivial flaws. Mike had learned certain academic forms, such as the form appropriate for generalization: "Mothers of the past decades...." But the forms were empty; he hadn't actually risen above his sense of pique at his own mother, as he revealed when he complained in the following paragraph that his mother hadn't gone to his high school graduation because he had refused to break up with his girlfriend. Mike wasn't using writing as a tool for reflection; for him, it was still a cumbersome and long-winded way of talking. The last four sentences show a writer who has run out of things to say but feels obliged to keep his pen moving.

Mike was thoroughly embarrassed at having exposed intimate details of his life, but his classmates rallied around him. When he looked up from his manuscript, Betty, a kindly, white-haired woman who had returned to college after thirty years, said, "If you're happy, that's what counts." Everyone nodded and murmured agreement. "She'll come around," said Philip, one of the class stars. "They don't want their babies to grow up," said Debbie, herself a young mother. Betty instantly agreed: "I raised three in the sixties, and it was *hard times.*"

Tabachnikov, a very patient woman, finally ran out of patience. "What about *the paper?*" she asked.

"It was good," somebody muttered. Others agreed. And that was it. Tabachnikov staged these public readings in order to help writers improve their work and to give the other students a chance to think critically about a text. But few of the students were accustomed to thinking in critical terms; others, like Philip, were restrained by tact. Most of the students felt that sincerity was an unassailable virtue: what mattered was to say what you felt. But sincerity was often indistinguishable from self-absorption. The only subject most of the students were comfortable writing about or talking about was themselves. Discussions about texts dwindled into silence; discussions about moms threatened to turn into full-blown therapy sessions. Philip developed a running joke in which he capped particularly touchy-feely comments with "Thank you for sharing."

Tabachnikov assigned short essays on specific readings, and open-ended pieces that were to be refined throughout the semester. For this major project virtually all of the students wrote about themselves; and virtually all of their work amounted to unreflective, if heartfelt, narration, the egocentrism that writing theorist Andrea Lunsford has singled out as a sign of the cognitively immature student.

At least one-third of the twenty-five students in class wrote at Mike's level or below. Most of them, perhaps all, had come through ESL or remedial English. A smaller group, of four or five students, read fluently and spoke to the point, and were able to use writing as a cognitive tool—a device for probing and reshaping thought. None of these students had taken remedial English or College Skills; City College hadn't had to develop abilities latent in them. Of this group only one student wrote the sort of clean, dutiful prose prized by high school English teachers. This was Marta, a big blonde from Spartanburg, South Carolina, who was also the only student in class to have received a run-of-the-mill middle-American education. The others all made at least occasional errors in punctuation, capitalization, syntax. But two of them, both women of Chinese parentage, wrote wonderfully. Here was Amelia's tale of herself:

"My childhood was spent behind four walls. My parents never allowed me to go anywhere. I was, to them, an object to keep forever untouched and uncorrupted by the outside world.... I looked at those people who I thought had acted unreasonably with their children and I noticed they were all of about the same age as my parents. They had gone through revolutions, wars. They had 'experience.' Their own sacred version of experience.... I decided to call my Mom and talk about it with her. But she avoided the theme. 'Leave the past alone,' is all she said. But I knew she was still in pain. For some reason, I saw her having my face. At that moment I realized that I was nothing but a younger version of her. I hadn't been touched by the 'dirty and deceiving' hands of experience. I was to them, the innocence they had lost prematurely.... And it is then when I started to ask myself if I should feel sad or happy for their overprotective attitude towards me."

Amelia's writing was sincere—painfully so—but not egocentric. Her subject, in fact, was how the dawning of consciousness had drawn her out of herself. And Amelia understood that writing was something manipulable in a way that speech was not. She glided back and forth between reality and dream with a fluidity that left her literal-minded classmates thoroughly confused; but she understood that the dream gained its force precisely by the way it obtruded on waking reality. Amelia wrote with a luxuriance that struck me as, if not Chinese, then certainly not American. In another essay she penned a sentence worthy of La Rochefoucauld: "Creativity is the happy part of your sorrow." Writing, she said, is like "navigating in the wide, blue, open sea while capturing fish. Writing is harvesting what you have sowed after a long year of work." Amelia amplified these metaphors into extended conceits; she didn't penetrate her subject so much as embellish it, and then embellish the embellishments.

It was in students like Amelia that City's diversity became something more than mere demographics, and more than the delightful spectacle of a multicultural classroom. Amelia had preserved something particular from the homogenizing influence of the public schools. She had developed a voice, a linguistic style that suited her own experience. Perhaps multiculturalism, in its achieved form, was a polyphony of just such well-trained voices.

In her course description, Ann Tabachnikov had written that the class would "work on writing that gradually builds a bridge between the private and the public self." Over time the students would shift to "writing that uses their personal experience to illustrate and explore expansive and universal themes," and finally to "essays which deal primarily with issues and ideas, rather than personal experience." Tabachnikov was aiming for cognitive growth, of the kind that Marilyn Sternglass talked about and measured with her nine-stage scale. But Tabachnikov was hoping to move the students from naive egocentrism to abstraction in a single semester, which was a great deal to hope for. In the second month of the class she began to prod the class toward the intermediate stage. She asked them to write about a paragraph from an essay by Loren Eiseley, "The Judgment of the Birds," a spookily beautiful example of just the kind of intellectual movement she was asking of them. Tabachnikov instructed the students to focus on Eiseley's use of language; she wanted them to examine writing as a form, a thing external to the writer.

The result was not encouraging. Adalberto, one of four Dominican students in the class and the one with the gravest language problems, was so at sea that he simply clung to bits of the original text. His entire essay read, "In the paragraph that I chose the author is using the language to express how a person seeking for his soul go out to a separated place. They go to a place where they can be along and be able to find their soul. He also put it like when Moises when to the desert to be in peace and talk with god for instruction, and also to get and idea what they have to do." Debbie cited a passage in which Eiseley climbs a hill at dusk: "Right away I got a vision in my mind. Maybe it's the way he descrived the scenery. Another example he gaved: Blue air was darkening into purple along the bases of the hills [a quote from the original]. Right then I got a since that it was getting dark." Even the stars of the class appeared not to recognize that language existed separately from meaning, though they clearly understood what they were writing about and even used a few terms of art—*personalization, metaphor, simile.*

After class a student named Richard came up to me and asked if I could read his piece. Richard had always looked to me like a big, sad bear. He generally came in late and slouched in a chair as far from Tabachnikov as possible. Richard never spoke, and he looked out at the class through his sleepy, distant bear eyes. Now he said to me, "I know we're supposed to do an analysis, but I don't know if this goes real deep." He showed me a few lines he had scrawled on a piece of paper during class. It was hard to make much sense out of them; we agreed that we would talk in the cafeteria.

Richard was a lost soul. In his first year at City College he had taken nothing but remedial courses and the notoriously undemanding introductory black studies course. Like so many other students, he had muddled through without having to break a sweat. Now, however, his own January clearance had arrived. He hoped to be an engineer, and he was taking algebra and trigonometry, and falling behind in both. He wasn't doing well in World Civilization, and he was obviously failing English 110. He simply wasn't doing the work. Richard slouched in his chair, just the way he did in class, and said, "My problem is that I'm lazy. I'm not really all that motivated. If I'm under pressure, I'm fine—that's how I got through elementary school, junior high school, high school. I could do it at the last minute, and I always got good grades."

I asked, "Is that working in college?" and Richard very quietly replied, "No." Sometimes he did a couple of hours of homework, sometimes none at all. But Richard didn't seem lazy so much as feckless. Anything could knock him off his perch. He had gone on an expedition with his little brother to a discount shopping mall in Reading, Pennsylvania. They had missed the last bus home and waited all night on the curb, and so Richard hadn't managed to write his Eiseley paper. At least he had gotten an assigned journal entry out of it. Richard said, "I really need to be angry to write something. If you're just going along and everything is fine, you can keep it to yourself. But if you're angry, instead of picking up the phone, you can write it down." And so he had written about his trip, and his discovery that "my brother is a bastard."

Richard didn't want to talk about his past, though he alluded darkly to "some very bad things that happened when I was young." From his writing it was clear that at some point Richard had begun to think of himself as a failure, and perhaps that that feeling had become self-reinforcing. For a paper on whether schools emphasize problem solving at the expense of expressiveness, Richard wrote, "Schools generally do teach students to be problem solver. in elementary school i ways felt i ways different than the rest of the kids. special in my own way. in what way i ask myself, i really don't remember. But i knew i was special. This all change as an adult but part of the feeling still stay with me." The very randomness of Richard's punctuation, capitalization, and spacing was a sign of what he thought of as laziness, but what might have more fairly been called despair. He seemed unable or unwilling to marshal even what he knew on the page. After his junior year in high school, Richard wrote, "I felt as if there was no purpose in bieng." And that was exactly the impression that Richard gave.

In mid-November, about two-thirds of the way through the semester, the class talked about a *New York Times* review of *Batman 2* that Tabachnikov had distributed. Tabachnikov was hoping to push them toward the third stage she had described— "issues and ideas, rather than personal experience." But few of the students had shown any mastery of the second stage, and even fewer were comfortable at this level of abstraction. Only a handful understood what the reviewer meant when she said that she had been delighted by the perversity of the villains; the thought was too unfamiliar. Only one student laughed when Tabachnikov read a wry passage from the piece. Some of the vocabulary was unfamiliar—not only *zeitgeist*, but *lurid* and *skewed*. But the real problem was translating from the level of the word or the sentence to the level of the paragraph or the whole—a higher-level version of the problem that Rudi Gedamke confronted. Some of the students seized on a particular word, like *sad*, to misconstrue the whole tone of the review. They seemed unable to reach a global sense of what was, after all, a relatively short and accessible piece of prose. Tabachnikov asked the students to write a brief essay about it, but their essays, like their comments, were largely uncomprehending.

At the end of the term the students handed in a portfolio that consisted of their major autobiographical essay and whatever other work showed them to best advantage. Most of the portfolios came carefully sheathed in plastic covers; the papers were neatly typed, often in one of the exotic fonts available in the City College printers. What was inside, however, showed how few of the students understood writing as a form, a thing external to themselves and to the words they heard inside their heads. Yvette, a timid, moonfaced Dominican girl who was still partially lodged in the ESL program, wrote a version of Mike's gripe about his Mom. It was terribly sad, rather than nattering or rancorous, but it still felt like unfiltered talk. "Every little girl has a dream," Yvette wrote, "and that is to stay with her family for ever. And never to grow up to face no kind of problems. I was very happy when I was a little girl, I thought I had everything. My father was very nice, but he died two years ago. My mother tries to give me everything except time and love. I have a brother who is very nice and two sisters that I really love. But everything in life is not happiness."

Tabachnikov had written, "Your lead is generally good." The second sentence, she had noted, was a fragment; *no* was the wrong word. She had not said, "Your writing is childish." And what would have been the point? Yvette's writing, in this diarylike form, was scarcely separate from Yvette herself. She had talked to Tabachnikov about her work, read it to the class, and then revised it. But she had no sense of her work's shortcomings, which were not in the work but in the thought process that it reflected. In her final draft she made only a few trivial changes. And the same could be said for Mike or Debbie or Adalberto or Richard or most of the others who had reached English 110 as naive writers. They had not tinkered with their work, perhaps because they did not view the work as something separate from themselves. And so they had paddled along in their egocentricity—their "expressiveness," to use the term favored by enthusiasts of personal writing.

At the opposite end of the class were the few better students, who not only were more persistent than the others but had a great deal more to say. When the class wrote about expressiveness, Rebecca, a Chinese American student, was the only one to move beyond her own musings. Rebecca wrote about works of art. Of Courbet's painting *The Trout*, she observed, "Even the size of the picture helps to convey his traumatic state of mind." She wrote about the sequence of emotions evoked by Vivaldi's *Four Seasons*.

Rebecca had decided to become an engineer, but only out of a desire for professional security; her soul prompted her elsewhere.

In her final, greatly expanded draft of the expressiveness essay she damned the school system, comparing it to "an assembly line constructing an automobile. Instead of automobiles it's constructing students or future productive workers." As a child, she wrote, she had fallen in love with art, but was disgusted to find that art class was just more technical training; her creativity was never acknowledged. "My frustration with these teachers was blazing like wild fire. Once I even gathered all my art work and set it ablaze in a rage of anger. The conflagration from the art work glowed and raised as high and hot as the disappointment and frustration I had bottled up inside me."

Rebecca was an impressive figure. She was tall, and her long hair was parted down the middle, and she had a disconcerting way of sweeping one side of it back and looking straight at you. The look was a little bit flirty, and a little bit challenging. She never ducked away or squirmed when I went to talk to her, as other Chinese students did. She was taciturn and almost melancholic; her parents had raised her on stories of hardship. Their lives had been swept away by the Cultural Revolution, and they had all but starved to death in the chaos of that time. Emigrating to Queens, they became the poor relations of a highly successful family. Rebecca had cousins at Harvard, Princeton, and MIT; an aunt taught biology at Princeton. I never met another student at City with so richly pedigreed a family. When I asked Rebecca why she hadn't gone to the Ivy League, she said, almost bitterly, "Those schools are for upper-class people." Rebecca had been accepted at Brooklyn Polytechnic, but when her scholarship had been cut she had been forced to withdraw in favor of City, which has the only engineering school in the CUNY system.

Rebecca had refused to count her modest blessings, as her parents counseled. She raged against their ingrained fear of life and their traditional views. They considered engineering an inappropriate profession for a woman. Rebecca didn't even like engineering, but she saw it as a prestigious profession where intelligence was rewarded. For all her strong-willed resistance, she felt a deep sadness toward her family and her past that generations of City College students would have recognized instantly. In her own autobiographical paper she wrote, "As I get closer and closer to fulfilling my hopes and dreams, I find myself drifting further and further from my

parents, sometimes even losing sight of them.... They don't understand the complexity of college. They don't understand why I spend
so much time reading now. Or why I keep such irregular hours."
Rebecca didn't regret her freedom; but she was paying for it in
anguish. "Will they ever look into my eyes," she asked, "and think
they are looking into the eyes of a stranger?"

Rebecca was a new version of the old-fashioned City College
student—a bright public school graduate too poor to afford private
college. Two or three students in the class fell into this category. Then
there was Marta from Spartanburg, who was fleeing the dead hand
of middle-class rectitude. And there was one student in a category
I could hardly describe. Joyce was a black woman whom I took to
be about fifty. Her reading comprehension was poor, and the gaps
in her vocabulary were yawning. I was amazed to find that she was
the most copious writer in the class. Joyce didn't write drafts of
stories, but new versions of them. Her personal essay weighed in
at about 2,000 words, or two or three times the length that most students settled for. Joyce simply loved to write. When she was nine,
she recalled in one of her stories, her parents had begun to fight.
Writing became her solace. "I lived in my own fantasy world," Joyce
wrote, "by making up stories about make believe families that were
happy and trouble free. I thought as I wrote these stories, that the
problems in my own real family would go away."

When she was thirteen Joyce invented a style of literary collage.
A teacher had assigned the class to make a composition by taping
personal objects into a notebook. Joyce wrote, "So I used this idea
and applied it to my writing. The only thing was that now, it was
more like a comic strip. I would cut out the people in the fashion
magazines and use them as though I was creating a play. My main
concern was the expression of the faces that I would use; whether
they would be happy or sad. I had become very good at creating
scenes and I influenced some of my friends to do the same." It sounds
like the sort of things that winds up in SoHo galleries nowadays.

Joyce's writing, in fact, had the quality of folk art: minutely
wrought, yet strangely naive. It was hard to say whether she had
retained the ability to conjure up a child's world or still actually dwelt
in such a world. When she wrote about her family she sounded like

Yvette—a little girl huddling against the gathering cold of loss. And in one of her stories she explained that she had learned about human nature, sexuality, and social mores on her frequent trips to the zoo. "When I was younger," she wrote, "I had been told that when the new year has come in, animals kneel as though they are praying. Many years before that, man has thought of the animal as being stupid and thoughtless. I believe that this is not true. Times are changing so much and so are our animals. Its changed so much that dogs, who have been known to be nothing but a dumb mut with no sense of self knows how to cross a street without getting hit by a speeding automobile."

"Times are changing so much and so are our animals" is a wondrously bizarre sentence, implying as it does that cats and dogs have joined the march of human progress. It sounds like the conceit of a Disney movie. Joyce had developed her imaginative powers all on her own, while her critical faculties, left to the haphazard care of school, had idled. Joyce had grown up poor, in a big family held together by a strong mother who insisted that everyone get a high school diploma. But after high school Joyce had a child out of wedlock, and then another, and her education ground to a halt. In 1984, when her kids were eight and five, she had enrolled in community college.

"*That* was hard," Joyce said to me as we rode down the escalator after class one morning— "working, taking care of my children, going to class." It had taken her five years to get a degree as a medical secretary. Then Joyce had raised her sights. She decided that she wanted to get a master's in speech pathology. This was her second year at City. She supported her family by working four nights a week, from 10 P.M. until 8 A.M., as a counselor at a group home for the developmentally disabled. It was a killing regimen, but Joyce was thinking about expanding it by becoming a full-time rather than part-time student in the spring.

You could read the hardness of Joyce's life in her eyes, and in her lined forehead and sagging cheeks. I was wrong about her age; Joyce was not yet forty. Still, she had something in her that had not been extinguished by the battering of inner-city life. It was hard to guess how a college education would act on Joyce's folkloric turn of mind. It may have been too late for her to break out of old patterns of thinking and to absorb new analytic skills. But she was the open admissions student par excellence—held back by poor schooling and the entanglements of the ghetto, pushed forward by ambition and a faith in education.

City College's admissions policy had given Joyce an opportunity she never would have had otherwise. But Joyce was one of a very few students who had the gifts needed to take advantage of that opportunity. At the other end of that spectrum—the spectrum of determination—were sleepwalkers like Richard. Owing to City's ethos of advancement Richard had reached freshman composition in a state of virtual illiteracy. But now the demands were rising, and he wasn't equal to them. A week before the end of class I found Richard in a brown study. He said that he had dropped out of the lower of his two math classes. "I knew I was going to fail," he said. He had been late for so many classes that his fate was already sealed. At least, he said, he could focus on his other math class.

But when I saw Richard after the term was over he told me that he had failed trigonometry as well. "I was spending so much time working on the other class," he said, "and when I pulled out I guess it was too late to catch up." He had failed World Civ, and he had failed English 110 as well; the only class he had passed was weightlifting. Richard realized that he would have to forget about electrical engineering, but he had no idea what else to major in. When Tabachnikov told him that she had no choice but to fail him, Richard said, "This has been good for me." Tabachnikov, who like Grazina Drabik hunted for signs of progress, saw Richard's acceptance as a sign of growing maturity. But to me it felt more like the peace that comes with surrender.

Tabachnikov did not take a particularly sanguine view of the class's attainments. Despite her continual exhortations, she said, hardly any students had revised their work; and her overall effort to move them beyond "this is what it feels like to be me" had failed. Something deeper than inattention or inexperience or second-language problems was at work, she conceded. But Richard was the only student that she hadn't passed. The others, at least, had done the assignments. She had, for example, given Yvette a B. "What Yvette set out to do, limited as it was, she accomplished," Tabachnikov explained. And that was true. Yvette had not been lazy or contrary; she had done her best. Tabachnikov added, "I don't see what purpose can be served, academically or psychologically, by making Yvette do English 110 again." And that, too, was true, just as Pete Martinez was probably right when he said that it wouldn't do Renato any good to take Social Studies over again. More experience was not going to make Yvette a significantly better writer; all the reading and the writing she had done for this class, after all, had not made a noticeable difference. She had been promoted this far; and Tabachnikov was not going to be the one to halt her progress.

But something very serious had been sacrificed in this generous and possibly inescapable transaction—intellectual vitality. This was the cost that Jim Watts did not want to reckon and that Grazina Drabik purposefully ignored. Philip, the class skeptic, once complained—in private, of course—that class discussion dwelt at the level of lunchtime chatter. "When you're in a class," he said, "you have to use a certain amount of ... I don't want to say 'intelligence,' because I don't want to come off as being critical." That would have violated his, and the class's, sense of decency. But that was the word Philip meant, so he left his sentence unfinished. Students were content to shoot from the hip, as Ronen Wilk had put it. Discussion was dragged down to the level of the lowest common denominator, the level of "expressiveness." How, then, were students to grow? What was pushing them forward? For all its warmth and geniality, there was a terrible emptiness at the heart of the class.

That void wouldn't have been so poignant had there been no one in the class but Mike and Debbie and Adalberto, and Yvette. But City was not, in fact, a remedial college, and it was still able to attract some of the gifted, sometimes untutored, young people who came out of the city's schools or emigrated from abroad. Intellectual merit still mattered at City, and to spend time with students like Amelia, Rebecca, and Philip was to know what the college could be. These students needed intellectual rigor; perhaps they would get it in the more challenging settings that lay ahead of them.

The greatest victims of the lowest common denominator may have been the students in the middle, who were neither obviously gifted nor dreadfully handicapped; or students like Joyce, who seemed at once limited and talented. An intellectually lively atmosphere might have galvanized them; instead they paddled along with the others, earning B's for showing up on time and doing the homework, just as they had in high school. They needed to be pushed hard, but City couldn't afford to do that; if it had, the students on the bottom would have been lost. And so they floated on into the regular curriculum, where their teachers would have no choice but to adjust their standards, and their expectations, to those that their students brought with them.

Part III

The Struggle
for Hearts and Minds

13

Dr. J's Theater of Racial Outrage

F aculty and staff members at City College often told stories of "rescuing" a student, usually black, from his own self-defeating rage. Rudi Gedamke felt that he might have gotten through to Curtis, who sat in the back of the class with his cap tugged over his eyes, after their climactic confrontation in Rudi's office. Another professor spoke of having paired off a hostile, militant black student with a Central European immigrant; after the two had spent a term working on a joint project, he said, the black student came to him and admitted that he had been compelled to rethink his racial stereotypes. Teachers and administrators told these stories because nothing made them prouder. This kind of psychic transformation went to the heart of their commitment to the open admissions ideal. But they also told these stories because they felt so disturbed by the alienation and hostility of some black students. That hostility felt, in part, like a refusal to recognize the sincerity of their commitment, and City College's commitment, to helping disadvantaged students. It felt like a repudiation of their most deeply held ideals.

These dramas of alienation and rescue rarely involved Caribbean or African students. Those students, having grown up in all-

black worlds, had not had the feeling of occupying the lowest rungs
of a racial pecking order; nor, in many cases, had they dwelt at the
bottom of the socioeconomic order. Many non-American black students identified themselves in pointedly nonracial terms. Soon after
I arrived at City College I met a Nigerian student named Rasheed
who was working toward his civil engineering degree. Rasheed took
great pride in his ability to rise to impossible academic demands.
"In the last four or five days," he said, "I have slept six hours—total."
Rasheed's identity was bound up with his work and his aspirations,
rather than with his skin color; he was openly contemptuous of racial
politics. "I've always been treated better by white people than black
people in this society," he said. "Most of my friends at City are white.
I work at Waldbaum's, and one of the black guys there said to me,
'You look black, but you're really white.' But I know what I am. I
tell these guys, 'You're still fighting the war, but there *is* no war.' The
benefits are there for everybody. You just have to take them."

Rasheed had been born into a middle-class family; many African American students at City had grown up in a world of failure
and despair. They took the subway out of that world every morning
and returned to it every afternoon. Unless, like Tammy, they had
miraculously preserved a sense of possibility amid the wreckage, it
was easy to feel that failure was foreordained. And in certain parts
of the African American community, this bitter intuition has become
an article of faith and the foundation of an ideology of repudiation
and resistance. The ideology is supported by conspiracy theories that
show the white world mobilized to destroy the aspirations or even
the lives of black people: white administrators rig the school system
to control and suppress young black men; white, perhaps Jewish,
doctors, hatched the AIDS virus in a laboratory and released it into
the ghetto; white politicians ensure a steady supply of guns and
drugs in the inner city.

These tall tales rest on the hard fact of persistent white racism
and persistent black poverty. But they are dangerous, and not only
because they promote hatred and fear; they also perpetuate the intellectual and cultural isolation of the black community. It was precisely
this isolation, both real and self-imposed, that formed the core of
the rescue stories. Black intellectuals such as Henry Louis Gates, Jr.,

chairman of Harvard's Afro-American Studies Department, have publicly condemned the propagation of racial myths, in part owing to a fear of rising black anti-intellectualism and cultural isolation. But a larger number of scholars have refused to criticize the extremists, reasoning that the fatalism they speak to is well founded in reality, even if the theories themselves are not. Law professor Derek Bell has even argued that black intellectuals disavow militants in order to enhance their prestige with whites. And so a war has been fought, in classrooms and public forums and academic journals and the media, over the hearts and minds of black people, and especially young black people. Though there are several sides in this war, the issue being contested is identity: where will black people situate themselves inside the larger American culture?

These issues of identity, exclusion, and difference were debated constantly at City College; race had replaced capitalism as the driving force of polemics and political activity on campus. I often met students, not all of them black, who believed reflexively in the conspiracy theories propounded in parts of the black media. And I heard them bandied about in class. In the course Psychology of Black Experience, which I attended several times in the spring of 1992, the students had no trouble agreeing that "the European seeks mastery over nature," while "the African strives for mastery over oppression and oneness with nature." The terms *African* and *African American* were used interchangeably, to distinguish black people from *European Americans*, as if in willful blindness to the diversity of cultures and values in and all around the classroom. At a later class, held soon after Los Angeles police officers had beaten black motorist Rodney King, a student said, "Justice is blind, and a lot of cops are going to have to start dying. They need to see their lives flash before their eyes." Others in the class nodded agreement and talked about what it felt like to be mistreated by the police.

There was power to be had, and even wealth and fame, in mining this vein of grievance, and plumbing the depths of suspicion and paranoia. It was a temptation difficult to resist, and one that many street-level leaders, politicians, radio talk-show hosts, and clergy freely indulged. Only at City College, though, had a titled, tenured academic figure made himself an impresario of racial bitterness and rejection. This was Leonard Jeffries, chairman of City's Black Studies Department. Jeffries was City College's greatest celebrity, its greatest hero, its greatest villain. He was a notorious man, and he made City a notorious place. And yet Jeffries' antitype also taught at City College. This was Edmund Gordon, a distinguished black psychologist and educational reformer who briefly replaced Jeffries as department chairman. Gordon was a representative, and an exemplar, of the camp of inclusion and of intellectual legitimacy. And so on the City College campus a vague and indistinctly demarcated intellectual struggle assumed, amazingly, the form of melodrama.

I first saw Leonard Jeffries in the spring of 1992. He had just been removed as chairman of the Black Studies Department by the CUNY Board of Trustees, largely as a result of a speech he had given in Albany in which he called one of his critics "a sophisticated Texas Jew" and seriously discussed the theory that blacks are benign "sun people" while whites are violent and rapacious "ice people" (a theory I had just heard in milder form in the psychology class). The board had appointed Edmund Gordon in his stead. Jeffries' core followers, as well as many otherwise disengaged black students, viewed Gordon as a sellout and Jeffries as a martyr to racial politics.

Now Jeffries had been asked by a group called the Statewide Africana Studies Movement to address a rally in the big, featureless plaza that fills the space between two wings of the NAC building. Jeffries, who espoused an "Afrocentric" philosophy, was wearing a dashiki and a particolored African cap. Behind him, in classic Black Panther fashion, stood a tall, unsmiling student in dark sunglasses and a trenchcoat, his hands clasped before him. Off to one side, Brother Steve, a roly-poly young man known as Jeffries' "bodyguard," scanned the crowd with the professional eye of a Secret Service agent. By the time Jeffries began to speak, the crowd had reached about 500—a huge gathering by City College standards. And Dr. J, as he calls himself, did not disappoint.

Jeffries' subject was the systematic effort by the white power structure to keep black people down. He explained the College Preparatory Initiative as a subterfuge designed to "whiten up" City College by limiting access to black students, and thus to thwart the increasingly successful consciousness-raising activities of the Black Studies Department. Jeffries' speaking style was both formless and seamless, a manner that assumed that everything is connected to everything. He hopped from century to century and nation to nation —it was all the same. Just as "Abraham Lincoln didn't have a damn thing to do with your emancipation," so "You're here not *because of* the liberal Jewish alumni, but *in spite of* the liberal Jewish alumni." The enemy was Lincoln, the Jews—not the overt racists but the scheming liberals, their will to domination masked by a show of sympathy.

Jeffries wheeled around slowly as he spoke, a practiced orator; his voice was always light and sardonic, mocking and incredulous. Enormities amused, rather than enraged, him. "You cannot trust a good white boy," he said, and the crowd snickered. And then he smiled knowingly and added, "But I think many of you want to be wannabes. 'I want to be one of them.' Don't be surprised if it's in your heart, because it's in the culture." The culture preached assimilation, but the reality was that black people could not succeed. "Where are you going to get a job?" Jeffries asked, throwing out a hand. "Companies are moving out to the suburbs. You think you're going to get a job out there? You think you're going to get a *house* out there?" Jeffries hooted; and the crowd, or much of it, hooted with him.

Jeffries spoke for well over an hour, without pause, without notes, as fluent and long-winded as Fidel Castro. In fact he mentioned the Fidel Castro–Che Guevara study group, which he planned to establish, along with the African Research Council, to counter racist Eurocentric scholarship. The white world had repudiated black people; now blacks would have to create a world of their own. His voice rose, and he cried, "We have to take over the college!" There was a momentary hush—CUNY had been torn apart by a strike the year before, and while a few students were eagerly awaiting a new one, most dreaded the prospect. Cheering and applause broke out. Then Jeffries raised a hand. "I'm not saying 'Torch it,' " he said with a sly grin. He only meant that students should take over the campus "spiritually and intellectually." But the threat, and the invitation, hung in the air. Jeffries was toying with the crowd and putting the entire college on notice. He was saying, "You've dismissed me; but *I* have the power."

Did he? It was hard to say for sure. The hard-core militants, whose views of the world were wholly bounded by Jeffries' edicts, probably numbered no more than a few hundred, and many of them seemed to have a tenuous relationship with City College. But they were active, and clamorous, and in subtle and not so subtle ways they corrupted the intellectual atmosphere. Students were often afraid of expressing a critical view of Jeffries, or of anything pertaining to race, for fear that a militant might be lurking in their midst. Like Jeffries himself, they understood the uses of intimidation.

Soon after Jeffries' speech the Africana Studies Movement called a meeting to protest his ouster. A black student told me that I was unlikely to be admitted and suggested that I seek permission from the president of the student government, which, along with the newspaper and the Student Center, fell within Jeffries' traditional sphere of influence. The student government was located on the ground floor of the NAC building, and as I walked down the corridor I felt I was crossing an invisible border into unknown territory— Leonard Jeffries' private fiefdom. One wall was plastered with posters filled with cryptic diagrams and rapturous praises of Nubian culture and other articles of Afrocentric faith. The posters lead to the student government office. The president, as it turned out, was not in. "Anyway," said a student in the office, "you're going to have to talk to Queen." Queen, whoever she was, had signed one of the posters. She was next door, in the office used by the Africana Studies Movement. I knocked, and the door opened just wide enough for me to see a huge picture of Malcolm X. Someone said, "Queen's not in. Wait here" —meaning outside. The door closed, and I stood in the corridor, trying to look inconspicuous.

I failed. A student with Rasta braids and an African-style knit cap spotted me from down the hall and circled warily toward me. "What are you doing behind the door?" he demanded. I explained that I was waiting, not hiding, and asked if he thought I might get into the meeting. "No, you won't," he said—an assertion, not a prediction. I waited anyway, just to see if Queen would actually materialize. Two minutes later he circled back and said, "I *told* you not to wait by the door." And now there was no mistaking the threat in his voice. I left.

City College boosters made a point of belittling the influence of Jeffries' personal claque. But they ignored the unthinking acceptance that Jeffries enjoyed among a far wider circle of students. I often talked to students who had almost no idea what Jeffries propounded but supported him nonetheless, because, like Malcolm X, he sounded like he was challenging the white power structure to a fight. As A. J. Franklin, a professor in City's clinical psychology program, put it, Jeffries "verbalizes a lot of the frustration that many African Americans have. They may not necessarily embrace that particular perspective, but they embrace the frustration." But most students didn't distinguish between the two; to embrace the frustration *was* to embrace the perspective.

Jeffries was not so much a practicing intellectual as a charismatic, authoritarian leader who had the legitimacy that comes with academic position. He drew his strength, and his convictions, from the demimonde, the street world where ancient grievances and suspicions are perpetually revived—the world, that is, that has reared many City College students. He had argued, at various times, that AIDS was, indeed, a conspiracy to destroy poor blacks, and that homosexuality was an un-African practice spread by Europeans. He was fascinated by the subject of melanin, and often implied, though rarely said outright, that blacks were superior to whites not only culturally and morally but biologically.

Indeed, in a coincidence so odd as to seem like the contrivance of an ironic god, City College had a white philosophy professor, Michael Levin, who had also formulated a theory of racial difference, but from the opposite point of view. As Levin phrased his hypothesis to me, "On average, blacks are less intelligent and more impulsive than whites, and this accounts for the difference in attainment and poverty between blacks and whites." To make such an argument at City College required a real taste for ostracism, and Levin, unlike Jeffries, had no followers and was universally disparaged on campus. He did not try to win converts among students; he had either the tact or the respect for his own field never to raise his theories in his logic class. In fact I knew several black students who had taken his class and found it, and him, completely unobjectionable.

Nevertheless, Levin helped make the world safe for Jeffries by establishing a symmetry of crackpot ideas. One day I happened to see Richard Severin, a black studies major I had met in the freshman composition class, riding the subway to school. Richard stoutly defended Jeffries as a truth teller. When I asked Richard what he thought about Jeffries' biological theories, he said, as students often did, "No one has come up with any real criticism; it's just personal." "But what do *you* think?" I asked. And Richard said, "What do *you* think about Professor Levin?" —as if, being white, I had Levin as my racial standard-bearer, just as Richard had Jeffries. Perhaps Jeffries had succeeded in persuading Richard that there was no race-neutral truth, or race-neutral approach to the truth—just racial blocs jockeying for power.

Jeffries, unlike Levin, had no field separate from his Afrocentric dogma. He taught no high-level classes in black studies; the department, in fact, had no such classes. Year in and year out, Jeffries taught Black Studies 101, the introductory class, as well as World Civilization. The Black Studies Department had, in fact, "colonized" the World Civ program when it was established in 1987, according to Jim Watts, the chairman of the History Department. "They had the Fruit of Islam in there, they had Len's bodyguards in there," says Watts. He and others had since reduced the number of sections taught by black studies professors, but Jeffries continued to use the class to reach beyond the hard core of acolytes that attended black studies classes. He had assured Watts that he used the standard texts and taught a more or less conventional course.

By the fall of 1992 I had already sat in on a number of black studies classes. Some of them, like The Psychology of Black Experience, had struck me as absurdly polemical; others had not. Moyibi Amoda, a Nigerian who had served in the department since its foundation, invited me to sit in on his introductory black studies class. Amoda was always nattily dressed in a suit; the outfit felt like a rebuke to Jeffries' absurd Afrocentric pretensions, though Amoda would never have intended it that way. He was a proud man, gravely courteous, reflective, and warm. He was the one tenured member of the department who spoke to me openly; perhaps he had been delegated to do so. I was wrong, he said, to think that the Black Studies Department had abandoned rigorous standards. He was eager to have me see his class to show me how wrong I was.

Amoda's class was a model of old-fashioned scholarly propriety. He stood in front of the students in his off-white suit and read his lecture from notes, in a formal manner rarely practiced anywhere at City. He read, and the students took notes. There was no back-and-forth. What Amoda said was thoughtful and nuanced and quite contrary to the monolithic idea of racial identity advanced elsewhere in the department. "You already are a son of America," he told his black students; "you already are a daughter" —it came out daw-*ta*, in Amoda's clipped and refined accent— "of America. If you went to the gate of Mali, and heard the griot talk, you would be like a Greek standing outside." Amoda said, "There's no such thing as a group person, a race mind." And then, perhaps for my benefit, he delivered a stern lecture on the upcoming exam. Amoda had proved his point: he, at least, taught black studies as an academic subject, not a political program or a racial mythos.

Was it possible that, for all his public bullyragging, the same would be true of Jeffries himself? One morning in early November I saw the chairman making a stately progress through the halls, trailed by several pilot fish. I introduced myself and asked if I could sit in on his World Civilization class, which was beginning in a few minutes, at noon. Jeffries looked distinctly amused. "There's a white media conspiracy out to destroy me," he said, "and I'm sure you're part of it. But I don't care. I'm not afraid of you or the *New York Times* or any of them." And so, with a few butterflies in my stomach, I walked around the corner and into Jeffries' classroom. Brother Steve was amiably greeting students from a post just outside the doorway. Jeffries hadn't yet come in, but a tall, thin, saturnine figure in a white knitted cap was setting up Afrocentric books against the blackboard. His name was Taiwo Ogunade, and though he described himself as a member of the department, he was in fact another member of Jeffries' personal entourage.

The class filled up slowly. By 12:10 Jeffries still hadn't arrived, but thirty-five to forty students had. Perhaps half a dozen were Hispanic, and the rest, black. I smiled at the students sitting nearby. They looked at me, and their looks weren't particularly hostile, but they weren't friendly, either. I became aware that I was smiling to myself to show that I wasn't anxious. In fact I was having trouble finding a place to rest my eyes. Fortunately, I could preoccupy myself by looking around the classroom. A handout was taped against one wall: "Edmund Gordon must resign from City College." There were all the books lined up against the blackboard, books on ancient Egypt and the supposed African discovery of the New World, books about monstrous, global conspiracies—not quite the texts that Jim Watts had in mind. The blackboard itself was already filled with vaguely Masonic-looking symbols that I had seen on the posters near the student government office—triangles inside circles. At the center of one of these glyphs were the words *inner core spiritual values*. The words *thesis*, *antithesis*, and *synthesis* each appeared at one of the three points of the triangle. Underneath the circle were the words *interaction*, *search for truth*, and *polarity/duality*.

Jeffries arrived fifteen minutes late and gave the class the African salutation, "Hotep!" The students chanted back, "Hotep!" Jeffries was dressed in dashiki and cap. He was a slightly portly man, and always in motion, waving his arms and striding across the room, swiftly pivoting on his heel. His energy filled the classroom, and the lethargy of a moment before gave way to an air of tense expectancy. "I want you all to be on your best behavior today," he said, "because we have a visitor from the media." The display of almost formal courtesy took me by surprise. I chose to overlook the edge of sarcasm, and I relaxed ever so slightly. Then, as if searching his memory, Jeffries said, "There was a James Traub who wrote an article critical of us in the *Village Voice*." I had been expecting this; a year earlier I had written about the speech that led to Jeffries' firing. I braced for the attack. But then Jeffries said that that article was one of the few that had examined his ideas on the merits. That was better than most. He turned toward me for the first time and said archly, "Now, would you happen to be *that* James Traub?" I said that I was. Jeffries was toying with me, as he had toyed with the crowd; I was at the outer edge of the spider's web.

Jeffries turned back to the class. "When you read a critique of Dr. J in the press," he said, "you read that he doesn't have any qualifications, no publications, no degrees, nothing. So let's talk about credentials." Jeffries wrote down his name on one side of a triangle-in-a-circle, mine on the other. He then began to reproduce his résumé. He had attended Lafayette College, where he had been elected head of the Jewish fraternity. He still had many Jewish friends. He had received his master's in international affairs from Columbia in 1963, and then his Ph.D. "And where did you go to college, Brother Traub?"

I mumbled an answer. I planned on saying as little as possible; I knew that this was not a debate that was to be won on the merits.

"Graduate school?" Jeffries queried blandly, as if he were conducting a job interview. I said that I hadn't gone to graduate school. "No graduate work?" said Jeffries incredulously. "Nothing? Not even any *professional seminars?*" The class hooted. And the unstated question hung in the air: "And yet you presumed to criticize Dr. J?" Jeffries turned back to his own column. For his senior thesis at Lafayette, in 1959, he had written about the urban crisis. "I want you to know that I was a man before my time," he said. "I was predicting the sixties." And he sent Taiwo out to retrieve a copy of the thesis from his office. Taiwo exited, returned. Jeffries read from his senior thesis. After college he had won a Rotary Club scholarship to study in Lausanne, where he had learned "perfect French." And he then began speaking French—perfectly passable French—while looking straight at me as if daring me to keep up. Jeffries was constructing a little drama in which I was the emblematic white critic. Here he was demonstrating his superiority even in that ultimate attainment of European culture, the French language. I remained mute, thus sealing his case, and Jeffries switched back to English. In 1958, he said, he had been assigned to introduce Justice William O. Douglas to President Sekou Toure of Guinea.

"How old were *you* in 1958?" he asked me—lightly, mockingly. I shifted uneasily in my seat. "Four," I said. The class tittered. (Jeffries later said that he had not made the introduction until about 1962.) Jeffries went on and on, piling honors on his own shoulders.

The class had been silent, but now a student in front of me asked, "But how were you treated by the Europeans, Dr. J?" The question sounded suspiciously like a setup. Jeffries flashed a smile and said, "In Europe I was treated not just as a man but as a black prince!" He spoke of the black regiment that had allegedly liberated several Nazi death camps—this had been the subject of a recent documentary—and it became unclear whether Jeffries was talking about the feeling of Europeans about the troops, black people generally, or himself; they seemed to be conflated in his mind. The same student started to ask part two of his question, but Jeffries was too deep in the role of black prince to notice. "Women *ran* to me to give me their children," he said. "When I went to the drugstore, girls were running, literally running, to serve me toothpaste." Jeffries once told an interviewer that men in Europe had offered him their wives in exchange for a homosexual encounter—a vivid proof of the decadence of high white culture, as well as his own allure.

The student in front of me finally managed to wedge in his question: "But ironically, Dr. J, when you came back to America, how did the descendants of those same Europeans treat you?" "Like dirt!" Jeffries cried, whereas in Africa, "they treated me not as a prince, not as a hero, but as a *god*!" The constant stream of praise burbling in the background of the class swelled into shouts of rapture.

Jeffries finally began to do some pyramid analysis on the blackboard. In his analytic scheme, which has a kind of Hegelian gloss to it, circles represent systems, while triangles, or pyramids, represent values. The core of Jeffries' Afrocentric philosophy was the belief that peoples of African descent have a "humanistic, spiritualistic value system," whereas European Americans have values that are "egotistic, individualistic, and exploitative." The other peoples of the world, including Asians, Arabs, and Meso-Americans, appear to have no place at all on the pyramid. Jeffries spoke of Africans as "sun people" and Europeans as "ice people," as if meteorology were destiny. Stranger still was that Jeffries insisted that the effects of the savannah and the cave determined cultures hundreds or thousands of years after the native peoples had left them and had mingled with one another. The clear inference was that the difference was, in fact, biological. To make such an argument at a place like City College seemed particularly absurd. Rasheed would have been amused by the idea that he shared a primordial set of values with the foot soldiers of the Africana Studies Movement.

Jeffries explained that the circle on the far right, which represented the European American world system, held an upside-down pyramid to symbolize the perverse values the system was founded on. It was a failed system— "land-poor, people-poor, and resource-poor" —until slavery made it possible to exploit the New World colonies. Again, Jeffries' passion for neat schemas made him leave a few instances of pre–New World prosperity, such as Dante's Florence or fifteenth-century Antwerp, out of his equation. Jeffries explained that the system evolved—and here he ticked off the words written around the circle—from chattel slavery to wage slavery to its modern form, debt slavery. The imperative of enslavement came from someplace beyond history—something inherent, apparently, in white people. Jeffries neglected to mention that the Arab slave trade lasted longer than the Atlantic version, or that the economy of the Arab world had depended far more thoroughly on the slave system than had that of the European powers. The Arabs, after all, were now brethren in the struggle against the dominion of the European American system.

Jeffries was angry now, and he wheeled from the blackboard to face the class directly. In Brazil, he said, "black youths are being killed like *dogs* in the street!" The class shuddered. Jeffries was talking faster and faster, pacing across the room. Interruption was unthinkable. He began to ride his favorite hobbyhorses, one after the other. He talked about Hollywood, and the old racial stereotypes in the movies. He said, "This is the institutionalization of racism that *the Jewish community is largely responsible for!*" Now, for the first time, Jeffries was shouting. He talked about sun people and ice people. And then he came back to the Jews, the Jews who had run City College and had opposed open admissions. "We've never been given *anything* by the Jews!" Jeffries shouted.

Nor was Jeffries through with me. I had described Cheik Anta Diop, a Senegalese author whom Jeffries regards as seminal, as a brilliant, eccentric polymath, but I had added that he did not say what Jeffries claimed he said. Furious, Jeffries said to the class, "He" —I was no longer "Brother Traub" — "has no qualifications, no insight into this field, and yet he has the . . ."

"Audacity," the student in front of me said helpfully.

". . . the *audacity* to say that I talk about melanin, while Diop never says a word about it." And now Jeffries wheeled on me. "Did you *read* Diop?" he demanded. I said that I had. Jeffries then read the first paragraph of Diop's *Civilization or Barbarism*, which merely said that the first *Homo sapiens*, being African, must have been "pigmented." He put down the volume with a contemptuous look—the look of Q.E.D.—and the class jeered. The drama that Jeffries had staged was coming to a thoroughly satisfying conclusion.

Finally Jeffries reached his great, consuming obsession—the involvement of the Jews in the slave trade. He was speaking rapidly, almost automatically. "We started looking into it," he told the class, "and we saw who was involved. The evidence just came *rolling in*. We found the involvement of the Dutch, and the French, and the Portuguese, and the English, and the Bremen Germans, and the Danes and the Swedes, and the Catholics, *as well as the Jews!*" And now he was rattling off dates, and stray facts, and titles and authors. "Don't just listen to Dr. J," he said. "It's in the books. It's all there. But I've talked about the Jews, so the whole power structure, the whole Jewish-controlled media, has set out to destroy me." Now Jeffries was pacing rapidly, and he was shouting at the top of his lungs. "On this altar of principle," he cried, "I'm being slaughtered, my family is being slaughtered, a whole *community* is being slaughtered! But we won't bow down. We won't give up. *A luta continua!* The struggle continues." Jeffries turned away to look out the window, and the class burst into applause.

The performance was over. The wrathful black god slipped away into the sulphurous smoke, and in his place stood the smooth and mocking black prince. Jeffries still wanted to have his way with me, and when the class ended he beckoned me over. Now, with his claque eagerly looking on as if at a one-sided boxing match, Jeffries chided me, challenged me, slapped me around some more. There was Diop and slavery and New World colonialism and whatnot. It was a game; but it was also an obsession, an unappeasable hunger. As I retreated, promising to read the books and listen to the tapes and see the world as Jeffries saw it, I found Moyibi Amoda at my elbow. Perhaps he had heard through the black studies grapevine that I was there. Now he rode down the escalator with me, his hands in the pockets of his camel's-hair coat.

"Well," Amoda asked, "what did you think of the class?" I told him how upsetting, and authoritarian, and ultimately how absurd, the whole experience had been. He listened attentively, scanning my face, taking a reading. He was terribly grave, and almost urgent. I had to understand where Jeffries was coming from, he said. We were standing in a foyer outside the faculty lounge. When a black student walked by, Amoda fell silent. Then Kamuti Kiteme, another tenured black studies professor, walked by, and Amoda waved, and again stopped speaking—Kiteme, whom he had known for over twenty years. I understood that Amoda was taking a risk merely by being seen speaking to me in public. He spoke of Ralph Ellison, of a black man's rage against "invisibility." He spoke of Gandhi— Gandhi!—who had cast off his Western clothes. I told him that I found the comparison grotesque; but Amoda was dead earnest. He talked about himself, about what it meant to be a black man in a white world. I felt nothing for Jeffries; but I was moved that Amoda would extend himself so far to defend the great mission that he felt that Jeffries represented.

And then Jeffries himself came down the stairs, trailed by Taiwo. Amoda tried to explain what I had said, to play the honest broker. Jeffries interrupted him with a look of impatience and disgust, and embarked on a tirade about global white supremacy and the Jewish-controlled media. It was as if Jeffries knew that Amoda was trying to create common ground, and wanted to trample it into insignificance. It was as if he wanted to prove that I was right about him, and Amoda wrong. Amoda stopped, started, stopped again, and looked on stoically.

The Black Studies Department at City College, like black studies departments at many of the nation's leading colleges and universities, was established as a direct result of pressure from black students and faculty in the late 1960s. The creation of a School of Black Studies was, in fact, one of the five demands of the militant students who conducted the lockout at City College in 1969. The college's administrators tried to mollify the activists by creating a single department of urban and ethnic studies, but in 1971, after a terribly bitter debate, the department was broken up into its component parts, the most prominent being black studies. The new college president, Robert Marshak, appointed a search team, consisting of the activists themselves and headed up by Amoda, to find a chair for the fledgling department. It was clear from the outset that black studies was to belong to its own partisans in a way that would have been unthinkable for an ordinary academic department.

Leonard Jeffries had taught political science at City in 1969, though he had not, despite his own claims to the contrary, been significantly involved in the student uprising. He had then become the founding chairman of the Black Studies Department at San Jose State University. He was an important figure among the "cultural nationalists," a group within the Black Power movement that was distinguished for its wholesale repudiation of white culture and its celebration of Africa and things African. He had just completed his doctoral dissertation, on subnational politics in the Ivory Coast, when he was interviewed, and then recommended, by City's search committee.

Robert Marshak had promised to award full-professor status as well as tenure to a qualified candidate. With no publications to his credit, Jeffries was clearly not such a candidate. One member of the search team, Frank Laraque, says that black students and faculty threatened to provoke a crisis were Jeffries not immediately tenured. (Amoda denies that any such threat was leveled.) Marshak, who was in any case eager to placate black students and faculty and unite them behind his vision of the "urban-grant college," agreed to give Jeffries tenure on arrival—another sign that the Black Studies Department was to have rules of its own. And Jeffries then proceeded to make a fool of Marshak by never again producing a single scholarly work. In fact Jeffries produced almost no written work at all. At times he spoke of having written a fifty-page "booklet," but the work was in fact commissioned for the junior high school market and was never published.

Over the years Jeffries gave the City College administration any number of reasons to remove him as chairman of the department. In the fall of 1982 a black student, Oswald Facey, claimed that Jeffries had shoved and "verbally abused" him while he was campaigning for student office. Facey was running against the ticket that Jeffries backed—an act, apparently, of lèse-majesté. In an interview in the *Campus*, Facey called Jeffries "a racist." The *Campus* called for Jeffries' resignation, citing his nonstop meddling in student government. The new college president, a black psychologist named Bernard Harleston, ordered an inquiry, but Facey failed to testify, and the issue was dropped.

Two years later, in the course of a meeting with Mitchell Seligson, a candidate for director of City's international studies program, Jeffries launched into a diatribe in which he declared that Harleston was the pawn of a Jewish conspiracy, and said to Seligson, "Why does a Jew like you want to work at a place like this?" Seligson withdrew his candidacy and wrote a biting letter to Harleston. Another investigation was launched, and this time it was conclusive. Martin Tamny, an associate dean of social sciences who had been present at the lunch, confirmed that he had heard Jeffries' remarks, as did the others who were present. Tamny recommended that Jeffries be stripped of his chairmanship. Harleston sent Jeffries a letter saying "such comments and remarks . . . are intolerable and indefensible"—and then declined to take any action.

Tamny was appalled that Harleston had passed up a golden opportunity to dismiss Jeffries. The chairman, apparently, had taken the president's measure. But perhaps he had taken his own colleagues' measure as well. Tamny says, "Seligson was outraged that no one had said anything at the time. If anyone should have said anything, it probably was me. I've thought about that meeting hundreds of times; I don't know why I didn't speak. I suppose it was because that was the sort of thing one heard from Jeffries all the time." Jeffries had never been challenged before; why now?

Yet another inquiry was begun in 1988, after a white student wrote a four-part series in the *Campus* describing Jeffries' outlandish teachings. The student said that he had actually enjoyed the class, and he refused to testify before a panel. But the article made public something that students had known and administrators had chosen to ignore: that the chairman of a major department was teaching racist mythology in class. They knew, as well, that most of the other tenured members of the department taught their own variant on Jeffries' Afrocentrism. None of them had published in scholarly journals for years. For all its flurries of militance, the department was fundamentally inert. Its makeup had barely changed since Jeffries had arrived, giving the department the mothballed quality of the

Stalinist era Politburo. No one even knew how many black studies majors there were, but the number seemed to be about half a dozen. Black Studies wasn't a field so much as a state of mind; you didn't have to actually take the courses to share in the consciousness.

Jeffries, in fact, deserved to be fired as chairman not because of his periodic enormities but because of the way he and his department demeaned the aspirations of their own students. One of his tenured professors, Perezi Kamunanwire, actually had another full-time job as Uganda's consul general in New York. Other professors shuttled between the campus and Africa, often leaving students in the lurch for weeks at a time. Several of them, including Jeffries, often neglected to hand in grades at the end of the term. Students would receive an Incomplete, which would automatically convert to an F after a semester. Jeffrey Rosen, the dean of social sciences, tried to explain to Jeffries that the department was harming its own students, but, Rosen recalls, "Len said that black students had to work, so they weren't able to hand in their homework. I pointed out that the same students were handing in homework in their other classes. That's not a conversation that's going to go very far with Len."

Jeffries himself was too much the bully to be a teacher, and not just toward white visitors. He treated his students as a chorus; dissent was unheard of, and an air of spurious consensus reigned. Students who gagged at the farrago Jeffries was spooning out knew better than to let on in class. Ericson Pierre, whom I had met the previous summer in ESL, had been persuaded by some of his friends to take Jeffries' World Civ class, mostly because it would be easy. When I saw him one day late in the spring of 1993 he said, "I regret taking this class, because I'm not learning anything. This man thinks he knows everything, so how can you ask him a question? I don't speak in class, because I don't want to get in trouble. If I try to say anything, they will say, 'You are black on the outside, but white on the inside.' "

Ericson had been trained in lycée, where students expected to bend beneath the whip; he was amazed to find that Jeffries didn't seem to care if anyone worked or not, so long as they parroted the dogma. Jeffries, he said, assigned ten essays and a research paper, but didn't specify length or subject and didn't return the papers. "I don't think he reads them," Ericson said. "I think the old lady does" —Mother Franklin, another Jeffries hanger-on who acted as class doyenne. Most students, he said, copied papers from other students. But at least you could count on a good grade. At one of the first class sessions, Ericson said, Jeffries had admitted that he had been asked not to give out so many A's, but promised that he wasn't about to stop. He had a formula, he said with a smile: " 'A' is for African, 'B' is for black, 'C' is for colored."

Foreign students, especially, often wandered into a black studies course under the mistaken impression that they might learn something about black history. Another Haitian student told me that she had decided to take the introductory black studies class from Kamuti Kiteme. The professor hadn't shown up for the second or third class and had sent Taiwo, the departmental pinch hitter, in his stead. Of the four Jeffries classes that I sat in on during the year, Taiwo taught two, prosing on about the superiority of Yoruba culture and the merits of traditional practices like clitorectomy, while students brazenly walked out the door. The Haitian student had been thoroughly offended at Taiwo's rambling monologue, and then outraged when he showed up for subsequent sessions. Where was Kiteme? Back in Kenya, apparently. She was naive enough to go to the department to complain. A beefy young man in an African cap was sitting at the secretary's desk. "You can talk to me," he said. "I'm with the department." When she poured out her tale of woe, he shocked her by saying, "If you're uncomfortable it means you're not ready to deal with the issue." Only later did she learn that she had been talking to Brother Steve.

But this was not a woman who took her education lightly. She had heard about Edmund Gordon, the new chairman of the department, and she proceeded to write him a letter about her experience, including the episode with Brother Steve. Gordon called her within a week and asked her to come speak with him. He heard her out, and when she had finished he said that he had tried to raise some similar concerns himself. "But there's nothing I can do," he said, as if Jeffries were his boss rather than the other way around. "There's nobody else on my side." The woman thanked Gordon for his solicitude and his candor, and added, "I'm sorry to say this, but I'm never going to take another black studies class."

Jeffries had effectively destroyed black studies as a legitimate field of inquiry at City College. And yet every three years, when his supremely loyal colleagues nominated him for another term as chairman, the college provost and president, and the CUNY Board of Trustees, routinely confirmed the decision. Any of them could have moved against Jeffries at almost any time; but no one did. Jeffries ruled through fear; and through fear he kept his power. Whenever his position was threatened, Jeffries knew that he could play the race card. "He explained that all of Harlem would rise if anyone touched a hair on his head," says math professor Bernard Sohmer. "I think Marshak believed it. And Harleston was constitutionally incapable of dealing with any kind of conflict." And perhaps Martin Tamny's explanation applied to them, as well as to himself, as well as to everyone else in a position of responsibility at City College: they had been turning a blind eye to Jeffries for so long that they could no longer bring themselves to confront him.

Jeffries gained his first real taste of notoriety in 1989, when he served as the key contributor to *The Curriculum of Inclusion*, a stunningly confrontational report on multicultural education in the public schools issued by a state-appointed panel. Current curriculum, Jeffries wrote, reflects "deep-seated pathologies of racial hatred" and a "wholesale policy of destroying the positive aspects and attributes of African Americans." The ensuing uproar made Jeffries a hero in some quarters, and he began, to his immense satisfaction, to travel the lecture circuit. In July 1991, Jeffries gave his stump speech to the Empire State Black Arts and Cultural Festival in Albany. The speech itself was a tastings menu of his preoccupations: "the melanin factor" and "the factor of ice," the slave trade, the Egyptian origin of Western civilization, multicultural education. He held up books and magazines and diagrams of triangles inside circles.

It wasn't Jeffries' cranky racial theories that got him in trouble so much as his feverish obsession with the Jews. He railed against the Jews who controlled Hollywood, and the Jews who financed the slave trade, and the Jews who ran the affairs of City College, and then again the Jews who financed the slave trade. He was, he said, only talking about "rich Jews"; yet the word seemed to stick in his mouth. He talked about "my Jews" at City College, and he called

Bernard Sohmer City College's "head Jew" —a reference to the "kabala" of Jews that, according to the Black Studies Department, secretly ran the institution. And he mocked one of his persistent critics, the education scholar Diane Ravitch, as a "sophisticated Texas Jew" —a coinage that had the ring of timeless anti-Semitism. Columnist Pete Hamill called the speech "pure Goebbels."

The speech upset City's delicate racial balance. Jewish students were taunted in small ways, something that had been unthinkable until then. Philip Altzman, a graduate student in physics who wore a yarmulke, said that he was frequently harassed. The head of City's Hillel chapter, Rabbi Roy Mittleman, sent out a slightly panicky letter to alumni quoting a student to the effect that "there has not been a single day this semester I have not had to deal with racist, anti-Semitic propaganda posted on the walls in the form of fliers and in newspapers around campus." Mittleman and a group of students received an audience with Harleston to discuss their fears. The president's response, according to one participant, was, "There's such a thing as freedom of speech; and I resent the notion that there's anti-Semitism on campus." Harleston wasn't altogether wrong, since, for all the polemical hot air, City was a far more racially harmonious campus than most; but the presentiment that an edge of personal anger had been added to the obligatory rhetoric made students fear for the future.

At first, Harleston and CUNY chancellor Ann Reynolds reacted murmuringly to the speech. But once many of New York's public and political leaders began to express their outrage, CUNY was forced to act. In late October the Board of Trustees voted to give Jeffries a probationary one-year term as chairman. This was a thinly disguised device designed to give Harleston the opportunity to ease Jeffries out painlessly and to find a replacement. In early February, Harleston, having failed to attract any number of younger scholars, turned to Edmund Gordon, whom he had known for forty years and who had acted as his adviser since 1984. It was Gordon, by an odd coincidence, whom the New York State Board of Regents had asked to rewrite *The Curriculum of Inclusion*. Gordon's appointment was formalized by the CUNY board in March. A few months earlier Jeffries had predicted that his dismissal would provoke violence that "would make Crown Heights [the site of a virtual race riot that summer] pale in comparison." In fact Jeffries' ouster provoked not a ripple in Harlem, and nothing more dangerous than a rally on campus. His bluff, finally, had been called.

When I first met Edmund Gordon, late in the summer of 1992, he illustrated the difference between himself and Jeffries with a story about his "evaluation," in fact his wholesale rewriting, of the New York State curriculum study. "When I presented the report," he said, "I got a standing ovation from the board. But Leonard Jeffries also complimented me on it. I had not repudiated the findings of the original report, but I had put it in an intellectual framework that people could agree or disagree with." The story was meant to illustrate several things at once. Gordon had a Left perspective on the vogue issues of the day; the students would be able to identify with him. But he was a consensualist, a finder of common ground. He cared deeply about the means of discussion, and he would bring to City College a new, intellectually serious language of discourse. But he was also saying, perhaps unconsciously, that Jeffries' approval mattered to him, and that he would find a way to work with the department rather than stand up to it.

Gordon was also explaining why he had taken a job that sensible, younger scholars had declined. He felt a deep sense of responsibility to Harleston, who had been a target of withering, and quite deserved, criticism over his handling of Jeffries. But Gordon was also thinking about the idea of rescue; and the prospect meant more to him than it could have to almost anyone else at City College. Gordon was an educational psychologist who had devoted his career to the issues surrounding the teaching of disadvantaged youth. City College, and its great experiment in open admissions, spoke to his deepest personal ideals and professional convictions. And he was a black intellectual of another generation who worried that the intellectual standards he had grown up with were losing their force. He surprised me, given his politics, by saying that affirmative action "has let too many of us get away with less than our best work." And he felt that the oppositional element of black culture, so deeply ingrained at City College, was working to undermine intellectual achievement itself. "What really concerns me," said Gordon, an elfin figure with a neatly trimmed salt-and-pepper beard, "is the department's anti-intellectualism, which speaks to an anti-intellectualism in the black community."

What upset Gordon most was the department's effect on black students, who so desperately needed intellectual nourishment. He was familiar with the vogue theory that by learning about their own heritage black students could increase their self-esteem, but, he said, "I have trouble with that. I'm convinced that what makes me feel good is a sense of competence. Learning about the achievements of your own people may encourage engagement with the subject matter, but it won't encourage competence. And I would opt for competence, not simple engagement." The goal of multiculturalism, in Gordon's mind, was not to make students feel good about being black or Latino or Asian, but to promote in all students the intellectual sophistication that comes of possessing "multiple perspectives."

Gordon was a man of another era. He had been shaped not by the civil rights movement or the Black Power movement but by the great ideals of the 1930s and 1940s—the vision of a dedicated black bourgeoisie, of an intellectual cadre aspiring to the highest levels. Gordon's hero and, he said, "personal mentor" was W. E. B. Du Bois, a tireless activist and organizer for black people and at the same time an irreproachable scholar. He referred often to Du Bois's injunction that "the talented tenth" of black people dedicate themselves to serving the community. Before taking up his intellectual life, Gordon had served as a Presbyterian minister and social worker, a guidance counselor, and a pediatric psychologist. He had been one of the founding figures of the Head Start program, as well as a leading authority on the whole range of issues surrounding race, disadvantage, education, and development.

A few months after Leonard Jeffries gave his fateful speech, Gordon's career had been capped with a festschrift given by his former students at Columbia and Yale, where he had been chairman of the Afro-American Studies program. Gordon had managed to become one of the leading black intellectual figures of his generation without ever writing a big book or even making any really seminal contribution. He was widely respected and universally liked, a kindly figure who found jobs and grants for young scholars, and never lost control of his ego, his temper, or his quiet, mellow voice. Sometimes he brought homemade soup to faculty meetings. There was a little bit of Mr. Chips in Gordon.

I went away from my conversation with Gordon feeling that City College was lucky to have persuaded him to take over the Black Studies Department. At the same time, it was hard to imagine Mr. Chips surviving in Leonard Jeffries' Black Studies Department. Precisely those qualities that would make Gordon a fine role model would, I feared, unfit him for Jeffries' politics of confrontation. In fact we had held our discussion in an office in the administration building because Jeffries had refused to vacate his own office. He was suing CUNY on First Amendment grounds, and he had decided, and of course the department had decided, to acknowledge Gordon's existence as little as possible. Even the departmental secretary at first pretended that she had no idea who Gordon was. Nobody with an office in the department was willing to make room for Gordon, and it wasn't in Gordon's nature to force an issue involving his own personal status or comfort; so well into the semester he continued to conduct his business from the administration building. One afternoon in the early fall I walked into the black studies office and was surprised to see Gordon sitting in a chair next to the secretary's desk. He was running the department from the chair, like Saint Louis dispensing justice from under a tree.

Gordon had ambitious plans for the department, and he was eager, in his restrained way, to move ahead. He had been promised three new tenure-track positions, one of them a distinguished professorship. He hoped to create a CUNY-wide graduate program, not in black studies but in "intercultural studies," as well as a postgraduate research body that he had tactfully named the Du Bois–Diop–James Institute for Research on the African Diaspora in the Americas and the Caribbean. (C. L. R. James was a well-known Jamaican scholar.) By the fall, Gordon understood that the department was bent on resistance, but he believed that his diplomatic, reassuring style would eventually carry the day, as it had so often in his life. A few professors were coming to him privately, he said, to tell him they admired his work and to wish him well.

Nor had Gordon arrived in the department alone. He had arranged appointments in black studies for bell hooks, an essayist and feminist scholar (who spelled her name without capital letters); Venus Green, a historian; and Fred Dunn, whose field was the philosophy of education. I used to drop by Dunn's office, and we would talk behind closed doors. (Green wouldn't even talk to me.) Dunn said that he wouldn't have dreamed of taking a job in black studies before Gordon had taken over. Gordon, he said, "is a cat that I like a lot, that I respect enormously." Dunn was a cat that I liked a lot. In fact he reminded me of a cat, a very big cat, slow and smooth and self-contained. And sharp—Dunn wore cashmere sweaters and silk socks and Italian loafers, and he kept his big head perfectly shaved and shiny.

Dunn considered Afrocentrism a form of politics rather than scholarship. "I don't like the line," he said mildly, or perhaps cautiously. "The line is too rigid, too divisive. It didn't move from the sixties. *I* was down in the sixties; I was a nationalist. I still have a broad streak from the sixties. But I'm interested in movement. I have no interest in hating white people. I *am* interested in moving black people." Dunn found that his students hungered for simplistic categories—above all, racial categories. They were, he said, "an easy sale" for Jeffries. Students would ask him if he considered himself African, and Dunn would reply, "I'm undeniably African by ethnic background. But clearly my nationality is American. If you want to ask me that question you're going to have to make it much sharper— *much* sharper. I'm a good chess player. I'm a pretty good basketball player. I'm a lot of things." It wasn't just an answer, it was an illustration of intellectual method. "I'm trying to show them that it's the wrong question," Dunn said. "We're in the academy; my job is to force some critical thinking."

Gordon had allies, but in truth he was way overmatched. The black studies faculty met every five or six weeks. From the outset, in September, Jeffries commandeered these meetings. "He would do these half-hour spurts," Dunn said, "usually about how Ed was an unprincipled liar, and he was part of the CUNY administration, and he was bent on destroying the Black Studies Department as it currently exists." The other tenured faculty, including those whom

Gordon considered marginally sympathetic, would remain quiet or chip in their own criticisms. Gordon, a man of monumental restraint, said nothing, except once, when Jeffries raised the fact that Gordon's wife was white. "You can criticize me all you want," snapped Gordon, "but leave my wife and family out of it." Jeffries had violated Gordon's gentlemanly code, the sort of archaism that made him seem like such an odd man out at City College. Jeffries made no further references to Gordon's wife, but he continued to dominate the meetings and ensure that nothing of consequence was discussed or at least decided.

Gordon made no more headway with black studies students than he did with faculty. He was the target of rallies and meetings and petition drives, and of a widely distributed flyer titled "Ten Good Reasons Why Edmund Gordon Must Resign." Reason number six was, "The Chair of the department of Black Studies is a sensitive position. The appointment of Gordon, who is interracially married is insensitive and highly questionable." When Gordon finally procured an office next to the Black Studies Department, and put a sign-up sheet on his door, someone scrawled, "Get out motherfucker." How could anyone, much less a diplomat like Gordon, deal with such unreasoning rage? Gordon was thinking about calling a public meeting but, he said, "I don't think it will do much good if it simply attracted Len's followers. They would just heap abuse." A younger man, or a more aggressive one, might have accepted the need for confrontation. But that wasn't Gordon's way.

There was, in fact, a great mass of black students who were repelled by Jeffries and his little squad of enforcers, and who might have responded to Gordon had he known how to reach them. Many of the more intellectually sophisticated black students were embarrassed and even insulted by the crudity of Jeffries' appeal. One day in the early spring I happened to see Aisha, the bright and mercurial girl I had met in Rudi Gedamke's class. I mentioned Jeffries, and Aisha started complaining about friends of hers who had fallen under his sway. "He's like a priest to them," she said mockingly. "I say, 'How can you believe all this stuff?' But if he says it, they believe it." Aisha had even had the cheek to corner the fearsome Jeffries outside of class. She proudly recalled the exchange for me. "I said, 'How can you possibly say that all white people are bad? Why don't you blame something on *yourself* for once. All white people are not evil.' " And Jeffries had replied, "You're totally out of touch with your black identity," and suggested she take his black studies class to get back in touch. Aisha applied and was told that the class was already full.

Jeffries' presence on campus, and his outsize fame, utterly eclipsed City's sizable cadre of gifted black students and intellectually serious black faculty. Michelle Wallace, a professor of English Literature, a well-known feminist author and one of City's leading black intellectuals, said that it infuriated her that Jeffries "has become the representative voice of the black community, and of City College" — not only among whites who loathed him but among blacks who revered him. Jeffries had turned City into a symbol of racial posturing. Wallace had grown up a few blocks from the City College campus and had received her bachelor's degree from City during the first years of open admissions; her mother had graduated from City as well. For her, the school was every bit the shining city on a hill that it had been to Rudi Gedamke, or to generations of Jewish immigrants before him. Open admissions had meant to Wallace that City College would become the focus of black intellectual aspirations, as it had been for the Jews. And instead, because of Leonard Jeffries, City had become a symbol of the most farcical and delusional elements of black thought. "Jeffries is like a cancer on the body of City College," she said bitterly. "He's killing the whole system."

Wallace felt impelled by her vision of City College to sharply, and publicly, draw the difference between myth making and real intellectual activity. "A number of us need to take on this job," she said, "if black studies is ever going to be a serious area." But standing up to a bully like Jeffries was dangerous work, and far more so for a black figure at City than for a white. Most of Wallace's colleagues refused to break racial ranks, no matter what they thought of Jeffries privately. When I asked A. J. Franklin, one of the most prominent black scholars at City, what he had thought of Jeffries' Albany speech, he hesitated and then said carefully, "I'm not in a position to refute it or not to refute because I'm not a historian." Was it anti-Semitic? "I've struggled with that," said Franklin. And what had he concluded? He hadn't reached a conclusion yet. And since he hadn't seen or

heard the whole speech, and didn't plan to, it was unlikely that he
would reach a conclusion anytime soon. And so, while a figure like
Michael Levin could be ignored as a crackpot, Leonard Jeffries cap-
italized on silence to claim that he spoke for black people generally.

Between those people who turned their back on him, those
who kept a prudent silence, and those whom he didn't know how
to reach, Edmund Gordon was a very isolated figure at City College
by early 1993. There was something noble in his cheerful stoicism,
but his *mission civilatrice* was not advancing very far.

In the spring semester Gordon taught two seminars and took
on more than a dozen students for independent study projects. I
made a point of regularly attending a two-and-a-half-hour class, The
Pychosocial Development of the African-American Male. Gordon
said that during the first session, which I missed, "the students took
me to task. They wanted to know who I was, and they were dubious
about what I was doing there." In Gordon's emollient vocabulary,
dubious translated as *hostile*. At least four of the students, he thought,
were followers of Jeffries. (In his other seminar, which focused on the
black child, students had accused Gordon and his coteacher, Irving
Hamer, of assigning too few Afrocentric texts.) Gordon had explained
himself, and added that he expected "Ivy League" work from them.
He handed out an extensive and very catholic reading list, and told
them a paper of twenty to sixty pages would be required. None of
the students had ever written a twenty-page paper, much less a sixty-
page paper. "And I bet those kids in the Ivy League don't have to
work or support a family," one student said to me tartly before class
the next week.

Gordon *looked* somewhat Ivy League, with raffish touches that
dated from the early 1970s. There was the beard, and the beret, and
the strange, Hobbit-like footwear—birkenstocks, in both open- and
closed-toe versions. He always wore a tie, but his ties never seemed
to reach more than halfway down his yellow shirts. The overall effect
was grandfatherly—a gentleman of the old school, fusty, faintly ab-
sentminded, and deeply courteous. Gordon had hearing aids in both
ears, and when the class abandoned itself to digression, as it often
did, he would sometimes sit back and let the noise wash over him.

Gordon made sure that coffee and cookies were always available at a side table. Everything about the way he conducted the class bespoke a respect for the intellectual endeavor in which he and the students were jointly engaged. During the first session I attended, Gordon referred continually to the work of others, noting where he personally differed but always holding out the possibility that they were right and he was wrong. The explicit subject of the class was dysfunctional behavior among young black men, but the subtext, as it was in Fred Dunn's classes, was intellectual method itself. "You do need canons of professional competence," Gordon said in a soft voice, rounded at the edges with the remains of a southern accent. "But since none of us can be completely objective we have a responsibility to say what our biases are. Thus I will say that I am black, male, of the twentieth century, I tend toward the Left, I try not to be sexist, and so on. I'm not objective, but I declare my subjectivity."

Gordon was preaching the morality of scholarship. It was a far, far cry from *"A luta continua,"* and the fifteen or so black students around the table were almost entirely silent, and even a bit fidgety. Then Gordon mentioned that his father was Jamaican, and alluded to the relatively high level of achievement of West Indians in the United States. Clark, a handsome, very light-skinned student at the far end of the table, said, "Caribbean people were trained to be part of their society, to like it." (The students demanded that I not identify them at all, so I am using invented first names.) Gordon translated: "What Clark is saying is that when blacks have bought into the European system, that influences their place in the system." Martha, sitting just to Gordon's right, said, "It comes from being more disciplined. There's more of a will to do with black West Indians than for those of us who were born and raised in the U.S." And there then ensued the most interesting conversation about race I had ever heard, or ever would hear, at City College.

It turned out that most of the students were either first- or second-generation West Indians. This striking fact could not be explicitly acknowledged, because doing so would have brought a touchy issue too close to home: the hierarchy of black achievement existed right there at City College. A certain level of candor was impossible, and yet Gordon had happened on a subject that almost everyone in class had given some thought to. "People came here as immigrants," said Martha, "and people are always willing to do something in a new country that they wouldn't do at home." Malina added, "Over there they were less oppressed than we were here. Maybe they have a bit less of a burden in terms of what the African American went through."

Many of the students didn't know whether to say "they" or "we," or indeed exactly how to feel about the privilege that seemed to have been conferred with their background. Being born into the talented tenth had been a source of pride when Edmund Gordon was a boy, as had aspiring to join the dominant culture. Now privilege was suspect, and assimilation was a source of embarrassment, even shame. Clark talked about how scrupulously his Guyanese parents had monitored his vocabulary and even his manners. "Sunday night is practice night," he said. "Everyone wears a suit and tie to the table. My father watches to make sure I'm using the knife and fork properly. I have this tendency to slide my hand down on the fork, and he corrects me." Clark had something almost courtly in his manner, but what he had apparently absorbed at the dinner table he had resisted in his mind. He saw the bourgeois ethic as a prop for the neocolonial society. "The motivation of a postcolonial power," he explained, "was to maintain the easy attachment that the people had. You want to make sure that the people who get to the top will represent the system so well that they will keep that system."

Gordon let the conversation wander for much of the class; perhaps he was glad just to have stirred up debate. Finally he said, "I do need to call your attention to about six other variables." And he quickly ran through a series of hypotheses on the issue of black social and economic status, suggesting additional reading as he went. The class went quiet again.

Signs of trouble began to appear the following week. A few students had left; the class was down to twelve or thirteen. Gordon began by explaining what the students should include in their outline of the research paper: "The definition and specification of the group under study" or "the level of confidence you have in the data you've collected." The students looked at each other dubiously. Finally Martha asked timidly, "Do you have a topic that you're going to suggest?" Gordon did not; the idea had probably never occurred to him. Later, when Gordon led a discussion of a scholarly article he had assigned, the class swung strangely between confusion over basic terms and a blithe willingness to question Gordon's own understanding of the material. It was as if they had no idea of the gulf between them and him.

A few days later, in the cafeteria, I saw a girl I recognized from the class, and I asked whether she was enjoying it. Not really, said Margaret. "I thought it would be a good class because I'd get a chance to really express myself on racism. It's a seminar, where you can say what you think. I don't believe it's good to hold things inside." Gordon struck her as phlegmatic and reserved; worse, he was an Oreo. At one point he had said, "I fear that I gave up a good deal of my blackness in the course of moving into a mixed world." Margaret had been scandalized. "My feeling is that if you have your identity, that's sacred," she said. Gordon's point had been that black identity is necessarily affected by living, and succeeding, in a white world, as it had been for Clark's father or his father. He had added, "My kids dragged me back into my black identity." But Margaret hadn't heard, or acknowledged, that part; something that was sacred, after all, could scarcely be compromised and regained. Anyway, she said, Gordon was assigning way too much work. She was going to drop the class.

From week to week I could feel Gordon lowering his expectations. "Does anyone know what a classic is?" he asked; and "Does anyone know what an empiricist is?" He had mentioned Gunnar Myrdal several times, but no one had bothered to learn who he was. Despite himself, Gordon was growing ever so slightly peevish. "When a professor calls a work to your attention," he said, peering over his half glasses, "it's worth stopping by the library and at least browsing it." And then he smiled, incongruously, to remove the force of the sting. I was starting to feel dismayed myself. These students were a full step farther along than those I had met in the core classes or in English 110; they were upperclassmen, and most were social science majors. And yet they lacked the most rudimentary academic habits. That first discussion had been misleading; like the students in freshman composition, they seemed at sea as soon as the discussion moved beyond the personal. And what was just as discouraging was that Gordon had failed to attract the talented black students I knew who shunned black studies. It might be a long time before the field would be sufficiently disinfected for their tastes.

Most classes began with a discussion of readings that Gordon had distributed the week before. In mid-March, toward the middle of the term, Gordon asked the students to comment on an article that asserted that black males had, if anything, more traditional bread-winner attitudes than white males, but that they had been deprived of the opportunity to satisfy their aspirations. Gordon pushed his glasses up his nose, looked down the table, and asked Vivian, a few seats away from him, to describe the author's argument. Vivian looked stricken, and then mumbled, more as a question than an answer, "The author talks about studies where black men talk about their feelings about manhood." "All right," said Gordon. "Martha, could you take us a bit further?" But Martha said, "What this paper is about is black male identity." "Chan?" Chan always sat just to Gordon's left. Chan looked down at the table and whispered, "I thought the same thing." Gordon tried, ever so gently, to prod Chan into a response. "What does this tell us about the idea of responsibility in the black male?" he asked. But Chan only gave him that anxious and beseeching look I had seen so many times before.

Gordon was clearly miffed. This was supposed to be an upper-level class, and the students seemed unable to interpret a perfectly simple text. Gordon explained the difference between mere literacy and critical reading. There was no mistaking his inference. It was a painful, awkward moment. Gordon then turned back to the text, explaining that the author was saying, among other things, that the high rate of black male violence might be explained not as wanton hostility but as a natural consequence of frustrated aspirations. Clark suddenly intervened: "It's not natural," he said. "It's because weapons are available." And weapons were available in the ghetto, Clark said, for the same reason that drugs were available—because that suited the purpose of the ruling class. Clark saw that Gordon had raised an eyebrow. Clark was the one student in class who seemed to recognize Gordon's intellectual merits and to look to him for approval. "Doesn't it seem so to you?" he asked.

"I don't think it's deliberate," said Gordon evenly. "I don't think it's a conspiracy."

Clark cut him off. "I disagree," he said heatedly. "It's got to be. And I can prove it." This was a favorite locution of Clark's, who had probably been winning arguments effortlessly all his life. Clark's proof was that the embargo on cigars from Cuba worked; how could huge shipments of drugs be getting through unless the government wanted it that way?

"It *has* to be," said Martha, "because they're the ones who have the control."

Gordon knew that he was losing the class, but he tried one last stand. "Suppose someone were to say that we're too honorable a society for that?" he asked. The class groaned as one. Someone said, "Puh-leeze!" And now the class was off and running. Students who had been timid a few minutes before were shouting at one another. Delbert, who worked at a hospital and always wore a tie to class, tried to explain that capitalism, by which he meant market forces, had a lot to do with the presence of guns and drugs in the ghetto.

"It's not just capitalism," said Clark; "it's national interest."

"It's survival," Martha interjected. "They have to make sure that their race survives." That sounded like an echo of Frances Cress Welsing's bizarre theory that racism was caused by white fears of "genetic annihilation."

Shoba had been waving her hand and trying to get attention. Shoba had admitted that she had a reading problem; usually she had trouble following the class discussion. Now she cried, "It's not national interest! Capitalism is more important." Clark insisted that Shoba was wrong, and said, "I can prove it to you in a single sentence." Clark improvised a really outlandish argument about the gold standard and national debt. "I'm not down with you," said Shoba. "But we can agree to disagree."

I looked over and saw that Gordon had opened a book. Apparently he had decided to let the flood spend itself. The argument raged over vast stretches of territory, or rather over a series of labels that stood for territory. Clark called on Gordon again: "Who controls the UN, honestly?" Gordon talked about multinationals, international finance, global capital flows. The class drifted off again. Martha said, "There's a book called *The Unseen Hand*. Has anybody seen it? Everything is falling into place. It's all part of a plan. And now they have one elite group that's going to rule the world." That, Martha explained, was the New World Order.

Gordon finally roused himself and tried to steer the conversation toward shallower waters. He talked about the civil rights movement, the need for political engagement, careful analysis, honest leadership. The conversation paused, and then rolled on. I looked at the notebook of the woman next to me; it was full of circles and triangles. The class had the quality of a failed exorcism.

When I stopped by Gordon's office a few days later, he was as smoothly cheerful as ever, but it was obvious that he was discouraged. I asked if he had been surprised at all the talk about *The Unseen Hand* and global conspiracies. "That's not just City College," he pointed out. "That's a widespread perspective in the African American community. What I try to do is put this conspiracy, or the impression of it, in perspective. When a particular set of values dominates a society you don't *need* a conspiracy to honor them." But Gordon conceded that he had been unpleasantly surprised, not so much last week as ever since arriving. "I had not realized the extent to which both the faculty and students had kind of bought into a dogma," he said. Gordon recognized that in class, as in the world of black studies generally, he remained an outsider, but he was an optimist by nature. "My feeling has always been that the basis of education is relationships," he said. "I hope that once the kids stop viewing me as an enemy and a stranger, and see me for who I am, then they can start to work with me."

But the class had exposed not only the students' conspiratorial turn of mind, but the way in which they used bombast and hollow polemics to conceal the absence of intellectual structure, or even of a base of knowledge. This was precisely the phenomenon that Leonard Jeffries exploited: many of the students who gravitated to him had never been asked to think their way through an argument before. Here were depths that Gordon could not easily contend with, and he was much too honest to minimize them. Gordon conceded that he had been much more surprised by the students' intellectual failings than by their politics. "Not only have they not learned to read for critical information," he said, "but the level of actual absorption is not very high." They were mired somewhere in the middle of Rudi Gedamke's College Skills curriculum.

Gordon understood that his real mission was to set the highest possible intellectual standards for black students at City College. "I don't want to sound arrogant," he said, "but this serves to remind me how much people like me are needed here. I don't know how much the faculty in general worries about this; I *know* that it's not a concern of the Black Studies Department." He was needed, but he also had seriously misjudged the depths of the problem and thus the nature of his rescue mission. And these were twenty-year-olds, not eight-year-olds. Gordon recognized that he had come upon them late, perhaps too late, in life. He said, "I think what's required for serious academic work not only includes some knowledge of the skills but some dispositions that probably get laid down pretty early." Gordon didn't expect many of the students he was seeing to turn into good thinkers. He didn't want to consider it; his sense of futility contradicted a life's work in reform and the faith in education that Kenneth Clark had once wielded against Irving Kristol. "If I concede," he said, "I would have to go into retirement. For me the position has to be taken in the affirmative: 'Yes, it's possible.' And you have to try it."

A few weeks later I took a seat in the far corner of Gordon's seminar room, next to Clark. A student in the middle, Steve, who rarely spoke in class, raised his hand and said that he was upset that a stranger had been permitted in the classroom. Steve had obviously steeled himself to say something difficult; his voice was wavering, and he had squared his shoulders toward Gordon and away from me. "We don't know what he's here to attack," said Steve. "It's not fair. At the very least, he should go hear Michael Levin as well." There was the unholy symmetry again.

Apparently Steve had been deputed to speak for a group of students, because others now joined in. I felt ambushed. Steve had always been particularly friendly to me, and I had often sat next to him. The class was all black, and I assumed that a few of the students bristled at my presence, but I had never felt it. Gordon had encouraged me to speak up in class, and I had found it exhilarating to be able to talk seriously about race in that setting—the exhilaration of diversity. I thought that I had been accepted; and so what I felt, first, was the pang of exclusion. I was angry to hear Steve talk about me in the third person. But I couldn't be disingenuous: I *was* an outsider, just as Gordon was. Some of the students probably thought of me as in league with him in some way. But Gordon, at least, was there for them, while I had purposes of my own. I had explained myself, as I always did, but I could scarcely explain myself away. Clark said, "You're always writing things at strange times. I never know what you're writing down." Clark, and Steve, and probably others, had seen me writing madly during the donnybrook the other week. What was *that* all about?

Of course, wherever I went in City College I was an outsider and a stranger. Why shouldn't students be wary of me, for all that I listened sympathetically as they unspooled their lives? Throughout my time at City there had been students who avoided me, or looked at me sidelong; others had confided in me out of nothing more than naive trust. But what made this class different was the issue of race. I wasn't just an outsider, but a white one, as I had been when I was standing at Queen's door. Steve had come close to saying that I was an adversary by definition, that I wanted a "white truth." I got hot about that; I said that I might not be unbiased but that, like Gordon, I made a point of examining my biases.

A few students said that race was irrelevant, that the reason I didn't belong in class was that I was a journalist and as such must be out to destroy City College. But Shoba, who despite her name was African American, disagreed. "If you were a black journalist, it would be totally different," she said. "If you were [Professor Alvin] Poussaint of Harvard, nobody would mind if you were sitting there. I don't care what anybody says, it's a race thing." I was asked to step outside while my fate was decided. For twenty minutes I sat in the black studies office, and with every passing minute I felt more and more the hopelessness of trying to find a race-neutral position in that class and among those students. Some of them, I knew, strained against identity politics and the reduction of all things to race. But most of them simply didn't believe in such a thing as race neutrality or in the more compromised, but indispensable, space created when all admit to their biases. The bias of skin color was inescapable, definitive. Diversity had its limits.

Finally I was escorted back into a very quiet, very tense classroom, though the tension now came of nervousness, not anger. Gordon explained that I would be permitted to remain under a set of conditions that obviously represented an uneasy compromise. One of the terms was that I stay only for the first hour. I said that I would think about it, but I didn't have to think about it long. The next week I came back to tell the students that I didn't want to be an interloper in their class, and I thanked them and took my leave.

After that penultimate class, though, I sat down to talk with Clark in his office. Clark was a Westinghouse Fellow and had a job with the honors program. He was a star, glib, charming, and well read. He could make a passing reference to Hume or Berkeley, and he knew enough—just enough, I thought—to make it sound convincing. He was exotic looking; he had taken to wearing a tiny cowrie shell wrapped into one of his tight corn rows, so that he looked like a merman from a Derek Walcott poem. I had always enjoyed listening to Clark talk, in part because he so patently loved the sound of his own voice, but also because he cared about getting things right, even though he often didn't. When I asked Gordon if he felt that he were reaching anyone, he mentioned Clark. He, too, had noticed that Clark looked to him for affirmation.

Clark said that he knew I had been in Jeffries' class; these things got around. It was Clark's belief that Jeffries upset people because he told painful truths. "When I think about the Jews," Clark said, leaning back in his chair, "I'm constantly reminded of the fact that they funded a huge amount of the slave trade. That's not anti-Semitism; it's just the historic truth." Clark felt the same way about white people generally: "They're living off the benefits of their oppression of black people." Clark was too handsome and charming and successful to be angry; he could attack white people and Jews without wishing to cause the slightest discomfort to the white Jewish person he was talking to. Clark was delighted when his beautiful girlfriend showed up at his office door. He asked her to sit down and wait while he finished his conversation, and then he returned to the job of showing me the error of my ways.

My view of Clark had been shaped by his stories about his Guyanese father—the suit and tie, the knife and fork. I had him pegged as a disciplined, high-achieving West Indian immigrant with somewhat florid political views. I had simply assumed that Clark was too smart, and too focused, to buy the Jeffries line. Talented students saw through Jeffries; how could they not? And yet as Clark leaned back and expostulated, with an almost professorial air, incredible things came out of his mouth. "Why did the U.S. support Castro?" Clark asked. We didn't, I replied. "Sure we did. The man played baseball; they thought they had him under control." Castro was our ticket to ward off real revolution in Cuba. And what about integration? That was a white scheme designed to head off the Black Power movement, and the authentic black aspiration for separate but equal status. Martin Luther King was the domestic Castro. Clark must have seen me looking at him the way Gordon had looked at him before. He smiled at my incredulity, a charming smile, and said, "Listen, and you will hear."

Clark was glad to have had the opportunity to watch Gordon in action. "He has achieved great professional success," Clark observed. "I want him to show me how to do that." But Gordon was wrong to think that he had convinced Clark of anything. "Intellectually we have profound disagreements," he said, with an air of majestic self-assurance. He was planning to do graduate work in Egyptology, a field that the Afrocentrists had annexed to black studies. And, suddenly solemn, he said that he had to agree that marrying a white woman was not "the correct thing to do." Clark was a popinjay, a flashy dresser of the intellect. And yet he was a young man with considerable powers, not the least of which was his self-love. He was entranced by his own thoughts, and dazzled by the elegant simplicity of his conspiracy theories. Perhaps he would snap out of it. But after spending an hour in Clark's one-man salon, another thought occurred to me: Leonard Jeffries, head of the Jewish fraternity and big man on the Lafayette College campus, must have once seemed just such a glib, pleasing, and self-entranced figure.

Toward the end of the spring semester I had lunch with Moyibi Amoda in the faculty lounge. Amoda was one of the Jeffries loyalists whom Gordon felt he might win over, at least to a position of neutrality. Amoda had remained correct but distant. I asked him what he thought of Gordon's work. He paused for a long time, whether out of tact or exactitude I couldn't tell. "I have read the material that Gordon has given me," Amoda finally said, "and I have found that as a thinker Gordon processes matters of race into a framework that he flatters himself represents a consensus." This was Amoda's roundabout way of saying that Gordon was bound by convention. Gordon, he said, was not a "paradigmatic thinker." I asked if he was saying that Jeffries *was* such a thinker.

"I'm saying that Len is sensitive to that," Amoda said, with the care of a man who knows that his words might have consequences. He spoke of Thomas Kuhn's theory of the paradigm shift. Applying this metahistorical apparatus to Leonard Jeffries struck me as an utter travesty. After twenty years Amoda had lost his perspective on Jeffries, and on the intellectual world beyond the confines of the department. He himself had stopped doing academic work years beforehand. After lunch Amoda took me down to his office. He pointed to the two big, tippy filing cabinets in the corner of his office and said, "Gordon claims that he came to this department and found that the faculty was in need of improvement, that we had done nothing; but is he even *aware* of the work that we have done?" Proud, indignant, Amoda bent over one of the filing cabinets to show me the fruits of his two decades at City College—grant proposals, curriculum development plans, in thick, yellowing folders. They dated from ten years ago and more, and none of them, not a single proposal, had come to pass. Amoda was an erudite man who insisted on fine distinctions. And this was what his scholarly work had come to. He had paid the price of surrendering his loyalty to Jeffries—stagnation, nostalgia, bitterness.

At the end of the spring term Gordon finally agreed to subject himself to the public hazing that he had avoided so far: he accepted an invitation from the Statewide Africana Studies Movement to speak at a public forum. Like his entire tenure as chairman, the scene had an element of incongruity that amounted to the surreal. Gordon looked tiny, and prim, and extremely isolated as he sat at the front of a steeply raked auditorium in NAC. The evening was conducted according to the inane form of a quiz show. The host, Brother Ozzie, read off a series of questions to which Gordon was to supply answers. "What is your qualification to be chairman of black studies?" Ozzie asked. "What is your qualification in African studies or Afro-Caribbean studies?"

Gordon started to answer, then stopped in order to thank Ozzie for having invited him to speak. He then began to tiptoe through the landmines. "Black studies," he said, "is a field that's emerging, it's a field that's changing." The field could not be clearly defined. He confessed that he did not have "tremendous knowledge" of Africa, but added, "if you will permit my immodesty, I would say that after Kenneth Clark there may not be another social scientist who knows more about African American issues than I do." That should have been enough, but Gordon knew that it wasn't. He could not be understood to be saying what he actually believed, that black studies was the study of the black person's experience in America. "Professor Jeffries is a prominent Africanist," he said, "and I'm a prominent African Americanist, and I think with our two strengths we could make this an excellent program."

The questions became increasingly tendentious, if that was possible. "Dr. Gordon," Brother Ozzie asked, "do you believe in academic freedom?" Gordon's self-control might never have been so sorely tested since his days growing up in Jim Crow North Carolina. But he was equal to the task, and he never acknowledged the transparent hostility of the questions. Question 8 was "Could you tell us the name of some of the slave forts and dungeons in Africa?" Some of the students around me snickered. Gordon, incredibly, named a slave fort, or maybe a dungeon. But this was too much even for him, and he asked Brother Ozzie, "Is that leading somewhere?" But Brother Ozzie had apparently received no instructions on answers. He simply read the next question: "You are seventy-two years old. You are past retirement age. How do you feel about your position?" Shoba, who was sitting in front of me, said, "This is *so* tacky." But Gordon answered that one, too, betraying only the slightest hint of impatience.

The final question was the backbreaker: "Many people are concerned about your interracial marriage to a white Jewish woman." A groan went up from parts of the audience, and Brother Ozzie said, "This is a *very* sensitive question."

"I certainly agree," said Gordon. "It's sensitive and none of your business." A few students pounded on their desks. Gordon continued, "I think to substitute one kind of racism for another kind of racism is morally and politically defeatist." I thought perhaps Gordon had finally broken the chains of his diplomacy, that he was ready to wheel on his persecutors and give them what they deserved. Gordon would have lost some, maybe most, of his audience, but he would have won a few real adherents. And he would have stood up for what was right. But Gordon considered those kinds of calculations self-defeating. And so he then spoke proudly of his wife, Suzanne, a retired pediatrician—who was not Jewish, though he didn't say so—and of his children and grandchildren.

The tone of the evening became more abusive still when audience members were given an opportunity to ask questions. They called Gordon "arrogant" and "a pawn." But Gordon never lost his composure and cordiality. "I hope you'll make an appointment to come in and talk to me," he would say when the torrent of abuse finally slowed. At one point Jeffries walked in, trailed by Taiwo, and appeared to hand a card to a student. The student then got in line, and from the card read a long and particularly nasty question involving the difference between "the critical African mind" and "the critical European mind." Gordon batted that one back, too. Jeffries was trying to cut him to ribbons; and here was Gordon trying to hold fast to Jeffries' coattails. "I count him as a friend," he said, and "my problem with Professor Jeffries' speech has much more to do with style than substance." He even called the department "Africana Studies," a coinage to which he and the college objected, though the department used it anyway. In short, he went as far toward Jeffries and his followers as he could without forsaking his own integrity.

Leonard Jeffries' lawsuit against City College and CUNY came to trial in April. Jeffries contended that he had been fired for publicly expressing beliefs that his superiors found offensive. The defendants claimed that the speech had merely been the last straw; it was his administrative incompetence, anti-Semitic outbursts, and lack of scholarly production that had moved them to act. Jeffries himself took the stand, wearing a floor-length homespun dashiki and a black cap with celestial symbols picked out in gold thread. The courtroom was packed with his admirers from "the community," as well as Taiwo, Brother Steve, and the other members of the claque. They obeyed the judge's admonition to remain silent, but you could hear a low murmur of approbation as Jeffries recited his list of accomplishments. He spoke of "the beautiful, multicultural mix" of students in black studies classes. Except for getting hung up on "epidural melanin" research and a few other outré topics, Jeffries showed a fine appreciation for his audience. A sharp cross-examination might have unhinged him; but when none was forthcoming from CUNY's attorney, Jeffries retired with his bearing intact.

It was clear from the outset that federal judge Kenneth Conboy, a Republican appointee, felt that Jeffries had the facts on his side. Perhaps Conboy was also eager to prove that Jeffries was wrong in thinking that the system was rigged against an outspoken black man. But the facts *were* on Jeffries' side. The college and the university had accepted Jeffries' renomination as chairman every three years no matter what he had done. Only when the speech had turned Jeffries into a disastrous image problem had the university acted. And that meant that Jeffries had been deprived of his First Amendment rights. It wasn't even a hard call. In mid-May the jury found in Jeffries' favor, awarding him $400,000 in damages. And in early August, Judge Conboy restored Jeffries to the chairmanship for two years—despite what he called the "hateful, poisonous, and reprehensible" statements made in the speech.

Gordon was, he admitted, more than a little relieved. Now he could stop beating his head against a wall, and work on bringing young black scholars to other departments at City and developing the graduate program and research institute he had proposed. The department itself would wither on the vine. Kiteme was soon to retire; another tenured professor was ill. Fred Dunn, who had been more than outspoken enough to alienate the lifers in the department, went back to his old job as head of education for the municipal employees' union. The department's executive committee had already refused to vote on a distinguished professorship for bell hooks; she would take up lodging in the English Department instead. No one with any ability would agree to join the department now that Gordon wasn't chairman; and the college would certainly refuse to accept one of Jeffries' fellow travelers. Perhaps in two years' time the college would move against Jeffries again, this time for the right reasons, and with the evidence to prove it.

But for now Jeffries had won, and Gordon and City College had lost. And it wasn't just a court case that they had lost. It was the opportunity to challenge Jeffries where it really mattered—in the arena of ideas. By his diplomacy, it was true, Gordon had lived to fight another day. But what was the virtue in that when Jeffries had emerged from his ordeal as a hero and a martyr? Michelle Wallace, of the English Department, said, "There *should be* an antagonism between Ed Gordon and Leonard Jeffries. Leonard Jeffries is not rational. It's not possible to absorb 'sun people' and 'ice people' into a rational view. My view of Leonard Jeffries is that he's a maniac; and you can't assimilate a maniac. Jeffries should be marginalized. But Ed Gordon is too much of a gentleman, an Ivy League gentleman, to understand that."

Silence was Leonard Jeffries' friend; and through collegiality and timidity, and racial blackmail and racial solidarity, he had succeeded in holding black students, and the Black Studies Department, in thrall for twenty years. And now the uproar that he had finally raised was dying away, and a gratifying silence was descending once again. Michelle Wallace's vision of a new Harlem Renaissance with City College at the forefront, and Edmund Gordon's vision of an inner-city Yale, would have to be shelved. No doubt they were unrealistic in the first place, not only because of one malevolent figure but because of what he represented—the deep currents of anti-intellectualism, and the appetite for consolatory myths, that ran through large parts of the black community. Perhaps, if the vision of a new kind of City College was to be realized, black students and black faculty needed to be liberated not only from Leonard Jeffries but from the Leonard Jeffries inside themselves.

Part IV

Over the Rainbow

14

Engineering Separates
the Men from the Boys

Because City was not a remedial college but a proud institution with strong ties to its own past, it had a surprisingly large class of elite students. This group was lodged in the very upper reaches of some of the humanities majors, the premedical program, and above all in the School of Engineering, which alone typically accounted for 300 to 400 of City's 1,200 annual graduates. In contrast, all the humanities departments together produced fewer than 50 graduates, the sciences about 60, and the highly selective Sophie Davis School of Medicine, a CUNY-wide program located on the City campus, about 75. City's other professional schools, in education, nursing, and architecture, together produced as many graduates as the Engineering School, but they lacked its reputation, on campus, in CUNY and in the professional world, for exacting standards and high achievement.

Engineering students at City College lived in a world of their own. They sat in the cafeteria with their books open, and pored over equations as they shoveled food into their mouths; or they sat in the library, or in their clubs, or in hideaways all over campus, working. They thought of themselves as a breed apart and were disdainful of the low standards that obtained, from what they could tell, elsewhere in the college. They could ace World Humanities by putting in a couple of hours of homework a week, at least if their English was good enough; but they were up to their ears in calculus. I often met engineering students who, like Wagner Ortuno and the other members of the Latin American Engineering Students Association, were stunned at the low levels of math and science ability they saw around them. Hugh Thomas, an electrical engineering student from Grenada, said that he had been amused by what passed for competence on the math assessment exam. "My ten-year-old brother could solve those problems," he snorted.

I found something of this same sense of superiority among faculty members in the School of Engineering. One day in early January 1993 I went to visit Sheldon Weinbaum, one of five distinguished professors in the school. I had just come from talking to counselors in the SEEK program, and I felt weighted down with their sense of despair. Weinbaum, by contrast, was full of righteous anger—that the state was shortchanging CUNY at the expense of SUNY, that City College was forever being slighted in the press and in public, that the great achievements of minority students were going unnoticed. "City College is clearly the jewel of City University," Weinbaum declared. "City is the college of choice for minorities in the CUNY system. If people would just look at the reality, they would make City into a university center" —a designation used at select SUNY campuses. Weinbaum was one of the college's tireless gadflies; recently he had organized a lawsuit designed to force the state to fund CUNY as richly as it did SUNY.

But Weinbaum's loyalties were pledged not so much to City College as to the School of Engineering. He was incredulous that I had dallied so long in the remedial and liberal arts backwaters of the college. "There's nothing special about the liberal arts at City College, except for a few programs," Weinbaum said with a dismissive wave. The School of Engineering, together with the sciences, had received $30 million in federal grants in recent years, in recognition of City's leading role in training minorities in those fields. City College chapters of national bodies, like the American Society of Mechanical

Engineers, generally bagged more trophies for student achievement than did their counterparts at private schools such as Columbia. It was no wonder that from time to time engineering faculty had proposed that the school secede from the college.

The issue of standards barely arose in the School of Engineering; nor did the nostalgia and bitterness that often accompanied it. Lateef Jiji, a professor of mechanical engineering, was sitting at a table in Weinbaum's office when I arrived. Jiji felt the same combination of pride and frustration that Weinbaum did. "The standards in the Engineering School are *higher* than they used to be," he said. "If you had the graduates from the forties and fifties, the supposed Golden Age, come back, they would have to work much harder to get the same grades." The faculty, Jiji said, was far more research oriented than it had been a generation or two before, and had more rigorous expectations. It infuriated Jiji, as it did Weinbaum, to hear the school dismissed as a second-rate institution, especially by old alums. "Everyone hears it in the air," he said, " 'Oh, you go to City College—it's not good, it's open admissions, it's blacks.' That's racism. It's as simple as that. They don't want to accept the fact that these students are as good as they were."

In many respects City clearly wasn't the institution that it had been, and it wasn't racist to say so. It wasn't the college but the Engineering School that was the jewel in CUNY's crown. How had that come to pass? All the distinguished professors and the federal funding—all the benefits that the institution itself could offer—wouldn't have meant a thing if competent students didn't go there. As the only engineering program in the CUNY system, it attracted students from around the city and, indeed, the world. Students from the Caribbean often said that they had heard of the school at home, and chose it over the engineering school at the University of West Indies.

Engineering is considered a wonky and second-rate profession by many upwardly mobile Americans, but among foreign students it enjoys an exalted status. In most Third World countries engineers are far more in demand than are doctors or certainly lawyers; the educational system is designed to produce technicians. Foreign-born students constituted about 80 percent of the Engineering School's enrollment, and they tended to be highly capable in the disciplines of the field. Hammeed Assaidi, the student with the explosive stammer whom I had met in ESL class over the summer, summed up the intuitive feeling of many foreign students when he said, "Math, it's like in my head. It's easy. Writing takes too much practice."

Some of these students appeared to be one-dimensional math wizards. But that impression was often misleading, as I had discovered with Wagner and his friends. Engineering students tended to have a broad ability to think conceptually, though this ability was often held in check by language problems, as was the case with Hammeed. And their education and training had predisposed them to hard work. Successful engineering students tended to be contemptuous of the work habits of lesser mortals. One afternoon I was sitting in the cafeteria with Robert Alexander, a grave and dignified computer science student from the Dominican Republic— and another fugitive poet—when a group of demonstrators staged a guerrilla theater piece in protest against planned tuition hikes. Robert recognized one of the protesters as a hanger-on in a computer science class. "These guys don't know what it's like to work," he said with sudden vehemence. "They don't know what it's like to get into a book for three nights consecutively without sleep, just to make sure you get a 90, or even an 80." Robert, like Wagner, had put himself through school, had taught himself English, and was preparing to graduate.

Any entering City student could enroll in the Engineering School; all you had to do was declare an engineering or computer science major. The ease of access, however, was deceptive, because students could take only introductory engineering courses until they satisfied a mass of requirements, including three levels of calculus, differential equations and linear algebra, and modern physics and quantum physics. The casualty level in some of these courses was appalling. In some classes as many as three-quarters of students fell by the wayside and either had to try again or choose a less demanding field. Mario Cobo, a Colombian student whom I met in an engineering tutoring program in the early spring, called the physics classes the "weed-out courses." "There's no question of separating the men from the boys," he said. "*Everyone's* a boy. It's more like who says, 'I'll give up,' and who says, 'I'll keep at it.' " Of the sixty students in Mario's modern physics course the previous summer, only five, he said, remained at the end.

Students who began anywhere below the highest level of remedial math were considered virtual lost causes in engineering. "Deep math remediation will not produce a scientist or an engineer," said Michael Arons, City's provost and the former chairman of the Physics Department. David Rumschitzki, a professor of chemical engineering, said that he virtually never saw a student who began in mid-level remediation. Of all those aspiring engineers that I had met in College Skills and Social Studies—Andrew, Simeon, Anton, and Renato—only a tiny fraction would ever even begin the engineering program; the weed-out classes for them would be upper-level remedial math, or English, or the core curriculum. And once they made it to the frontier of engineering, the trek to a degree would be even more perilous. Fully half of engineering students left the program after their first year, generally owing to poor performance in math and science courses.

Elsewhere in City College and in CUNY, the struggle between traditional expectations and the students' shortcomings was resolved in favor of the student, through sympathetic promotion and backing off from standardized tests; but not in the School of Engineering. No one argued that the high failure rate in the modern physics course was evidence of discrimination, or suggested that students mired in trigonometry be permitted to take courses in electrical engineering. Perhaps this was in the nature of the subject matter, or of the people: science and math courses deal with the kind of material that is not subject to interpretation; engineers do not go in much for polemics. But it also mattered that the end product of an engineering education is an engineer. Society cannot afford to meddle with the qualifications of an engineer, as it can with, say, a social worker or a psychologist. It's not only that the consequences of failure are so much greater. A social worker who reads haltingly may still be good at her job, while an engineer who can't do calculus is unlikely to be good at hers. And so standards, in engineering, were not seen as the stalking-horse for some elitist social agenda.

At the same time, the Engineering School was not about "picking winners," in the pejorative, antiegalitarian sense in which scholars of higher education such as Alexander Astin used the term. City College could not attract the sort of hothouse plants who go to MIT or Cal Tech, at least not in large numbers; but neither would it wish to. What made Sheldon Weinbaum or Lateef Jiji proudest was that so many of their successful students were impoverished immigrants, the first in their families to attend college. These were students who needed help, academically and in all the other ways that City College students needed help.

There was a great deal of communal self-help in the Engineering School. Many of the ethnic clubs in Baskerville Hall functioned as engineering study groups, since the overwhelming fraction of their Chinese or Haitian or Nigerian membership planned to be engineers. These clubs also provided the kind of emotional support that Wagner Ortuno's group, LAESA, offered. LAESA, in fact, was unusual in that it was much more than a fraternal organization. Sometimes the club brought in speakers, or organized trips to professional conferences. Two gunmetal-gray filing cabinets were full of old exams and textbooks. Over the years Wagner and his friends had seen a lot of young Hispanic students fall through the cracks or switch majors when the going got tough. They made a point of recruiting fledgling Latino engineers into the organization. Wagner had become a virtual big brother to the childlike Renato Lopez, the SEEK student, whom I often saw sitting on one of the broken old chairs in the Ecuadorean Club. LAESA now had an extensive tutoring program for students like Renato in English, math, and science. One wall of the room was covered with a monthly calendar where tutoring assignments were noted in black magic marker. And then on Saturday mornings Wagner and the other upperclassmen offered GED and ESL instruction to the Hispanic community of upper Broadway—all in their copious spare time.

The Engineering School had an extensive program of its own for disadvantaged students. The Program for the Retention of Engineering Students, or PRES, offered tutoring in introductory math and science; "enrichment courses" that focused on problem-solving, test-taking, and analytical skills; personal and career counseling; and opportunities for federally funded research work. Open only to black and Latino students, the program grew from 45 to 358 students in its first five years. PRES was a remarkable success by any standard. A 1992 evaluation found that PRES students had a higher retention rate than a cohort group of comparable students, as well as higher grade-point averages and pass rates in math and science classes.

One reason for the program's success was that it was very well funded. The shortage of minority engineers is widely considered a national problem, even a crisis—both because of concerns about national competitiveness in an increasingly technological environment and because relatively few white, middle-class students are entering the field. Fortune 500 companies, foundations, and governmental bodies like the National Science Foundation are eager to support attempts to increase the flow of minority engineers. PRES had received over $1.5 million in outside funding since its inception in 1987. The program even included a part-time psychological counselor, which would have been unthinkable in, say, the SEEK program, where the staff had shrunk year by year.

But resources, again, were not and could not be the whole answer. PRES's success had a great deal to do with its selectivity. Students became eligible for the program only if, on entry, they placed into calculus or precalculus, the highest levels of remedial math. When I asked Ramona Brown, the program director, why the minimum threshold had been set so high, she resorted to City College's favorite word, but with an uncharacteristic twist: "Corporations are interested in students who have potential. They don't have to be at the very top, but they have to be in the pool of students who probably could complete the degree." Brown assumed, like Michael Arons, that students who began in Math 74—intermediate algebra and geometry—had too slender a chance of success to justify the use of scarce resources. The effect of this process of selection was drastic. When the program began, Brown recalled, 700 incoming students had opted for a major in engineering. Of those, 300 had placed into calculus or precalculus. And of that group, only 30 were eligible minorities. It was discouraging to see how vast was the gap between the educational backgrounds of the Asian and white students, on the one hand, and black and Latinos, on the other; but this was a deep-seated problem that Brown could do nothing to correct. She would accept students at the margins, but she acknowledged that she was engaging in a form of triage.

One afternoon in the middle of the spring semester I went to hear one of PRES's weekly career counseling sessions. It was held at 3 P.M. on a gorgeous Friday, and the fact that thirteen students had shown up was something of a triumph, especially since most of them were underclassmen interested only in summer jobs, and the speaker, Robert Tilbey, who worked for a diversified firm called AMP, had none to offer. Tilbey, an earnest, bespectacled young black man with an air of professional joviality, was very conscious of his status as role model; it was probably no coincidence that AMP had sent him to the City College campus. Tilbey talked about the basics—put your best foot forward, talk about why you want the job, "interview your interviewer." He talked a lot about résumés: "Don't include your height and weight," or your "family status," or whether or not you wear glasses.

When Tilbey had finished his presentation, Brown got up and asked the thirteen students to give him a big hand. They did their best. Then she explained that I was there, and that I was hoping to talk to students. My heart sank; in the past this kind of announcement had lead to mass flight. But not this time: these students were eager to tell me of their experience. I swiveled around to talk to a black student sitting behind me. His name was Ellsworth Royer; he had been raised in St. Croix and then had moved to New York with his family in his last year of junior high school. Higher education was considered mandatory in Ellsworth's family. Four of his six brothers and sisters were attending CUNY schools; there were three Royer boys in the Engineering School alone. Ellsworth had graduated seventh in a high school class of 400.

Ellsworth had problems, but they were not academic. "I never knew my father," he said. "He abandoned my mother when I was a baby. But everyone tells me that I look just like him. And you know how people say that children end up being just like their parents? I just hope that I'm a different person from my father." Ramona Brown had told me that many PRES students needed personal counseling more than tutoring, and that for some reason the better students, and often the ones from more prosperous backgrounds, seemed to have the most severe problems. Ellsworth frowned and said, "I feel a lot of pressure"—a phrase I had heard many times at City College.

By now it was 5 P.M., but most of the students were still lingering, listening to Ellsworth, waiting their turn to talk to me. For many of them, as for Wagner, City College was more home than home. They lived like monks, and the campus was their monastery. Ellsworth's friend John Barclay, who was sitting next to him, said, "You have to ask yourself, 'Is it worth it?' Why am I going through all this?" John was another well-educated, ambitious West Indian student. He was from Trinidad, and like virtually every Trinidadian I had met at City College he believed devoutly in the virtues of education. But he was acutely aware of the sacrifices he was making. He was working toward his Ph.D. in computer science. Since he had spent four years working after high school, he wouldn't graduate until he was past thirty. John did not come from a world where people postponed life and family until their thirties.

John was a thickset young man, with a smooth round face and a tiny cross-shaped scar, like a brand, just above the right edge of his upper lip. The scar, and his bulk, made him look formidable, like a Leonard Jeffries bodyguard; but his deep, melodious voice and reflective manner canceled out the first impression. "Why bother?" he asked again, looking at Ellsworth but not really expecting an answer. "It's not for the money; the difference just isn't that great. It's more that I want to set a trend for my kids, to attain the highest level possible." Most students at City College were so overwhelmingly concerned about landing a decent job and putting their insecurity behind them that it was remarkable to meet someone motivated by an ideal of excellence.

The PRES students were different in important ways from the students I had met during the fall. They tended to come from a slightly less disadvantaged background and to have performed better, often much better, in school. Many of them, like Ellsworth, suffered from the same social and psychological problems I had seen in students farther down the ladder, yet they seemed less disabled by them; even those who weren't immigrants had something of the immigrant's fierce drive to succeed. Before Robert Tilbey had begun to speak I had chatted with Karen Hazell, a young black woman with a short flattop Afro, a nicely tailored jacket, and long pendant earrings. She said she had to leave early. "I've got my four-year-old back home," she said. "I pick him up from school at six, but since it takes me an hour and a half on the subway, I have to be gone by four-thirty."

Other students I had met at City had been dragged down by the burdens of single-parent motherhood but Karen seemed to have a lot of cork in her. She was a tallish woman, with perfect posture, high, sharp cheekbones, and a certain refinement of voice and manner. When we met again several weeks after the career counseling session, Karen said, "I always wanted to be an engineer. I was the one in the family they always turned to when they had to fix something. I'm real interested in gears and cars and things like that." I had heard this from innumerable engineering hopefuls at City, but Karen had the education to match her talents. Her mother, a retired high school teacher, had pushed her into going to Brooklyn Tech, a selective and specialized high school intended for future science majors and engineers. Karen had gotten as far as precalculus, and she regretted that she hadn't gone farther. Like many students at Tech, Karen had graduated with a Regents Diploma.

After working for a few years Karen had been accepted at Northeastern University in Boston. In two and a half years she had piled up $15,000 in student loans and a very unimpressive grade-point average. "I played around *a lot*," she said with a smile. Karen returned to New York, found a job while she continued to take classes toward an engineering degree, and then got pregnant. "I just don't believe in abortion," Karen said. "And at first I thought: How bad can it be? Little did I know that it would kill me." She was only half joking; she wondered whether her carelessness, the carelessness of countless girls she knew, had destroyed her prospects. The word she used was *ruined*; and then she said, "No, I don't want to say that. My friends all tell me that I'm too negative." I was surprised to hear her say so; perhaps her effervescence was a bit of an act.

In fact Karen had not figured out any miraculous solution to the problem of single motherhood. A few days earlier her son, Malik, had sprained his knee jumping around the bed, and Karen had had to find some way to juggle doctor's visits, child care, and classes. Even in normal times Malik made her student's life close to impossible. Karen could stay in school only from 10:00 to 4:30, which put her at a serious disadvantage, and at home she got virtually no work done until 9:00, when Malik went to sleep. I asked Karen if she found enough time to work.

"I don't think I really do," she said ruefully. "I'm always tired; it really doesn't matter what I do. During exam time I'll stay up three, four nights a week. Sometimes I'll take a nap from nine to one, and then stay up the rest of the night." She did a lot of her reading, and even some of her writing, on the long subway rides to Flatbush and back. I wondered if she managed to concentrate any better than Che, the student from Rudi Gedamke's class who also used the subway in lieu of a library. Somehow Karen had managed to maintain a B-plus average, but the courses were getting harder and harder. "I was taking 14 credits," she said, "but I just dropped a big one—Calculus 3." She would have to retake the course in the summer.

For the first time Karen was seriously questioning her goals. "I may be in the wrong major," she said. She was thinking about switching to the science teaching program in the School of Education. And then as soon as she said it she must have remembered what her friends had told her about being negative, and she tacked in the opposite direction. "I have this feeling," she said. "I started out in engineering, and I'm going to finish in engineering." Even if she didn't, Karen would probably make a very fine physics teacher, which the world may have needed more than it needed another engineer.

Karen was not an average City College student, but nobody would have thought to call her privileged. Like Ellsworth and John, she suffered from the kind of handicaps endemic in the inner city. Together, they offered a vision of what City College might have been like had Buell Gallagher evicted the strikers that spring morning and had open admissions thus been implemented in the more modest, three-tiered form called for in CUNY's 1968 master plan. The school would not have been white and middle class; the demographics of the city, and of the public schools, had changed too much over the last quarter century. Nor would it have been a meritocratic funnel; the topmost slice of graduating seniors would go off in any case to the best private colleges, where scholarship money was available. City would have consisted instead of relatively successful graduates of the public schools and immigrants who had received a solid education abroad. They still would have needed the boost that City could give them, but not so big a boost. Would that have been bad?

I had had this discussion with Neville Parker, a civil engineer who directs the college's Transportation Institute. He, too, was Trinidadian, but, like Clark, the student I had met in Edmund Gordon's seminar, he considered the island's rigorously selective educational system a vestige of colonialism. "There was all this talk about standards," Parker said. "But the very people who had a vested interest in the system were the ones who were talking about the standards going down." And the same was true, he thought, at City College. When he had enrolled in City's evening session in 1959, he said, students were studying geometry and trigonometry, "but nobody ever called it remedial. It tempts one to think that the words are used emotively"—to stigmatize the black and Hispanic students who were taking such courses now. Parker considered the whole debate over ability a thinly disguised attempt to maintain the status quo. He didn't believe those differences were real. He would have had City College admit virtually anyone who graduated from high school, and he wouldn't have practiced the sort of discrimination by ability on which the PRES program rested. "If you're out to teach people who are ready, then you're not a teacher," Parker said angrily. "I would go so far as to say that that's charlatanism."

And yet it was a fact, not a racist claim, that students who began in geometry rarely made it through the engineering program, just as it was a fact that students who began in College Skills or remedial English—most of them black or Hispanic—were not becoming deft readers and writers a year or two later. City could choose to ignore these facts, because they were painful, or because they could easily be twisted by polemicists of the Left or Right; or it could accept them, and then do its best to push back the limits. That was what the PRES program, and the Engineering School generally, were all about. Parker's brand of egalitarianism would have lead City College to a noble, politically irreproachable doom.

Chemical engineering was both the smallest and the most elite field in the Engineering School. Only fifteen or twenty students graduated each year. The faculty had only twelve members. And both the faculty and the students had a reputation for excellence. Chemical engineering students boasted that they did better in their required civil and electrical engineering courses than the majors in those fields did. The comparison worked only one way, since no one else was required to take chemical engineering courses. And no one wanted to—other engineering students conceded that chemical was the toughest of the four fields. All of the departments required more than the 128 credits that were standard for graduates in the liberal arts and sciences; but some chemical engineering classes were considered so difficult that the figure was all but meaningless. And the most difficult chemical engineering class, by far, was in design.

All engineers took classes in design; mechanical engineers had to draw up plans for things like automatic gutter sweepers, and then build them. In chemical engineering, which involves the study of chemistry on an industrial, rather than a test-tube, scale, students were expected to design entire factories, which is what they would be doing once they got a job in the field. The students in Professor Irven Rinard's design class for the spring semester were expected to simulate an efficient, profit-making factory for the production of various petroleum-based chemicals used in the manufacture of nylon. The class was held in Steinman Hall, an aluminum-skinned cube that would be the ugliest building on almost any campus other than City College. During the class, which met twice a week from 9 to 11 A.M., the sound of hammering punctuated almost every exchange; workers had been retooling Steinman for five years.

Several students had run aground on the immensely complex computer program they were using to model their factory, and Rinard spent much of the morning talking about systems issues and how they could be translated for the purposes of the Aspen computer program. How much cool water do you have to pump into a cooling unit known as a heater block in order to sufficiently reduce the temperature of water heated in a chemical process? How much pressure do you need? How much energy do you need to start up a plant?

He moved quickly, and the students listened attentively. I was struck by how crisp and targeted the questions were. The students posed hypotheticals that showed they grasped the issues. Or so it seemed— I was too far out of my depth to be able to say for sure.

Afterward virtually the entire class adjourned to a windowless basement room in Steinman. The room looked like a bomb shelter, except that it was lined with DEC workstations. "What do all of you call this place?" I asked, trying to sound chipper. Everyone thought for a moment. Someone answered, "The basement." "B-23" —the room number—someone else said. Nobody bothered with cute names, any more than they bothered with posters, radios, hotplates, or any of the other amenities that make academic work more bearable. I didn't recognize any of the chemical students—they didn't seem to haunt the cafeteria. In the monastic world of engineering students, they were the Trappists.

"You folks spend a lot of time here?" I asked Arthur Martin, a tall, handsome West Indian student. "Oh, pretty much every night," said Arthur complacently. "If we have a research paper to do most of us will be here all night. And then we'll get here about eleven or twelve on Saturday and usually stay until about nine." They even had special IDs that gave them access to the building on Sundays and holidays, when it was closed. "My family really can't understand what I'm doing," said Arthur. "Saturday morning, everyone's getting into their clothes to go out, and I'm getting dressed for school." Arthur was, in fact, a highly respectable dresser. A few weeks later I saw him relaxing outside Steinman in a classic college-boy sweater, a V-necked cotton knit with stripes along the collar. He looked as if he had just walked off the cricket pitch.

Arthur was a classic moving-on-up immigrant. He had grown up in the Virgin Islands, but his father, an electrician, had so low an opinion of the Islands' American school system that he sent Arthur and his little brother to the British island of St. Kitts to finish their education. "I'm the first in my family to go to college," said Arthur. "There's a lot of pressure. But in terms of school, it's never been all that hard for me. I always knew that I was going on with my education." Arthur had studied chemistry, biology, and physics by the time he finished the ninth grade. "I was planning on being a doctor," he said, "but I never liked biology. I decided to do chemistry instead. It took you a week, two weeks, to learn in biology what you did in an hour in chemistry." Now Arthur was in his second-to-last semester, and chemistry didn't seem so easy. He was taking four or five other classes, but most of the work he was doing was for design class—which was worth 2 credits.

A week or so later I decided to drop by B-23 again to see if the design class really did live in the place. Arthur was talking to a friend in a vestibule off the upstairs lobby. "There's nobody down there now," he said, "but you should have been here two days ago. We were finishing our designs, and they were due on Tuesday. We spent the entire weekend in the basement. We even slept there." The students kept pillows in an upstairs lounge; sometimes they would rest there before resuming their labors.

"So," I said, "now you're kicking back?"

"Well, we're relaxing for the next two days. But then we have the environmental analysis due, and we'll be getting back our designs from Professor Rinard, so we'll be there full-time again."

In Steinman B-23 I had, for all intents and purposes, left behind the City College that I had experienced thus far. In fact when I said to Brendan Mee, the one white, middle-class student in the class, that I was writing a book focusing on open admissions, he said, "Is this an open admissions college?"

"What do you think?" I asked.

"I would say that City is an open admissions college," Brendan said. "But I wouldn't say that this department is open admissions." Certainly Arthur, who had earned 77 credits at the University of the West Indies before enrolling at City, would have had no trouble gaining admission to City College at any moment in its history; nor would Marcia Anglin, a Jamaican student who had earned a diploma in chemical technology from the University of West Indies; nor would Brendan, who had already earned a degree in history at Columbia. None of them had been substantially educated in the New York City public schools; even Brendan had received much of his schooling in England. This was not because the public schools didn't produce students like them, but because those it did were snapped up by the fancy private colleges.

The design class was the elite of the elite. Its students were even farther from the City College norm than were the PRES students. Among them there were no African Americans and no Hispanics. A few came from relatively privileged backgrounds. But they all had been very well educated before arriving at City, whether it was in Lebanon or Jamaica or China or Greece. They resembled, more than any other group at City College, the students of City's Golden Age, relentless strivers who used the educational system to overcome social and economic handicaps. If there was anything sad about the comparison, it was that the class of 1943 had been reared in New York and trained in its schools, while this sliver of the class of 1993 had been raised and educated abroad.

Irv Rinard's students had chosen City College primarily because it was so much cheaper than Columbia or Cooper Union or any of the other fine private institutions that would almost certainly have admitted them. But they had also chosen City because of the School of Engineering's reputation, and the department's as well. There were several such preserves at City College, where talented teachers taught talented students. They were preserves not because ordinary students weren't welcome, but because access was so difficult that they dropped off before reaching the gate.

Had Neville Parker had his way, the school's, and the department's, reputation would have suffered, and students like Arthur and Brendan, who had no ideological stake in the open admissions ideal, would have found a way of going elsewhere. City needed them even more than they needed City; and it kept them by insisting on standards of performance that were not enforced elsewhere in the college because the old meritocratic impulses ran headlong into the new democratic commitments. That was how City College had reconciled its tradition with its new character: in its uppermost reaches an old-fashioned rigor obtained, while everywhere below the college adjusted itself to the needs and disabilities of its students.

15

In Which City College Declines to Embrace Its Newness

I n early December 1992 a body called the Chancellor's Advisory Committee on Academic Program Planning submitted a report that was to serve as a blueprint for curriculum redesign throughout City University. The authors of the report, all of them CUNY professors and administrators, proposed that a system full of redundancies and historical relics be rationalized and brought up to date. Lightly attended majors and graduate departments would be "consolidated," whereas popular programs, especially those with a clear professional orientation, were slated for expansion and reform. Among the changes suggested for City College were enhancement of the Education School and of programs in health care. However, the committee recommended, in its coolly bureaucratic language, that City's majors in philosophy, classics, French, Spanish, and anthropology, among other fields, "be taken to the Second Level of review for possible phasing out," generally to be merged with the more populous program at Hunter.

The Goldstein report, as it was called after committee chairman Leon Goldstein, president of Kingsborough Community College, caused an uproar throughout the system that made the reaction to the College Preparatory Initiative look tame. The colleges thought of CUNY as an administrative apparatus, and a nuisance at that, not a unified institution that ought to be rationalized at their expense. Faculty and administrators were infuriated by what they took to be a bid by Chancellor Ann Reynolds to usurp their authority to determine the colleges' identity and mission. And the report was proposing the virtual evisceration of liberal arts programs at several campuses. Within weeks the faculty of the CUNY Graduate Center, which wasn't even affected by the report, issued a statement predicting that the proposals, if adopted, "would initiate a cascade of decline at CUNY," including a mass exodus of scholars in the liberal arts. The group asked Reynolds to publicly repudiate the report "so as to counteract, in so far as possible, the harm it has already done."

The sound of engines being gunned could be heard across the university, and nowhere more so than at City College. Outraged professors wrote to the chancellor, to the vice chancellor, to the newspapers. Charles Evans, the mossbacked chairman of City's Philosophy Department, sent a letter to the *New York Times* invoking the sainted name of Morris Raphael Cohen and suggesting that the message implicit in the proposal to eliminate the philosophy major was, "College students who attend school north of 125th Street do not need critical thinking." Professors who had never shown much interest in black and Hispanic students suddenly began to play the race card with abandon. Perhaps all those diatribes from Leonard Jeffries had been turned to good effect.

A special meeting of City's Faculty Senate was called for late January, just before the start of the spring term. The mood in the auditorium, in the bowels of the NAC building, was ugly. It was unanimously agreed that City College would accept not so much as a single one of the report's proposed subtractions. The only question was how best to say "Nuts to you." A professor of political science said, "We *can't* respond to a document that we all understand is impossible." Others took up the cry for a militant intransigence. "This is a classic trap," declared the chairman of the Psychology Department. They would be suckered into a response, and the Goldstein report would be adopted anyway. That wouldn't have been wholly inconsistent with Ann Reynolds' tactics with the CPI. But in the fury of the response you could also feel the paranoia of an institution that felt chronically misunderstood and had shielded itself from criticism with a romanticized self-image.

Jim Watts, who was sitting next to me, was a perfect instance of this phenomenon. It was Watts who had insisted to me that City's standards hadn't diminished even a trifle since he had begun teaching history in 1965. He had given himself utterly to the school, and he defended it passionately, as if even the smallest concession could bring the waters flooding through the dike. Whenever I saw Watts he would say, "Why are you wasting your time on Leonard Jeffries? He's a putz"; or "Why are you mucking around in all those remedial courses? If you want to see the real City College, go to one of the history electives. We've got the best students you'll find anywhere, great kids, *and nobody knows it!*" City College's reputation drove Watts crazy. And now he was boiling. He rose, his voice brittle with rage, and said, "We're going down the wrong road. Are we to think that [Vice Chancellor Richard] Freeland and Reynolds are going to read our response and say, 'Oh my God, I didn't know that about the liberal arts'? 'I didn't know that about City'? Is that the logic that we're dealing with? I don't think so. Why are we putting ourselves, as the purveyor of a superior liberal arts education, in a defensive posture?"

Once everyone had had a chance to vent some spleen, the discussion cooled off, and it was agreed that the Faculty Senate would, in fact, respond to the Goldstein report, but with an unequivocal dissent. After the meeting adjourned, Philip Baumel, a professor of physics who had been at City even longer than Watts had, made his way over to where we were sitting. A deeply disillusioned, even bitter, man, Baumel had predicted that open admissions would fail, and now he believed that his worst fears had been borne out. He and Watts were old friends, and old adversaries. Baumel, too, opposed the Goldstein report. "Hidden in the language of this report," he declared, "is a vocationalism that I find nauseating." But Baumel also said, "You know, Jim, they *are* wrong about the liberal arts. But it's not so easy to make that case when you look at the problem we have with remedial students. That's a very large part of City College, whether we like it or not." But for Watts, that world didn't quite exist. He believed in those students abstractly, but he didn't see many of them in the upper-level history classes he taught. He didn't fathom their problems. And so he changed the subject.

What Baumel was saying, and Watts was denying, was that City College had ceased to be the institution it once was, and had become something whose identity was hard to fix. That, certainly, was the way some members of the Goldstein committee viewed the situation. One of them, Abraham Ascher, was a professor of history at the Graduate Center who had graduated from City in 1950. Ascher had very happy memories of the school, and especially of philosophy, a field in which he minored. "It was, for an undergraduate institution, a rather distinguished department," he said. It had been, Ascher said, very painful to contemplate eliminating philosophy, as well as classics, not only at City but at several other campuses as well. But, he asked, "Are they truly liberal arts colleges in the way that they were twenty-five years ago? The answer is no. And since this is a fact, why continue? Why not accept the reality of it?" Ascher said that the committee had been guided by the numbers; and though some of the figures were out of date, and others flat wrong, they implied a different institution from the one Jim Watts was describing. City had all of twelve students taking classics courses. Even in philosophy, the sacred preserve of Morris Raphael Cohen, City had only nine majors. And the pattern wasn't limited to the liberal arts. In the 1950s, City had had several hundred physics majors. Its physics faculty now was more distinguished than it had been then; but now City had eleven physics majors.

The Goldstein report was proposing that students be given what they wanted—what was useful to them—rather than what the college thought they should want. Ann Reynolds, for one, had trouble understanding what all the hubbub was about. "We have to begin thinking about City University in the nineties," she said. "Students have voted with their enrollment cards. We have infinitely more business majors, more communications majors, than we had ten years ago. We have lots more health sciences majors. We have far fewer students majoring in history and Romance languages." Reynolds, a zoologist by training, considered the Goldstein report a "student-oriented" document. She suggested that philosophers and French teachers stop complaining about the report and start thinking about why students weren't taking their classes.

Richard Freeland, the vice chancellor for academic affairs, was not given to using marketplace metaphors to describe the educational process. A historian of higher education, Freeland was plainly uncomfortable defending the report, which had cast him in the role of anti-intellectual bureaucrat. He said, "Most academics, and I would include myself, would find it hard to imagine a liberal arts setting that did not include philosophers, or a liberal arts curriculum that does not include philosophy courses." Freeland took comfort from the fact that the report proposed to eliminate majors but not the fields themselves; students would still be able to take philosophy courses from philosophy professors, at least in theory.

But as a historian of education, Freeland knew that the curriculum shifted according to larger intellectual patterns, the economy, and the demographics of college-goers. A century earlier, after all, many colleges had offered little *besides* philosophy and classics. Nothing was immutable, and certainly not the shape, or the limits, of a liberal arts education. "These numbers are painful to face," he said, "and people don't want to face them. That's why there has been the reaction there's been. But as academics, we do have to face facts and truth." City College, Freeland said, "is a very different place from what it was, and it's going to have to find some way to embrace that newness." And that was just a tactful way of expressing what Abraham Ascher had said more bluntly.

City College took the position that the numbers were wrong and, in any case, conveyed a false impression of the college. The Faculty Senate's response to the Goldstein report called the school's excellence "the best-kept secret in New York City." "Surely," the authors noted, "there is no other college or university in the country whose public image is so falsely and so completely shaped by accident and eccentricity." That was shorthand for "Leonard Jeffries and Michael Levin." But the response included a sentiment, almost universal at City, that Leonard Jeffries would have been happy to endorse: underlying the criticism of City College was "a palpable subtext of racism in which the entire city is implicated." What Freeland really meant, as Charles Evans had alleged, was that black and Latino students didn't belong at a serious liberal arts college.

This charge was given a certain amount of credence by the proposal, contained in the report, that "ethnic studies" departments be strengthened at some of the same colleges scheduled to lose their philosophy majors—including some, like City, that had as many philosophy as black studies majors. Wasn't this a way of saying that minority students could waste their time on a curriculum of self-esteem while middle-class whites studied anthropology and French? It was, in fact, almost impossible to read this recommendation as anything but a sop to CUNY's minority lobbies, and an expression of the liberal racism that gives in all too easily to self-serving black demands.

But the numbers remained. Why did Hunter have eight times as many students taking upper-level French courses as City? Why did Queens College have more than double City's physics majors, with nothing like the quality of City's Physics Department? It wasn't for lack of trying. City was justly proud of the minority students who majored in the classic liberal arts fields, but their numbers were small because of the students' own predispositions and disabilities. Physics, for example, is a subject for students who like to figure out high-level puzzles; no other major field in science has so little direct vocational application. And Queens and Hunter attracted the sort of middle-class students who could afford to spend four years solving high-level puzzles, or reading good books, even if they were going to head into law school or business school the moment they had finished their college idyll. City College attracted students who were hell-bent on pulling themselves out of poverty; the liberal arts and sciences were an unaffordable and even frivolous luxury, even for students like Rebecca, the fiery spirit I had met in freshman composition. Others had language problems that made the humanities daunting.

Of course, City had attracted desperately poor students fifty and sixty years before. But those students had received a solid grounding in the liberal arts before arriving on campus. They believed in, and were comfortable with, the kind of abstract endeavor involved

in studying math or physics or philosophy. The same was true, if
to a far lesser extent, with contemporary students at Hunter or
Queens. And it was not true at City, where the overwhelming fraction of well-educated students were immigrants who had their sights
trained on engineering and medicine. Among the New York public
school products, a huge chunk dropped out before reaching the
upper levels of the college, and the survivors tended to sort themselves into the less demanding fields—education or the social sciences. And this group of students was overwhelmingly black and
Hispanic. Race, in other words, was correlated with the factors that
worked against liberal arts enrollment. But racism hadn't caused
City's predicament, and it wasn't racist to call attention to that predicament. Waving the bloody shirt of racism was a way of distracting
attention from painful numbers and a painful reality.

A few days after the Faculty Senate meeting, I paid a visit to
Paul Sherwin, City's dean of humanities. Sherwin hadn't joined in
all the holy rolling over the Goldstein report. Constrained by his position to be diplomatic, he was also circumspect by nature and rarely
indulged in the pleasure of speaking for effect. He was a patriot,
but with a more balanced and less possessive attitude toward the
college than Jim Watts or the other stalwarts of the "Nuts to you"
faction. I expected from Sherwin a few measured words of reproach
for the Goldstein report. I was wrong. Sherwin wanted the world
to know that he was prepared to fall on his sword. "If the Philosophy Department goes," he declared, "I would quit. I cannot imagine City College without a philosophy department. If it's not doing
its job in teaching philosophy, then it's not serious about the liberal
arts, and then the whole enterprise isn't worth sustaining. It would
be a sham."
    Paul Sherwin was one of City College's "institutional people,"
one of a small core of faculty and administrators who had been at
the school for years, who believed in its mission, and who had accepted the responsibility to advance that mission. Over the years
he had dedicated himself to ensuring that City remained, or once
again became, a liberal arts college of a high order. He didn't believe
that he could make students take philosophy classes; he believed

that he could make them want to do so. And he felt that with a strong enough program in the humanities, City could attract more traditional liberal arts students. The Goldstein report represented a mortal threat to everything he had worked for, as well as to his underlying faith that City College could shape its own destiny rather than be shaped by larger forces. The chancellor's study looked like a monstrous self-fulfilling prophecy. How was City to attract high-quality philosophy or classics professors without a major? How would it attract or keep superior students?

Sherwin felt connected to City's majestic past, but not too connected. His father had graduated in the City class of 1938, but he himself, in the great tradition of academic upward mobility, had gone to Yale, where he had studied English and written a dissertation on Milton and the lyric poet William Collins. Even after years of a desk job, Sherwin could deliver ringing encomia on behalf of the underappreciated Collins. He was a tall, thin, and slightly stooped man, with wire-rimmed glasses, a high crown of ginger-colored hair, and a thick mustache. He chain-smoked Camels and typically did something else while he talked—took phone calls, riffled through papers, called out to his secretary. There was always a sports jacket folded carefully over a chair near his desk, but I never saw Sherwin in anything but a shirt, usually in some postmodern hue, such as sea-green. He was harried, but he never quite lost his composure. In the overwrought and heavily Jewish culture of the City College faculty, Sherwin, who was also Jewish, came about as close as anyone to maintaining WASP sangfroid.

Sherwin had gone straight from graduate school to City in 1971, thinking he would do good works teaching open admissions students for a few years, and then fulfill his destiny teaching graduate seminars at an expensive private university. But he found that he liked teaching open admissions students; he even liked teaching remedial English. And so he became a fixture at his father's alma mater, one of City's large class of aging Young Turks. His timing, however, was not propitious: he had arrived at the tail end of the great hiring surge that accompanied open admissions. When City was forced to undergo a brutal retrenchment in 1976, the English Department had twenty or so nontenured faculty members; afterward, only three or four remained. The faculty had shrunk from 150 to 50, and even they spent most of their time teaching freshman composition and remediation. Fewer English students justified a smaller faculty, and the staleness and stagnation inside the department in turn kept students away. In 1971 there were more than 500 English majors; by 1985 or so the number was down to 50. And this process of supply and demand chasing one another downward was repeated throughout the humanities. No tenure-track appointments were made in any of the liberal arts fields after Sherwin's arrival in 1971, a drought of almost biblical proportions. City bottomed out in the decade from the mid-1970s to the mid-1980s.

In 1985 a number of faculty members accepted offers of early retirement; this depleted the ranks of the English Department, thus enabling Sherwin, who had just become humanities dean, to at last make some new appointments. Marilyn Sternglass was hired in composition, and Joshua Wilner, another Yale man whose father had graduated from City, in English literature. In 1991, Wilner, a young Young Turk, became the chairman of the department. As CUNY's budget briefly swelled in the mid-1980s, money was available to hire one or two new faculty members per year in some departments. Another round of early retirements in 1991 and 1992 eliminated some older faculty members—in fact decimated several departments—but also opened up more space for new hires.

But by that time the abundance of the 1980s had vanished as swiftly as it had arrived, and the budgetary spigot was twisted shut. CUNY's budget decreased every year from 1988 to 1993, even as the number of students in the system increased. Once again City could not afford new "lines" for tenure-track hires; but the departments still desperately needed fresh blood. Sherwin now set out to find soft money—non-tax-levy funds—in order to make new hires. He embarked on a one-man fund-raising campaign, devoting countless hours to persuading foundations and alumni that Leonard Jeffries was not City College, and that City was not a brackish swamp of remediation. And by and by, he succeeded.

Sherwin found that older alumni, those who predated the Golden Age, were less agitated by the change in admissions standards and felt a greater sense of identity with the new student. He persuaded a small family fund, the Winston Foundation, to make a $1 million gift, over a period of eight years, to commemorate the eighty-fifth birthday of Simon Rifkind, who was stepping down as head of the fund. Rifkind, a legendary judge, lawyer, and public figure, was a graduate of the class of 1922. The Simon Rifkind Center for the Humanities became Sherwin's all-purpose funding source. He also used the gift to leverage a $600,000 matching grant from the National Endowment for the Humanities. During the late 1980s and early 1990s Sherwin managed to raise a remarkable $5–6 million.

Sherwin was like one of those talent-show competitors who keep twelve plates spinning on rods at once. He would raise enough money to authorize a new hire, and then keep that person airborne with a steady stream of soft money until a regular line opened up, at which point he would lower the professor to the terra firma of the operating budget and use his own funds to hire someone new. Sometimes Sherwin kept as many as eight professors aloft at the same time. And he was pouring soft money into precisely those fields that might have been considered archaisms.

In 1988 Sherwin made the first new hire in philosophy since the age of Cohen, or so it seemed. In 1990 he came up with a tremendous coup by hiring a young philosophy teacher at Harvard, Juliet Floyd. Two years later he persuaded yet another Yalie, Jennifer Roberts, who had chaired the Classics Department at Wellesley, to come to City. Roberts was working out a double major in classics and English, and preparing to teach courses in history and women's studies. Already the first tiny crop of classics majors, just three or four, was taking root. Roberts had revived an old classics section of World Humanities; she had forty students reading Greek literature in translation, with plans for another section on Rome.

The English Department was actually smaller in 1993 than it had been in 1984, when the hiring freeze was still on, but almost one-third of the faculty was new. Many of the new hires had received a thoroughly avant-garde training and were thus almost by definition more appealing to many students than were the guardians of the canon who otherwise constituted the department. "The fit with the institution was better," as Sherwin said diplomatically. The English Department became fashionable for the first time in over a decade.

By 1993 the number of majors had reached 140. Another 150 students were pursuing graduate studies in literature, composition, and creative writing. And the effect was similar in the other departments that were slowly being rejuvenated. In history the number of students taking elective courses more than doubled, to 341, between 1985 and 1993. Philosophy was growing, if more modestly. Better-prepared students appeared to be enrolling at the college, which in turn made it easier to hire good faculty.

Paul Sherwin, and the other institutional people such as Jim Watts, were pressing against the limits of City's identity. As Josh Wilner said, "It would have been very easy for people to say to Paul, 'That's not City College anymore. You're holding on to a dated idea. We're going to invest our money elsewhere.' " That, after all, was precisely what the Goldstein report had in mind and what Richard Freeland meant when he suggested that City "embrace its newness." City College was a new kind of institution in the history of higher education, an affirmative action, antipoverty program in the inner city. Two-thirds of the students dropped out, and most of the survivors just wanted a decent job. The kind of rigorous liberal arts education that Sherwin was spending his precious funds on was meant for a very different kind of institution, one with well-prepared, middle-class students. Sherwin was madly spinning his plates on behalf of City's small elite. Shouldn't he have been more concerned with the majority?

The Goldstein report was full of fine language about the primacy of the liberal arts, but what it was really saying was that a public university like CUNY has a responsibility to students and to society to put its economic function first. In fact the report was only one aspect of a larger effort to match CUNY graduates with job opportunities. Ann Reynolds had also instituted, with no particular controversy, a program called the Workforce Development Initiative, which was designed to train CUNY students in emerging technologies and projected areas of growth, such as health care. Reynolds was a popular figure with legislators in part because she soft-pedaled the noble rhetoric about the liberal arts and was shrewd enough to describe her annual budget request as "nothing less than an economic recovery plan for our City and State." Reynolds understood that higher education had to serve technocratic purposes in order to justify the expenditure of tens of billions of dollars in public funds. The Goldstein report was thus a creature of the American system of mass higher education, just as the Zook Commission report had been forty-five years earlier.

Why not, then, accept this new reality—not only the reality conferred by City's admissions policies but the larger reality of vocationalism? Why push at the limits? The answer was simple: To do otherwise was intolerable. To accept these limits was to admit the truth of the charge that the anonymous writer who smugly called himself "Justice" had laid at Townsend Harris's doorstep 150 years earlier: That a college for working men would have no place for those studies that are valued not for their utility but for "the free and enlarged views they give of human life and human relations." The vocational or utilitarian principle was vastly more central to higher education now than it had been in "Justice's" day; but for all that, college simply could not survive its reduction to a marketplace instrument.

The university is the one site in our culture where knowledge is valued for its own sake, or rather for the free and enlarged views of human life that it affords. Should it lose that sense of purpose, a college would be just another social-service institution. Its sense of standards, of high purposes, would be mere pretensions. And nobody would care especially whether it lived or died. That was why Philip Baumel found the Goldstein report nauseating; that was why Richard Freeland was hoping to have it both ways. In its response to the chancellor, City's Faculty Senate wrote, "It is in their commitment to a liberal arts education for every student, regardless of his or her ultimate professional objectives, that a university and the society which that university serves affirm free and open-ended inquiry as an individual and social good." This sentiment ought to have been too obvious to need restating, as the authors themselves noted; but apparently it wasn't.

The report surfaced a contradiction in City's aspirations for itself: it wished to maintain the elite standards set forth in the postwar Rockefeller report without jeopardizing the egalitarian commitment at the core of the Zook Commission study. City's institutional people had to overlook the harsh facts that Rudi Gedamke knew so well; they had to overlook the dynamic of advancement, which delivered semiliterate students to the core curriculum and beyond. City was a strangely hybrid institution, and it may very well have been getting worse and better at the same time. The remedial program was seeing ever more deeply damaged students, while the uppermost branches of the liberal arts were beginning to bloom once again—in large part because of a growing number of relatively well prepared and well grounded immigrants and non–New Yorkers. City was increasingly separating into two parts—the college of the remedial *Inferno* and the college of Jim Watts's *Paradiso*. This growing gulf represented a critical failure of the open admissions ideal, but it made possible City's renewed life as a vigorous liberal arts institution.

An article that I wrote criticizing the Goldstein report appeared in the *New York Observer*, a local weekly, in late March. About a week later I found two surprising messages on my answering machine. The first was from Victoria Chevalier, an English major and one of several dozen students who had received one of the academic fellowships that were City's preeminent mark of distinction. Victoria's message said, "Many of us are very upset about your article, which perpetuates the worst stereotypes about City College," and asked me to come and speak with a group of fellows. The other speaker, who did not identify herself, said, "We found the tone and content of your article appalling and we would like you to come to a meeting to . . . discuss this." Apparently she had been about to say something like "confess" before thinking better of it.

I was dumbfounded by the rage, and when I reread the article I felt reassured that I had, in fact, defended City College against its threatened denudation. Various faculty members who read it had also seen it as sympathetic, if not quite as single-mindedly as they would have wished. I agreed, trepidatiously, to meet the following week at a seminar room on the sixth floor of the NAC building. I knew an invitation to a beheading when I heard one, but I also knew that the students had every right to interrogate me. When I arrived at the appointed place, I felt reassured to see Tracy, a well-educated and well-traveled black woman who was the only student I ever saw

at City College reading a copy of *Town & Country*. Tracy wanted to
pursue graduate studies in the history of psychiatry, and we had
talked of her plans. Now she said, "I guess I've been brought here
to denounce you." That certainly confirmed my worst fears. Tracy
moved off, visibly uneasy, although I couldn't tell if she was worried
about carrying out her mission or about being identified with me.

I took a seat at the head of a big square table next to Vern
Ballard. In my article I had used Vern, whom I had met in a literary
theory class the previous spring, as an example of a minority student who had discovered philosophy by accident at City College and
who would have lost something precious had the major been eliminated. Vern was a mild-mannered and abstracted young man who
deplored controversy. He was my safe harbor; but he looked miser-
able, and I had the feeling that he wasn't about to put himself in
the lion's jaws on my behalf.

Looking around, I saw virtually every talented student in the
humanities that I had met at City. I had admired Victoria ever since
I saw her stand up to an English professor of the ancien régime who
complained that students were being addled by theory. At the far
end of the table was Ron Tyson, a bespectacled black man in his forties who by sheer force of intelligence and erudition had dominated
a class on slave narratives that I had attended in that very room. Ron
had just been awarded a full scholarship to pursue his Ph.D. at
Columbia. To my right was Tammy Pate, a black woman who had
been Charles Frye's teaching assistant in the SEEK class the previous
summer. These were the students, black and Hispanic and white,
many of them older and thus serious and self-reliant, whom Paul
Sherwin and Jim Watts and Josh Wilner held out as prizes to the
Ivy League scholars they were trying to lure to the unfamiliar reaches
of Harlem.

After some nervous clearing of throats and shooting of glances,
Victoria, sitting around the corner to my left, initiated the proceed-
ings by holding up a copy of my article and saying to the others,
"This article maintains that City College has no need for its humanities departments, no need for liberal arts . . ." "Wait!" I cried. "I don't
think any such thing. I didn't *write* any such thing." The woman next
to Victoria angrily cut me off. This was Helen O'Connell, who had

left the other message on my machine. "This article," Helen said, smacking the table with the offending pages, "is a heap of shit." And then she got up and stormed out of the room. I was stunned. I had expected to be trashed, though I still didn't know why; but I hadn't expected to feel like I was back in Leonard Jeffries' class.

There was a commotion, and then Frank Hernandez, an older student sitting to my right, spoke up furiously. "I'm sick of people criticizing City College," he said, waving his arms. "This is my degree I'm thinking about, and I'm seeing it get devalued every time another article appears." I slumped back in my seat, resigned to letting the blows rain down on me. The premise of most articles about City, Frank said, was "We can't educate these kids anyway, so let's just let them sit in the cafeteria and enjoy themselves rather than going out and breaking windows and holding people up." Just as I was about to say, "That wasn't *my* premise," an argument broke out in an altogether different direction. Tammy Pate, completely mistaking Frank's point, turned on him and all but called him a racist. "If *that's* what you think then I'm glad you're graduating," she spat.

Now it was Frank's turn to air a festering grievance. "This is it!" he shouted, rising from the table. "This is what happens any-time you try to discuss any kind of subject around here. You imme-diately get slammed and called a racist. I've been here three years and I can't tell you how glad I am to be getting my degree this spring." Frank started to leave, and I said, "No, no, stay!" I was developing some sympathy for Frank. He sat down, glaring in all directions but mine. Victoria stepped into the charged silence and resumed the business at hand. She picked up her copy of my article—by now everyone had received a photocopy—and started in: "How could you have written ... ?"

I had written that "City is scarcely the same school as it was in the days when it had strict admissions standards," but that never-theless it had a coterie of talented students who were hungry for serious intellectual work. Victoria and Helen and some of the others had been so outraged by the first point that they didn't notice the second; and they attributed to me the sentiments of others whom I quoted, just as Tammy had with Frank. They seemed not to believe in the idea of a middle ground, of the principled striving-after-objectivity that Edmund Gordon talked about. Ron, who had talked to me about politics and race with a bracing intelligence and candor, whom I thought of as a friend, assailed me pedantically on the definition of "journalistic objectivity," even though he appeared not to have read the article. Even Ron! I felt the ground sliding away from my feet.

My shellacking lasted for a little over an hour. Afterward, I was grateful for the students who came up to say that things had gotten out of hand, that the article wasn't as one-sided as they had been led to believe. It was discouraging that they had been so easily railroaded in the first place, and that others had been so blinded by polemics. Perhaps the teacher who had upbraided Victoria hadn't been all wrong. Still, this was the first time I had been inside the coterie that I described in the article. And I understood that a large part of their anger came from pride. These students lived in a world where people read serious books and thought serious thoughts. It was a small enough world to have a hothouse intensity, but big enough to be sustaining. To them, it was the real City College. And, as Jim Watts said, nobody knew it. City College, in the public mind, was almost entirely defined by its failings—by what it used to be and no longer was. The Goldstein report had reinforced that impression. These students were unwilling to acknowledge the large element of truth in the report's numbers. What they knew was that their own truth had been buried in those numbers. City's reputation was an insult to their abilities and efforts; it was hardly surprising that they were hypersensitive to criticism.

It appeared, in the spring of 1993, that some blood was going to be spilled over the Goldstein report. New York's governor, Mario Cuomo, singled out the report as a sign that CUNY was thinking seriously about its future and its role in a changing economy. Ann Reynolds thus understood that she would have to see the planned reorganization through in order to argue for more state funding. But she had promised that she would not act unilaterally; this time, she would consult for real. And the reaction throughout the system had been so adamant that Reynolds risked provoking a virtual insurrection if she went ahead and implemented the proposal. The restructuring foreseen in the Goldstein report was actually fairly modest, and much of it might have occurred without the chancellor's prompting; but it stood for, or could be made to stand for, an assault on the most cherished ideals of egalitarian higher education. It was this penumbra, as much as the specific recommendations, that roused the fury I had seen in students and faculty.

In the end, it was Reynolds who blinked. In June she authorized a resolution to establish procedures to review academic programs. The chancellor would coordinate the process, but the colleges themselves would control it. Her hope was that the colleges would now be free to make needed changes without giving the impression that they were buckling under to a domineering chancellor. But it was also a face-saving device. The threat was lifted from Sherwin's ongoing project and from City College's struggle to reshape its identity.

16

Reading Bakhtin, Thinking About Propp

C ity College's English Department, like English departments on a great many campuses, was divided between an older generation of historical critics and connoisseurs and a younger generation of theoreticians. The divide at City was especially sharp because the older generation was so very old—most had been around since the 1960s—and because the younger generation had been forced to survive a much more rigorous process of selection than had the veterans. The younger scholars tended to have something of a cult following among the better students. Soon after I started visiting City, in the spring of 1992, I asked Steve Urkowitz, a member of the department's new generation, what upper-level class he thought I should sit in on. "Carla Cappetti's literary theory class," he said immediately. "You'll be amazed at the level of the discussion."

Cappetti taught English 331, one of two courses in critical thought required of all English majors. The class had traditionally been taught as an introduction to literary analysis, but Cappetti was an authority on modern critical theory, a field that a number of her colleagues considered self-indulgent left-wing twaddle. Her course outline included such headings as "Linguistics, Formalism, Semiotics: Language and Parole, Synchrony and Diachrony, Signified and Signifier, Denotation and Connotation, Story and Plot, Defamiliarization." She assigned impenetrable authors—Benjamin, Bakhtin, Propp, Barthes, Derrida, Lacan. Most English students tried to sign up for a less grueling, and more orthodox, version of the class. But for the best students in the department, who had breezed effortlessly through most of their classes, the course had the appeal of Mount Everest.

Cappetti refused to compromise the difficulty of the material, no matter how much the students moaned. Insisting that they could rise to the highest order of complexity was her own form of idealism. As the class was about to embark on a discussion of Jacques Derrida's "Structure, Sign and Play," Cappetti commented, "I'm the last one to believe that complex writing has to be unclear or indirect. But sometimes the difficulty of the prose is commensurate with the difficulty of the thinking." Cappetti had a singsong and slightly monotonous voice, and she labored over the vowels, in her northern Italian accent, like a careful hiker picking her way among boulders. Authors like Derrida, she said, "are asking new questions, questions that have not yet found a language." Cappetti herself then illustrated the problem of the unsayable by observing, "In Derrida we have the intention to produce a center without a center, or a structure without a structure—so to speak."

Much of the life of the class came from the students' counterattack in the face of a threat to their accustomed modes of thinking about language and literature. They were offended by Barthes's "Death of the Author," as well as by an essay by Ian Hunter arguing that not only literature but criticism itself could only be seen as an unconscious expression of larger historical and cultural forces. They bridled at the loss of intellectual autonomy. "The critic has the responsibility to seize on the most progressive strands available at the time," said Chris, a kid with earrings in both ears who was sitting to one side of me. Judy, who did not share Chris's political assumptions, snorted derisively. Judy was a very well read woman with a twenty-three-year-old daughter and a job teaching riding at a stable on the Upper West Side. She was putting up a serious fight on behalf of tradition. "Isn't Hunter himself just as limited by his *own* historical moment?" she asked.

"What's the alternative?" Cappetti shot back. "Silence? Or is it best to admit these limitations, and remain conscious of them?" No one had a decisive answer to her question.

"I may have misread him," said John, a student in the creative writing program. "I've misread everyone else so far." And everyone laughed—they were all wandering around in the dark. Many of the students had never before encountered any mode of reading except the appreciative, and they were suffering from radical disorientation. Cappetti, however, was pleased with the class. I talked with her in the corridor of Townsend Harris Hall while the students worked on one of her regular half-hour essay quizzes. "It's true that these students don't have very much background," she said, "but I think in some ways that they have more of an intuitive understanding of critical theory because of who they are. These theories deal with marginalization and the suppressed viewpoint of the minority, and these students are themselves members of minority groups. They don't have the sensibility of the dominant group." Cappetti had taught much better prepared students in Europe and the United States, but she loved teaching students whose minds had not yet been trammeled and confined.

Demographically, the students were no more representative a sample of City College than were the chemical engineering students I would later meet, though the skew was in a different direction. All of them were native English speakers. Half were white, a ratio that was not unusual in upper-level humanities classes. Several of them wore khakis and wire-rim glasses and would have looked perfectly at home at Columbia or Harvard. There were middle-class students like Cindy, the young woman from Nebraska with the G-man dad whom I had met when I first came to City. Still, middle-class white students at City tended to be an unconventional lot. I often sat next to Danny, who with his black beret, thick black glasses, long sideburns, and single earring looked the very picture of a Beat poet. Danny was, in fact, a military brat who hadn't quite imbibed the martial code. He had enrolled at City on a lark and bounced around a few departments. Then a girl he liked told him that she was taking

Cappetti's class. Danny saw the name of George Lukacs on the reading list. That was enough—he had been reading Lukacs as part of his self-education in Marxism. He signed up, "and everything just exploded." Danny had been a young man in search of a theoretical structure. Now he spouted structuralese with impressive fluency.

It was here, too, that I met Vern Ballard, whom I was later to describe in *The Observer*. Vern was a tall, thin young man with high, sharp cheekbones and a long, delicate jawline. His most striking feature was his haircut—chopped-off dreadlocks that looked like a Roman candle frozen a moment after explosion. Vern didn't make much of a first impression. He was a shy soul who rarely spoke above a mumble. His manner was quizzical and perplexed. But the breadth and depth of his interests was extraordinary. Vern was taking or auditing six or seven courses, and he had a Mellon fellowship in philosophy and a computer science fellowship he used to study artificial intelligence; he worked fifteen or twenty, and sometimes thirty, hours a week helping faculty members use computers, and he did some tutoring out of the goodness of his heart. He was taking Cappetti's class out of sheer curiosity. A light curtain of haze seemed to hang between Vern and the rest of the world; it might have had something to do with sleep deprivation.

I talked to Vern in the cafeteria one afternoon—he had just pulled an all-nighter to finish a philosophy paper—and he listed, rather reluctantly, his various accomplishments. I asked him if he came from an academic background. He popped his sleepy eyes open wide. "My mother's dead and my father raised us on welfare," he said. He had grown up in West Virginia and then in Harrisburg, Pennsylvania. His father had held, and lost, various government jobs, and was now working as a clerk for the Harrisburg Department of Transportation. Vern talked about his father with resignation, but not anger. "He's a dreamer," he said. "He always wanted to help kids on the street, so he would hold festivals on the weekend, and we would organize the whole thing ourselves—my father, my sister, and me." Vern's father always hoped for a job in social service, but he was too dreamy to actually go out and get one. He sounded like Vern himself, but without the focus or dedication. Vern's sister was a "religious fanatic" who also worked as a clerk.

Vern had discovered in high school that he loved to dabble with computers, but he never thought to do more than dabble. He then enlisted in the army—it was hard to imagine someone as gentle and airy as Vern in the military—and after his tour was over he enrolled in Harrisburg Community College. Then he transferred to Temple, and when he had grown weary of commuting to New York, where his girlfriend was attending Barnard, he transferred again to City. "It's funny," said Vern, "but until now I never even knew what grades I got. I just never looked. And when I finally saw them I had done a lot better than I expected."

Despite his formidable Rasta haircut, Vern was basically a space cadet. He loved to read and think, and always had, and he thought nothing of his own remarkable achievements, and never believed that he would go any further than his father had. "In fact," he said, "when I look back I've already gone further than some of the people I went to school with, even the people I looked up to." Vern had probably gone further than all of them. He was the darling of several departments and had begun an e-mail correspondence with Marvin Minsky, the colossus of artificial intelligence. He insisted that he suffered from a learning disability involving the capacity to recall concepts, but he admitted that no one believed him. Vern was slowly realizing that he was not at all the person he had expected to be. "I think," he said in his slow and dreamy way, "that my insecurity has helped me keep my feet on the ground. If I began thinking of myself as an academic or something, I might really get lost."

Cappetti assigned a great deal of writing, and some students who rarely spoke in class showed in their written work that they were making real inroads on the material. Vern described the Underground Man, the self-deluded narrator of Dostoyevsky's *Notes from the Underground*, as "an apparition for whom time has no order, for he is lost in his mind's imagination and a mnemonically conjured past." He also charmingly described this pathetic figure as "an unrequited masochist." Still, Vern's essay was essentially descriptive and did not quite come to grips with the assignment, which was to apply Benjamin's "Theses on the Philosophy of History" to the Dostoyevsky work. Vern was still new to critical thinking.

The essays varied enormously in quality. Several students took a deep plunge into the theoretical—none more so than Danny, who interpreted the story as a struggle between the soul and "the inhuman forces of industrial capitalism." Danny closed with a majestic flourish: "Dostoyevsky's narrative whimper is the deathcry of the Cogito in the modern age, 'I think therefore I cannot be.' " Others in the class were way out of their depth; several students thought they were expected to show that Dostoyevsky would have accepted Benjamin's theories if he had known about them. Most of them, however, made a brave attempt to apply a critical apparatus to a text, and even threw off a few sparks in the process. All of the papers were coherent, and none of the authors made serious errors of grammar, diction, or spelling. The average student in the class was more intellectually sophisticated than the best students I had met in English 110; I could imagine no one in that group, except perhaps Rebecca, Amelia, Marta, and Philip, feeling even marginally capable in Cappetti's classroom.

For the last class of the term there were no essay quizzes, no combing through texts for evidence of repression or omission. It was kick-back time. Cappetti reviewed the work of the term— structural linguistics, Russian formalism, the Frankfurt school, the post-structuralists. She knew that her classes were sparsely attended, and in her drawn-out, laborious cadences she made a rare plea for support: "If you have friends who you think would enjoy this course, please recommend that they do so." That drew a snicker. A few students felt they had wasted their time and would forget about the arcane language they'd learned as soon as the class ended. Others knew that few of their friends would be willing to endure such an ordeal.

Cappetti asked the students to tell her what they had liked or disliked about the class. John, the creative writer, responded that he felt it had made him a more critical reader. In the beginning, John had bristled at the dislodging of the author from the center of the critic's attention. Now he had decided that the world was big enough for himself and Jacques Lacan. Vern then cleared his throat and delivered the most extended comment I had heard him make: "I expected a lot less from this class than I got," he said. "Right now I'm taking a computer science course that's breaking down the structures that I had learned in high school. The same is true with this class. I had always taken language for granted. Basically, I read without thinking. I had this book on the shelf over my bed for two or three years, a book by Terry Eagleton [a structuralist literary critic]. I couldn't make any sense out of it. I took it down the other day and read it again, and I had a real feeling for what he was saying." Vern was fascinated by the idea that he was studying logic from a set of converging and overlapping perspectives.

Several students later told me that English 331 was the best class they had taken at City College. Danny said that he had found the class "disturbing"; he felt that he would never again be able to think of literature in the familiar way. The course had been powerful precisely because many of the students were relatively naive, or at least inexperienced, readers. And perhaps, as Cappetti thought, the fact that they weren't traditional students had allowed them to make up with intuition what they lacked in knowledge or sophistication. It might also be true that for these very reasons the students would succumb all too easily to the glamour and the schematic simplicity of theory, as perhaps Victoria had. I could see that tendency in Danny. The students probably should have had a more thorough grounding in literature before taking the course.

But Cappetti was not a dogmatic teacher, and it seemed unlikely that she would turn out a race of logic choppers. She had forced her students to scrutinize the foundations of their own thinking; they had seen that one can read and think in such-and-such a way, and not only in the way they had always read and thought. It was supposed to be disturbing. This kind of open-endedness, this collapsing and re-forming of convictions and modes of thought, was, after all, the very essence of a liberal arts education.

The Goldstein report posed no threat to City College's English Department and thus would not have limited—at least not directly—City's ability to hire scholars like Carla Cappetti. I was interested to know what had become of City's Philosophy Department, which the report *had* targeted. Philosophy recalled, as no other field did, the era of City's vanished glory, when legions of sallow, undernourished boys gave themselves over to the pleasures of abstract speculation.

Indeed, the very unworldliness of philosophy, and its insistence on depth and rigor, has made it an emblem of the liberal arts ideal. Philosophy diverts the student's attention from phenomena to their meaning, from the actual to the possible. It clears a student's mind of cant, as Morris Raphael Cohen used to say, though it may put nothing else there in its stead. Philosophy is the highest form of intellectual exercise. That was why Paul Sherwin declared that a college without a thriving Philosophy Department was a sham.

I met City's star philosophy professor, Juliet Floyd, immediately after my interrogation in the seminar room, which she had sat through quietly with an expression of curiosity on her face. She introduced herself, and we agreed to meet for lunch the following week in the faculty lounge. Floyd didn't fit the City College faculty mold, which is to say that she spoke softly, moved slowly, ate sparingly. She was a languid woman with an academic pallor, short blond hair, and striking pale eyes. Apparently she was good at what she did, since over the years she had been offered jobs by Notre Dame, the University of Texas, Georgetown, Williams, Wesleyan, Wellesley, and Boston University. But she had gone from Harvard to City College. She said, "When I told my adviser that I was taking a job at City College he said, 'Juliet, *why*?' "

I thought that was a fair question. "First," she said, "there was the opportunity to really help create a department." One other philosopher had been hired two years before her, and another, a colleague from Harvard, would be arriving the following year. Jennifer Roberts, the classicist, would be teaching some philosophy as well. A nucleus was forming. "And," Floyd added, "I did feel that sense of mission." Since arriving she had become something of an amateur authority on Morris Raphael Cohen and the history of City College, and she had sought out kindred souls throughout the campus—a mathematician, a chemical engineer. There weren't many.

Floyd had been on campus for three years, and her sense of mission hadn't flagged, although she was wary of boosterism. "The faculty," she reported, "is completely divided between those who say, 'Everyone is educable, the school is great,' and those who say, 'The place has fallen apart, standards have gone to hell.' " Her own view of City College had been largely formed by her experience teaching the core philosophy class, which very few students took before their second or third year—which is to say that Floyd saw only the survivors. She had carefully anatomized this somewhat unrepresentative group. "The top third," she said, "has a lot of potential. The best of them are as verbally polished as the middle third of students at Harvard. And there's a higher level of motivation." Floyd had also observed that while Harvard was full of glib students who could barely write, City had a fair number of students who sounded helpless but wrote surprisingly well. "The middle third," she said, "is a mixture. They could go either way. Many of them don't really know where to go, and they don't have parents to tell them what to do." Others produced solid, pedestrian work. And the bottom third?

Floyd reflected for a long moment. "Different schools have different tails," she finally said. "Wellesley, for example, has no tail. City College has a *major* long tail. And what you see in this group is heartbreaking. They've been tricked by the system into believing that they can do what in fact they can't do. My job with them is to say, 'You have a grave problem writing. It will not be solved in a day, or in a few days. You have to get some help.' " Floyd was amazed at what students didn't know. One day she had realized that most of her class had no idea what a dissertation was, or what it was that scholars did. And so she put off the lesson and talked about graduate school and the life of a professor. "The students were fascinated," she said. Experiences like this made her more certain, not less, that she had made the right choice.

She invited me to attend her seminar on Wittgenstein's *Philosophical Investigations*. The fact that City College had such a seminar was a surprise to me, and probably would have been a surprise to the authors of the Goldstein report as well. Here was philosophy with a vengeance. The first day I attended the class, in mid-April, I saw a few familiar faces. Vern was there, maintaining his usual silence and wearing his habitual look of perplexity. So was Carla Janzen, a philosophy major, premed, and Mellon fellow who looked, with her flowing blond locks, like she had stepped out of a Merchant-Ivory production of a Forster novel. I had stopped by Carla's table in the cafeteria one day when I heard her arguing with a friend over whether the human personality had chemical origins. Then there was Abner Quinones, a friend of Carla's and also a philosophy major, and David Beckett, a wire-rims-and-khaki type I had met in a class on the slave narrative.

The class discussion was conducted at a higher level than anything I had heard before at City College, even if it often strayed far from the dense tangle of Wittgenstein's thoughts. The focus that day was on Wittgenstein's exploration of whether any important distinction separated real understanding from what appeared to be mechanical versions of understanding, such as rule-following. Opher Rabban, an Israeli student who was a philosophy major and a devout reductionist, insisted that Wittgenstein's distinction between the acquisition of knowledge and understanding was null. "There *is* no difference," he said. But a black woman, Robin Lewis, said, "I didn't really understand an American history course I was taking, but I got an A. Maybe I had acquired the knowledge without understanding it. And I can read sheet music, but I can't re-create a piece of music from it in my head. Can it be said that I understand the signs on the paper, or am I mimicking yet again?" Even Vern piped up, addressing the same question: "My sister could do math earlier than I could, but I knew how to make change before she could. She could count to one hundred, but she didn't know that ten dimes make a dollar." It occurred to me that it might be precisely this ability to relate an abstraction to lived experience that was the chief outward sign of understanding—and if so, that this class was doing an impressive job of fathoming Wittgenstein.

It was easy to see why students considered Floyd a good teacher. She explained Wittgenstein clearly, which seemed amazing enough in itself. But she was also a keen and sympathetic listener. Some students were way out of their depth, and others would resort to the showboating that is endemic in a college full of prima donnas, like Harvard, but relatively rare at City. And Floyd would patiently hear them out, nod respectfully, and say something like "I think that speaks to the distinction Wittgenstein was making in his analogy of the chess game." Abner, for example, would often ask questions that sounded completely off the wall to me, but Floyd, who may have known what Abner meant better than he himself did, would reproduce the question so as to make it perfectly relevant. Abner felt good, and the discussion advanced.

The fourteen or fifteen students in the class represented an even thinner slice of City's student body than those in Cappetti's class—not only ethnically or racially, but culturally and academically. Some had transferred to City after several years at fancy private colleges: Sheldon Weinbaum's son Danny had been enrolled at Brown, and Kevin, a withdrawn and troubled young man who wore a leather flying-ace cap indoors and out, in cold weather and hot, had left Bennington with nothing lacking for his degree except a senior thesis, which he hadn't been able to bring himself to write. Michael Steinberg had left City in the 1960s, earned a bundle in the furniture business, and now returned to school. Michael may very well have been the only student at City who lived on Park Avenue (although I knew one who worked as a doorman on Park Avenue).

Three or four graduate students were taking the class, and Ethan Aiken, a math professor who was a friend of Floyd's, audited regularly. Robin Lewis had received her degree at Amherst after a stint at Hampshire. I saw Robin sitting with Michael one day after class. It was a gorgeous afternoon in early May, and they were taking some sun on one of the stone benches outside of the administration building. I asked Robin why she'd come to City to do graduate work in English. "My tuition at Amherst and Hampshire cost me $80,000," she said. "I couldn't even think about going to a place like NYU for graduate studies." City charged her $475 a course.

But money wasn't the real issue for Robin. Now that she'd seen City, she regretted that she hadn't attended as an undergraduate. "I can't tell you how much I envy students like Victoria or Helen," she said—they were all friends. "They're all walking around the hall saying, 'Did you read Bakhtin? What did you think about Propp?' And there's such accessibility here! It's amazing to me that I can just sit down and have lunch with a bell hooks or a Michelle Wallace. That kind of thing was unthinkable at Amherst." City's demographics also meant a lot to Robin. "Hampshire and Amherst were almost totally white," she said. "You couldn't talk about race; everything was so politically correct." She had just heard bell hooks deliver a feminist critique of Malcolm X. The fabulously incorrect Taiwo Ogunade had stood up and, in the course of defending Malcolm, had babbled about his own five wives. "I really wanted to vomit," Robin said. "Yet at the same time I thought, 'This is great.' It was more like" —and here she gestured beyond the stone gates to the north of the campus— "real life."

By the end of the term Floyd felt that the Wittgenstein seminar was the best class she had taught so far. To have held onto a dozen students for so difficult a course would have been a noteworthy achievement anywhere. But she was also pleased with the eclectic mix, with the level of the discussion, with the quality of the written work. Only a few of the students had been so overwhelmed that they had dropped out or been unable to write a satisfactory term paper. Of the others, Michael had written a paper in the form of a detective story that Floyd found delightful; Opher had rewritten his thesis three or four times until she gave him an A; Danny had done fine work; and Vern and Robin had both proven so exacting and obsessive that they were still shaping and reshaping their work in the middle of the summer. The big surprise was Abner, who wrote very well and showed signs of wide reading. Abner was one of those City College students whose gracelessness concealed a real intelligence.

These students, like the students in the chemical engineering design class, represented a tiny elite. But it mattered greatly that City had such an elite and that by all accounts it was growing. An outsider like Robin could come to City and instantly feel the pulse of a real intellectual life. Scholars like Juliet Floyd could withstand the smirks of their colleagues to come to benighted, Jeffries-ridden City College. "Can you see why I'm so engaged with this place?" Paul Sherwin asked me one day. "Can you see why it means so much more to me to be at a place like this than to be, say, chairman of the English Department at Princeton?" I could. If not for Sherwin, City wouldn't have people like Juliet Floyd; and if not for Floyd and others, City might well have become a combination of a remedial college and an advanced technical institute for the training of engineers and architects. Sherwin felt that he was bringing the richest intellectual gifts to students who otherwise might never know them.

Still, it was impossible to forget how very small this elite was, and how unrepresentative of City's entering class. And because City was not in control of its admissions policies, its tail would remain vastly longer than its head. Juliet Floyd took comfort from the fact that the best students were isolated from the rest of the college by fellowship programs and the like, but she worried that the fragile ecosystem she was helping to create would be swamped by the teeming world beyond. She wondered whether the college was really willing to commit itself to excellence. "I don't want to sound arrogant," she said, "but I don't know whether the will is there to fight for people like me. We have a sense of standards which the people who have been here for twenty years don't have. It's so important for students to see that." She knew that she was a threat to the entrenched order.

Floyd believed that City's egalitarian admissions policy was no threat to its aspirations for excellence. The SEEK students, after all, weren't dragging down the standards of her philosophy seminars; good students were still coming to the college. That was true; but it didn't take account of the culture fostered by the admissions commitment. Teachers who knew that they couldn't insist on the highest standards without losing much of their class had succumbed to the ethos of mediocrity that Floyd found so worrisome; they waved as students went on to the next level, still locked in the simplest patterns of thought. And this was so despite City's very high attrition rate, which one could interpret either as proof of the school's high standards (as Jim Watts did) or as a sign that the majority of students were unable to meet even fairly forgiving standards. There weren't enough angels in City's *Paradiso*; and there wouldn't be so long as the vast majority of entering students were so deeply unprepared for college.

17

When I Come Here,
Is All I Do Is Work

I n the late spring, as I climbed up into the bracing atmosphere
of City's most rarefied liberal arts classes, I was also swimming
along the submarine levels of the school with the students I had
met over the summer. The SEEK students had all advanced one notch
to Social Science 2, College Skills 2, and English 2—not so much
because they had demonstrated their aptitude at the lower level as
because so little was to be gained by keeping them there. They
weren't swimming so much as being swept along by the tide.

Would they have responded more if more had been demanded
of them, as the College Preparatory Initiative assumed was true of
high school students? Perhaps; but they seemed so deeply disengaged that it was hard to imagine the intellectual task that would
have quickened their energies. Nothing had been demanded of them
before; and now, when alarm bells should have been going off, they
sat in the back of the class and whispered to each other, or idly turned
the pages of their Cliff Notes. And so when I visited them in their
College Skills class toward the end of the spring term, they were
very much the same students I had met almost a year earlier.

Renato Lopez was calmer than he had been, but still "high schoolish," as his counselor had said. Once he grew so obstreperous that his College Skills teacher, Carole Bermann, ordered him to move to a desk with no neighbors. Thereafter Renato crossed his arms on his desk and lay down. Paula Sarmiento, a shy and giggly girl who lived in the shadow of her friend and fellow Ecuadorean Jenny Villegas, still never spoke in class, never took notes, and rarely seemed to pay attention at all. Paula's hair changed from month to month; now, after a long chestnut phase, she had dyed it black, like Jenny's.

In a social science class a few days later, Jenny sat in the rear corner, sharing with Renato a catalog of summer school classes available at Lehman College. Jenny had told me that she was going to transfer to Lehman, although earlier in the year she said she was planning to shift to Baruch College, the CUNY school that specializes in business. As we filed out of class, I asked Jenny why she had decided to transfer. "Because I want to do computer science," Jenny replied, "and the requirements in math are less." I was amazed that Jenny was thinking of so tough a field. "Why computer science?" I asked. "I don't know," she said with a helpless look. "It's something."

"But why computer science as opposed to something else?"

We were threading our way down an escalator in the NAC building, with Paula trailing in Jenny's shadow. Jenny made a pianist's motion with her fingers. "I like typing," she said. Typing? I asked Jenny if she knew what computer scientists did. "You know," she said, "they look in the back of the computer." Like Mario, Rudi Gedamke's student who misunderstood the difference between a dentist and a lab technician, Jenny had no conception of the hierarchy that stretched from rote work to skilled trades to the professions. To her, computer science was the college name for the job that computer technicians or even data processors did. Jenny said she had friends making good money looking in the backs of computers. She had no idea that she was aiming at something exponentially harder.

A week or so later I went to see Carole Bermann, a burned-out veteran of twenty years in the SEEK program. "This was," she said, "one of the worst classes I ever had." Julissa, by far the most able of the five students I had followed since the summer, was one of the few bright spots. She had worked hard and aced her exams; she had also passed English 110. The others depressed Bermann. Jenny had shown some improvement, as she had during the fall, but she had still failed every test that required reading comprehension, and had failed the reading assessment test. And when the crunch came, she hadn't made much of an effort. Paula had tried, at least more than before, but she hadn't come close to passing a test. "She's so weak in everything," Bermann said with a sigh. "I mean, she made some progress, but . . ." —there was no happy way to complete the sentence. She wanted to recommend Paula for ESL, but she knew the department would balk at taking someone who spoke English well enough and had been here for eight years. "It's a problem with language," she said, but she didn't sound convinced.

Renato had also passed the reading test, though with the lowest possible passing grade. Bermann considered this a comment on the test rather than on their improvement. Like Rudi Gedamke and Pete Martinez, she thought the decision to lengthen, but not renorm, the test was a farce. Renato, too, had failed all of her tests, hadn't even taken the final, and continued to be a discipline problem. She and Martinez had passed Renato the previous semester with the hope that he would start to grow up. Now Bermann said grimly, "I should have followed my gut instincts and not put him in the class in the first place. He's going to repeat, but not with me." And Jane? Jane was the black student who never spoke in class and seemed to make no contact at all. Bermann put her palms to her face and shook her head. "Jane's not going anywhere," she said. "You can't connect with her; I've tried. She's just like, 'I don't understand, I don't understand.' Pete says, 'I wonder why she keeps coming to school.' " Bermann laughed, and it would have been easy to say that there was something cruel in her laughter. But if there was, it was only the cruelty of the burned-out case. Her idealism had been sapped by years of frustration, and she no longer bothered with the pieties.

Anyone who spent much time in this demoralizing world survived by focusing on the few hopeful stories; mine was Sabour Clarke, the black student who had written about hand-to-hand combat. I had seen Sabour occasionally since the fall. He was hard to find, since his mother didn't have a telephone, but I ran into him

a few days after I saw Carole Bermann, and we agreed to meet in
the downstairs student lounge, where he hung out. The lounge was
supposedly a place to read or talk quietly, but when I arrived and
found Sabour, half a dozen students were throwing a ball back and
forth, lunging for it, and then falling all over each other in a wild,
noisy scrimmage that ended about six inches from our feet. We decided to go elsewhere, and as we left, Sabour looked back in dis-
belief and said in his deep, syrupy voice, "And these guys are juniors
or seniors."

On our way upstairs we saw Clark, the glib theoretician from
Edmund Gordon's class, and he and Sabour immediately greeted
one another. Clark was wheeling a fancy bicycle, and he and Sabour
talked bike technology for a minute. They often cycled together, and
they had become friends. Sabour was also friends with Anton, the
bright, moody student from Rudi Gedamke's class. Sabour had smart
friends. He was inarticulate, but he had more inside than he showed.
I told him I was glad that he was tight with Clark, although he should
watch out for his politics. "Yeah," said Sabour, "he's got a very big
vocabulary." He tried to say the word two or three times, but he
couldn't get it right.

Up in the relative tranquillity of the cafeteria, Sabour observed
that he had always had older friends. Looking out from under the
bill of his cap with his big sleepy eyes, he said, "I carried myself more
mature when I was young. Even when I was a freshman, my friends
were juniors and seniors." With his shaved head Sabour looked old,
and at twenty-one he was in fact a rather old college freshman. He
had been left back in the second grade, and then again in the fourth—
for "kid stuff." After fifth grade, he said, "I decided to straighten
out my act." A lot of Sabour's friends had never straightened out
their act, but he had a kind of inner cool that protected him. He was
serene, but not passive.

I asked Sabour if he felt that the last year had changed him
at all. He didn't know what I meant. He realized, he said, how hard
it would be to find a job. I said that I was thinking more of internal,
mental changes. Sabour gave a little nod and said, "I'm *reading* more.
I used to buy the *Daily News* and just read the sports section. Then
I started reading the whole paper. Now I'm buying the *New York*

Times. If I see a book I'm interested in, I'll pick it up, I'll read it. It's like spontaneous reading." Sabour didn't mean read so much as "check out." "When I was in high school," he said, "I'd come home, play basketball, run around, that kind of stuff. Now I turn on the news or I'm reading a book. It's funny you asked because I really didn't notice it until now. I guess subliminally I've changed." And even if he couldn't pronounce *vocabulary* he was obviously picking some up.

Sabour hadn't done as well in class as he would have liked. He hadn't taken math seriously and had earned only a C. That was an ominous sign, since he would have to take three more, increasingly difficult, semesters of math in order to qualify for the program in architecture. In his other classes he had earned two B's and a Pass. But Sabour recognized—now that he thought about it—that college was changing him. "A lot of the teachers," he said, "their tone is like, 'You're a grown man, we shouldn't be telling you things. You've got to be responsible for yourself.' And I'm getting to be more reponsible. Now when one of my friends comes over to the house and says, 'Come on outside,' it's like, 'No, I've got to work,' 'No, I've got to stay inside.' "

Sabour said this almost wonderingly; he was seeing himself in a new way. There was naivete, and bravado, in his confidence, but also a stern, adult resolve. "I *know* that I'm going to graduate with an architecture degree," he said, "either here or someplace else. And if there's nothing, then I'll find some other job." Sabour was taking an art class and finally learning how to draw those orthogonals he had invented for himself. He was a long way from a degree, in architecture or anything else. The odds were still against him; any number of things might come along and defeat him. But Sabour was not, I thought, likely to defeat himself.

Though the SEEK students were still almost wholly submerged in remediation, possibly never to escape, several of the ESL students I had met over the summer had emerged into the bright and sometimes blinding light of the regular curriculum. Hammeed, Ericson, Jean, Hyunsun, Servio, and Fernando all took English 110, the freshman composition course, in the spring. Gloraida had dropped out of school and moved to Puerto Rico, Atik had been forced to leave school to tend to his sick mother, Mones and Abukar had had to sacrifice some or all of class work in order to make money. But probably only three or four of the original seventeen students would still be taking ESL courses by the following fall.

Some of the students had moved unimpeded through the regular curriculum, though I couldn't tell if that was a comment on their latent abilities or on the generosity of their teachers. Fernando, the courtly, middle-class Dominican student, still spoke an extremely rudimentary English, but he had passed English 110 and was preparing to transfer to SUNY Buffalo. Ericson, the bashful Haitian student with the brilliant smile, had failed the reading test, and had made it through his composition class with only the barest amount of work. The class had been a waste, though not nearly so big a waste, he thought, as World Civilization 101 with Professor Jeffries, which he had taken on the advice of some militant Haitian friends.

Ericson hadn't really encountered the reality of college, yet for the following semester he was planning to take courses in philosophy, world humanities, chemistry, and calculus. And his English didn't seem up to the challenge. He lived in an all-Haitian world, and though his lips no longer trembled violently when he had to switch to English, he still took a good ten minutes to begin speaking in full sentences when I called him at home. His Haitian friends, he said, made fun of his mistakes when he tried to speak to them in English. Still, Ericson was determined to pursue a career in engineering, which he had set his sights on as a *premier* in his lycée in Port-au-Prince.

Hammeed Assaidi, the Yemeni student whose English seemed to have been run through a blender, was very much the dark, stocky, and endearingly overeager young man that I had met the year before; he still had his rather weedy black mustache. Hammeed had breezed his way through his math classes and was ready to take his first civil engineering course in the fall; but he had been advanced into English 110 without taking, much less passing, the reading or writing assessment exams, as the system now permitted. His English 110 teacher had given him a Pass but asked him to take the course once again. "In my writing I improved a lot a lot," said Hammeed. He let me look at a sheaf of his papers, and I saw that it was true.

An early essay on Buddha's "sermon at Benares" was a formless pastiche of the sage's aphorisms, rendered in Hammeed's private idiom: "He said if someone take his desire of having more things for himself. Selfishnes is sickness that together efect many people. A person may lose his friends and his relation to everyone who may know because of selfishnes." But in a second draft of an essay he wrote toward the end of the semester, Hammeed methodically contrasted two short stories involving requited and unrequited love. "Love," Hammeed wrote, "is an emotion that always happens almost to all of us." Despite his confusion over the placement of adjectives and adverbs, Hammeed wrote with much greater command than he had shown earlier. And he concluded, in the American style, with personal opinion: "Finally, in my point of view which has come from my experience, most boys and girls are suffering in their marriage because their families are arranging their marriages by choosing their future partners. This is happening in many places where the culture and tradition of the society determine the choice of a marriage partner, a person may lose his right to choose the girl that he wants."

Hammeed was beginning to compose, to use writing as a way of bringing order and even calm to the wild tangle of his English. His speaking style was still far more free-associational than his writing. He coined his own verb tenses, as in "I have been heard it over there." He still backed and filled madly as he spoke, and he often misunderstood and mispronounced simple words. But his vocabulary was far wider than it had been, and he was vastly more coherent. He had adopted the semiofficial City College newspaper reading habit: the *Daily News* five times a week, and the *New York Times* on Tuesday, when the science section appeared. After two years in a New York City high school and one in college, he was still a long way from being able to wield English as an academic language. It was altogether possible that he never would; but his growth over the course of a year had been enormous, and there was every reason to hope that it would continue.

Hammeed worked in a grocery store on upper Broadway, which he deeply disliked, and after the semester ended we met at the City College cafeteria during his lunch hour. Hammeed's uncle, who was part owner of another grocery store, accompanied him, allegedly because he happened to be heading in that direction anyway. For all his modern sentiments, Hammeed was a traditional boy, and he was slightly put out when I insisted on paying for his lunch. The uncle, short and wiry and dark, was waiting for us at the table, and he immediately said something to Hammeed in Arabic. Hammeed translated for me: "He want to know who pay for the lunch." I tried to make amends by explaining that I hadn't given Hammeed a chance to pay. After lunch, when I went to photocopy his essays, Hammeed almost jammed dollar bills from his pocket into the change machine.

Hammeed said that he had been working in the grocery store six hours a day, seven days a week, during the school year. Now that it was summer he was working twelve hours a day, which helped explain why he had been so delighted to hear from me and to meet me at the campus. His life was sheer drudgery. Come the fall, he would go back to working six hours a day, while taking an insanely ambitious schedule of core courses and higher-level math and engineering courses. "Do you really think you can manage?" I asked. Hammeed shrugged. I noticed the crescent-shaped scar that he had at the edge of his hairline. "I don't have no girlfriend," he said. "I don't spend time with nobody, I don't have time to go out. When I come here, is all I do is work."

Hammeed's uncle had listened politely throughout the conversation, but finally he put in a question. Hammeed translated: "He want to know how many years I can get a degree." I explained that City College students took an average of slightly more than six years to graduate, and that since Hammeed had to support himself, and had gone through the ESL program, he probably wouldn't make it in much less. The uncle listened quite carefully—it turned out that he understood English well enough—and then said to me directly, "Do you think he can finish in three years?" That was why he had come: he wanted to know how fast it was humanly possible to graduate. That was the gale-force wind that Hammeed had at his back. This was one student who would never have to worry about motivation. Like so many other immigrants at City, his problem was pressure, not apathy. He bore the weight of large expectations, including his own. I wondered if Hammeed would find the time to get an education, much less a life, while he clambered hand over hand toward his degree.

18

The Real City College

J
im Watts was always after me to sit in on history electives, read student papers, attend department functions. I had, in fact, read a sheaf of papers from a class that Watts himself taught and had been duly impressed; and I had attended a class on the Civil War and Reconstruction taught by Lou Masur, another of City's recent hires from Harvard, and had been delighted to find ideas and textual citations being batted back and forth across the classroom. This was the real City College, Watts kept insisting; and though I had seen too much of the college to concede that, I recognized that City had several dozen classes in the liberal arts where students did reasonably serious work. But Watts wasn't convinced that I was convinced; his boosterism was relentless. In early May, with the spring semester winding down, he called to invite me to the department's annual awards luncheon.

Jim Watts did not believe in timid celebration. He had taken over a corner of the faculty lounge, and waiters were passing around wine and cheese to faculty, guests, and award recipients. The college photographer was there. CUNY vice chancellor Richard Freeland, Watts's erstwhile nemesis from the struggle over the Goldstein report,

would be arriving later to deliver the closing remarks. With the threat
of the report receding, Freeland could now be treated as a fellow
historian and local eminence. After the guests had been seated and
the entree served, Watts made a few remarks. I had first met him
a year earlier, when he had just assumed the chairmanship. He had
been overweight then; now, after a year of budget cuts and CPI and
Jeffries and Goldstein, he had taken on a good deal more ballast.
His salt-and-pepper beard looked stretched along his jaw, and his
tan suit jacket rippled at his ribs. But this was the kind of moment
Watts lived for. He gripped the podium hard and launched into his
favorite spiel: "An intellectual renaissance is upon City College. . . .
These students embody the excellence of the entire college. . . ." Then,
one by one, the winners of the fourteen annual awards, prizes, and
scholarships were introduced by their professors, shook hands all
around, and pocketed their check.

The winner of the General Tremain Prize for the best essay on
the Civil War was Francisco Hernandez; and I immediately recognized the older student who had first gotten huffy with me, and
then gotten even huffier with another student, during my tribunal
a month or so before. At the time his name had been Frank, and
it turned out that he was politically incorrect enough to use only
the Anglicized form of his name. Frank was introduced by Robert
Twombly, a historian of architecture who was described as his mentor. Frank, said Twombly, had examined City College's archives to
find the records of two southern students who were expelled from
the school in 1860 after they had joined the infant Confederacy. It
turned out that Frank specialized in primary research material. He
had also written a paper for Twombly based on letters between
Henry Guggenheim and Frank Lloyd Wright that he had unearthed
in the archives of the Guggenheim Museum. Frank had used the
letters to argue that the tempest raging over the design of an addition to the museum was a recapitulation of the conflict over Wright's
original building.

I talked with Frank after lunch. He reminded me a great deal
of another pudgy Hispanic with a mustache, New York's former
schools chancellor Joe Fernandez—tough, wisecracking, quick on the
uptake, with the pride that comes of having made it much farther

than he ever could have dreamed. "There are three cousins in my family," Frank said, "and I'm the only one to have graduated from *high school*. It never even occurred to me to go to college." Both of his grandfathers had been lawyers associated with the Batista regime in pre-Castro Cuba, and Frank's family, like much of the Cuban middle class, had fled the island for New York after losing everything in the aftermath of the revolution. The family moved to Miami, and for twelve years after high school Frank worked in real estate, finally rising to be the sales manager of a public housing project.

"I realized," Frank said, "that this was the end of the line. I wasn't going any further without an education, so I enrolled at Miami-Dade Community College and got my associate degree. Then I realized that wasn't going to do me much good." He was accepted at CUNY for the spring semester in 1991, but was sent to City rather than Hunter, his first choice. Feeling sorry for himself, Frank was wandering down the halls of the NAC building one day when he saw a name on a door—Robert Twombly. "Not *the* Robert Twombly!" thought Frank. Frank was an architecture buff; he worshiped Twombly's study of Frank Lloyd Wright. And here he was, at City College of all places. Frank arranged to meet his hero; and his career at City took off.

Frank lived the prototypical City College student life. "As soon as I got here," he said, "I got a job as a waiter at Tony Roma's" —a rib joint on the East Side. "I would come straight from school, work four to ten, sometimes one to ten on weekends, and then go home and collapse. I couldn't get rid of the smell of barbecue sauce no matter how many times I showered; it was in my clothes, my hair, everywhere." Amazingly, Frank completed the 80 credits he needed to graduate in five semesters. "You can figure out what that means," he said proudly. "This semester I'm taking 16 credits; last semester I took 20 credits" —seven courses. Was he reading Frank Lloyd Wright's correspondence in Tony Roma's kitchen? No; Frank said that he managed to do most of his work on the weekends.

And now Frank was graduating from City as a shining star. He had the $400 check for the General Tremain Prize in his pocket and a wall full of acceptance letters from law schools back in his apartment. His mother was over the moon with joy—by choosing the law,

Frank was renewing the family line. Frank had been so sought after that he could actually work up a good head of indignation at Fordham, which had merely invited him to join next year's law school class. Because Frank's Hispanic background made him a member of a disadvantaged minority group, he had been wooed like a basketball prospect, a practice that Frank himself appeared to consider normal. He had finally decided to attend Cardozo Law School (at Yeshiva University) in downtown Manhattan, which offered a full scholarship. But Cardozo also had a sentimental advantage. When Frank was a little boy living in New York, his father drove a truck between a printing plant in New Jersey and the offices of *Forbes* magazine, just across from Yeshiva's building. "And so when I talked to the interviewer from Yeshiva," Frank said with a big, meaty grin, "I told him that it took me twenty-seven years to get across the street."

A week or so after the awards ceremony I was haunting the student lounge when I saw Andrew, the Ghanaian student I had met in Rudi Gedamke's class, sitting by himself on a couch, his hands resting limply in his lap. Andrew's resolve had melted away in the course of that semester, as his parents squabbled and his loneliness deepened; Rudi had ended by offering him one of his contracts. I asked him if he had kept his half of the bargain by working with Rudi. "I've just been so busy," Andrew said. "At the beginning of the semester I said I was going to go see him, and then I never had the time." I had the sickening feeling that Andrew was slipping away, and I said sternly, "You've got to go see Professor Gedamke. He means it when he says he wants to help you."

"I know, I know," said Andrew, giving me his ever-obedient smile. He promised to see him when the fall semester began. Andrew had said the same thing to Rudi every time they had seen one another— "I'm busy, I'm coming." Rudi hadn't decided whether he would let Andrew keep the C he had given him, or convert the grade to an Incomplete, which would compel Andrew to take the course once again. In the fall he would sit down with Andrew's SEEK counselor to thrash it out. Of the six students Rudi had put on contract, three had worked with him at least sporadically during the spring, and he had made their C permanent. Che, the quiet, dreamy-eyed kid who sat in the far corner, had never shown up at all. And Margaret, the older woman who could barely read or write, had withdrawn from City College. Rudi followed the fortunes of many of his other students, and his reports were for the most part gloomy. The students who needed him most were seeing him least.

When I asked how the past semester had gone, Andrew flipped his hands back and forth in a gesture that meant "Not so hot" —a sign that things must have been very bad indeed. "I had to drop Chem 103," he said abjectly. "I was always falling behind, and I couldn't catch up. I think I should have studied more." Andrew admitted that he also might have gotten no more than a C in Math 75, the advanced geometry course. And then he embarked on a lecture on the virtues of hard work and discipline that I had heard him deliver before. He must have found the words reassuring; he spoke them as if they were some sort of talisman.

I asked Andrew about his family. "Everything's fine," he said emphatically. "I just don't see my father anymore." I murmured, "I'm sorry." Andrew flared up: "I don't care. He doesn't want to have anything to do with us, and that's fine with me." Andrew sounded petulant, and his petulance felt like the thinnest cover for his fear and hurt. And he started in on another sermonette about self-reliance. When he was finished, I said, "Good luck, Andrew." And Andrew flashed me his nervous, overeager smile.

I happened to walk by the lounge about two hours later. And there was Andrew, still sitting with his hands in his lap, his eyes unfocused.

Tammy, the student I had met through Marilyn Sternglass, experienced life as a series of never-ending crises; she staggered, righted herself, and then staggered again. In January, between semesters, I had gone to visit her at home in the South Bronx. I took a subway and a bus, retracing Tammy's own complicated route to school, and as the bus moved northward the grim urban landscape turned almost feral. On both sides of the street there was open land covered with trash and bits of brick and leaves and weeds, land that was returning to a corrupted state of nature. On Tammy's corner, at 169th Street and Third Avenue, there was another open lot, and men squatting in doorways, and a sign for the Martin Luther King Health Center's Alcoholism Unit over a truck dock at the back of a grocery store. Tammy was late to meet me because the elevator in her building had broken down, as it did almost weekly, and she had had to walk down from the fifteenth floor. She would go back up when it was repaired.

Tammy was very depressed. It was the month between semesters, the worst of times for her. Tammy had meant it literally when she said that school was all she had. When school was out, she had virtually nothing to do—except fret. She had a job as an usher at Radio City Music Hall, but she couldn't work full-time, and spend hours commuting, *and* go to class and get her work done; so she worked only once or twice a week, and weeks went by when she didn't work at all. Tammy and her mother scraped by on her mother's $400 a month in SSI payments, plus Tammy's meager income and the unused portions of the state and federal grants she received through school. In part because she was virtually penniless, and in part because she had trouble doing anything nice for herself, Tammy almost never went to movies or dinner or took even the most modest trips.

Tammy found plenty of things to be depressed about. Her birthday had just come and gone, and neither her father, nor her many siblings, nor her friends, had so much as called. "My mom says she's praying for me to get a new set of friends," she said with a roll of her eyes. We were sitting on a low concrete wall at the back of the Webster-Morrisania Houses, an area she kept away from after dark. Tammy didn't really know anyone in the building, because she spent virtually all of her time on campus. Her life outside of school revolved around two people—her mother, Mary, and her boyfriend, Jay; and now, she said, she and Jay were breaking up. But that was more an expression of her mood than anything else: a few minutes later Tammy said that Jay was urging her to move in with him.

Jay had a good job working at a hospital in Westchester, and he had a nice apartment near where Tammy used to live. But she was resisting. "I feel like if I moved in," Tammy said, "Jay wouldn't respect me anymore. I want to get married to Jay someday, and I don't want him to take me for granted." Tammy was acutely aware of the perils of sexual availability—and it wasn't just a matter of Jay's respect. In her family, women became pregnant at sixteen, as regularly as clockwork. "I talk to my sister and I'm kind of disgusted by the way she had all these kids without even thinking about it," Tammy said. She had no trouble understanding the consequences of casual mistakes.

Tammy was feeling lonely and listless; but she had felt lonely and listless before. What really upset her was that her whole future had suddenly been imperiled. A few days earlier she had gone to the campus to find out why her financial aid check hadn't arrived. The clerk who looked up her records said, "Oh, but you've been de-registered." —because of Tammy's nightmare and nemesis, the math assessment exam. City had a rule that students had to have passed all three of their assessment tests by the time they reached their 60th credit. The previous semester had put Tammy over the top, but, according to Tammy, no one had notified her. Now, with her arms wrapped around her to ward off a chill wind, she said, "When I found out that I had been deregistered, I literally got sick. I got a light feeling, like I couldn't stand up. I couldn't even talk. I just looked at that person and didn't say a word. School means so much to me—I'm sure that's why I reacted like that. When I came home I couldn't even bring myself to tell my mother. I was in a daze; I didn't know what I was going to do."

Tammy's life took so much willpower. Nothing happened by itself. She couldn't turn to her parents for help—her father was useless and her mother was helpless. Tammy's mother couldn't bear to see her suffer, and so, at low moments, when Tammy would talk about dropping out, her mother would say, "Maybe that would be best." Mary wanted to have Tammy by her; she worried that the moment was soon coming when she would be all alone. Tammy felt that pull but knew she couldn't surrender to it. And so, once she had recovered her composure, she went back to the campus and talked to the dean of academic standards, the registrar, and the financial aid people. She promised to pass the math exam no later than August. Jay agreed to pay for tutoring. And so she was reinstated. It was as if a death sentence had been commuted.

The experience had left Tammy feeling shaky and vulnerable. We had gotten thoroughly cold standing outside, and Tammy took me into the lobby of her grim brick building. Someone had called in a fire, or tripped an alarm, and firefighters, huge in their heavy coats and hats and axes, went rushing by and raced up the stairs— the elevators were still broken. By and by they came trooping back down. Nobody paid much attention; false alarms were an almost daily event. Tammy was looking out a big grimy window at the fire truck and the people aimlessly milling in the street. She was over-whelmed by forebodings; sometimes her voice cracked, and she would struggle to master her feelings. She said quietly, "I know if I don't make it through school then I'm just going to be standing right here like I am now, or I'll be out on the street." I tried to say encouraging things, to remind Tammy of everything she had already achieved; but I, too, felt the weight, and the bewildering variety, of her problems. And I couldn't refute Tammy's premise. If she dropped out of City College, she might very well be sucked back into the world of her mother, and her brothers and sisters, and her friends, and their parents and brothers and sisters.

I didn't see Tammy again until the end of the semester, when we agreed to meet for lunch at the cafeteria. I waited for her in the fluorescent purplish glare of the lobby, which was just beyond the cafeteria. A woman was standing at the newspaper vending machine across the lobby, and I did a double take when I realized it was Tammy. She had braided her hair into tight corn rows and then swept them straight back over her head, a Nefertiti look that gave her an almost queenly air. Even her skin looked brighter. Nefertiti might not have chosen to have her nails painted with billowing white waves and studded with tiny rhinestones; but Tammy had to improvise her fashion statements. What mattered was that she was doing some-thing for herself. It was obvious that something good had happened.

The major event of the semester had been Tammy's desperate campaign to pass the math assessment exam on the fifth or sixth try. She had approached the exam as if her life hung in the balance, which to some extent it did: if she failed, she might have been forced to leave City College. She had gone faithfully to the tutor Jay had paid for, and she had studied the mistakes she made on her prior exam, as City College policy permitted. "I knew I had to get to the test with plenty of time to spare," Tammy said, "so I went to sleep real early. I got on the bus—of course I was doing more problems on the bus—and when I got to the science building there was a whole line of students waiting outside. And they were all working on problems, too." Tammy was probably not the only one for whom this exam meant so much. In the past, Tammy had not finished the exam in the regulation fifty minutes, and she felt that her poor vision was to blame. This time, though, she finished five minutes early, so perhaps her problems in the past hadn't been entirely optical. Still, she wasn't at all confident that she had passed, which required 25 correct answers out of 40. A few days later she found that she had scored a 26.

That was justification enough for the hair and the nails. But though she had dodged one bullet, the fusillade had barely slowed. She had just come from astronomy, which she had chosen as the least onerous of mandatory science courses. "I'm going to fail," she said flatly. Tammy opened up her notebook, as if I might be able to help by scanning her notes. I saw the words *velocity* and *luminosity*, and then a confused welter of signs and arrows. "I write down everything the teacher says," Tammy said, "but I don't know what he's talking about. The sun is a G-2 star—that's the one thing I've picked up so far." Everyone in the class was confounded, Tammy said, but she most of all. On the first exam the class average had been 56; she had scored 28. On the next, she had tumbled to a 10. She could drop the class, but then she would have fallen below the minimum standard for a full-time student and thus lost her financial aid. So she would have to take an F and then avail herself of another generous City College policy that allowed students to retake a course they've failed. It would be another heroic trudge, like the math exam.

Tammy could never relax; the consequences of failure were too terrifying. And so even minor setbacks could lead to a bout of depression. Her squabbles with Jay, her problems with math, and her close call with de-registration, Tammy said, had made this her worst semester at City College yet. She had become more and more anxious, and now she was worried that she was running out of time. It had taken her four years to compile her first 80 credits—what Frank Hernandez had done in two and a half years while working full-time. The state tuition assistance program, or TAP, covered only five years. And so

Tammy was trying to persuade herself, or delude herself, that she could graduate next spring. In fact there was no way she could complete another 48 credits in less than two years. How was she going to survive?

"Jay's talking about paying for my schooling," Tammy said, inspecting her decorated fingernails. "He said he would drop out of school until I got on my feet. He's really, really, *really* concerned about my finishing school." Jay was in the Engineering School, and his family, from the Virgin Islands, took education very seriously; he was offering to make an extraordinary sacrifice. But even the terms of Jay's generosity made Tammy uncomfortable. He had joined a Muslim community in Brooklyn, and he had begun to preach values that Tammy regarded as reactionary. "He expects women to be subordinate. I've told him I'm not the humble type. I'm not the housewife type, either. I'm more career oriented. He says of course I should have a career and everything. But then he says that he wants to have a big family, eleven kids, and you're going to have to cook and clean and submit. And I'm not the submitting type." Tammy flushed with pride as she made these womanly declarations. A note of toughness came into her soft voice and into her cautious, doubting manner.

There were still more catastrophes, more episodes of fear and terrible self-doubt, in Tammy's saga. She was seeing a City College therapist and trying to talk her way through her woes, worrying all the while that her standing in psychology would be hurt if she were discovered. She had pinned all her hopes on psychology, perhaps because she felt that by learning to tend to the pain of others she could master her own suffering, or put it to use. But there was more to it than that. Tammy didn't simply want to lose herself in others. She wanted to raise herself out of the world she had been born into, and whose grasp she so desperately feared. She had preserved enough self-esteem, despite everything, to want something fine for herself and to hold herself to high ideals. She still was probably no better than even odds to graduate; but those were pretty good odds by City's standards.

The day before graduation, on a blazingly hot afternoon, I went to see if my friends in engineering were around. I found Wagner

Ortuno in the Ecuadorean Club, across the hall from LAESA; the presidency of LAESA had passed into the hands of his successor. The Ecuadorean Club had a TV and a microwave and a fridge—and a blackboard that was often covered with equations. Albert Einstein gazed out from a photo high up on the wall, with "$E = MC^2$" printed in big block letters. Wagner had been giving a lot of thought to his future. Throughout his career at City he had clung to the tradition of student activism he had grown up with in the Dominican Republic. In the CUNY-wide tuition strike of 1989, Wagner had lead the Ecua Squad, a team of committed activists who shut down buildings, confronted the police, and, Wagner said proudly, "did all the dirty work." He had been a central figure in a failed strike two years later. This past year he had run for president of the student body against the Jeffries party. Wagner had been the candidate of moderation, fielding a multiracial slate and pledging to focus on practical student concerns rather than the usual revolutionary posturing. But the other side had won, as it virtually always did; a sizable fraction of the few students who cared about such things were Jeffries followers.

Wagner was rethinking his position. "I've been reminding people that we're students," he said, resting a hand on a filing cabinet. "We came here to study. Maybe political activity is like a sine curve." Wagner sketched an oscillating line with his hand. He had ridden the curve up; now he was riding it down. Wagner was thinking about how much he owed to his mother, who had always been after him to do his homework, and to his father, who had provided him with an example of dogged hard work. His father lived in New York now, and he would be coming to see Wagner graduate. And his girlfriend, too? Wagner's girlfriend was history; she had gotten tired of seeing him once a week, on Sunday, when he wasn't hanging out at the club, studying in the library, or tutoring young students and older members of the community.

Wagner had big plans for the future. He had been working for Con Edison, as many engineering students did, but he had decided against the corporate life. "I was thinking about it," he said, "and I realized I don't want to be twenty, thirty years with the same company, punch out at lunch, punch in, go home at three-thirty. That's not what I want to do with my life." No, Wagner wanted to strike out on his own, to start a new business. Or perhaps he would teach; after all, he had been a teacher ever since he had come to City College. He was trying to convince his friends from the club to teach high school, and form an import-export business with him on the side. They were afraid to wander far from the primrose path, but Wagner was prodding and pushing. "I feel like I can be the first drop of water in the pool," he said, with his grandiose sense of his own destiny. "You know, if one drop goes, the others follow."

I left Baskerville Hall and crossed Convent Avenue. Usually students were playing touch football on the roadway. I remembered the Chinese kid I had seen drop a plastic golf ball on the road and take a hack with an eight-iron; a security guard had hurried over after his first whiff. Now Convent Avenue was empty in the blinding light. The whole campus was empty. Wagner was there because there was no place else he wanted to be. And I had heard that the students in Professor Rinard's chemical engineering design class were still working on their projects, even though the school year was over. I walked into Steinman Hall and threaded my way down dim corridors to the cinderblock bunker of room B-23; lo and behold, it was jammed with students.

No one even looked up when I walked in. The students I had met before—Brendan, Arthur, and Hassan—all happened to be out, but others, whom I didn't know, were hunched over their DEC workstations. Two Greek students, John Gatzonis and Joanne Thomatos, were at the computer nearest the door. The manufacturing process they had chosen to model for their project had turned out to be an antiquated one, used only in older plants in Third World countries. They had spent weeks trying, and failing, to show how the process could make economic sense. Now, instead, they were busy demonstrating why it couldn't. They had fallen way behind; but then, so had everyone else.

It was hard to remember that these students had other classes—lots of them. In fact so many of the engineering courses were worth only 2 credits, despite requiring hours of homework, that everyone in the design class was taking at least five other courses in order to record the 12 credits needed to retain full-time status. John was taking six academic courses and physical education, which was worth 1 credit. Joanne had five courses, and two physical education classes. It seemed almost ludicrous. "Actually," said John, "Numerical Methods is almost as much work as Design, but nobody has the time to do it. Our professor gets really mad, but there's nothing he can do." Once John cleared his design project out of the way, he planned to tackle his lab work from two other courses. And since he wasn't graduating until January, there was no reason not to keep right on working through next week, or whatever it took. I thought I detected in his tone of voice the quiet satisfaction of the true masochist.

"How long are you guys going to be here tonight?" I asked.

"Oh, I don't know," John answered. He swiveled around in his chair to face Marcia Anglin, a Jamaican student I had met earlier. Marcia was at a workstation across the room. "Marcia," John asked, "how long are you going to be staying here tonight?"

"I guess about eleven, twelve. You?"

"About twelve."

In those final days I sometimes tried to imagine an alternative City College, one in which excellence would be the rule rather than the shining exception. It was probably an idle exercise, since, as the timid formulation of the College Preparatory Initiative had shown, the open admissions commitment was sacrosanct. And it wasn't just a question of political reality. Even to say that a student like Renato, or Paula or Che or Margaret or Richard or Philip, shouldn't be admitted to City College felt almost intolerably cruel. That was what lent the admissions policy such moral weight. Could I, as Jim Watts had asked, deny them admission in the name of standards? Perhaps not, though if it is true that the remedial undercollege is threatening City's upper stories, then it is also true that City simply has to stop taking so many students who need so much help.

But aside from the harm to the institution, it is fair to say that City shouldn't be admitting these students because the experience isn't helping *them* enough. Perhaps City hasn't figured out how to help them, or perhaps, as I thought, their problems are too profound to be addressed in a college setting. In either case it's clear that eventually, and probably quite soon, they will join that funereal roll call of dropouts that Rudi Gedamke sounded in his memo. The SEEK

program made sense when City's admissions standards were pro-
hibitively strict. Now that even terribly educated students can gain
admission, it is pointless to offer special dispensation to students
whose poverty supposedly prevented them from reaching even that
modest level. Doing so comes perilously close to saying that *anyone*
should be able to enroll. At the same time, to abolish the SEEK program altogether would be to foreclose the principle of potential, on
which it was founded. It would ignore students like Tammy or
Sabour, who dithered their way through high school but now are
ready to take their destiny in their hands. A fair alternative would
be to retain a much smaller version of SEEK, in which students who
otherwise would have to go to a community college could be recommended for senior college admission by high school teachers, counselors, or administrators.

Then there are the students who did well enough in high school
to meet City's admissions criteria, but were so poorly educated that
they languish in remediation for several semesters before reaching
the regular curriculum. Their chances of survival are poor, though
slightly better than those of the SEEK students. Would I, if I were
king, restore City's old admissions standards so as to exclude them?
No, in part because it would be meaningless; grade inflation has put
an 80 or 83 average well within the reach of even the most noncha-
lant student. A more meaningful stricture would be to demand that
students entering City, and the other CUNY senior colleges, have
taken and passed a full menu of academic courses, as was expected
in the days before open admissions. I would make the CPI mandatory and require students who haven't satisfied its requirements to
do so before enrolling at a senior college or, alternatively, to pass a
series of proficiency exams.

One obvious flaw with such a system, as well as with the CPI
in its current form, is its inability to interpret transcripts from Haiti
or Santo Domingo or Lahore. Translating the records of students from
English-speaking countries, or countries with European educational
systems, might not be insuperable; and such students, at least the
English-speaking ones, would probably pass proficiency exams without much trouble. But the same couldn't be said for Chinese or
Dominican students. Their records would be opaque *and* they might

not have the English to pass exams, no matter what their academic background. It would be a terrible loss, both to these young men and women and to City University, if they couldn't be admitted until they have developed sufficient language skills to demonstrate the full range of their ability. City's Engineering School, among other things, would be decimated. And so, if I were king, I would make such students wait until they have enough English-language capability that an interviewer can get a full sense of their academic experience—thus eliminating much or all of ESL 10—and then admit them, or assign them elsewhere, based on a combination of their record, the interviewer's conclusions, and their performance on proficiency exams. As with SEEK, in other words, I would exercise discretion.

My hypothetical City College might be smaller than the current one, but it still would consist overwhelmingly of students of color, students without money, first-generation college-goers. The college still would have a remedial burden to shoulder, and its students would suffer from forms of adversity unknown to the classes of 1940 or 1960. But it would be dedicated to academic excellence, its degree would be respected everywhere, and it would be immune to the cavils of the Goldstein commission. It would lift up rather than kneel down. Sheldon Weinbaum, the engineering professor, argued that City should have been designated a "university center," a term used in the New York State system to set apart the campuses with graduate institutions and high academic standards. City as it exists now has not earned the distinction; but under the right circumstances, it could. And a City College fully restored to its former glory, only now with black and Hispanic students, and students from every corner of the world, would offer a majestic symbol of the diverse, multicultural society that is America's future.

Yes; but what about the casualties? If CUNY *had* been structured like SUNY, many students who didn't gain admission to City would go to one of the lesser senior colleges. And they would have few grounds for complaint. Open admissions, after all, is driven less by the demand for access to elite institutions than by the demand for access to four-year colleges. And here is the heart of the problem: If City, or CUNY, tightened admissions standards, thousands of students now going to senior college would have to go to community college, or to vocational institutions, just as was envisioned under CUNY's 1968 master plan. And very few students who qualified for senior college would be eager to accept something less.

The idea makes me queasy as well, and it isn't just a matter of economic opportunity. As Steven Brint and Jerome Karabel, the authors of the foremost history of the community college, write, "Our reservations about vocational education hearken back to an indigenous American tradition of commitment to the ideal that the educational system should be as devoted to the formation of democratic citizens as it is to the training of workers and that one of its principal tasks is to empower ordinary people." What if the cost of dedicating ourselves to academic excellence was relegating even more students to education-as-workers rather than education-as-citizens? How would this comport with the Jeffersonian vision that gave rise to our system of public education? There is no philosophically satisfying answer to this question, although there is a very sound practical answer: students who drop out of a four-year college are not receiving education of any kind. They need to be helped; and if a two-year degree or vocational training will help them to get a good job and lead a decent life, then it isn't to be denigrated. And why the zero-sum formulation? Americans often return to college later in life, when the spirit moves them. Indeed, one of the most inspiring institutions at City College is its Center for Worker Education, which offers evening courses to older students, many of them motivated by nothing more tangible than a yen to gain the education they passed up the first time around.

The economic question is actually harder to put to rest than the philosophical one. The credentials just shy of a four-year college degree are only marginally worth having. W. Norton Grubb, a numbers cruncher at the National Center for Research in Vocational Education at Berkeley, recently found that a college degree is worth about 80 percent more in average earnings than a high school diploma; even controlling for the differences in demographic characteristics between high school and college graduates, the degree itself is still immensely valuable. Certificates from job-training programs, he concluded, offer no measurable advantage over high school diplomas only. Recipients of associate's degrees from two-year colleges can expect to earn as much as half again more than high-school-only job seekers, although demographic difference accounts for much of the gap. A vocational degree from a community college is worth more than an academic one, and either degree improves the average income of women more than that of men. Grubb concludes that critics like Brint and Karabel who consider a community college degree virtually worthless have overdrawn the case; but the encouragement he offers is extremely modest.

The problem lies not only in the schools but in the labor markets. Economist Ivar Berg has explained how in the years since World War II the labor market has adapted to mass higher education by raising the ante of job requirements. Thus insurance agents are now required to have college degrees, though Berg cites evidence showing that nonpedigreed agents do as well as or better than the credentialed. The system has become self-reinforcing. Colleges advertise themselves as the royal road to a white-collar job and require only the most modest record of high school achievement for admission. Students get the message and go off to college in vast numbers. Employers are appalled at the education level of the average high school graduate, and find in any case that they have a huge pool of college graduates from which to choose.

The most obvious way to break the circle, and of course the heart of the whole open admissions dilemma, is to start producing well-educated high school graduates. As Berg writes, "America should be doing a far better job in insuring that *all* of her people reach adult life with 12 years of quality training and education," rather than 16 years of mediocrity. Of course, that's easy for him to say. Everyone agrees that we should be producing better high school graduates, but no one has yet found the key to doing so. A more readily attainable way to slow the credentials chase is to raise the prestige of vocational education, keeping in mind that it need not preclude a liberal arts education later in life. President Clinton's national service program, which forgives student loans in exchange for a year of community service, applies to two-year as well as four-year institutions. Secretary of Labor Robert Reich has put job training at the center of the administration's effort to promote American economic competitiveness. In 1993 Congress appropriated $100 million for programs designed to give meaningful, on-site job training to students in high school, and in the spring of 1994 passed the School-to-Work Opportunities Act, which combines high school vocational education, on-site training, and possible postsecondary education as well. If vocational training actually led to good jobs, and if it were seen as an essential element of a national campaign to upgrade the skills of the American worker, rather than a second-rate alternative for kids who couldn't hack college, then it might slow the rush of high school graduates into colleges that can't give them a decent education.

Graduation Day was Friday, May 28. It was a fine morning, and when I reached the campus at 9:30, half an hour before the beginning of festivities, hundreds of family members were already sitting on the folding chairs set up in the plaza in front of the NAC building and all the way back to the administration building one hundred or so yards away. The mothers looked uncomfortable in their tight full-length outfits; little girls in frilly dresses and Mary Janes scampered underfoot. Down Convent Avenue to the south, graduating students in their gowns were forming up in ranks—here the tiny handful from computer science, there the great mass from the Education School. Everyone, of course, was snapping pictures of everyone else.

A reviewing stand had been set up on NAC's second-floor balcony. Lavender bunting—the school's color—was wrapped around the poles holding up the stand; lavender flowers hung from the front rail; the lavender City College flag hung just below the American flag, and a huge lavender banner that read "1847–1993" had been fixed to the facade above and behind the stand. It was almost shocking to see City College decked out in all this gaudy grandeur; the school was so threadbare most of the time that now it looked like a dumpy old professor wearing a shiny tux. Lavender is not the ideal color for formal wear.

Charles Marks, the grand marshal of the commencement, advanced to the microphone in the reviewing stand. Marks, in civilian life a professor of English, apparently had a lock on the marshal's job by virtue of his ability to speak from the diaphragm and to deploy ordinary English words as if they were Latin. When he said "ro-tun-da," the word echoed majestically off the wings of the NAC building. Marks introduced the City College band for the national anthem, and the Reverend Clarence P. Grant for the invocation, and CUNY board member Thomas Tam for official greetings, and then sundry speakers and recipients of honorary degrees.

Along with other newsfolk I was standing on the upper part of a ramp that led to the reviewing stand. I was squinting into the sun when I realized that a gentleman in a dashiki and African cap was standing by my elbow. "Good morning, Professor Jeffries," I said. Jeffries returned my greeting, and then was silent for a moment. "A lot of people are spreading lies about me," he said quietly, but with his usual air of menace. He was looking away from me, toward the vast crowd of students on the plaza below us. "Some woman reporter said that I didn't even have my Ph.D. when I was hired at City College."

"*I* didn't say any such thing," I answered. I wasn't looking at Jeffries either. Jeffries had shot my heart rate up by about double, and as I mastered my emotions I peered very hard at something or other in the middle distance. I had just finished writing an article about Jeffries, and the fact checker reported that Jeffries had ranted at him for fifteen minutes before hanging up. Now Jeffries mentioned some minor fact that he felt I had gotten wrong. I said that I had learned it from him. Then we stood silently again. Apparently he had nothing further to say. Why was he standing there? A paranoid thought flashed across my mind: he was fingering me, Mafia-style, for his minions, who would follow me after the ceremony and beat me up, or Lord knows what. After I had waited long enough that it wouldn't seem as if I were fleeing him—a long time, or so it seemed— I walked up the ramp to the press table, feeling slightly absurd. I had permitted Jeffries, in a tiny way, to intimidate me. Of course, who hadn't?

The speakers were a good deal less stodgy and orotund than I expected. Daniel Goldin, an engineer from the class of 1962, bitterly assailed his own generation's failure of will, and urged, "Don't let the system beat you back, don't be afraid of failure, don't play it safe; go for it, grab it, make America and the world great again." Wilbur Pritchard, an engineer from the class of 1943, the fiftieth reunion class, said, "Looking around me, I don't see that there's been any significant change. The inner idea hasn't changed one bit." Vice chancellor Richard Freeland, now fully rehabilitated after the fiasco of the Goldstein report, spoke of Jim Watts's awards luncheon, saying that he had been "impressed and humbled by the quality of the work described and by the feeling of the faculty members for it."

Like Pritchard, Freeland spoke directly to the burden and the shadow that City College could never escape—the past. "Historically and today," Freeland said, "the scholars of your faculty bring you an international reputation; historically and today, your students attract the admiration of others." Historically and today—there was no better way to flatter City's vanity, and soothe its anxiety. Was there the tiniest bit of hedging in that less-than-stirring phrase, "attract the admiration of others"? Perhaps Freeland wasn't quite sure if a City College degree had held its exchange value over the years.

And then the degrees were conferred en masse, the students roaring and flinging their caps in the air. The valedictory address and the Ephebic Oath were delivered, the alma mater—"Lavender"—was sung, the benediction was pronounced, and then to the strains of Mendelssohn the students filed out onto Convent Avenue. With that, City College's 146th year had come to a close. I wandered through the crowd eddying around the plaza, and there, in a cap and gown and with a big smile, was Frank Hernandez. Frank was standing on the shallow steps leading down to Convent Avenue with his girlfriend, who had once been his boss at Tony Roma's, and his jubilant mother and solemnly proud father, who many years before had unloaded stacks of magazines across from Yeshiva Law School. They were thrilled and awed by the spectacle, and they greeted me with the gravity due a papal nuncio.

Frank was heading upstairs for—what else?—the History Department celebration. Jim Watts had already told me that I was expected. This time Watts had really laid it on thick—champagne, wine, sandwich platters, fresh fruit. All the award winners were there, with their moms and dads, if they had them, or their wives or girlfriends or boyfriends, or nobody at all. There were black students and Hispanic students and white students; the most exotic creature in the room, to my mind, was Jadwiga Pieper, a pale, intensely serious young woman with brilliant blue eyes and bristlingly short brown hair who had come to City from the University of Berlin to do Latin American studies. The City College campus was itself a kind of fieldwork for her.

Jim Watts had even brought his college-age daughter to witness his moment of glory. He had been showing off his students to her like prize roses, and now he collared me as well. "Look around you," Watts commanded. I did as I was told. I could feel The Speech welling up in Watts's soul. "This is the *real* City College," he declaimed in his raspy voice. "I'll compare my History Department to any other department in the city, and I guarantee—*I guarantee*—we'll come out better. We've got some of the best students I've ever seen. And the same is true over at English and Political Science. . . ." It was not for me, with Watts's daughter listening loyally, to do anything but nod. And when the speech came to an end, I congratulated Watts and took my leave.

I rode the escalator down from the fifth-floor history office. The NAC building was empty now. In a week, the summer session would start and the students would come flooding back, but this was one of the rare moments when there was absolutely no reason to be on campus. The escalator ended at the second floor, and I walked out toward the big concourse in front of the library, from which another escalator descended to the ground floor. Black and especially Haitian students always gathered at the circular ledge around the escalator. As I was leaving I noticed three or four students leaning against the ledge, among them Mones, the sad-eyed teacher who had fled Port-au-Prince, leaving his wife and two children and sickly father behind.

"Mones," I said, "what are you doing here? It's graduation day."

"Oh, yes?" he said. Mones appeared not to have noticed. He was a man in harness; he was too busy straining against the load that was his life to raise his eyes to the world around him. He had a math textbook with him; the other students were his tutees, though I still couldn't fathom what they were doing in the deadly quiet. Perhaps, like Mones, they had nowhere else to go once school ended. The tutees, in fact, were Mones's entire source of income, and thus his sole bulwark against destitution. They had also warped his career at City College. Because he had had to spend his mornings tutoring, Mones had been unable to take the advanced ESL 20/30 course in the fall. This past semester, though, he had finished ESL. "How did you do?" I asked.

"My professor give me a B," said Mones. That seemed quite creditable to me, given Mones's continuing problems with spoken English. But Mones was very disappointed—an emotion he rarely showed. "I think I will go and talk to him during the summer," he said. For Mones, the effort never ended. Over the summer he would take FORTRAN, to give him a solid base in computer science. And the next semester he would resume his impossible life as a part-time student. He needed to get his master's in math in order to fulfill his dream of teaching high school in the United States, and to be able to bring his family over; and he still didn't know how many undergraduate credits he would need, if any. He already had undergraduate and graduate degrees from Haiti, but that wasn't good enough. And so Mones would keep battling his loneliness, his debilitating migraines, his halting English, and the poverty he dragged behind him like a dead weight, because he knew that if he succeeded he could banish the past, reverse his ill fortune, and enjoy the fruitful life that for many generations America has held out as the prize to those who sacrifice and strive.

I said good-bye to Mones, and he pumped my hand and gave me that smile that seemed so thin a mask over his pain. His students politely said good-bye to me, too. As I rode down the escalator toward the sunny, empty plaza, where the buildings and grounds people were already sweeping up the debris and stacking the folding chairs, I thought, "*That* was the real City College."

Sources

The primary source for this book was several hundred interviews conducted over a period of eighteen months with City College students, professors, administrators, and alumni. I made extensive use of student papers, and internal documents produced by City College and City University. What follows is a list of books, studies, and articles from which I also drew information and guidance.

American Council on Education. *Higher Education for Everybody?* Washington, D.C., 1970.

Ballard, Allan. *The Education of Black Folks.* New York: Harper & Row, 1973.

Bartholomae, David. "The Study of Error." *College Composition and Communication*, vol. 31, no. 3 (October 1980).

Berg, Ivar. *Education and Jobs: The Great Training Robbery.* New York: Praeger, 1970.

Bizzell, Patricia. "What Happens When Basic Writers Come to College?" *College Composition and Communication*, vol. 37, no. 3 (October 1986).

Brint, Steven, and Jerome Karabel. *The Diverted Dream.* New York: Oxford University Press, 1989.

Brubacher, John S., and Willis Rudy. *Higher Education in Transition*. New York: Harper & Row, 1958.

Cahan, Abraham. *The Rise of David Levinsky*. New York: Harper & Brothers, 1917.

Carnegie Commission on Higher Education. *A Chance to Learn: An Action Agenda for Equal Opportunity in Higher Education*. New York: McGraw-Hill, 1970.

Cohen, Morris Raphael. *A Dreamer's Journey*. Boston: Beacon Books, 1949.

Commission on Financing Higher Education (the Rockefeller Commission). *The Nature and Needs of Higher Education*. New York: Columbia University Press, 1952.

Council for Basic Education. *Open Admissions: The Pros and Cons*. Washington, D.C., 1971.

Crossland, Fred E. *Minority Access to College*. New York: Schocken Books, 1971.

Dawidowicz, Lucy. *The Golden Tradition*. New York: Holt, Rinehart & Winston, 1967.

——. *The Jewish Presence: Essays on Identity and History*. New York: Holt, Rinehart & Winston, 1977.

Dyer, Conrad M. "Protest and the Politics of Admission: The Impact of the Black and Puerto Rican Students Community (of City College)." Ph.D. dissertation, City University of New York, 1990.

Freeland, Richard. *Academia's Golden Age*. New York: Oxford University Press, 1992.

Gitlin, Todd. *The Sixties: Years of Hope, Days of Rage*. New York: Bantam, 1987.

Glazer, Nathan, and Daniel Patrick Moynihan. *Beyond the Melting Pot: The Negroes, Puerto Ricans, Jews, Italians and Irish of New York City*. Cambridge: MIT Press, 1970.

Glenn, Charles Leslie, Jr. *The Myth of the Common School*. Amherst: University of Massachusetts Press, 1988.

Gorelick, Sherry. *City College and the Jewish Poor*. New Brunswick, N.J.: Rutgers University Press, 1981.

Gross, Theodore L. *Academic Turmoil: The Reality and Promise of Open Education*. Garden City, N.Y.: Anchor Press/Doubleday, 1980.

Grubb, W. Norton, et al. *Betwixt and Between: Education, Skills and Employment in Sub-Baccalaureate Labor Markets*. Berkeley, Cal.: National Center for Research in Vocational Education, December 1992.

Grubb, W. Norton. "Postsecondary Vocational Education and the Sub-Baccalaureate Labor Market: New Evidence on Economic Returns." *Economics of Education Review*, vol. 11, no. 3 (1992).

Gruber, Howard E., and J. Jacques Voneche. *The Essential Piaget*. New York: Basic Books, 1977.

Healy, Timothy. "The Case for Open Admissions: New Problems—New Hopes." *Change* (summer 1973).

Higher Education for American Democracy. A Report of the President's Commission on Higher Education. Washington, D.C., 1947.

Hook, Sidney. *Out of Step: An Unquiet Life in the Twentieth Century*. New York: Harper & Row, 1987.

Howe, Irving. *A Margin of Hope: An Intellectual Autobiography*. New York: Harcourt Brace Jovanovich, 1982.

———. *World of Our Fathers*. New York: Harcourt Brace Jovanovich, 1976.

Johnson, Paul. *A History of the Jews*. New York: Harper & Row, 1987.

Katznelson, Ira, and Margaret Weir. *School for All*. New York: Basic Books, 1985.

Kriegel, Leonard. *Working Through: A Teacher's Journey in the Urban University*. New York: Saturday Review Press, 1972.

Kristol, Irving. "Memoirs of a Trotskyist." *New York Times Magazine*, January 23, 1977.

Lavin, David, et al. *Right versus Privilege: The Open Admissions Experiment of the City University of New York*. New York: Free Press, 1981.

Lazere, Donald. "Back to Basics: A Force for Oppression or Liberation?" *College English*, vol. 54, no. 1 (January 1992).

Lu, Min-zhan. "Redefining the Legacy of Mina Shaughnessy: A Critique of the Politics of Linguistic Innocence." *Journal of Basic Writing*, vol. 10, no. 1 (spring 1991).

Lunsford, Andrea A. "Cognitive Development and the Basic Writer." *College English*, vol. 41, no. 1 (September 1979).

———. "The Content of Basic Writers' Essays." *College Composition and Communication*, vol. 31, no. 3 (October 1980).

Mann, Horace. *Lectures on Education*. Boston: W. B. Fowle and N. Capen, 1845.

Marshak, Robert E. *Academic Renewal in the 1970s: Memoirs of a City College President*. Washington, D.C.: University Press of America, 1982.

National Adult Literacy Survey. *Adult Literacy in America*. Washington, D.C.: Office of Educational Research and Improvement, the Department of Education, September 1993.

Nichols, David C., and Olive Mills, eds. *The Campus and the Racial Crisis*. Washington, D.C.: American Council on Education, 1970.

Noel, Lee, et al. *Increasing Student Retention*. San Francisco: Jossey-Bass, 1985.

Otheguy, Ricado. *The Condition of Latinos in the City University of New York*. A report to the Vice Chancellor of Academic Affairs and to the Puerto Rican Council on Higher Education. June 1990.

Petrosky, Anthony R., and David Bartholomae. *The Teaching of Writing*. Chicago: National Society for the Study of Education, 1986.

Ravitch, Diane. *The Schools We Deserve: Reflections on the Educational Crises of our Times*. New York: Basic Books, 1985.

Report of the Subcommittee of the New York State Legislature Relative to the Public Educational System of the City of New York (Strayer Committee). 1944.

Riesman, David, and Christopher Jencks. *The Academic Revolution*. New York: Doubleday, 1968.

Riesman, David, and Verne Stadtman, eds. *Academic Transformation: Seventeen Institutions Under Pressure*. New York: McGraw-Hill, 1973.

Rose, Mike. "Remedial Writing Courses: A Critique and a Proposal." *College English*, vol. 45, no. 2 (February 1983).

Rose, Mike, et al. "Perspectives from an Analysis of Classroom Discourse." *College Composition and Communication*, vol. 42, no. 3 (October 1991).

Rouse, James. "The Politics of Composition." *College English*, vol. 41, no. 1 (September 1979).

Rudy, S. Willis. *The College of the City of New York: A History*. New York: City College Press, 1949.

Shaughnessy, Mina. *Errors and Expectations*. New York: Oxford University Press, 1977.

——. Various essays collected in *Basic Writing*, vol. 3, no. 1 (fall/winter 1980).

Sternglass, Marilyn. "Writing Development as Seen Through Longitudinal Research." *Written Communication*, vol. 10, no. 2 (April 1993).

Tinto, Vincent. *Leaving College*. Chicago: University of Chicago Press, 1987.

Trow, Martin. "Reflections on the Transition from Mass to Universal Higher Education." *Daedalus*, vol. 99, no. 1 (winter 1970).

U.S. National Commission on Excellence in Education. *A Nation at Risk: The Imperative for Educational Reform*. 1983.

Wagner, Geoffrey. *The End of Education*. South Brunswick: A. S. Barnes, 1976.

Waxman, Chaim I. *American Jews in Transition*. Philadelphia: Temple University Press, 1983.

Williams, James. "Politicizing Literacy." *College English*, vol. 54, no. 7 (November 1992).

Acknowledgments

C ity College has been a whipping boy in the press for so many years that the institution had every reason to be gun-shy when I showed up. My presence engendered all sorts of overheated fears and hopes—mostly fears—but I was given the run of the place and welcomed almost everywhere I went. Literally hundreds of students talked to me freely, none more so than Sabour Clarke and the young woman I refer to only as Tammy.

Several teachers let me take up residence in their classroom, and even invited me to become an active participant. This was especially true of Rudi Gedamke, Grazina Drabik, Edmund Gordon, Gloria Silverstein, Ann Tabachnikov, and Juliet Floyd. Marilyn Sternglass was especially generous in trying to persuade me of the wrongness of my views and in permitting me to speak with her students. Other professors made themselves available whenever I needed enlightenment; this group includes Paul Sherwin, Jim Watts, Bernard Sohmer, Josh Wilner, Fred Dunn, and Lawrence Plotkin.

The administrators who helped me immeasurably include Charles DeCicco and his assistant, Jackie Hughes; Ramon Berenguer;

and, above all, my friend Arnaldo Melendez. At CUNY, Marilyn Maiz lead me through many of the intricacies of testing.

Very large portions of my manuscript were read by my friends Phil Weiss and Jim Sleeper, both of whom showed me the error of my ways without bruising my ego—a triumph of tact as well as of surgical precision. Yehuda Mirsky was instrumental in filling in the blanks of my historical knowledge. They are, of course, all absolved of complicity in my mistakes, or for that matter in my opinions.

My agent, Joy Harris, was both a tiger and an angel. My editor, William Patrick, read my manuscript, and discussed it, as if he cared about my work every bit as much as I did.

My wife, Elizabeth Easton, read every word, questioned the dead patches, and then apologized profusely for doing so. The apologies were never necessary. I would be a fraction of myself without her.

Index